The Modern Poet

THE MODERN POET

Poetry, Academia, and
Knowledge since the 1750s

ROBERT CRAWFORD

OXFORD
UNIVERSITY PRESS

OXFORD

UNIVERSITY PRESS

Great Clarendon Street, Oxford OX2 6DP

Oxford University Press is a department of the University of Oxford.
It furthers the University's objective of excellence in research, scholarship,
and education by publishing worldwide in

Oxford New York

Athens Auckland Bangkok Bogotá Buenos Aires Cape Town
Chennai Dar es Salaam Delhi Florence Hong Kong Istanbul Karachi
Kolkata Kuala Lumpur Madrid Melbourne Mexico City Mumbai Nairobi
Paris São Paulo Shanghai Singapore Taipei Tokyo Toronto Warsaw

with associated companies in Berlin Ibadan

Oxford is a registered trade mark of Oxford University Press
in the UK and in certain other countries

Published in the United States
By Oxford University Press Inc., New York

British Library Cataloguing in Publication Data

Data available

Library of Congress Cataloging in Publication Data

Data available

ISBN 0–19–818677–0

1 3 5 7 9 10 8 6 4 2

Typeset in Garamond by Kolam Information Services Pvt. Ltd, Pondicherry, India
Printed in Great Britain
on acid-free paper by
Biddles Ltd,
Guildford and King's Lynn

Acknowledgements

I would like to thank the following people who have helped me, directly or indirectly, with the making of this book: M. H. Abrams, Michael Alexander, Dorothy Black, Thomas Bonnell, Marilyn Butler, Neil Corcoran, David Daiches, Leith Davis, Ian Duncan, Douglas Dunn, Nils Eskestad, Lilias Fraser, Jill Gamble, Christine Gascoigne, Howard Gaskill, Henry Hart, Seamus Heaney, W. N. Herbert, Chrystel Hug, Kathleen Jamie, Helen Kay, David Kinloch, Barbara Korte, Donald Mackenzie, Phillip Mallet, John Matthias, Edwin Morgan, Frances Mullan, Les Murray, Tom Normand, Jay Parini, Don Paterson, Leah Price, Richard Price, Norman Reid, Neil Rhodes, Nicholas Roe, Susan Sellers, Christopher Smith, Jane Sommerville, Jane Stabler, Fiona Stafford, Emily Todd, and Andrew Zawacki. In addition I owe a debt to my students, friends, and colleagues at the University of St Andrews, and to the staffs of the British Library (especially its Lending Division), Edinburgh University Library, Glasgow University Library, the National Library of Scotland, and St Andrews University Library.

My wife Alice sustained me heroically through this and other labours; my children Lewis and Blyth cheered me more than I can say. My employer, the University of St Andrews, gave me two semesters of research leave in which to work on the book. While authoring *The Modern Poet* I was writing poetry and co-editing several anthologies. These activities complicated the task, but also encouraged me to smile at some of the matters discussed here. For their patience I would like to thank my co-editors Simon Armitage, Meg Bateman, Mick Imlah, and James McGonigal, as well as Tony Lacey, Robin Robertson, and Anna South. At Oxford University Press Sophie Goldsworthy and Matthew Hollis deserve gratitude, as does J. S. A. Pritchard for her careful copy-editing.

Versions and sketches of short sections of this book have appeared in *Comparative Criticism*, *Critical Survey*, the *London Review of Books*, *Proceedings of the British Academy*, and the *Times Literary Supplement*. I am grateful to the editors of these periodicals for their support and encouragement.

As author, I have ensured that none of the copyright material in this book exceeds the amount permissible under 'fair dealing', as advised by Oxford University Press.

R. C.

St Andrews

2000

For all in similar boats

and

In Memory of ROBERT FERGUSSON (1750–1774)

Contents

Abbreviations

A.   Robert Anderson (ed.), *The Works of the British Poets*, 13 vols. (Edinburgh: Mundell & Son, 1792–4), vol. i, preface

CP   Hugh MacDiarmid, *The Complete Poems*, 2 vols. (London: Martin, Brian & O'Keeffe, 1978)

EA   W. H. Auden, *The English Auden*, ed. Edward Mendelson (London: Faber & Faber, 1977)

PC   I. A. Richards, *Practical Criticism* (1929; repr. London: Routledge & Kegan Paul, 1978)

Introduction

This book is for readers of poetry. Some will love poetry's music, its risk-taking with language, its visionary reach. Others will approach and return to poetry because in their professional lives they study or teach it as an academic subject. These groups of readers should not be mutually exclusive. The chapters that follow are written to make sense to people outside academia. Presented in plain, clear prose, they are also designed to interest and occasionally to provoke a specialist academic audience. Sometimes it may be hard to address both the classroom and the wider public. Yet since such difficulties are what *The Modern Poet* is about, it seems best to acknowledge them at the start. My argument is that sometimes awkward, but often fruitful links between academia and poetry condition how the figure of the poet has developed in English-language societies since the mid-eighteenth century. This formulation of the modern poet shapes our reading and our writing. If, like most literate human beings, at some time you have written a poem, have read poetry for pleasure, and have studied it, then this book offers you a detailed argument about the developing relationship between these overlapping activities.

To read or write poetry is to change one's mind. The mind-altering, imaginative power of verse is what makes it so enjoyable. If words are among our greatest possessions, then poetry is language operating at its limits, and pointing the way beyond. In it imagination and articulation fuse at their highest intensity. This makes poetry such a rich resource. Yet writing verse (or reading it) is a critical as well as a creative activity. Very rarely does the author's critical sense approve every word of a first draft. Almost always phrasing can be improved, expressions shortened, sharpened, or otherwise rewritten. If the alert reader relishes every word of a poem, then he or she is making a value judgement, regarding that piece of work as excellent among its kind. The writer of a poem is also that poem's first reader. In the world of publication and circulation, poems' meanings are made collaboratively, arising and often changing as a result of various people's input. Sometimes the making of a poem works this way before publication, if poets show their drafts to friends for comment before the full shape and wording of the text is decided. Even if the poet works in complete privacy, other people have a part in the poem, since words, phrases, images, and topics come from many (often untraceable) sources that have become part of the authorial consciousness. In another, equally important sense, the lone poet is both a writer and a reader; the process of reading, altering, then rereading (sometimes silently, sometimes aloud) makes its vital contribution to the creation of the poem.

A glance at manuscripts shows that critical skills are part of any poet's equipment. Even John Keats, who wrote to a friend that 'if Poetry comes not as naturally as the Leaves to a tree it had better not come at all', was a minutely careful reviser. In the very same letter he goes on to ask for 'one or two alterations' to be made to the proofs of *Endymion*.[1] Yet writing poetry goes beyond revision in that simple sense. It involves having one's mind changed, as rhythms, images, and ideas arrive apparently from nowhere, wafted on the thermals of language in that dream-state which characterizes poetic composition at full stretch. The poet's job is to arrive at and work in precisely that condition, though few can maintain their position there for long. Its excitement and trancelike air are caught by Norman MacCaig when he writes of how 'I lie, not thinking, in the cool, soft grass, | Afraid of where a thought might take me.'[2] There is a note of submission present, as if the poet is not so much someone who thinks as someone who is taken over by thought. W. S. Graham, in one of his most celebrated first lines, asks not 'How do we use language?' but 'What is the language using us for?'[3] This makes words sound as if they control the writer. The poet seems a medium (rather in the sense of a spiritualist medium) through which articulation passes. Les Murray, when asked where his poetic phrases come from, speaks of attempting to set up a kind of medium-like receptivity: 'As a poet, you set up a field in which they fall...you're waiting for the knowledge which you don't know you possess to fall into the field which you've set up. It's setting your own receiver.'[4] Murray's formula-

---

[1] John Keats, *Letters*, ed. Robert Gittings (London: Oxford University Press, 1970), 70 (to John Taylor, 27 Feb. 1818).

[2] Norman MacCaig, *Collected Poems*, new edn. (London: Chatto & Windus, 1990), 7 ('Summer Farm').

[3] W. S. Graham, *Collected Poems 1942–1977* (London: Faber & Faber, 1979), 191 ('What is the Language Using Us For?').

[4] Les Murray, talking with Robert Crawford, in Robert Crawford, Henry Hart, David Kinloch, and Richard Price, (eds.), *Talking Verse* (St Andrews: Verse, 1995), 170.

tion suggests that with practice the poet may learn how to become such a receptive field. Yet he also emphasizes 'the unconscious', so that making a poem involves not so much material deliberately found as something surprisingly given or transmitted to the poet. The maker of poems gets into a receptive condition, and waits, almost like the 're-ceiver' of a telephone. The poet is simply an instrument. Edward Thomas in the early twentieth century hopes to become such an instru-ment at the start of his poem 'Words':

> Out of us all
> That make rhymes,
> Will you choose
> Sometimes—
> As the winds use
> A crack in a wall
> Or a drain,
> Their joy or their pain
> To whistle through—
> Choose me,
> You English words?[5]

There is something movingly tentative about the way Thomas islands that single word 'Sometimes'. He gives it a line to itself, as if to stress that he knows this prayed-for occurrence will not happen fre-quently, and can be only occasional.

If Murray's mention of the unconscious makes the process of in-spiration sound mysterious, then Thomas, with his talk of 'A crack in a wall | Or a drain', seems to demystify the act of poem-making, or at least to make it seem thoroughly familiar. At the same time, though, he is harking back not only to the classical, etymological sense of the English word 'inspiration'—poetry as a sort of divine afflatus or giving of breath—but also to the Romantic notion of the Aeolian harp, that passive bardic emblem. The miniature Aeolian harp, introduced to Britain by James Oswald, was designed to be hung on the branch of a tree. It was activated not by a human hand but by the breeze which played upon its strings. Murray's 'receiver' and Thomas's 'drain' are more recent versions of that eighteenth-century emblem of poetry, the little harp whose music is mysteriously given by the air. Thomas's poem 'Words' begins with pedestrian images, yet ends with celebration of the

---

[5] Edward Thomas, *Collected Poems* (London: Faber & Faber, 1936), 94 ('Words').

maker dancing with language and even 'In ecstasy' as a poem is made. Such ecstatic delight lifts the poet out of the drains and into the oddly irrational zone often associated with verse composition—a kind of crazy dreaming, a visionary state that might be so far beyond the normal as to be called mad. Famously, for Shakespeare's Athenian Duke Theseus in *A Midsummer Night's Dream* 'The lunatic, the lover, and the poet | Are of imagination all compact'. The Duke presents the image of 'The poet's eye, in a fine frenzy rolling'.[6] That ecstatic 'fine frenzy' is the Shakespearian version of the Latin *furor poeticus*. This trope of poetic inspiration is theorized in European literature at least as early as Plato's *Phaedrus* (written almost two and a half thousand years ago), where Socrates argues that there is a 'kind of possession and madness' that 'comes from the Muses'. He goes on to say,

> This takes hold upon a gentle and pure soul, arouses it and inspires it to songs and other poetry, and thus by adorning countless deeds of the ancients educates later generations. But he who without the divine madness comes to the doors of the Muses, confident that he will be a good poet by art, meets with no success, and the poetry of the sane man vanishes into nothingness before that of the inspired madmen.[7]

Here and elsewhere the *Phaedrus* engages with a question often posed today: Can the writing of poetry be taught? Plato's Socrates appears to think it cannot. However, he does see poetry as bound up with the process of education. The *Phaedrus* returns later to the relationship between poetry, academic institutions, and knowledge. It suggests that at least the 'necessary preliminaries' of the art form are teachable.[8] If poetry's creation involves, in part at least, critical skills, then today we assert that such abilities can be developed in schools and universities. We tend to believe that writing involves critical alertness, and that reading, as an imaginative act, demands creativity. Yet the mutual imbrication of the creative and the critical can still be problematic in an era of aggressively marketed Creative Writing workshops, competitions, courses, university degree programmes, and other aspects of 'poebiz'. The awkwardness of the relationship between the creative and the critical is not new. Plato perceived the difficulties, and solved

---

[6] William Shakespeare, *A Midsummer Night's Dream*, ed. Harold F. Brooks (London: Methuen, 1979), 103–4 (v.i. 7–8 and 12).

[7] Plato, *Phaedrus*, trans. H. N. Fowler (London: Heinemann, 1914) (Loeb Classical Library Plato, I), 469.

[8] Ibid. 543.

them to his apparent satisfaction. For later centuries, though, Plato's very solution became an abrasive part of the problem.

Plato admired poetry, but considered it potentially corrupting because it encouraged distortion of the truth. As the first academic and founder of the original Academy, he is remembered not least for expelling the poets from his ideal state in Book X of *The Republic*. Earlier in that same work he discussed the kind of strictly controlled poetry that could function in education. He made it clear that the most protean and lively poets had no part to play in the ideal learning system, which could cope only with poets who are 'severe rather than amusing'.[9] Plato here sounds like the dour proponent of a police-state. Actually, he greatly enjoyed poetry. There seems regret in his conclusion that poets, those inspired madmen, will be hard to integrate into his proposed system. By the time he ends *The Republic*, however, he has decided that the poets will have to go.

Plato's view of poets was not shared by all his students. One of the most distinguished of these, Aristotle, wrote the first of many academic treatises on poetry. Yet Plato's attitude in *The Republic* can be seen as the clearest early indicator of a mutual suspicion or hostility between academics and philosophers on the one hand, and poets on the other. Over the centuries, and not least during the Renaissance, poets have often felt the need to fight back against what they saw as a dismissal of their vital art. In English the most important early example of this is Sir Philip Sidney's 1595 *Apology for Poetry* which clearly targets Plato as it mounts its *Apology* (which, in modern English, means 'Defence') in the face of poetry's detractors:

And first, truly, to all them that professing learning inveigh against Poetry may justly be objected, that they go very near to ungratefulness, to seek to deface that which, in the noblest nations and languages that are known, hath been the first light-giver to ignorance, and first nurse, whose milk by little and little enabled them to feed afterwards of tougher knowledges.[10]

Presenting poetry as a kind of foundational knowledge is only one of the ways in which Sidney attempts to outflank Plato. He also states that the earliest Greek philosophers were poets. Sidney did not define poetry

[9] Plato, *The Republic*, trans. Desmond Lee, 2nd edn. (Harmondsworth: Penguin, 1987), 157.
[10] Sir Philip Sidney, 'An Apology for Poetry', in Edmund P. Jones, ed., *English Critical Essays (Sixteenth, Seventeenth, and Eighteenth Centuries)* (Oxford: Oxford University Press, 1922), 2.

as verse. Rather, he went back to Plato's own native language to explain that the Greek word for poet 'cometh of this word *Poïein*, which is "to make": wherein, I know not whether by luck or wisdom, we Englishmen have met with the Greeks in calling him "a maker"'.[11] Among such makers, users of literary art, Sidney included 'even Plato', who also 'feigneth', and much of whose 'beauty depended most of Poetry'.[12] Sidney links poetry to 'delightful teaching' and to the 'treasure-house of Science' (in English the word Science then had its Latin sense of 'knowledge'), but he also gives it a particular excitement as 'heart-ravishing knowledge' which can communicate and teach much more effectively through 'an image' rather than through the philosopher's 'wordish description'.[13] The aristocratic Sidney proclaimed that 'of all sciences...is our poet the monarch'.[14] His linking of poetry to inspir-ational teaching and to knowledge is a strategy which allows Sidney (whose contemporary Francis Bacon equated knowledge with power) to enhance poetry's status in the eyes of those who liked 'professing learning', and to defend it against those charges that can be traced back to the earliest academic, Plato. At the same time, whether he praises the Greek philosopher, outmanœuvres him, or considers him 'a natural enemy of poets', Sidney reveals a worry and a combativeness that have not gone away.[15]

Such anxieties are still prevalent, and the poet's wariness of the academic is scarcely confined to one language or culture. At late twen-tieth-century Princeton University (with its Institute for Advanced Studies) the French poet Michel Deguy in his poem 'Étude avancée' ('Advanced Study') seems stunned and lost: 'J'ai déjà oublié ce qui va commencer' ('I've already forgotten what it is to begin').[16] Deguy is a highly intellectual poet as well as a lyrical one, and today Princeton University is noted for employing poets as teachers on its Creative Writing programmes. Yet Deguy's most striking presentation of the poet aligns that figure not with intellectual system-building, but with wild destruction when the poet as 'traitor' sides with the feral and monstrous feudal winds which rush about the surface of the earth, evading human capture and destroying structures: 'Le poète est le traître qui ravitaille l'autan' ('The poet is the traitor who provides supplies to

---

[11] Sidney, 'An Apology', 7.   [12] Ibid. 4.   [13] Ibid. 12, 3, 5, 17.
[14] Ibid. 26.   [15] Ibid. 45.
[16] Michel Deguy, *Given Giving*, trans. Clayton Eshleman (Berkeley and Los Angeles: University of California Press, 1984), 180 and 181.

the southwind').[17] Whatever culture they come from, poets may incline towards the scholarly: it is the Russian 'maker' Joseph Brodsky who produces the Alexandrian statement that 'a footnote is where civilization survives'.[18] Yet for every such inclination, a countering gesture can be cited: it is the Alexandrian poet Cavafy who longs for the uncivilized primitives, presenting them in his famous Greek poem 'Waiting for the Barbarians' (with an amount of irony which may be minimal) as 'a kind of solution' attractive to the poet of a sophisticated society.[19]

These two poets are writing in the period of self-conscious 'modernity' which may be defined as having been ushered in by the eighteenth-century European Enlightenments. Though the adjective 'modern' can be used by historians to cover the last 500 years, and by literary critics to cover only the last century, Jürgen Habermas points out that 'The process of detachment from the models of ancient art was set going in the early eighteenth century by the famous *querelle des ancients et des modernes*.' So it was, Habermas argues, that 'The "moderns" . . . articulated the self-understanding of the French Enlightenment as an epochal new beginning.'[20] It is in this period, when the verb 'modernize' enters the English language, that there develop so many of the systems of modernity which we now take for granted. Anthony Giddens has stated that ' "Modernity" can be understood as roughly equivalent to "the industrial world" '; and whether we think of the industrial revolution and the concomitant systematization of capitalist ideals of free trade as expounded by Adam Smith, or the rationalist debates about the nature of personal identity developed by David Hume, or the social and educational ideals promoted by Jean-Jacques Rousseau (involving both the contractual model of the state and the admiring of the 'noble savage'), the eighteenth century presents us most forcefully with the development of those structures we regard as modern.[21] That century declared and constituted what has become the world's paradigmatic developed modern nation, the United States of America. It is when, historically and ideologically, self-aware modernity was initiated. Whether or not we now label ourselves 'postmodern', we are

[17] Ibid. 22 and 23 ('Le Traitre'/'The Traitor').

[18] Joseph Brodsky, *Less than One* (Harmondsworth: Viking, 1986), 99.

[19] C. P. Cavafy, *Collected Poems*, trans. Edmund Keeley and Philip Sherrard (London: Hogarth Press, 1975), 15.

[20] Jürgen Habermas, *The Philosophical Discourse of Modernity*, trans. Frederick Lawrence (Cambridge, Mass.: MIT Press, 1987), 8.

[21] Anthony Giddens, *Modernity and Self-Identity* (Cambridge: Polity Press, 1991), 15.

defined in terms of that constituting 'modernity'. *The Modern Poet* will argue that the figuration of the poet which we still take for granted also has its roots in the Enlightenment, particularly in the Scottish society that produced Smith and Hume, and was so conscious of divisions and connections between the primitive and the civilized. The word 'modern' in this book is not used to mean 'modernist' or 'contemporary' but to signal a new conception of the poet which emerged from Enlightenment modernity and which (while it has evolved since the 1750s) continues to be powerful today. That is why, throughout *The Modern Poet*, the adjective 'modern' is taken to denote a period from the mid-eighteenth century to the present, a stretch of history in which such terms as 'Modernist' or 'postmodern' enact only variations on an underlying note of Enlightenment and post-Enlightenment modernity.

Twentieth-century poets such as Deguy, Brodsky, or Cavafy, who may veer at times between attraction to barbarism and to sophistication, and who may even wish to combine the two, are not being straightforwardly inconsistent. Rather, they are enacting a variation on the centuries-old pattern which this book characterizes as that of 'the modern poet'. Such a cultural design, it will be argued, is bound up with the place of poetry in modernity, and specifically in the modern academy. It might be that some readers feel poetry over the last hundred years has become immured in classrooms. There is a popular perception of much twentieth-century poetry as rebarbatively obscure, demanding the kind of study possible only under seminar conditions. This attitude may have been developed by some of last century's most academically nurtured poets, particularly T. S. Eliot who wrote in 1921 that 'it appears likely that poets in our civilization, as it exists at present, must be *difficult*'.[22] Yet even Eliot a dozen years later told the students and professors of a Harvard University lecture hall that he would 'like an audience which could neither read nor write', and linked the poet with the most primitive as well as the most educated mentality.[23] Such a connection is typical of the modern poet as presented in this book, but it is one which has a history that goes back considerably further than the twentieth century.

---

[22] T. S. Eliot, *Selected Essays*, 3rd edn. (London: Faber & Faber, 1951), 289 ('The Metaphysical Poets').

[23] T. S. Eliot, *The Use of Poetry and the Use of Criticism* (1933; repr. London: Faber & Faber, 1964), 152.

The notion that poets should be primitive or 'savage' was generally alien to English-language writers before the mid-eighteenth century. In Renaissance works like Spenser's *Shepheardes Calender* or Drayton's *Poly-Olbion* there may be occasional details that pre-empt 'the modern poet'. Writing about Renaissance poetry's 'system of authorial roles', Richard Helgerson has called attention to the way 'Spenser's idea of a poet was an unstable but necessary union of two ideas'—the unpolished and the polished—which are 'embodied in two roles—shepherd and knight'—though 'not even Spenser could maintain the precarious equilibrium'.[24] The most striking anticipation of the later, post-1750s authorial role of the modern poet occurs in an uncharacteristic passage written by Sir Philip Sidney. There is a passing moment in his *Apology for Poetry* where the Elizabethan aristocrat makes a remarkable admission:

I must confess my own barbarousness, I never heard the old song of Percy and Douglas that I found not my heart moved more than with a trumpet; and yet is it sung but by some blind crowder, with no rougher voice than rude style; which, being so evil apparelled in the dust and cobwebs of that uncivil age, what would it work, trimmed in the gorgeous eloquence of Pindar?[25]

Sidney passes on to other things, developing his defence of poetry, but, in imaging that possible combination of the barbaric and the eloquently sophisticated, he anticipates the subject of this book. What for Sidney was only a transitory pang and notion became, when poetry and the teaching of English literature in the academy first converged, the emergence of the modern poet. The development of 'the modern poet' is itself part of Enlightenment modernity; with it what Sidney regarded as a tangential speculation would become part of the cultural mainstream. Poets would be assumed to have at once the 'eloquence', sophistication, and education which Sidney indicates when he names Pindar; at the same time they would possess the 'barbarousness', wildness, and intuitive, even shamanistic knowledge that Sidney hints at when he hears for a moment the 'rude' nameless voice of his ballad-singing 'blind crowder'. It was an emerging relationship between poetry and the universities which produced during the Enlightenment this volatile combination that we may term 'the modern poet'. The volatility

---

[24] Richard Helgerson, *Self-Crowned Laureates* (Berkeley and Los Angeles: University of California Press, 1983), 99–100.

[25] Sidney, 'An Apology', 32.

involved from the outset has continued to energize and complicate the relationship between poetry, academia, and knowledge.

Few academics since Plato have attacked poetry directly. Yet even in recent times poets have still felt threatened. Arguably throughout the last century they duelled with academia (often in its own lecture halls) at least as fiercely as Sidney fenced with Plato. Today it is hard to find teachers who quote the Greek philosopher's views on poets with approval; it is more likely to be poets who are expressing hostility towards the groves of learning, viewing the academicization of poetry as a recent and dangerous phenomenon. During the later Middle Ages, then in the sixteenth and seventeenth centuries, many poets had been university educated, and, on occasion, had participated in educational projects; William Cowley, for instance, was closely involved in the early development of the Royal Society.[26] In the mid-eighteenth century, however, the Scot Robert Fergusson (1750–74) became probably the first significant poet to study English poetry as part of his university course. Fergusson reacted very much against the Anglocentric grain of his teaching, and chose instead to champion Scots vernacular language. Famously, he addressed to his teachers a poem in Scots which ironically attacked his St Andrews 'Principal and Professors' using the sort of Latin headings ('*Imprimis . . . Secundo*') that might have been found in a lecture or scholarly textbook.[27] Over two centuries later, quarrels between poets and their academic teachers, colleagues, or contemporaries can be just as lively. Les Murray's essay 'The Suspect Captivity of the Fisher King' was first delivered as an address to the University of New South Wales. Like Fergusson's poem, it is ironically structured to resemble the points of a lecture, and includes the following:

17 Failed authors are liable to blame their failures on anything at all, even on tenured employment in a university. Such authors are, however, more likely to punish successful full-time writers than fellow academics.

19 Academics and authors despise each other most when each has it in mind to exploit the other; when this impulse is dormant, each merely considers the other his dependant, if not his natural servant.[28]

[26] See Helgerson, *Self-Crowned Laureates*, 225–9.

[27] Robert Fergusson, *The Poems*, ed. Matthew P. McDiarmid (Edinburgh: Blackwood for the Scottish Text Society, 1954–6), 2 vols., ii. 183 ('To the Principal and Professors of the University of St Andrews, on their Superb Treat to Dr Samuel Johnson'); on this poem see Robert Crawford, 'Robert Fergusson's Robert Burns', in Robert Crawford (ed.), *Robert Burns and Cultural Authority* (Edinburgh: Edinburgh University Press, 1997), 1–22.

[28] Les Murray, *Blocks and Tackles* (North Ryde: Angus & Robertson, 1990), 153.

Taking the mythical 'Fisher King' from 'the legend of Parzifal' as personifying poetry, Murray argues that 'All academies are police academies' and that today's poet or Fisher King 'has allowed poetry to be taken over and used by the police'.[29] Many readers may be more familiar with the story of the Fisher King from the 'Notes' to Eliot's *The Waste Land* than from opera-going. There seems an irony in Murray's use of this now most academicized myth to defend poetry against academia. Yet the apologia is spirited. Murray's anthology *Fivefathers: Five Australian Poets of the Pre-Academic Era* looks back with some affection to a time before Australian poetry entered 'the university age' in the 1960s. Discussing 'the association of poetry with the universities' generally, Murray has spoken of this as, at best, 'an uncomfortable, scratchy relationship'.[30]

Murray's provocative remarks are contemporary with the American poet and critic Dana Gioia's controversial *Atlantic Monthly* article 'Can Poetry Matter?' which earned its author 'hate mail...typed on letterheads of various university writing programs'.[31] Gioia's point was that there was a growth in the quantity of poetry published in the United States, but this had been accompanied by poetry's constituting a subculture made up largely of teachers and students. 'Based mostly in universities, these groups have gradually become the primary audience for contemporary verse. Consequently, the energy of American poetry, which was once directed outward, is now increasingly focused inward.' Gioia's article is shrewd, though less punchy than Murray's lecture. As a poet he is not hostile to academia *per se*: 'The campus is not a bad place to work. It's just a bad place for all poets to work.' While regretting the overwhelming academicization of poetry, Gioia goes on to make some more detailed points about it:

Even within the university contemporary poetry now exists as a subculture. The teaching poet finds that he or she has little in common with academic colleagues. The academic study of literature over the past twenty-five years has veered off in a theoretical direction with which most imaginative writers have little sympathy or familiarity...Poets have created enclaves in the academy almost entirely separate from their critical colleagues. They write less criticism than they did before entering the academy. Pressed to keep up with the plethora

[29] Ibid. 155.
[30] Les Murray (ed.), *Fivefathers* (Manchester: Carcanet, 1994), 14; Clive Wilmer, *Poets Talking* (Manchester: Carcanet, 1994), 106.
[31] Dana Gioia, 'Hearing from Poetry's Audience', *Poetry Review*, 82/1 (Spring 1992), 27.

of new poetry, small magazines, professional journals, and anthologies, they are also less well read in the literature of the past. Their peers in the English department generally read less contemporary poetry and more literary theory. In many departments writers and literary theorists are openly at war. Bringing the two groups under one roof has paradoxically made each more territorial. Isolated even within the university, the poet, whose true subject is the whole of human existence, has reluctantly become an educational specialist.[32]

Peter Forbes, editor of the London magazine *Poetry Review*, chose to reprint Gioia's piece in 1992, presumably because he thought it relevant to the situation in Britain. British universities have been slower to involve themselves in 'Creative Writing', but the position is changing, and 'Creative Writing' is among the most rapidly growing areas of English Studies throughout the United Kingdom. Universities, such as East Anglia, Lancaster, and St Andrews, which employ professional poets and have offered postgraduate degrees in Creative Writing for some years now find themselves joined by a cohort of other institutions, some employing well-known writers on a regular basis, others buying in occasional lecturers on the cheap and relying on less established writers to do much of the teaching. An indication of this shift was a 1988 national conference of Higher Education Teachers of English at which one of several addresses in a section on 'English and Creative Writing' was given by Professor Philip Hobsbaum of Glasgow University. As the organizer of groups of writers in Cambridge, London, Belfast, and Glasgow which played a part in nurturing the work of authors as diverse as Seamus Heaney and James Kelman, Hobsbaum urged British academics to employ more writers at their institutions. His address was somewhat sketchy, but he pointed to the origins of English teaching in the eighteenth-century Scottish universities as involving the teaching of composition, and he suggested students might be taught how to make 'poems, or stories, or plays' rather than criticism. Hobsbaum pointed to the success of poets as teachers in British universities, instancing the cases of Edwin Morgan and Geoffrey Hill; yet he also drew attention to some writers' sense of academia as 'hostile to them'.[33] Nevertheless, there is an awareness among academics in Britain that creative writers are increasingly working within English departments of higher-education institutions. To take only a few high-profile instances, the

[32] Dana Gioia, *Can Poetry Matter?* (St Paul, Minn.: Graywolf Press, 1992), 2 and 13–14.
[33] Philip Hobsbaum, 'The Teaching of Creative Writing', in Philip Hobsbaum, Paddy Lyons, and Jim McGhee (eds.), *Channels of Communication* (Glasgow: HETE 88, 1992), 11, 13.

present British Poet Laureate, Andrew Motion, is a Professor who teaches Creative Writing; there are notable concentrations of poets working at several British universities, including Oxford (where, however, creative writing is not offered as an examinable academic subject) and St Andrews (where creative writing is taught at undergraduate and postgraduate levels). In a recent Research Assessment Exercise, which judges the quality of research produced by British academics, the English Panel saw the growth in the amount of creative writing submitted by university English departments as probably the most striking development of English studies in Britain.[34]

It may be that the relationship between poetry, university English, and Creative Writing in the UK is now encountering the sort of difficulties described by Gioia in the United States. Perhaps British poetry will become more and more academicized. Certainly, one can detect a hostility towards academia among some British poets. Where in Australia Murray worried in 1992 that 'One of the simplest ways of reducing poetry and its effect in human lives is to make it part of the exam process, by which humans are graded and in which most undergo a measure of humiliation', in Scotland the poet Tom Leonard had inveighed in 1990 against the idea that 'The best poems' were something to be taught by an academic 'professional caste of people'.[35] By 1997 the English poet Jon Silkin was calling attention to kinds of 'academic reading' of poetry as 'a form of ethnic cleansing'.[36] Though antagonism between poets and academia is nothing new, there may be a tendency to assume that it is a phenomenon bound up only with recent developments in the teaching of English in universities. Commentators usually concentrate on post-war America, where the teaching of creative writing, composition, and literature sometimes existed uneasily together.

Whether we are considering America, Australia, or Britain, we should not avoid the issue of money. Most poets earn relatively little, and lack a reliable regular income. Understandably, they envy the salary of a tenured academic. On the other hand, academics, mired in administrative paperwork, managerial prose of the 'quality assurance' sort, and examination marking, may covet what they see as the poet's freedom.

[34] As a member of the 1996 English Panel, I obtained the Chairman's permission to say this.
[35] Murray, *Blocks and Tackles*, 157; Tom Leonard (ed.), *Radical Renfrew* (Edinburgh: Polygon, 1990), pp. xvii and xviii.
[36] Jon Silkin, *The Life of Metrical and Free Verse in Twentieth-Century Poetry* (Basingstoke: Macmillan, 1997), 55 and 56.

The lure of a salary draws the poet into the classroom more often than the inducement of liberty tempts the academic out. Perhaps because they are too polite to discuss money, the most widely read institutional histories of literary teaching in the universities ignore creative writing, though there is now at least one, less well known account of the topic.[37] In *Professing Literature*, an influential 'history of academic literary studies in the United States', Gerald Graff says virtually nothing about the teaching of creative writing. His one mention of Norman Foerster's early 1930s establishment of the graduate curriculum at the University of Iowa states simply that 'This is an instructive story in itself (though it cannot be pursued here), for Foerster did not foresee that creative writing programs would quickly be detached from their initial synthesizing purposes and become autonomous enterprises—as would criticism itself.'[38] There is a strong suggestion that Graff excludes creative writing because he does not see it as part of 'academic literary studies'. However, recent work has drawn attention to the way in which, when English literary texts began to be taught at universities for the first time in the English-speaking world in the classrooms of eighteenth-century Scotland, what we would now call composition, creative writing, criticism, and critical theory were all bound together as part of the subject of Rhetoric and Belles-Lettres.[39] Even today in many university English departments these remain taught side by side, and it might be hard to say where one ended and another began. To see creative writing simply as something new to the universities is to distort the history of poetry and academic literary studies. Yet such a misreading prevails.

Often it allows academics to see what they do as clinically separate from the production of the texts they study. In some ways this may appeal to an age of professional specialization, but for the writing and appreciation of poetry it is damaging. Even Jerome McGann, a stimulating critic alert to the notion of 'a poetry of knowledge', manages to write about both Ezra Pound and James Macpherson without relating either to the university milieu so important to their work.[40] In constructing his own 'poetry concerned with all that is needed | Of the sum

[37] D. G. Myers, *The Elephants Teach* (Englewood Cliffs, NJ: Prentice Hall, 1996).

[38] Gerald Graff, *Professing Literature* (Chicago: University of Chicago Press, 1987), 1 and 138.

[39] Robert Crawford (ed.), *The Scottish Invention of English Literature* (Cambridge: Cambridge University Press, 1998), see especially the first two chapters and the final chapter.

[40] Jerome J. McGann, *Towards a Literature of Knowledge* (Oxford: Clarendon Press, 1989), 96–128; Jerome J. McGann, *The Poetics of Sensibility* (Oxford: Clarendon Press, 1996), 33–40.

of human knowledge and expression', Hugh MacDiarmid was certainly fierily aware of the university classroom, but other poets have often assumed there is no connection between what they do and the domain of academia.[41] Such a view may be comforting to many academics, and to numerous poets, since it presents the territory of each as uncontaminated by the other, allowing a firm distinction to be maintained between, for instance, what Graff calls 'academic literary studies' and the production of poetry. This artificial division, however, has been as helpful as the Berlin Wall.

That such a strong differentiation persists is in some ways surprising. Though a number of poets still regard literary theory as toxic, and some theorists appear to wish to dissolve away all sense of aesthetic pleasure in an acid bath of ideological awareness, many trends in modern criticism encourage contact between poets, theorists, and critics. Examples might include Harold Bloom's mixing of his prose and his verse in that brilliant, rather macho, agonistic work *The Anxiety of Influence: A Theory of Poetry* (1972), or of contentions (like those implicit in Roland Barthes's *S/Z*, for example) that reading can be a form of activity akin to writing. So we have the authoring, 'goal-orientated', purposeful, and scholarly 'active reading' of Lisa Jardine and Anthony Grafton, as well as the more dream-powered reading as creative writing ('A real reader is a writer') espoused in the 1990s by the French theorist Hélène Cixous.[42] Barthes, building on his theory of 'The Death of the Author' (which sees writing as produced less by an individual than by the cultural codes of a society), presents in *S/Z* a text that is imaginatively provocative. *S/Z* goads through its very organization, placing the piece of creative writing which it analyses (Balzac's story 'Sarrasine') as a mere appendix to Barthes's own critical reading, reversing conventional notions of host and parasite.[43] Les Murray fights back against this occupation of the writer's place by the critic, countering modern attempts to blur the distinction between criticism and creation by arguing that 'Those who say the author is dead usually have it in mind to rifle his wardrobe.'[44] It is

[41] Hugh MacDiarmid, *The Complete Poems*, 2 vols. (London: Martin, Brian & O'Keeffe, 1978), ii. 1004 ('The Kind of Poetry I Want').
[42] Harold Bloom, *The Anxiety of Influence* (New York: Oxford University Press, 1973); Lisa Jardine and Anthony Grafton, ' "Studied for Action": How Gabriel Harvey Read his Livy', *Past and Present*, 129 (1990), 30; Hélène Cixous, *Three Steps on the Ladder of Writing*, trans. Sarah Cornell and Susan Sellers (New York: Columbia University Press, 1993), 21.
[43] Roland Barthes, *S/Z* (Paris: Éditions du Seuil, 1970); *S/Z*, trans. Richard Miller (New York: Hill & Wang, 1974).   [44] Murray, *Blocks and Tackles*, 157.

hard not to suspect that in some sections of modern academia theoretical discourse has been seen as more important than poetry, or as replacing poetry, with producers of theory being valued more highly (in economic and other terms) than makers of verse. Introducing Hélène Cixous at the University of California, Irvine, in 1990, Jacques Derrida presented her not as a theorist but as 'very much a poet'.[45] Derrida was trying to praise Cixous, using the word 'poet' as a term of approbation. Yet some writers of verse will resent Derrida's use of such terminology. To them it may appear that, for a time at least, theory became the prized poetry of academia, displacing or at best menacingly policing the business of fiddling with stanza-breaks and line-endings. Poetry, verse was elitist, technically baffling, less interesting than prose. It was shunted down the corridor, a few doors beyond Media Studies.

Nevertheless, it is not simply recent academics who have been rifling poets' wardrobes; for a long time poets have also tried on academic gowns. One could say that Pope's 1711 'Essay on Criticism', an elegantly dressed poem containing a history of criticism and attempting to fend off the '*Critic Learning*' of France, was a poet's pre-emptive strike against the academicization of modern literary learning, just as the notes added to the *Dunciad Variorum* are Pope the poet's revenge on the scholarly control of texts.[46] A Shakespeare editor and scholar as well as a poet, Pope was already compromised by a whiff of chalk dust, but he was writing before the teaching of English literary texts entered the universities, so his 'brave *Britons*' in the 'Essay on Criticism' are still '*unconquered*, and *unciviliz'd*' by the kinds of critical policing promoted by the French Academy.[47] Still, Pope's ever-so-sophisticated siding with the '*unciviliz'd*' is a tremor that anticipates the figure of the modern poet, wild, yet menaced by the seminar room whose architecture increasingly surrounds him.

For a much clearer instance of a poet in academic attire, we might turn to one of Pope's twentieth-century admirers. Whether or not they are viewed as a spoof, few texts could be more academic than Eliot's 'Notes' to *The Waste Land*. Those additions serve to alert us to how much that poem is a product of its author's academic training. When

---

[45] Jacques Derrida, quoted on the front jacket-cover of Cixous, *Three Steps on the Ladder of Writing*.

[46] Alexander Pope, *The Poems*, ed. John Butt (London: Methuen, 1963), 167.

[47] Ibid.

Roland Barthes describes a text as providing 'entrance into a network with a thousand entrances...a perspective (of fragments, of voices from other texts, other codes), whose vanishing point is nonetheless ceaselessly pushed back', he is developing a theory of writing which has learned from modernist texts of earlier French literature and from the sort of poetry best exemplified in English by *The Waste Land*. In such poetry an allusive structure of embeddings produces just the kind of 'perspective of quotations, a mirage of structures' which Barthes sees as characterizing the literary code.[48] Where Eliot (quoting Dickens) entitled part of his text at one stage 'He Do the Police in Different Voices', Barthes presents literature as 'Le Tissu des voix' ('The Weaving of Voices'). If behind Eliot's poem lay works aware of such modern technologies as 'a surcharged phonograph' or 'a confused tangle of other voices most like the mutter and hum through a City telephone', then Barthes's view of literature as bound up with a coded 'réseau' ('network') uses a French term which, when Barthes wrote *S/Z*, was applicable not only to telecommunications but also to computing.[49]

Barthes is best remembered for his essay 'The Death of the Author', and it is no accident that the notion of the all-important individual author dies just as computing technology becomes more widely available. The place of the Godlike solitary genius is usurped by that of a system, a 'réseau' or network that structures and even appears to produce the piece of writing which may then bear a particular author's name. The notion that a text is generated through systems of circulation and cultural practices held sway in the later twentieth century with as much vigour as had the idea of individual authorial genius in the later nineteenth. Poetry, academic criticism, and technology grew increasingly bound together throughout much of the last hundred years, as part of those educational, technological, and literary *Discourse Networks* examined by Friedrich Kittler.[50] Now we can see that later nineteenth-century hymns to lone genius are cognate with what became the ideology and politics of the Superman. Equally, we may suspect that

[48] Barthes, *S/Z*, trans. Miller, 12 and 20.

[49] T. S. Eliot, *The Waste Land: A Facsimile and Transcript*, ed. Valerie Eliot (London: Faber & Faber, 1971), 5; Barthes, *S/Z*, 27 and 28; for Eliot and telephone technology see Robert Crawford, *The Savage and the City in the Work of T. S. Eliot* (Oxford: Clarendon Press, 1987), 134. For information about 'réseau' as a computing term in French around 1970, I thank Chrystel Hug and Laurent Catach.

[50] Friedrich A. Kittler, *Discourse Networks 1800/1900*, trans. Michael Metteer, with Chris Cullens (Stanford, Calif.: Stanford University Press, 1990).

the promulgation of the 'death of the author' is a reaction against earlier author cults, and is of a piece with developing global technologies such as the computer, which present authorship as a generation of codes and a weaving of textual materials. Barthes is no more thieving from Eliot's 'different voices', than he is straightforwardly stealing from computing technology, but the poetry, the criticism, and the computing of his era are all interrelated. More recently, in quite different kinds of American poetry, verse and criticism appear fused in such works as Jorie Graham's *Materialism*, which, with its use of long excerpts from Plato, Francis Bacon, Walter Benjamin, and others, offers a hybridizing of critical and poetic texts, while Susan Howe's long poem *A Bibliography of the King's Book; or, Eikon Basilike* seems suspended between poetry, criticism, and computer-informed scholarship, as do various texts by Charles Bernstein and the 'Language poets'.[51] Increasingly, contemporary poets and academics are rifling one another's wardrobes. In this new 'age of information', neither has a monopoly of knowledge.

Though most of this book is given over to examinations of specific modern poets, I wish to make it clear that the volume's title denotes not an individual but a form or trope, a cultural space or authorial role which many poets have occupied. Through a series of studies, the book tracks a shifting yet resilient and potent figuration of the poet's role, and examines how a number of poets have come to terms with it. Following on from the work of Barthes, Michel Foucault's essay 'What is an Author?' has been influential in teaching us to think of the author not simply as a person but as a constructed cultural site.[52] While it is not written in a Foucauldian idiom, *The Modern Poet* is informed by some of Foucault's ideas, and has been stimulated too by modern scholarship, particularly that of Gérard Genette, which attends to the significance of 'paratexts', the packaging of texts and the history of the book.[53] Not all poets working in the period occupy the cultural space of 'the modern poet', but a remarkable number do. I want to make it quite clear that I am not contending that every poet is or ought to be an academic, or that all academics are or ought to be poets. I am, however, arguing that the course of modern poetry and the development of modern academia are,

---

[51] Jorie Graham, *Materialism* (New York: Ecco Press, 1995); Susan Howe, *A Bibliography of the King's Book; or, Eikon Basilike* (Providence, RI: Paradigm Press, 1989).

[52] Michel Foucault, 'What is an Author?', in Josue V. Harari (ed.), *Textual Strategies* (London: Methuen, 1980), 141–60.

[53] Gérard Genette, *Paratexts*, trans. Jane E. Lewin (Cambridge: Cambridge University Press, 1997).

for better or worse, deeply intertwined, and that we should face up to this rather than following those poets and critics who would seek to ignore or deny the fact.

The Modern Poet does not offer a conventional history of poetry since the 1750s, the decade when literary texts in English clearly emerge as a subject of university study. To attempt such a full-scale account of the topics signalled in my subtitle would require many volumes. In order to produce a single book whose chapters may inform or underpin arguments about the poet's relationship with academia, I have selected a relatively small number of poets whose work seems pertinent. Inevitably, readers will be able to list other authors—whether G. M. Hopkins or Geoffrey Hill, Geoffrey Grigson or John Berryman—whose accommodation or quarrel with academia was important to their work. I have resisted the temptation to provide comprehensive coverage, while attempting to select a sufficient range of examples. I hope that the suggestive potency of my instances and arguments may provoke further exemplification and debate. There are certainly gaps in my narrative, occasioned by the decision to adopt a selective focus rather than try for an inclusive round-up.

However, as well as looking at a number of major works, *The Modern Poet* attends often to writings whose importance has been obscured or sidelined, and which some commentators have considered of little interest. This book emerges from and in part deals with a Scottish milieu which may be strange to non-Scottish readers. For that reason space is given over to significant aspects of Scottish material known to specialists, but not familiar to a wider audience. My initial chapters set this out in some detail, then move forward rapidly to relate it to more recent concerns in poetry throughout the English-speaking world. To see the industrial revolution Scotland of Adam Smith and David Hume as a cradle of Enlightenment modernity is hardly new. Still, to remind readers that the modernity of that culture was manifested also in its enthusiasm for the 'primitive' and to connect that Scotland to more recent poetry may well raise eyebrows. The speedy forward movement towards the end of the early chapters is aimed to short-circuit some accepted views of the literary past and present. It may unsettle readers who demand a more measured historical progression, but I hope that it serves to confound assumptions about the too readily presumed obsolescence of some of the texts and writers discussed. As much a gadfly as a guide, and presenting not simply lines of influence but also some heretical analogies, this book is designed to inform, to argue, and to provoke.

My early chapters share a preoccupation not only with poetry, but also with such scholarly matters as eighteenth-century annotation, reading lists, educational treatises, and anthologies. They try to show how ideas of a modern poetic canon were taking shape alongside the publication of the Ossianic poems and the evolution of the concept of the modern poet. Later chapters, which deal with nineteenth- and twentieth-century examples, supply further detailed evidence for the argument, and round out its nature. The way in which the cultural space of 'the modern poet' is marked out does evolve over time, rather than remaining static. However, the evolution is clearly that of a continuing reinvention of ways to fuse imaginative wildness and scholarly education, one still perceptible in such poets as Ted Hughes, Seamus Heaney, or Paul Muldoon. Readers of *The Modern Poet* must confront some odd juxtapositions and leaps, but they will be justified in expecting an argument which has an articulated shape to it, albeit one which begins in terrain that may be unfamiliar.

Janus-faced at the door of this book stands the poetry of Ossian. This was produced through the mid-eighteenth-century collaboration of James Macpherson and Hugh Blair. The word 'Ossian' has a blurring effect, since it allows for a constant slippage between Ossian (a supposed prehistoric Gaelic bard) and James 'Ossian' Macpherson, the eighteenth-century translator (some would argue author) of the Ossianic poems. Ossian is at once ancient and *à la mode*: in that paradoxical quality lies an important aspect of the work's modernity. It appealed to an Enlightenment culture fascinated alike by novel technologies and by the primitive or primal. To call it 'modern' is correct, but also richly slippery: Ossian is, to deploy a phrase of Marianne Moore's, 'archaically new'.[54] Rather than pretending that no such slipperiness exists, I want to draw attention to this as something powerfully productive of the textual effect we call 'Ossian'. That effect encompasses both the ancient bard and the modern Macpherson; indeed, it may also include Macpherson's friend Professor Hugh Blair, since he too is co-producer of the resonances created by the Ossianic poems. Though it was argued that he was a particular early Scottish Gaelic poet, Ossian (since at least the eighteenth century) has mattered far more as a textual effect rather than an

---

[54] Marianne Moore, 'Archaically New', in Bonnie Kime Scott (ed.), *The Gender of Modernism* (Bloomington: Indiana University Press, 1990), 349.

individual. Ossian's paradoxical effect is of simultaneous primitivism and sophistication. Ossian's very slipperiness opens up the cultural space of the modern poet. Here is the wild Highlander who comes from the start accompanied by up-to-date scholarly paratexts. He is simultaneously the production of 'barbaric' Gaelic translated by the Highland Macpherson, and of polite academic knowledge as represented by Blair, first Professor of Rhetoric and Belles-Lettres at Edinburgh University. As originally published, the Ossianic texts themselves encourage a slippage between the 'primitive' bardic and the sophisticatedly academic, since they operate in a stereophonic way that feeds primitive epic into one ear and the scholarly gentility of elaborate footnotes into the other. It is just because 'Ossian' is such a slippery text and term that it has the ability to bring together the apparently contradictory elements which make up the configuration indicated by this book's title. Uniting such barbarism and such sophistication, Ossian is the first full representative of the modern poet, at once primitive and a knowledge-crammed *alumnus*.

My first chapter goes into considerable and minute detail establishing the cultural background to that Ossianic *œuvre* which, though internationally protean, is often brushed aside. Recent research by Katie Trumpener has emphasized Ossian's importance for the development of eighteenth- and nineteenth-century prose fiction.[55] Ian Duncan (with regard to Scott in particular) has argued that 'The *Poems of Ossian* defined a new cultural position of *inauthenticity*, somewhere between translation and forgery, which would become the classic position of an "invented tradition" in modern letters.'[56] Nevertheless, Ossian's wider impact on poetry remains woefully underappreciated. In his sophisticated primitivism Ossian is a precursor of Burns and Byron, Scott and Wordsworth. Formally, he is vital to the growth of the prose poem and *vers libre*, while the value of Ossian's introduction of the 'fragment' into modern European and North American literature is hard to overstate. Chapter 1 of this book attends to the circumstances which gave rise to the Ossianic corpus, and to the significance of this invention of the modern poet, manufactured at the previously unimaginable intersection of the wilderness and the lecture room. This first chapter also shows how Ossian arrived crucially in the period when a university-sponsored poetic canon

---

[55] Katie Trumpener, *Bardic Nationalism* (Princeton: Princeton University Press, 1997).

[56] Ian Duncan, 'Introduction' to Walter Scott, *Rob Roy* (Oxford: Oxford University Press, 1998), pp. viii–ix.

was emerging. The practical development of that canon, and its shaping of our ideas of modern poetry, is the subject of Chapter 2.

The authorial role of the modern poet is far from confined to the age of Romanticism. On the contrary, its import in marking the conjunction of poetry, academia, and arguments about access to knowledge in developed nations is immense. If Blair was instrumental in the production of the figure of the modern poet, then, as pioneering editor of a vast national anthology, he was also a key developer of the way in which, as poetry and academia evolved in the centuries that followed, verse was presented to its readers as a body of work that represented the nation. Issues of native language and cultural imperialism, central to the production of the Ossianic corpus, are of great importance in the combined acts of legal, academic, and commercial judgement which shaped the national body of poetry. The second chapter considers these. It also links them to the way in which, as one of the earliest university academics to teach English literature, Blair constructed a model of the national poetic corpus. Such work still ghosts some of the most influential modern anthologies of poetry. It conditions the way in which poetry is disseminated, whether in deliberately academic works like the Norton anthologies or in smaller national gatherings.

In the mid-nineteenth century, Chapter 3 argues, the Romantic figure of the primitive-sophisticated modern poet is reinvented as that of the Victorian scholar-gypsy. This savant is attuned alike to the knowledge of academic scholarship and to a wilder world beyond with its different, less systematized ways of knowing. My third chapter examines the Oxford milieu which formed the highly sophisticated priests of knowledge A. H. Clough and Matthew Arnold. Both these poets contributed to the development of English studies in the English universities. Chapter 3 goes on to look at the way in which each writer sought not so much to escape his academic environment as to connect it with a Highland culture still regarded as more distinctively 'primitive'. Clough's 1848 *Bothie of Toper-na-fuosich* is a work of knowledge and revolution which follows in the wake of Ossian by uniting lecture room with Highland *nous*. Arnold's ideal of the scholar-gypsy is connected not only with his view of Clough but also with his Celticism and his defence of Ossian. Together Arnold and Clough made possible a reshaping of the figure of the modern poet which mediates between High Romantic wildness and the later developments of the Celtic Twilight, that dimly lit zone in which Yeats weaves his own gypsy scholarship.

In Chapter 4 the aggressive restatement of poet as primitive-sophisticate made by T. S. Eliot and Ezra Pound, fresh from the lecture halls of American academia, brings the figure of the modern poet into the vanguard of modernism. There the poet is at once linked to 'the savage' and to the professorial as Eliot and Pound, like Hugh MacDiarmid and W. H. Auden, contest academia's possession of knowledge at the same time as they revoice academic procedures. I should emphasize that I am not saying that poets of the twentieth century (or of our own) are 'modern' in exactly the way Ossian was modern, or that they were powerfully influenced by James Macpherson. Rather, in redefining the role of the modern poet, they drew on elements—of learned sophistication and deliberate primitivism—which had been combined earlier by their Romantic and Victorian predecessors. The cultural space of the modern poet has been subject to persistent reinvention. As words such as 'primitive' and 'savage' have grown faded or tarnished in recent usage, the term 'marginal' has been in the ascendant; MacDiarmid on the Shetland isle of Whalsay in the 1930s was hardly 'primitive', but (as his recurring omission from books purporting to present 'the poetry of the Thirties' indicates) he was certainly marginal. The Ossianic and Romantic linkage of primitive wildness and bookish sophistication is not identical with the later nineteenth-century trope of the poet as 'Scholar-Gypsy', any more than the ideal of the poet who combines 'primitive' gypsy lore with donnish learning is identical with Eliot's poet who is 'more *primitive*, as well as more civilized, than his contemporaries', or Les Murray's 'peasant mandarin'.[57] My aim is not to provide a one-size-fits-all straitjacket for every poet writing in the last three centuries. *The Modern Poet* does not contend that Ossian = Arnold = Eliot = Larkin. It is attuned to rhythm, style, and nuance. However, the chapters that follow do argue that, given the enormous differences between their *œuvres*, the connections between the orientations of the various poets treated are especially remarkable. These individual writers all develop the aesthetic of the primitive-sophisticated 'modern poet', and mark significant stages in its unfolding. In tracing such an evolution, this book alerts readers not least to assumptions about the place of the poet in culture and society, whether that society is the eighteenth-century Scotland of capitalist entrepreneurs enthusing over primitive Highlanders, or Ted Hughes's anthropologically alert

---

[57] T. S. Eliot, 'Tarr', *Egoist*, Sept. 1918, 106.

information era in which the shaman-poet's work is discussed and devoured by aficionados of advanced technologies of information.

Earlier in the twentieth century, preoccupied with the governing of knowledge, the modernist poetry of Eliot, Pound, Auden, and Mac-Diarmid displays a consciousness which can be called 'cybernetic'. That term, whose etymology means 'knowledge-governing', was invented later by Eliot's student friend Norbert Wiener. Eliot's links with Wiener are discussed in the fourth chapter. Modernist verse, which evolved through a dialogue (sometimes a quarrel) with academia, is, even more than the poetries of Clough and Arnold, a poetry of learning developed in an environment where issues of knowledge and power frequently overlap. Some of the poets take this very seriously, as the domineering Pound does when he sets himself up as an 'Ezuversity', or as MacDiarmid does in a combative poetry which at times anticipates later developments in computing. Others, like the Auden of *The Orators: An English Study*, use their self-conscious awareness of themselves as poets in dialogue with academia to send up the whole academic governance of knowledge, not to mention the specific subject of English Studies. Auden may be donnish in his insistence on 'dictionaries (the very best money can buy)', yet the room in which he uses these, 'The Cave of Making', has a primitive sound to it, confirming him as yet another post-Ossianic primitive-sophisticate, another modern poet.[58]

Since the figuration of the modern poet develops through a dialogue between poetry and academia, and because universities until the later nineteenth century were all-male institutions, the concept of the modern poet is very much a gendered one. The fifth chapter of this book looks at how poets related to academia in nineteenth- and twentieth-century America. 'Men, Women, and American Classrooms' attends to such diverse teacher-poets as Longfellow, Frost, Lowell, and Ginsberg. Whether tame or wild, they are seen as playing out patterns which confirm them as male modern poets deploying a calculated balance of sophistication and primitivism. Chapter 5 goes on to suggest that a shift in twentieth-century American verse has involved a regendering of the poetry of knowledge. This has been carried out by a number of writers, prominent among them Marianne Moore, Amy Clampitt, and Jorie Graham, all of whose interaction with academia and the world of learning has matured the figure of the modern poet. Towards the close

[58] W. H. Auden, *Selected Poems* (London: Faber & Faber, 1968), 121 ('The Cave of Making').

of the twentieth century, poets more and more combine a sophisticated, usually academically formed awareness of knowledge not with straight-forward 'primitivism', but with other kinds of marginality, whether of gender, race, or nationality. So such different poetries as those of Seamus Heaney and Selima Hill unite learned panache with the deployment of a status (Heaney's Irishness, Hill's femaleness) which might once have consigned them to the peripheries, yet which is now deployed (as Ossian's primitivism once was) to counterpoint their cosmopolitan sophistication.

When Cleanth Brooks and Robert Penn Warren published the third edition of their textbook *Understanding Poetry* in 1960, it opened with the grand statement that 'Poetry gives us knowledge'. Then, with an anxious glance at the existence of the 'robot', it went on to attempt to separate poetic 'knowledge' from 'information'.[59] My book ends with a coda, 'The Poet's Work', which looks at Philip Larkin and other poets writing in recent decades, seeking a balance between their perception of poetry as 'primitive' and their work in an academic environment. In so concluding, I make it clear that I write as a poet as well as a literary critic. I intend this book to be an intervention in the still forming geography of contemporary poetry in our information age, as well as a contribution to literary history and to the understanding of the historical relationship between the writing of verse and the growth of English studies in the universities.

The Modern Poet is written at a time when poetry and academia are, as usual, renegotiating their mutual relationship. As a contribution to such parleyings, the book aims to alert readers to the genealogy and formative importance of that interdependence. An increasing awareness of the way in which the origins of university English studies were bound up with the production of what we would now call 'creative writing', may be proceeding in tandem with an attempt to strengthen the poet's position in relationship to the modern university English literary curriculum. Reflecting on his life in academia and on the history of English studies, Frank Kermode comments that

If we could begin all over again, it would be useful to recall that poetry was once assumed to be a teachable subject. The demise of that notion is in part a consequence of developments internal to the poetic tradition, especially the

---

[59] Cleanth Brooks and Robert Penn Warren, *Understanding Poetry*, 3rd edn. (New York: Holt, Rinehart & Winston, 1960), pp. xiii, xiv, and 2.

decay of confidence in the accessibility and value of learnable techniques. There is no point in deploring that historical development, but it can still be argued that people who have actually written Petrarchan sonnets, villanelles, sestinas, ballades, and so forth, whatever the merit of their performances, actually understand more about poetry than people who haven't, and may have a better understanding of more modern, less communicable technical achievements. They will know better why poetry is important, if it still is.

Conscious of a suspicion of creative writing courses on the part of many teachers of literature, Kermode nevertheless concludes by expressing his satisfaction with a graduate class whose students had been taught to write poetry as a major element in their studies: 'Belatedly, I am almost convinced that this is where the study of literature ought to begin.'[60] The thrust of my book supports such an assertion, and deletes Kermode's 'almost'. Yet it suggests also the need to understand how academia's attitude to poetry may impact on poetry itself. It would be naive to pretend that if verse is taught in the groves of academe, the classroom will have no effect on verse. In such a process of education there will be students, the best probably among them, who will rebel against the idea of a poetry contained and controlled by teachers, and who will go in search of something wilder. In this they will follow Robert Fergusson and Robert Burns in their self-conscious reactions to the academic milieu and to those gifted eighteenth-century professorial pedants Robert Watson and Hugh Blair. Still, it would be wise to remember that even in the very early university English classes Professor Blair himself established a pattern of seeking out primitive sublimity.

If poetry and academia are renegotiating their relationship, then this should not simply be a case of academics telling poets what to do, converting them into efficient teachers. Poets do not exist for the mere purpose of serving the university system. If some of them are to work in that system, then they should profit from it. The gain should be more than financial. It should also take the form of less obvious forms of sustenance, intellectual and imaginative nourishment. Though *The Modern Poet* is not a catch-all history of the relationships between every poet and every academic, throughout the pages of this book there will appear poets whose work thrives on and incorporates kinds of knowledge and information which the university can provide. It will also be apparent

---

[60] Frank Kermode, *Not Entitled* (London: Flamingo, 1996), 197.

that an academic community may provoke fruitfully aggressive reactions in the poet. What matters is that poets should not be blandly agreeable, but should use the system, its books, knowledge, time, money, and opportunities to provide kinds of peculiar nourishment useful to the making of verse, rather than simply acting as diligent functionaries of the curriculum. A necessary badness—a wicked, selfish streak of *furor poeticus*—must coexist with a willingness to teach. Not all poets, not all academics, will be prepared to countenance such a *modus vivendi*, but some will, and it is to be hoped that they may function as critics, defenders of poetry in their prose, as well as poets.

The days when freelance poets might be given rein to discuss poetry at length in widely circulated periodicals or newspapers, or to publish books of criticism with mainstream publishers, has largely gone. There is a tendency for today's poets to confine themselves to reviews or short essays in specialist journals. Even up to the 1970s when volumes such as Ian Hamilton's *A Poetry Chronicle* appeared, these shorter prose pieces might be collected and more widely circulated as books. Nowadays, apart from the prose of a small number of major poets such as Les Murray, this is becoming an uncommon phenomenon. There are, though, poets as different as Tom Paulin, Adrienne Rich, and Douglas Dunn who are linked to universities and whose prose may find an academic as well as a non-academic audience. Such poets also have the time, training, and resources to ponder and construct larger-scale arguments about poetry, theory, and literary history which would be well-nigh impossible for the 'freelance' poet to consider. The 'free-lancer' is constantly subject to the immediate demands of journalism, short-space reviewing, lack of security, and need for ready cash. In earlier centuries it was taken for granted that poets as well as professional critics would address and develop conceptions of the history of poetry. The point was not that poetry belonged only to writers of verse and that they should exercise their rights over it, but that they might be particularly attuned to its development. In this way a consciousness of their heritage might nourish poets' own work at the same time as contributing to a wider appreciation of poetry and its place in the culture.

I have tried to author this book in such a spirit, and hope that it will have a wide appeal and resonance. At the same time, I needed to write *The Modern Poet* to make sense of my position as a poet and an academic. If I were to continue in both capacities, I required to have some awareness of how they might relate to one another. My aim was not to make the connection seem too easy, but to understand it as part of a much larger history. I gained a sense of reinforcement from investigating that cultural development, sensing certain continuities with the remote in time and place, as well as with the immediate communities in which I am involved. There are certainly other ways to be a poet, and to think about poetry. Some years back, as one of the participants in 'New Generation Poets', a British promotion in which twenty poets were selected by senior writers and others, then fanfared at home and abroad, with poetry being billed as 'the new rock and roll', I felt elated and sometimes ill at ease.[61] While it was good to have our work disseminated, to appear on radio and television, to read to large audiences, nevertheless, as rockers and rollers, many of us were unconvincing. Among the twenty were several poets who worked in universities or who had spent a long time in them. To stress this point would have made for boring marketing. I was impressed by how readily several journalists latched onto the rock and roll tag, keener to write about it than to print poets' work or discuss it in their papers. While the poet may still nurture a love of that wild energy most familiar to wide audiences through the culture of rock and roll, poetry is also a business of musing, reflection, and crafting in which nothing stageable or photogenic happens. The excitement is subcutaneous, a matter of dream, brain, nerve, and muscle, while the unleashing is simply words on a page, or a speaking voice which arrests hearers far less by its volume than by unexpectedly jumping to the right conclusions. Given that, the university, despite its dangers of desiccation, may be at least as hospitable to poetry's development as the arena of rock music. In any case, each of these worlds is subtly aware of the other, and of further constellations beyond.

Part of my own academic training involved the adoption of an impersonal voice. This had its advantages, since it appeared to control the ego. However, I was not always convinced that the scholars and critics who taught me were committed to so straightforward an aim. I realize now that when I was an undergraduate at Glasgow University, then a graduate student at Oxford University in the early 1980s, the norm of an impersonal scholarly voice was very much under attack.

---

[61] See e.g. Alison Roberts, 'Hit Parade of New Poets to Stop the Music on Radio 1', *The Times*, 13 Jan. 1994, 9; Mike Ellison, 'Rock-Style Stardom Beckons as a New Generation of Poets Quits the Attic for the Limelight', *Guardian*, 13 Jan. 1994, 22.

That voice had developed as part of a particular system. Its effect was to make the writer (whether male or female) one of the chaps, aloof in meticulous and studied neutrality. Masking my Scottishness and my concerns as a poet, such a pose also suppressed other cultural differences, including class. It was a voice which owed much to Arnoldian notions of criticism as 'disinterested', yet which often concealed particular designs. This impersonal tone has been contested not least within academia by feminist and black scholarship where the giving of personal testimony can become a self-consciously staged trope of its own. Nevertheless, it can also establish the writer as having an identity which is not that of the chaps. *The Modern Poet* draws on the accents and techniques of that 'impersonal' tradition of scholarship in which I was educated, and which I still value, but it also deliberately introduces on occasion the first person since I do not wish to mask my own interests as a poet, controversialist, and rewriter of literary history. If the aims of the poet and of the academic seem hard to untangle, then that is what this book is about. Instead of pretending that the university study of poetry in English has evolved separately from the writing of poetry, we need to face up to the fact that the two have been and continue to be fused in the figure of the modern poet.

CHAPTER 1

The Birth of the Modern Poet

One day around the year 1755 a young Highland schoolmaster fell asleep under an oak tree and found himself on Parnassus. There he met the goddess Minerva and together they walked beside a 'great River of Time'. This was principally a turbulent watercourse of books into which were hurled 'all the Works of Genius' to see if they might survive. Eventually the schoolmaster and Minerva reached the Island of Immortality, 'the Eternal Mansion of those Divine Geniuses whose Writings have escaped the Dangers of Time & been judg'd worthy of a Fame equal in Duration to that of the World'. Entering a circular temple of books, the two visitors saw the works of Homer and Virgil, *Paradise Lost*, Shakespeare's plays, and tragedies by Corneille and Racine. After surveying other volumes, the schoolteacher caught sight of

a beautiful Casquet enriched with Diamonds & precious Stones not unlike that which Alexander is said to have found in the Tent of Darius. In this the Goddess told me were deposited the precious Remains of several Ages and Nations which tho' but little known were judg'd worthy of Immortality. Upon opening it the first Thing I discover'd was the Odes of Sappho, one of Alcaeus and a few Fragments of the other Grecian Lyricks. There were also preserv'd here a good Number of Small Poems in Different Languages and Characters, some of them Compos'd in Lapland, others by our own Scottish Bards and others produced in the Wilds of America. What surprized me not a little was to find in this Collection several very ancient poems celebrating the heroic Achievements of British Heroes, which performances, tho' of infinite Value, were absolutely unknown except to a few who retain'd the Knowledge of the two Original Languages of this Island.

At this point, disturbed by a procession of Muses heralding the arrival of 'the Writings of the Great Mr. Pope', the schoolmaster woke up and hurried home, 'full of the wonderful Vision'.[1]

---

[1] Quoted from Edinburgh University Library MS La. III.251, pp. 137–48.

This vision is the product of an ambitious aspiring writer, striving for literary power by aligning himself with a sense of absolute critical judgement. Its author is a poet as well as a scholar. His vision, far more a piece of literary artifice than an actual dream, is written by a critical as well as a creative imagination. The creative intelligence here signals modernity in its anxiously self-conscious awareness of the weight and order of earlier literary monuments. It is also recognizably modern in its admission to the literary pantheon of critical texts by Boileau, Addison, and others, as well as works of what we might now call creative writing. In today's parlance what we have here is a prophetic formulation of the canon, one which bonds modern to classical authors, in the way that multivolume anthologies of a national corpus (which will be discussed in my next chapter) do slightly later in the eighteenth century.

In some respects the assembly of books in the schoolmaster's vision corresponds closely to the group of texts praised by the first university teachers of English when the subject began at around this time as 'Rhetoric and Belles-Lettres' in the Scottish universities.[2] That is the milieu in which the schoolmaster had been trained. Yet, unlike the multivolume anthologies of national poetry and the developing university subject of Belles-Lettres, this strikingly anticipatory vision offers a canon which includes both Welsh and native American poetries. It also contains work in Gaelic, the language behind the translated Ossianic 'Fragments' which will soon excite literary, artistic, and musical Europe.

A few years earlier, this same schoolmaster, whose name was Jerome Stones, had been a student at St Andrews University. On 27 November 1747 he borrowed some volumes from the university library. These included Thomas Ruddiman's 1710 edition of Gavin Douglas's Scots translation of the *Aeneid*; the second, 1736 edition of Thomas Blackwell's *An Enquiry into the Life and Writings of Homer*; and Francis Peck's *New Memoirs of the Life and Poetical Works of Mr. John Milton: with An Examination of Milton's Style, & Exploratory & Critical Notes on Divers Passages of Milton & Shakespeare* (1740).[3] Clearly Stones was interested

---

[2] See Robert Crawford, *Devolving English Literature*, 2nd edn. (Edinburgh: Edinburgh University Press, 2000), ch. 1, and Robert Crawford (ed.), *The Scottish Invention of English Literature* (Cambridge: Cambridge University Press, 1998).
[3] St Andrews University Library Receipt Book, Professors and Students, 1737–48 (St Andrews University Muniments, LY. 205.1), Jerome Stones's entry for 27 Nov. 1747.

in poetry, and in the then most prestigious genre of poetry, epic. Blackwell's work admired the 'sublime' and presented Homer as a '*Stroling Bard*' who lived when 'there was but little *Erudition* in the world' and so was 'truly *natural*'. At the same time, though, Blackwell explores the kinds of knowledge Homer possessed, and the lengthy Index to his book includes several entries under the heading 'Education, *Power of it*'.[4] The volume by Francis Peck offered a rather different kind of epic poet. For Peck, a Cambridge graduate who pioneered the annotation of modern English writers through juxtaposing their works with extracts from their contemporaries, 'Mr. MILTON was, by *nature*, a fine poet; but a great deal more so, by *art*. Yet he was fond of having it thought to be all pure *nature*.' Peck's Milton is a learned author, who works hard to deploy his academic learning in the service of poetry. The very language which Peck uses makes Milton sound like a poet with exams on his mind:

He proposed at first to write in *Latin*, but afterwards contented himself to write in *English*. Upon weighing the thing he was not sure whether he could arrive to be *Beta* in the former, though he was not without hopes (&, I think, his hopes did not deceive him) that he might come to be *Alpha* in the latter.[5]

If Peck gives Milton an alpha as a modern English epic poet, Blackwell regards Homer as equally to the fore among the writers of classical epic. Jerome Stones also carried with him from the St Andrews library the translated work of a third epic author, Virgil. The translator, Gavin Douglas, Bishop of Dunkeld and a former student at Stones's university, had produced in the early sixteenth century the first full version of a classical epic in a modern European vernacular. Two centuries later some Scottish readers were beginning to regard Douglas's work, with its copious elaborations and original prologues, as a classic of their literature. Yet the Scots language in which Douglas wrote required considerable glossing even for the eighteenth-century Scot. At a time when many Scots, particularly in the universities, were trying to 'purify' their written and spoken English of Scotticisms, while consigning vernacular Scots idiom to the past and to the lower classes, Douglas's work could be seen as a glory but also as an awkward embarrassment. In the later eighteenth

[4] Thomas Blackwell, *An Enquiry into the Life and Writings of Homer* (1735; 2nd edn. London: n. p., 1736), 67, 106, 129, 347 ff.

[5] Francis Peck, *New Memoirs of the Life and Poetical Works of Mr John Milton* (London: n.p., 1740), 3 and 5.

century, when they were being taught 'correct' English style by their professors, students at St Andrews scribbled on the flyleaf of the volume of Douglas's translation such remarks as 'Gavin Douglass was one of the Stupidest Idiots that ever breathed the Breath of Live.'[6] Attitudes towards Douglas might exemplify the way in which educated Scots at this time felt caught between their own supposedly barbarous speech and the sophisticated English language they aspired to. Jerome Stones, though, thought differently. For this ambitious student of epic poetry, Douglas was a source of inspiration, and the university library a resource that helped him shape for English-language writers the modern conception of the poet.

Stones was and has remained an obscure figure. Even his name is less than certain. As a St Andrews student he signed himself 'Stones'; in the few memorials of him, he is called 'Stone'. He was born in the parish of Scoonie, Fife, in 1727, son of a seaman (who died when Stones was 3) and a poor mother. Stones studied English, writing, and arithmetic at his local school, then worked as a pedlar or chapman, dealing in buckles, garters, and small items. Yet his intellectual concerns meant that soon he became an itinerant bookseller who was said to pursue this trade 'more with a view to the improvement of his mind, than for any peculiar emolument'.[7] A perfect example of the much mythologized multi-talented Scottish 'lad o' pairts', Stones taught himself Hebrew and Greek. His local schoolmaster John Turcan helped him with Latin. After a time Stones's brilliance was noticed by Thomas Tullideph, Principal of St Andrews University and a heritor of Stones's parish, who encouraged the pedlar to become a student. Stones matriculated at the University in session 1747–8 and amazed his (mainly younger) fellow classmates by his vivacity and learning.

We can see from Stones's library borrowings that the former pedlar was using the university in some ways like a typical Scottish student of the period. So, for instance, he took out volumes of Addison, a staple text for those 'provincial' Scots who wished to train themselves in the

[6] *Virgil's Aeneis, Translated into Scottish Verse by the Famous Gawin Douglas: A New Edition* (Edinburgh: n.p., 1710), title page of the St Andrews University library copy originally classmarked as QQ 4.28.

[7] Revd Swan of Scoonie, writing in Sir John Sinclair (ed.), *The Statistical Account of Scotland*, 21 vols. (Edinburgh: n.p., 1791–9), v. 111; other biographical information about Stones is drawn from *Encyclopedia Perthensis*, 23 vols. (Perth: n.p., n.d.), xxi. 440–1; and Donald Mackinnon, 'Collection of Ossianic Ballads by Jerome Stone', *Transactions of the Gaelic Society of Inverness*, 14 (1887–8), 314–69.

writing of correct English.[8] He also borrowed, like many of his peers in the 1740s, volumes of Rollin's *Method of Teaching and Studying the Belles-Lettres*, a work whose subtitle in English translation makes clear its purpose: 'An Introduction to Languages, Poetry, Rhetoric, History, Moral Philosophy, Physics, etc., with Reflections on Taste, and Instructions with Regard to the Eloquence of the Pulpit, the Bar, and the Stage, the Whole Illustrated with Passages from the most famous Poets and Orators, ancient and modern, with Critical Remarks on them, Designed more particularly for Students in the Universities.'[9] This was a manual much used by Scottish students who wished to train themselves in speaking and writing, and to acquire a polished literary education. As we now know, eighteenth-century St Andrews was both culturally marginal and one of the very first centres of the new university subject of 'Belles-Lettres', which later became 'English Literature' and which catered for those who wished to improve their literary taste and abilities.[10] Stones as a student was not simply learning for the sake of learning. He was self-consciously using the university to educate himself as a writer.

It is recorded that he produced humorous poems while he was a student. More importantly, his reading of Gavin Douglas was to result in the publication a few years later of a modern English version of Douglas's own prologue to the twelfth book of his Scots *Aeneid* translation. By the time Stones's poem was published in the *Scots Magazine* in 1755, thanks to the patronage of the Duke of Atholl he was living as a schoolteacher in the ancient seat of Douglas's bishopric, Dunkeld in Perthshire. Stones introduces his modern English version of the Scots poet with words which reveal both his eighteenth-century embarrassment at Douglas's Scots language and his pride in the earlier translator-poet's achievement in describing the coming of spring:

The most pompous description of that enlivening season I ever met with, in any book, ancient or modern, is Bp Douglas's prologue to his translation of the 12th

---

[8] See Crawford, *Devolving English Literature*, 16–44; Stones's borrowings of Addison are recorded in St Andrews University Library Receipt Book (see n. 3 above), entries for 11 and 27 Nov. 1747, 16 Dec. 1747; also Receipt Book, Professors and Students, 1748–53 (St Andrews University Muniments LY.205.2), entries for 26 Jan. 1749.

[9] St Andrews University Library Receipt Book, Professors and Students, 1748–53, entries for 18 and 31 Oct. 1748, and 19 May 1749.

[10] See Crawford (ed.), *The Scottish Invention*, especially introduction; see also Robert Crawford (ed.), *Launch-Site for English Studies: Three Centuries of Literary Studies at the University of St Andrews* (St Andrews: Verse, 1997).

book of Virgil. Such of your readers as can trace the beauties of that poem,
amidst the rubbish of antiquated orthography, and an obsolete dialect, must
meet with a pleasure in the perusal of it, not easy to be paralleled, and stand
amazed at the exuberance of its author's imagination. An attempt to accommod-
ate the delicacies of that performance to modern ears, is sent you inclosed.[11]

What follows is quite a close, competent translation of Douglas's Scots
into modern English, offering us scenes which might appeal not least to
an ambitious young poet now living in the Highlands:

> Deep in the bosom of th' inclosed ground,
> 'Midst shades, and vales, the raging bucks are found,
> And panting harts retire in mingling droves,
> To seek the covert of the thickest groves;
> There, red of hue, and fleeter than the wind,
> Her speckled offspring nurs'd the tender hind,
> The kids pursue the roes across the lawn,
> And the dun doe is follow'd by the fawn.[12]

This is not great verse, but in its measured way it is highly adequate.
More interesting is how Stones is converting this work of Scotland's
'antiquated' and 'obsolete' epic literary heritage into a format likely to
appeal to a modern audience whose taste has been formed by James
Thomson. Thomson was a poet admired by Stones, and *The Seasons* was
one of the Scottish poetic texts most praised by the university teachers
of Rhetoric and Belles-Lettres.[13] The young schoolmaster was also
interested in combining what he had gained from his own education
both inside and outside university with his commitment to Scottish
literary culture. This led him not only to translate the medieval Scots of
Douglas's epic, but also to produce a work which stands as a milestone
in the relations between English and Gaelic. Here Stones's efforts signal
the direction to be taken by the text which brings to full development
the distinctive cultural form of the modern poet.

Stones was no native Gaelic speaker, or, as he put it more colourfully,
'I am equally a stranger in blood to the descendents of *Simon Breck*, and

---

[11] A.Y. [i.e. Jerome Stones], 'Description of a May Morning, Translated from Gawin
Douglas, Bishop of Dunkeld', *Scots Magazine*, 17 (1755), 294. Stones is identified as author of
the pieces attributed to him in the present volume by his obituarist in May 1756 (see *Scots
Magazine*, 18 (1756), 314).

[12] A.Y., 'Description', 296.

[13] See 'To the Author of the Elegy on the Clergyman's Horse,' on p. 81 of EUL MS
La.III.251.

the subjects of *Cadwallader*. I have no personal attachment either to the *Welsh leek*, or the *Irish potatoe*. None of my ancestors that I know of ever came within view of *Penmanmaur*; and I can prove, that, for ten generations back, none of them has so much as had the second sight.'[14] Nevertheless, Principal Thomas Tullideph at St Andrews encouraged the talented and patriotic young Lowland linguist to study Gaelic. No Gaelic was taught at Scottish universities in this period. The language itself was regarded as barbarous and disgraced by most Lowlanders. However, the Gaelic-speaking philosopher Adam Ferguson (a student at St Andrews in the 1740s) had suggested that there were 'relicks of ancient poetry in the Highlands'.[15] This was a dangerous time for Gaelic culture. Only the year before Stones matriculated as a St Andrews student, the University, anxious to demonstrate its Hanoverian loyalties in the month following the Jacobite defeat at Culloden, offered the chancellorship of the University to 'Butcher' Cumberland, whom the professors officially praised as 'Rebelliumque Domitor' ('Conqueror of the Rebels').[16] Still, clearly among the professoriate, even in this period, there was some interest in Gaelic. In the 1720s, shortly after the first Jacobite Rebellion and before he moved to St Andrews, Tullideph had been the Church of Scotland minister in the united parish of Dron, Kirkpottie, and Ecclesmoghridain in Perthshire.[17] As its very name suggests, this parish was in an area where the Gaelic language was to the fore. When Stones, not long after the second Jacobite Rebellion, went to Dunkeld, he entered the Perthshire territory which Tullideph had known as a young man. Dunkeld was an area in which Gaelic was strong and Jacobitism not unknown. The local parish minister in Stones's time, for example, was not only a St Andrews graduate but also the only minister of the Church of Scotland who had not, during the recent Jacobite Rebellion, prayed in public for King George.[18] Stones does not appear to have been a Jacobite, but the Principal of Cumberland's St Andrews, an amateur poet with a fondness for

---

[14] A.Y. [i.e. Jerome Stones], 'Of the Progenitors of the English Language', *Scots Magazine*, 17 (1756), 93.
[15] Anon., 'Adam Ferguson', *Edinburgh Review*, 125 (1867), 63; Adam Ferguson, in Henry Mackenzie (ed.), *Report of the Highland Society of Scotland Appointed to Inquire into the Nature and Authenticity of the Poems of Ossian* (Edinburgh: Constable, 1805), appendix IV, 63.
[16] 'Praefatio ad Diplomam', in Francis Pringle, *Copies of Addresses and Public Acts, etc.*, manuscript book (St Andrews University Muniments, MS LF.1111.P8C99).
[17] Hew Scott, *Fasti Ecclesiae Scotticanae*, new edn., 8 vols. (Edinburgh: Oliver & Boyd, 1915–50), iv. 201–3 and v. 113 and 243.   [18] Ibid. iv. 155.

'eloquence', for Scottish vernacular culture, and for classical literature, encouraged his young protégé the aspiring poet-scholar to learn Gaelic and to pursue his investigations of ancient Celtic culture.[19]

This Stones eagerly did. Writing in the *Scots Magazine* in February 1755 about Johnson's newly published *Dictionary*, he complains about a lack of attention to the ancient Celtic language and to etymological study involving the modern Celtic tongues. In this year when Thomas Gray began his poem 'The Bard', Stones wishes more attention might be paid to such areas as 'the wilds of Lochaber'.[20] He reveals a strong commitment to what he describes as 'a language, which was once spoke by a great and mighty people, but now confined to a small corner or two, where it languishes, and seems to be dying away through mere old age'.[21] In September 1755 Stones writes to Tullideph from Dunkeld with a mixture of scorn and excited fascination about ancient and modern Highland culture with its Irish (i.e. Erse or Gaelic) poetry:

there is no People in the Globe of the Earth, whose Language may be proven to have undergone less Change ... than that of the Irish and our own Scottish Ancestors. That they never were friends to Commerce, or Intercourse with Strangers, both History, Tradition and the very Genius of the People strongly assure us. An Irish Poem I have in my Custody at present, ascribes all the Calamities that have happened both to the Nation, and the Royal family, for several hundred years, entirely to the Mixture of forreigners, among the genuine Gauls, and having testifyed the most implacable Hatred, against the very Name of English, and Lowlanders, the Poet assigns no other Cause for it, but that their Language, so far from being pure and unmixed like the Gallick, is a Compound of Dutch, Latin, and all the Tongues that were spoke at Babel. Again, so far from Learning having ever made such Advances among them as to effect the least Change in their Language, you may rest assur'd, that it has not hitherto so much as dawn'd in their Horizon; they have scarce a word in their Language proper to express the name of Science by, and the Peasants in the Highlands, are as far remov'd from what may be call'd the modern Taste of Life, as the Grecians were, five hundred years before the Trojan War ... I mentioned before, their Custom of singing the Praises of their ancient Heroes. No sooner did I hear some few Specimens of these Kind of Songs, than I long'd to have a Collection of them, which I have happily acquired, and a pretty large one too, after much Labour, and some Expence. Numbers of these Songs were composed as may be easily proven, sixteen hundred years ago, and yet there is hardly

---

[19] Tullideph's poems and 'Oratio de Eloquentiae' are in his Common-place Book (St Andrews University Muniments, LF.1109.T8C6), pp. 101–2, 110, and 7–8.
[20] A.Y., 'Of the Progenitors', 91–2.   [21] Ibid. 92–3.

a word in them, but the very Children understand. This shows how little the Language has chang'd in that Time.[22]

Stones describes a culture that is primitive, pre-scientific, warlike, and wild, a kind of living memorial to the noble savage. Yet this culture is also part of his own inheritance as an academically trained Scoto-Briton. Note how he writes of '*Our* [my italics] valiant ancestors'. These primitives 'far remov'd from what may be call'd the modern Taste of Life' become in Stones's account the focal point for the eye of modernity. That eye is unstoppably drawn to them, even sees itself as related to them. In Stones's writing we hear just one of the ways that a preoccupation with degrees of barbarity and refinement is part of Scottish Enlightenment modernity. Similar interests can be found in Adam Ferguson's *Essay on the History of Civil Society* (1767) or John Millar's *Observations Concerning the Distinction of Ranks in Society* (1771), or in the writings of Adam Smith, William Robertson, or other studies of subjects as various as belles-lettres and agriculture. The prevalence of such a topic has often been noted.[23] If we have poetry in mind, then in Stones's letters we see just how emphatically the most distinguished Lowland scholar of Gaelic in the mid-eighteenth century saw the Highlanders as Homeric. We can sense too how imminent are the Ossianic poems, those poetic works famously presented as collected in modern times but dating originally from the third century. Stones, as his manuscripts show, was a poet as well as a scholar. His writings are powered by a conjunction of the developing academic literary climate represented by St Andrews, and the young schoolmaster's own not inconsiderable poetic imagination. On the one hand, Stones is 'primitive' in his origins (most of his fellow students were far from pedlars) and in his taste for the culture of a Highland civilization still widely regarded as barbarous; on the other hand, he is highly sophisticated in his training, scholarly work, and the self-conscious development of a project both critical and creative. Uniting these characteristics, Stones typifies the Scottish Enlightenment. He also anticipates the intellectual and imaginative make-up of the modern poet. Pursuing his etymological researches with a view to proving the antiquity and wide dissemination of the ancient Celtic language, Stones, under Tullideph's guidance, was preparing his own

---

[22] Jerome Stones to Thomas Tullideph (fair copy of letter dated 'Dunkeld, Septr. 20 1755'), EUL MS La.III.251, pp. 6–7. Tullideph may be identified by his address at Kilmux in Fife on p. 23 of the same MS.

[23] For more on this, see Crawford, *Devolving English Literature*, especially ch. 1.

'Inquiry into the Original of the Nation and Language of the Ancient Scots'. He built on the researches of such earlier scholars as Bochart, O'Flaherty, and Lloyd, but surpassed them in his knowledge of Scottish Gaelic materials. He envisaged his work as two octavo volumes, with notes and commentaries. As part of his project, his anthologizing of Gaelic poetry grew:

I also collected numbers of ancient Poems, the Productions of Irish and Scottish Bards for my own Perusal, since by such as a learn'd Modern observes the Real Genius of a people is strongly mark'd and demonstrated. These pieces like the Language they were compos'd in and the people they serv'd to amuse are daring and incorrect passionate and bold. Like the Compositions of the Orientals one meets in them with unexpected Flashes of the Sublime which are succeeded by as unexpected Falls. All their Images like those of the first Ages, are natural though familiar, and striking though mostly borrow'd from common Objects. Homer compares Agamemnon to a Bull, and the Patience of Ajax to that of an Ass—thus here we have the mutual Strokes of two Combatants likened to the Thumping of Hammers, a Conqueror makes such Havock among his Enemies as a Hawk does among the smallest Birds, and a Virgin lamenting over her dead Lover tells us that his Hair was blacker than a Crow, and his Cheeks reder than the Blood of a Calf.[24]

Stones is here describing the nature, language, and imagery of Gaelic verse in ways that once again make it appear Homeric. Yet his concern with Gaelic was that of a poet as well as that of a scholar; indeed, I would argue that it is impossible to see these as separate interests. The poetic fruit of Stones's outsider's commitment to Gaelic culture appeared in the *Scots Magazine* in January 1756 when Stones published the first ever English translation of a Gaelic ballad.

Despite the 1751 publication in Edinburgh by the Jacobite poet Alasdair MacMhaighstir Alasdair (Alexander MacDonald) of a collection of Gaelic verse with an English preface lamenting the ignoring of the Gaelic language, before this point there had been very little crossover in Scotland between the indigenous literatures in Gaelic on the one hand, and in Scots and English on the other. The publication by Stones of his Gaelic translation initiates the idea that Scottish literature and culture were in a positive way plural. From the wider perspectives of the English-speaking world and of Europe, it is also a moment of

---

[24] Jerome Stones, 'An Enquiry into the Original of the Nation and Language of the Ancient Scots, with Conjectures about the Primitive State of the Celtic, and Other European Nations', EUL MS La.III.251, p. 42.

intellectual and poetic ignition. For Stones's translation and its presentation prepares the way for a greater work crucial to the inception of European and North American Romanticism. Stones prefaces his translation by emphasizing that he has collected neglected works which

for sublimity of sentiment, nervousness of expression, and high-spirited metaphors, are hardly to be equalled among the chief productions of the most cultivated nations. Others of them breathe such tenderness and simplicity, as must be greatly affecting to every mind that is in the least tinctured with the sister passions of pity and humanity. Of this kind is the poem of which I here send you a translation. Your learned readers will easily discover the conformity there is, betwixt the tale upon which it is built, and the story of *Bellerophon*, as related by Homer: while it will be no small gratification to the curiosity of some, to see the different manner in which a subject of the same nature is handled, by the great father of poetry, and a highland bard.[25]

As has been pointed out by Fiona Stafford and others, it is extremely likely that these words were read by the young James Macpherson, then, like Stones, a Highland schoolteacher.[26] Macpherson had started publishing in the *Scots Magazine* in May 1755. Though his poem 'The Highlander' was not published until 1758, he was eager to write poetry in English that drew on Highland themes. What the classically educated Macpherson (a recent graduate of Blackwell's Aberdeen) had not done at that date, though, was to translate Gaelic poetry into English or to relate it to classical examples. This is exactly the course that Stones had been pursuing. Though it appears to survive only in manuscript, his 'Vision' in which he imagines Scottish Gaelic poetry as part of the immortal heritage of great literature was, we are told by the minister of Stones's original Fife parish, 'published, and often reprinted since his death'.[27] Stones, whose literary projects included a Scottish rewriting of *Macbeth* as well as other Gaelic and English concerns, was at the intellectual and imaginative forefront of Scottish literature in the 1750s. Despite his relative obscurity, his aspirations may have fuelled the work of other writers in the following years.[28] The *Scots Magazine* (the one journal published continuously in Scotland between 1750 and 1759,

[25] [Jerome Stones], 'Albin and the Daughter of Mey', *Scots Magazine*, 18 (1756), 15.

[26] Fiona Stafford, *The Sublime Savage* (Edinburgh: Edinburgh University Press, 1988), 65. Other details about Macpherson's early publications are drawn from this.

[27] Swan, *Statistical Account*, v, 113.

[28] On Stones and *Macbeth* see Neil Rhodes, 'Shakespeare at St Andrews: Origins and Growth of a Tradition', in Crawford (ed.), *Launch-Site*, 30–3.

and the only magazine published in Edinburgh between 1750 and 1755) was the principal Scottish literary organ of its day.[29] Though modelled on the London *Gentleman's Magazine*, it had as one of its stated aims 'That the Caledonian muse might not be restrained by want of a publick echo to her song'.[30] In a Scotland eager for all kinds of 'improvement' this periodical was read avidly by the literati. In its pages in March 1755 the aims of the Select Society for improving literary and other cultural activities were set out.[31] Initiated by the painter Allan Ramsay, Adam Smith, David Hume, the future Lord Monboddo, and others, the Select Society by 1755 numbered among its members talented and ambitious writers such as the friends John Home (whose play *Douglas*, championed as a rival to the work of Shakespeare, was premièred in 1756), William Robertson (historian and Principal of Edinburgh University), Lord Kames, and Hugh Blair.[32] These and other aspiring authors were just the sort of readers who scanned the *Scots Magazine* for public evidence of the perky 'Caledonian muse'.

What Stones's work suggested to such an audience was that the Gaelic literature of their own country, though primitive and foreign to most Lowlanders, contained work comparable with that of Homer. Blackwell had written of Homeric epic's 'wide uncultivated country'. He had seen the material for epic as 'not to be found in a well-governed State, except it be during the Time of a *Civil War*' (as in the case of Milton's 'high-spirited Poem'). Blackwell's Homer was that '*Stroling Bard*' who 'took his Plan from *Nature*' and whose language could 'express all the best and bravest of human Feelings, and retained a sufficient Quantity of its *Original, amazing, metaphoric* Tincture'.[33] Stones presented in just such terms his embellished 'Albin and the Daughter of Mey: An old tale, translated from the Irish'.[34] He was also encouraging among the Scottish literati an appetite for a quasi-epic native poetry that was both primitive and capable of appealing to modern sensibilities; that was foreign and familiar. 'Albin and the Daughter of Mey' was produced

---

[29] Mary Elizabeth Craig, *The Scottish Periodical Press, 1750–1789* (Edinburgh: Oliver & Boyd, 1931), 29 and 33.

[30] Quoted in W. J. Couper, *The Edinburgh Periodical Press*, 2 vols. (Stirling: Eneas Mackay, 1908), ii. 72.

[31] Anon., 'An Account of the Select Society of Edinburgh', *Scots Magazine*, 17 (1755), 126–30.

[32] Davis D. McElroy, *Scotland's Age of Improvement* (Washington: Washington State University Press, 1969), 48–67.   [33] Blackwell, *Enquiry*, 27, 106, 325, and 46.

[34] On Stones's translation, see Micheal Mac Craith, 'The "Forging" of Ossian', in Terence Brown (ed.), *Celticism* (Amsterdam: Rodopi, 1996), 126–8.

a decade after the Jacobite civil war of 1745–6 by a self-conscious translator schooled in modern university literary study, yet was also 'natural' in being one of 'those compositions, which are the production of simple and unassisted genius, in which energy is always more sought after than neatness, and the strictness of connection less adverted to, than the design of moving the passions, and affecting the heart'.[35] His emphasis on 'affecting the heart' aligns Stones's presentation of his Gaelic ballad with the emerging literature of sensibility. His use of the 'Lochmey' Highland landscape of lamentation, its cairn and mountain-side decorously Englished, also set out in the opening stanza a terrain and a tone which other, far better-known writers and readers would adopt as their own:

> Whence come these dismal sounds that fill our ears!
>   Why do the groves such lamentations send!
> Why sit the virgins on the hill of tears,
>   While heavy sighs their tender bosoms rend!
> They weep for ALBIN with the flowing hair,
>   Who perish'd by the cruelty of *Mey*;
> A blameless hero, blooming, young, and fair;
>   Because he scorn'd her passion to obey.
> See on yon western hill the heap of stones,
> Which mourning friends have raised o'er his bones![36]

A year after publishing this narrative and lamentation over the death of a young man, the 30-year-old Jerome Stones was dead. He left the rest of his manuscript collection of Gaelic poetry untranslated. Blending in his career and in his writing elements of the unsophisticated, the primitive, and the highly educated, he is one of the writers who most nearly anticipates the invention of the modern poet. Yet his own poetry remains too constrained by convention. It foreshadows, but does not fully initiate, the transformations of Romanticism. However, within its Scottish context, it spurs that cultural shift. It helps create the taste which will constellate around and nurture the work of James Macpherson. Stones dies, and Ossian is born.

First, though, it is necessary to remind readers briefly of the story of the genesis of James 'Ossian' Macpherson's writing. John Home, playwright and member of the Select Society, met the young Macpherson, Highland schoolteacher and classically trained graduate of Blackwell's

---

35 [Stones], 'Albin and the Daughter of Mey', 15.   36 Ibid.

Aberdeen, on the bowling green in the Dumfriesshire town of Moffat in the autumn of 1759. A decade earlier, in the wake of conversations with Adam Ferguson, Home been encouraged by the English poet William Collins to seek in the Highlands 'Strange lays' by 'Old Runic bards'.[37] Neither Home nor Collins knew any Gaelic poetry, but in Moffat in 1759 Home realized that Macpherson could give him a good idea of the nature of Gaelic verse. He persuaded the reluctant Highlander to make a translation for him. Home took Macpherson's version back to Edinburgh, where his friend Hugh Blair was particularly interested in it.[38] In the winter of that year Blair was to commence the Edinburgh lectures on Rhetoric which led to his appointment as lecturer in Rhetoric (from 1762 Professor of Rhetoric and Belles-Lettres) at Edinburgh University.[39] Blair, 'being as much struck as Mr Home with the high spirit of poetry which breathed in [the translation], promptly made enquiry where Mr Macpherson was to be found'.[40] The poet and the academic met, with results which would alter the course of modern poetry.

Since most readers tend to avoid Ossian, and find it hard to understand the enormous impact made by his work throughout the developed world in the eighteenth and early nineteenth centuries, it may be worth quoting a little at this point. Here is the opening of the third of the 1760 *Fragments of Ancient Poetry*:

> Evening is grey on the hills. The north wind resounds through the woods. White clouds rise on the sky: the thin-wavering snow descends. The river howls afar, along its winding course. Sad, by a hollow rock, the grey-hair'd Carryl sat. Dry fern waves over his head; his seat is an aged birch. Clear to the roaring winds he lifts his voice of woe.[41]

This haunting, haunted music whose energetic wildness ('howls... roaring') is balanced by a geriatric delicacy ('grey...thin-wavering... grey-hair'd') so that it is at once new and antique, primitive and sophisticatedly knowing, both entranced and helped to form the Romantic ear. For modern readers it may beg parody; for an earlier audience it

[37] Roger Lonsdale (ed.), *The Poems of Gray, Collins, and Goldsmith* (Harlow: Longmans, 1969), 504–5 and 516. See also Fiona Stafford, 'Primitivism and the "Primitive" Poet: A Cultural Context for Macpherson's Ossian', in Brown (ed.), *Celticism* 79–96.

[38] For a fuller account, see Stafford, *The Sublime Savage*, 77–95.

[39] Blair's first lecture was given on 11 Dec. 1759; see Anon., 'Scotland', *Scots Magazine*, 21 (1759), 660–1.

[40] Hugh Blair, in Mackenzie (ed.), *Report of the Highland Society*, appendix IV, 57.

[41] *The Poems of Ossian and Related Works*, ed. Howard Gaskill (Edinburgh: Edinburgh University Press, 1996), 10.

demanded imitation. Biblically epic, yet crammed with lyric notes, it initiated and brought to fruition a tonal shift in Western writing. Long before Scott, it invents the Romantic vision of Scotland on which Scott's more ironically inflected work depends. It also consecrates Romantic landscape in general. An Ossian-filtered Scotland, along with the work of Burns, lies behind the Scotophilia of Wordsworth, Coleridge, Byron, Keats, and so many other Romantic poets, not to mention painters and composers. Ossian initiates a spatial change in the imagination, which comes to view the sublime northern and western landscapes of the British isles as crucial to poetic vision. Ossian's importance is formal as well as stylistic and thematic. After Ossian, the prose poem develops, as does *vers libre*.[42] Yet what is most important to the argument of this book is that particularly in its blend of primitivism and sophistication the evolving Ossianic text creates the modern poet.

Until lately, the importance of the Ossianic poems has been clouded (especially in Britain) by an obsession with whether or not they were forged. The historian Hugh Trevor-Roper denounced Ossian as a sham, in much the same way that Dr Johnson (no doubt anxious about the balance of power between oral and written texts) had done so two centuries earlier.[43] Trevor-Roper's essay was trapped in a long-running (often English v. Scottish) argument over whether or not Macpherson was a forger. While it was scarcely illegal in university English departments to present Ossian as providing a stylistic and thematic idiom for Romanticism, it was obligatory to utter the O-word with a knowing smirk. A recent critic can still dismiss with scorn the 'few last-ditch believers in Ossian'.[44] Yet other research, most notably that of Fiona Stafford, Howard Gaskill, Katie Trumpener, and Ian Duncan, has led to a fuller appreciation of the cultural significance of Macpherson's work.[45] We might even use Trevor-Roper's arguments about 'invented

---

[42] See H. T. Kirby-Smith, *The Origins of Free Verse* (Ann Arbor: University of Michigan Press, 1996).

[43] Hugh Trevor-Roper, 'The Invention of Tradition: The Highland Tradition of Scotland', in Eric Hobsbawm and Terence Ranger (ed.), *The Invention of Tradition* (Cambridge: Cambridge University Press, 1983).

[44] Kirby-Smith, *The Origins of Free Verse*, p. vii.

[45] Stafford, *The Sublime Savage*; Howard Gaskill (ed.), *Ossian Revisited* (Edinburgh: Edinburgh University Press, 1991); *Poems of Ossian*, ed. Gaskill; Fiona Stafford (ed.), *From Gaelic to Romantic* (Amsterdam: Rodopi, 1998); Katie Trumpener, *Bardic Nationalism* (Princeton: Princeton University Press, 1997); Ian Duncan, 'Introduction' to Walter Scott, *Rob Roy* (Oxford: Oxford University Press, 1998).

tradition' to make the point that Ossian helped Scotland to reinvent itself, and so functioned as an imaginative crucible, a reminder that national identity (like poetry) is dynamic and metamorphic rather than essentially unchanging.

Many of today's commentators may be more benignly disposed towards Ossian, Son of Fingal. Nevertheless, the signal importance of the way the Ossianic corpus was being produced through the meeting of the poet and translator Macpherson with the pioneering academic Hugh Blair has not been fully articulated. When he met Macpherson in the autumn of 1759 Blair was preparing his lectures on Rhetoric and Belles-Lettres whose plan was published in the *Scots Magazine* for that December. We can see from this outline that the shape of the lecture course (which changed relatively little over the next quarter-century) was clear from the start:

On the 11th of December , Dr Hugh Blair, one of the ministers of Edinburgh, began a course of lectures on composition. In his introductory lecture he gave a view of his plan: and proposed to treat of taste; of language and style; of eloquence, or public speaking, with the different kinds of it, suited to the pulpit, the bar, and popular assemblies; and to explain the principles of the various kinds of composition both in prose and verse.[46]

This structure corresponds with the form of Blair's enormously widely disseminated and influential *Lectures on Rhetoric and Belles-Lettres* (1783) and with the volumes of student notes of these lectures which circulated repeatedly in earlier decades. So, just as Blair was composing one of the first university courses in English vernacular literature, he was also working with Macpherson on the initial volume of Ossianic poems. This conjunction was crucial to the writings of both Blair and Macpherson. It also gave to the first appearance of the Ossianic poems a peculiarly self-conscious air. When Blair met Macpherson, the minister and future professor was a skilled editor. In 1753 he had produced a published edition of literary materials which had been presented to him 'in prodigious disorder'. Grandson of a bookseller and familiar with the Edinburgh literary world, Blair was also *au fait* with Homeric annotation and had been a member of a Church of Scotland General Assembly committee whose job was to turn prose passages of the Old and New Testaments into metre.[47] His was a creative as well as a critical mind,

---

[46] 'Scotland' (unsigned report), *Scots Magazine*, 21(1759), 660–1.
[47] Robert Morell Schmitz, *Hugh Blair* (New York: King's Crown Press, 1948), 7, 12, 18, 21.

and the subject of the lectures he was writing in 1759 was presented principally as 'composition'. If we read carefully Blair's account of his first dealings with Macpherson, we realize that he was a co-maker, not simply a critic of the Ossianic corpus. After having 'much conversation' with Macpherson on the subject of Highland poetry at their first meeting, Blair recalled that

> When I learned that, besides the few pieces of that poetry which he had in his possession, greater and more considerable poems of the same strain were to be found in the Highlands, and were well known to the natives there, I urged him to translate the other pieces which he had, and bring them to me; promising that I should (take) care to circulate and bring them out to the public, by whom they deserved to be known. He was extremely reluctant and averse to comply with my request, saying, that no translation of his could do justice to the spirit and force of the original; and that, besides injuring them by translation, he apprehended they would be very ill relished by the public as so very different from the strain of modern ideas, and of modern, connected, and polished poetry. It was not till after much and repeated importunity on my part, and representing to him the injustice he would do to his native country by keeping concealed these hidden treasures, which, I assured him, if brought forth, would serve to enrich the whole learned world, that I at length prevailed on him to translate, and bring to me, the several poetical pieces which he had in his possession. Them I published in 1760, under the title of *Fragments of Ancient Poetry, collected in the Highlands of Scotland*, and wrote the Preface which is prefixed to them, in consequence of the conversations I had held with Mr Macpherson.[48]

Blair emphasizes Macpherson's reluctance. This hesitation (also noted by John Home) corresponds to the general Highland suspicion of Lowlanders described by Jerome Stones. Again, Macpherson repeats Stones's concerns about the irregularity of the Highland poetry. However, with the help of Blair's expository preface based on Homeric scholarship linked to Gaelic material according to Stones's recipe, this unevenness is presented as a virtue. It is a sign of original 'primitive' power. Blair's account makes it clear that without his sponsorship and active intervention the Ossianic pieces would never have been assembled or published. It is Blair who desires and actually claims responsibility for publishing the book, which appeared in June 1760. Blair's modern biographer also credits him with the ordering of the poems.[49]

---

[48] Blair, in Mackenzie (ed.), *Report of the Highland Society*, appendix IV, 57–8.
[49] Schmitz, *Hugh Blair*, 141.

The published volume of these prose versions of Gaelic poems was as much Blair's production as it was Macpherson's.

It is essential to realize that from the start these Ossianic poems are presented both as primitive and scholarly. They have a peculiar textual self-consciousness. The June 1760 title page looks like that of a classical text, with its Latin motto from Lucan's *Pharsalia*.[50] The three lines of Latin end intriguingly with the term '*Bardi*'.[51] Yet it is the opening word of the title, appearing in large capitals, 'FRAGMENTS', which is most striking. As will be discussed below, the use of 'fragments' with regard to these texts was extremely significant and innovative. Blair the academic introduces 'the following fragments as genuine remains of ancient Scottish poetry'.[52] The title of the June volume may have been suggested by a London collection of *Select Pieces of Ancient Poetry*, noticed in the *Scots Magazine* in February 1760.[53] The word 'fragments' could have come either from Blair or Macpherson, both of whom were classically trained. It is the Lowlander Blair, though, not his Highland collaborator, who gives prominence in the preface to the name 'Oscian', only mentioned in passing in one of the poems. These are presented by Blair, in terms which recall Jerome Stones, as having enormous antiquarian interest: 'The date of their composition cannot be exactly ascertained. Tradition, in the country where they were written, refers them to an aera of the most remote antiquity: and this tradition is supported by the spirit and strain of the poems themselves; which abound with those ideas, and paint those manners, that belong to the most early state of society.' Though he leaves the 'poetical merits of these fragments' to the public, Blair implies it is high, and mentions a further 'work of considerable length' that may yet be recovered. This is a text involving 'Fingal'. It is called an 'Epic poem'.[54] When Blair supplied his summary, Macpherson had gathered no such 'Epic'. By the time of the second, October edition, however, 'It may be proper to inform the

---

[50] *Fragments of Ancient Poetry Collected in the Highlands of Scotland and Translated from the Galic or Erse Language* (Edinburgh: Hamilton & Balfour, 1760).

[51] Stafford (*The Sublime Savage*, 100) quotes 'the standard eighteenth-century translation of these lines by Nicholas Rowe': 'You too, ye Bards! whom sacred Raptures fire, | To Chaunt your Heroes to your Country's lyre; | Who consecrate in your immortal Strain, | Brave Patriot Souls in righteous Battle slain; | Securely now the tuneful Task renew, | And noblest Themes in deathless Songs pursue.'

[52] *Poems of Ossian*, ed. Gaskill, 5; unless otherwise indicated, quotations from Ossian are taken from this.

[53] 'New Books' (unsigned listing), *Scots Magazine*, 22 (1760), 109.

[54] *Poems of Ossian*, ed. Gaskill, 5–6.

public, that measures are now being taken for making a more full collection of the remaining works of the ancient Scottish Bards; in particular for recovering and translating the heroic poem mentioned in the preface.'[55]

Blair made this happen. As part of a scheme to raise funds for an Ossianic field trip, he had requested Macpherson to write him 'an ostensible letter concerning his Situation, and the reasons why without some Encouragement he could not venture on such an Undertaking'.[56] Macpherson did as he was asked. Writing to Blair in June 1760, he made clear his willingness to 'make a large, and I hope a valuable, collection of our ancient poetry'. He also stated, 'I cannot well spare the expence.'[57] Clearly Macpherson, the young Highland schoolmaster, is wary of being led into debt by the established gentlemen of Edinburgh; at the same time, he obviously catches a scent of financial as well as literary gain. Equally evidently, Blair, who persuades Lord Hailes to become an active participant in getting up a subscription for Macpherson, sees that the project may enhance his own status as a member of the literati. The production of the Ossianic corpus is a speculative commercial as well as a daring aesthetic project. As with so many Scottish Enlightenment concerns, at its heart is a relationship between imagination and hard cash. This is clear from Blair's ensuing, tough-minded correspondence with the London booksellers, and from Macpherson's later career.[58] Their genesis gives the Ossianic poems a certain modernity, situating them firmly not only in the arena of socially sponsored art but also in the evolving capitalist marketplace of literary production in which Dr Johnson maintained that 'No man but a blockhead ever wrote, except for money.'[59] If the sympathetic sentiments of the poems seem to link them to Adam Smith's newly published *Theory of Moral Sentiments* (1759), then their commercial sense (not to mention the division of labour involved in their production) is of a piece with the philosophy of *An Inquiry into the Nature and Causes of the Wealth of Nations* (1776). Smith the

[55] *Poems of Ossian*, ed. Gaskill, 3.

[56] Hugh Blair, letter to Lord Hailes, Bruntsfield, 23 June [1760], published in Robert Hay Carnie, 'Macpherson's *Fragments of Ancient Poetry* and Lord Hailes', *English Studies*, 41 (1960), 22.

[57] James Macpherson, letter to Hugh Blair, Balgowan, 16 June 1760, published in Carnie, 'Macpherson's *Fragments*', 23.

[58] For Blair's correspondence with booksellers see R. W. Chapman, 'Blair on Ossian', *Review of English Studies*, 7 (1931), 80–3.

[59] James Boswell, *The Life of Samuel Johnson*, 2 vols. (1791; repr. London: Dent, 1973), ii, 16 (5 Apr. 1776).

lecturer on Rhetoric and Belles-Lettres told his Glasgow University students that the Ossianic translations 'have very great merit'.[60]

During the spring of 1760 a few of Macpherson's short translations circulated in England. They aroused considerable interest in such literary figures as Horace Walpole and Thomas Gray. Gray, Cambridge don and author of 'The Bard', was '*extasie* with their infinite beauty'.[61] He corresponded with Macpherson, though scepticism about the poems' authenticity mixed with a prejudice against the Scots soon coloured the fascination felt south of the border. A strong sense of Scottish–English rivalry was bound up with the emergence of the Ossianic poems in the decades after Culloden, and has continued to surround the work to this day. One reason for Scottish enthusiasm for the Ossianic poems was that they provided Scotland with an ancient bard to set against the English poets. Eventually Burns would come to occupy the position of 'Caledonia's Bard', but in the mid-eighteenth century there were other contenders for that title, foremost of whom was Ossian.[62] Defending or attacking the genuineness of the Ossianic poems too readily became a measure of one's Scottish or English patriotism. In the context of the poems' (in)authenticity, Dr Johnson (whose visit to the Highlands was linked to his scepticism about Ossian's work) contended that Scotsmen loved Scotland more than the truth. The Scots wanted a poet who might outshine England's finest. 'Whaur's yer Wully Shakespeare noo?' a member of the Edinburgh audience is said to have shouted at the première of Home's verse drama *Douglas* in 1756.[63] In Hugh Blair's Edinburgh Scottish–English rivalries in the wake of the 1707 Act of Union (not to mention the Jacobite Rebellions) conditioned the reception of Ossian and the developing design of the modern poet. Jockeying between Scotland and England also shaped an evolving canon of poets which came to represent the nation, as we shall see in the next chapter.

In Edinburgh lengthy extracts from the *Fragments* appeared in the *Scots Magazine* as soon as that pamphlet was published. The story of its eager

---

[60] Adam Smith, *Lectures on Rhetoric and Belles-Lettres*, ed. J. C. Bryce (Oxford: Clarendon Press, 1983), 136.

[61] Thomas Gray, letter to Thomas Warton [*c*.20 June 1760], published in *Correspondence of Thomas Gray*, ed. Paget Toynbee and Leonard Whibley, 3 vols. (Oxford: Clarendon Press, 1935), ii. 680. For Gray's connections with Macpherson see also ibid. iii. 1223–9.

[62] *The Letters of Robert Burns*, ed. J. De Lancey Ferguson, 2nd edn., ed. G. Ross Roy, 2 vols. (Oxford: Clarendon Press, 1985), i. 83.

[63] See David Hutchison, *The Modern Scottish Theatre* (Glasgow: Molendinar Press, 1977), 10.

reception has been told elsewhere.[64] Much less well known is the way Blair used his university lectures to champion the new publication. A 1765 set of student notes of his lecture on the sublime offers us a wording which appears to date from the start of the decade. After discussing the sublime in the Bible, Milton, Homer, and Lucretius, the Professor tells his students,

In (a late publication) some fragments of Erse Poetry, we have also several instances: as—'Oscar my Son came down: the Mighty in Battle descended. His armour rattled as Thunder, and the Lightning of his eyes was terrible' (Frag. 6th) 'Thy voice was like a Stream after rain, like thunder on the Distant Hill' (Frag. 12th) 'Dermid & Oscar were one: they reaped the Battle together: their friendship was strong, as their Steel, and Death walked between them to the Field' (Frag. 7th).[65]

The quotations may be a little inaccurate and the detailed comment missing from these student notes, but there can be no doubt that Blair was using his university lectures as a vehicle to promote and explain the newly published Ossianic poems. Though the published 1783 Belles-Lettres lectures contain less Ossianic material than the versions given to the Edinburgh students, this is largely because it had been published separately in Blair's 1763 *A Critical Dissertation on the Poems of Ossian, the Son of Fingal*. A second edition of this appeared in 1765. Blair's *Dissertation* frequently formed part of later editions of Ossian, being bound together with Macpherson's translations. It was regarded as the standard guide to the poems, and was one of a number of books which brought Ossian into an emerging Scottish Enlightenment 'canon of literature'.[66] When Blair spoke to his Edinburgh University students of Rhetoric and Belles-Lettres, he devoted an entire lecture to Ossian's work.[67] This, the thirty-seventh part of Blair's thirty-nine-lecture course, came as part of the lectures on Poetry which paid particular attention to epic.

Macpherson's first epic poem, *Fingal*, appeared in December 1761. In the early part of that year Blair and Macpherson were in frequent

---

[64]   Stafford, *The Sublime Savage*, 96–132.

[65]   John Bruce, notes transcribed from Hugh Blair's *Lectures on Rhetoric and the Belles-Lettres*, vol. i (dated 1765 by Bruce), Edinburgh University Library MS Dc.10.6, pp. 95–6.

[66]   John Valdimir Price, 'Ossian and the Canon in the Scottish Enlightenment', in Gaskill (ed.), *Ossian Revisited*, 113; in the same volume, see also Steve Rizza, '*A Bulky and Foolish Treatise?* Hugh Blair's Critical Dissertation Reconsidered', 129–46.

[67]   For fuller details and text see Yoshiaki Sudo, 'An Unpublished Lecture of Hugh Blair on the Poems of Ossian', *Hiyoshi Review of English Studies*, 25 (Keio University, Yokohama, Mar. 1995), 160–94; my quotations are from manuscripts.

contact; the epic was developed with Blair's full encouragement and we know that as early as 1761 Blair was supplying his classes with an analysis of Ossianic poetry.[68] The earliest version of the Ossian lecture we have dates from 1765. It insists that 'it would be unpardonable to pass by the poems of Ossian... written in rude ages and in a barbarous nation, and which after remaining unknown to the learned for many ages has lately appeared and has been received with admiration. It has not only been read with pleasure in this Nation but is already begun to be translated into foreign Languages.' Blair's extensive consideration, presenting the poems as ones which 'abound with Fire, Vehemence and Spirit', compares Ossian the Celtic bard with Gothic and Runic poets. Blair finds Ossian's work far superior in beauty. Though Ossian is the product of barbarous ages,

Barbarity is a word of very undeterminable signification. In its most proper signification it excludes polished manners but admits of generous Sentiments, in particular with respect to Heroism... Ossian had all the advantages of following other Poets; he spoke of dark ages before him, and says the words of their Bards came only by halves to their ears 'They were dark as the Tales of other times, before the light of the song arose.' That darkness, and Ossian no doubt received great benefit from the Poems of others. He was himself a person of exquisite sensibility, a professed warrior, and the son of a celebrated Hero.[69]

Here, as Blair lectures in tones which seem to anticipate those of Miss Jean Brodie, we are taken to the heart of one of the central features of Ossian's appeal: he is in one sense 'barbarous', yet also a person 'of exquisite sensibility'. His quasi-Homeric poems simultaneously bear the mark of 'the essential Qualities of the Sublime' (defined by Blair as 'Grandeur and Simplicity') yet carry the sophisticated packaging of modern academia.[70] For, though Spenser's *Shepheardes Calender* of 1579 had appeared with a 'Glosse or scholion for thexposition of old wordes and harder phrases' accompanying the verse, the Ossianic poems were the first works of poetry in modern English to appear from the beginning with a full, straight-faced academic apparatus.[71] Pope's *Dunciad Variorum* of 1729 had parodied Shakespearian and classical scholarship; at Edinburgh University John Stevenson had read to Blair's class Pope's

---

[68] Schmitz, *Hugh Blair*, 48–9.
[69] Bruce, notes on Blair's *Lectures on Rhetoric* (EUL MS Dc.10.6), 201, 202, 205–6.
[70] Ibid. 90.
[71] Edmund Spenser, *Poetical Works*, ed. J. C. Smith and E. De Selincourt (London: Oxford University Press, 1912), 418 ('Epistle' prefacing *The Shepheardes Calender*).

notes on Homer.[72] But the preface to the Ossianic *Fragments*, the prefaces to *Fingal* and *Temora*, the university lectures on the poems, and the *Dissertations*, whether those by Blair, by Macpherson, or worked on jointly, are neither spoofs nor superadded materials. Rather they accompany the text from its inception, giving it the form of a classic and classical production.

Ossian is the most self-conscious text imaginable, constantly aware of its own intertextuality, of its linguistic status and its challenging place on literary maps. This is not simply a primitive poetry. It is also very much a self-aware poetry of advanced knowledge. Anyone looking at the opening pages of either book I or book II of *Fingal*, for instance, must be struck by the way in which the classically trained Macpherson, surely following Blair's academic lead, has placed long footnotes under the text. These explain the significance of the many 'exotic' proper names which are crucial to the effect of the work. The footnotes also adduce in the original languages (and in English translation) sometimes lengthy passages of Latin and Greek classics which parallel or otherwise relate to the main text. So, for instance, on the opening page from book II of the first edition of *Fingal* (1762) there appear four lines of the Ossianic work, with twenty-six lines of annotation in double columns underneath. These annotations explain that the location of the action is 'familiar to those who have been in the Highlands of Scotland'; they also supply comparable passages from the *Iliad* (in the original Greek, accompanied by Pope's translation) and from the *Aeneid* in the original Latin.[73]

Hugh Blair's full-scale *Critical Dissertation on the Poems of Ossian* appeared in 1763, just three years after the first *Fragments*. Blair worked on it as Macpherson's Ossianic corpus was still evolving. Never before in the history of poetry had a work been followed so quickly by an academic handbook. A studious commentator and university professor, Blair emphasized the 'study' of poetry as bound up with its production even in the supposedly primitive society of Ossian. Peter Murphy has drawn attention to the way Blair writes in his *Critical Dissertation* about Ossian's poetry as already 'institutionalized'; as Blair puts it,

the Celtic tribes clearly appear to have been addicted in so high a degree to poetry, and to have made it so much their study from the earliest times, as may

---

[72] Schmitz, *Hugh Blair*, 12.
[73] *Fingal: An Ancient Epic Poem, in Six Books* (London: Becket & De Hondt, 1762), 21.

remove our wonder at meeting with a vein of higher poetical refinement among them, than was at first to have been expected among nations whom we are accustomed to call barbarous.[74]

Professor Blair readily connects 'poetry' to 'study'.[75] Yet in his classroom he also hymns Ossian's wildly elemental power, breaking 'forth like a torrent of fire', so that, as in the later case of the 'heaven-taught ploughman' Burns, divine inspiration is replaced by the validation that comes from 'primitive' origins.[76] Macpherson's old-new work offers a sense of essential inspiration without involving its readers in potentially awkward theological complications. Sublime, yet accompanied by its own handbook, Ossian is *ab initio* both text and paratext, simultaneously barbarous and academic, ancient and modern. Protean, slippery, and fertile, it is prose and poetry, Gaelic and English, original and translation, primitively simple and ultra-sophisticated. Here is a product of lecture halls as well as of lochs and mountains. The textual effect that we call 'Ossian' mediates between each of these pairs of apparent binary opposites. Its very formal fluidity has been a constant source of its life.

That fluidity makes the Ossianic corpus crucially important as marking the first full appearance of the modern poet. Such a poet self-consciously combines these attributes, being at once 'primitive' (or, in more recent times otherwise 'barbarous' or marginalized) and book-clad. The modern poet's knowledge outflanks that of the existing cultural centre. Eighteenth-century Scotland was to produce several similar figures in Ossian's wake. The academically trained vernacular poet Robert Fergusson is one; Robert Burns is another. Fergusson acquires the knowledge of an advanced curriculum that involves the Anglicizing Rhetoric and Belles-Lettres. Yet he uses his education in the services of the Scots vernacular and carnivalesque street-life. In 'To the Principal and Professors of the University of St Andrews, on their Superb Treat to Dr Samuel Johnson' he contests cultural authority by speaking simultaneously in the language of the lecture room and the demotic pub (Johnson is addressed as 'Samy', the professors as 'billy boys'). Burns, who hailed Fergusson as his 'elder Brother in the muse',

---

[74] Peter Murphy, *Poetry as an Occupation and an Art in Britain 1760–1830* (Cambridge: Cambridge University Press, 1993), 21, quoting Blair.

[75] See Fiona Stafford, 'Hugh Blair's Ossian, Romanticism and the Teaching of Literature', in Crawford (ed.), *The Scottish Invention*, 68–88.

[76] Price, 'Ossian and the Canon in the Scottish Enlightenment', 111, discusses this.

adopted a similar strategy. He presented himself as a primitive 'rustic Bard' who scorned 'colledge classes'. Yet he made no secret of his wide reading which extended from classical authors to Milton and Adam Smith. That reading also took in the footnotes of Ossian.[77]

Later, as the nineteenth century progressed, those Cambridge students Coleridge and Wordsworth roughened the edges of their advanced educations by forsaking their *alma mater* for the mountains of the wild Lake District. Coleridge's 1796 lines 'Imitated from Ossian' find excitement in the 'restless gale' and '*dreary* vale', while carrying a long epigraph from an Ossianic poem.[78] The young Coleridge had contemplated going with Robert Southey to the even wilder environment of the Susquehanna, attempting the apparently contradictory blend of erudition and primitive simplicity which was the dream of so many post-Ossianic poets. Coleridge recalled that he wanted 'to have combined the innocence of the patriarchal Age with the knowledge and genuine refinements of European culture'.[79] He and Wordsworth were to produce in *Lyrical Ballads* a collection whose poetry declares its own natural simplicity. It opens with poems which protest the virtues of nature and the heart, while the poet sits on an Ossianic 'old grey stone' rather than poring over 'barren leaves' of books.[80] Yet the same volume begins with a famous and learned 'Preface'. This quasi-academic paratext functions like Blair's Ossian *Dissertation*. Moreover, in its stress on the emphatic and simple language of the 'low and rustic' whose environment ensures that 'the passions of men are incorporated with the beautiful forms of nature', it restates for a nineteenth-century English audience earlier Scottish arguments about Highlanders' sublimely simple language.[81] Though the mature Wordsworth chose to conceal them, modern scholars have increasingly unearthed echoes of Macpherson in his early works.[82] Commentators have pointed out Wordsworth's

[77] See Robert Crawford, 'Robert Fergusson's Robert Burns', in Robert Crawford (ed.), *Robert Burns and Cultural Authority* (Edinburgh: Edinburgh University Press, 1997), 1–22; also Crawford, *Devolving English Literature*, 98.

[78] Coleridge, *Poetical Works*, ed. Ernest Hartley Coleridge (1912; repr. London: Oxford University Press, 1973), 39.

[79] Samuel Taylor Coleridge writing in the *Friend* in 1809, quoted in Richard Holmes, *Coleridge: Early Visions* (London: Hodder & Stoughton, 1989), 66.

[80] William Wordsworth and Samuel Taylor Coleridge, *Lyrical Ballads 1805*, ed. Derek Roper, 2nd edn. (London: MacDonald & Evans, 1976), 51 ('Expostulation and Reply') and 52 ('The Tables Turned').

[81] Ibid. 21 ('Preface').

[82] See Fiona Stafford, ' "Dangerous Success": Ossian, Wordsworth, and English Romantic Literature', in Gaskill (ed.), *Ossian Revisited*, 49–72.

continuing interest in Ossianic themes, at the same time as making clear
that he knew Blair's work, possibly from infancy.[83] Like Blake, Wordsworth develops and transmutes the Ossianic concept of poetry, particularly that blending of straightforward simplicity and outflanking
intelligence which were the result of Ossian's academic-imaginative
genesis.

The Ossianic invention of the modern poet was massively influential
for most of the Romantic poets. Indeed, one could argue that it
produced them. Scott, whose whole vision of the Highlands (while
spiced with irony) is built on the legacy of the Ossianic corpus, gives
his first major long poem a title as well as a tone which owes at least as
much to Ossian as to the minstrelsy of the Borders. *The Lay of the Last
Minstrel* presents a 'Minstrel' who is both cannily and uncannily Ossianic:

> infirm and old;
> His withered cheek, and tresses gray,
> Seemed to have known a better day;
> The harp, his sole remaining joy,
> Was carried by an orphan boy.
> The last of all the Bards was he . . .

Scott gives us his Minstrel's 'unpremeditated lay' (though even that is a
Celticizing of Milton's 'unpremeditated verse'). Yet it is presented from
the very start with scholarly annotation in true Ossianic style.[84] A
thoroughly educated Edinburgh lawyer, with obsessive self-consciousness Scott turned footnotes and multiple prefaces into a form of high
art. In his study *Paratexts*, Gérard Genette sees Scott as anticipating
modernist practice.[85] This 'minstrel' went on to build at Abbotsford a
remarkable research library, museum, and archive to fuel his own work.
His most successful long poem, *The Lady of the Lake* (1810), was even
more unashamedly Ossianic. It invokes the 'Harp of the North!' and the
'ancient days of Caledon'. Though this is not the place for a full account
of the Ossianic 'human relic', Scott's work picks up on the quintessential

---

[83] See J. R. Moore, 'Wordsworth's Unacknowledged Debt to Macpherson', *PMLA* 40
(1925), 362–78; Stafford, '"Dangerous Success"', 49–72; Duncan Wu, *Wordsworth's Reading
1770–1799* (Cambridge: Cambridge University Press, 1993), 16, 92, 181–2, 185; Duncan Wu,
Wordsworth's Reading 1800–1815 (Cambridge: Cambridge University Press, 1995), 137.

[84] Sir Walter Scott, *Selected Poems*, ed. Thomas Crawford (Oxford: Clarendon Press, 1972), 49
('Introduction'); John Milton, *Paradise Lost*, ed. Alastair Fowler (Harlow: Longman, 1968), 436
(IX. 24).

[85] Gérard Genette, *Paratexts*, trans. Jane E. Lewin (Cambridge: Cambridge University Press,
1997), 284–8.

Ossianic theme of lastness, and of lone survivors.[86] It also tries to out-Macpherson Macpherson in its relishing of Highland Gaelic names: 'the wild heaths of Uam-Var ... Benvoirlich's echoes ... Menteith ... Lochard ... Aberfoyle ... Loch   Achray ... Benvenue ... Cambusmore ... Benledi ... Bochastle ... Vennachar.'[87] The lingering glee with which these names crowd the poem clearly re-echoes the Ossianic mode. More than anything else, it is the Ossianic corpus that hints why for the bard of Abbotsford 'Caledonia! stern and wild' is 'Meet nurse for a poetic child'.[88] Scott's poems prepare the way for his fiction, and the 'Highland Minstrelsy' of chapter 22 of *Waverley* (1814) takes over where his verse leaves off. Sir Walter's writings followed those of Ossian into the European imagination, making him the single most influential figure in the history of the novel. Scott was at once a sophisticated modern economic man and 'The Wizard of the North'. Small wonder that in 1805 he was so impressed by Macpherson's ability to produce work which would powerfully 'interest the admirers of poetry through all Europe'. Scott smiles at Ossian's bringing together of 'Achilles, with the courtesy, sentiment, and high-breeding of Sir Charles Grandison', but it is just such a union of ancient, 'natural' simplicity and modern sophistication which Scott will attempt as a modern poet.[89]

In 1807, two years after the publication of Henry Mackenzie's *Report ... into the Nature and Authenticity of the Poems of Ossian*, the young Byron sent its editor his own first book of verse. He was delighted to write of 'Oscar' and the 'last of Alva's clan':

> They feast upon the mountain deer,
> The pibroch raised its piercing note;
> To gladden more their highland cheer,
> The strains in martial numbers float.[90]

This is the Byron of the Ossianic prose poem 'The Death of Calmar and Orla' ('many are the widows of Lochlin! Morven prevails in its strength'). He may have 'roved a young Highlander o'er the dark heath' near his beloved boyhood 'dark Loch na Garr', but Byron is a Harrovian

---

[86] On Ossianic survivors, see Fiona Stafford, *The Last of the Race* (Oxford: Clarendon Press, 1994).

[87] Scott, *Selected Poems*, 140–3 (Canto First).

[88] Ibid. 123 (*The Lay of the Last Minstrel*, Canto Sic, part II).

[89] Sir Walter Scott, review of Mackenzie's *Report, Edinburgh Review*, 6 (1805), 445–6.

[90] Leslie A. Marchand, *Byron: A Portrait* (London: John Murray, 1971), 43; Lord Byron, *Poetical Works* (London: Henry Frowde, 1904), 16 ('Oscar of Alva: A Tale').

Highlander.[91] Eager to present himself as a Romantic wildman, he is as keen to be the sophisticate who in his 'Hours of Idleness' dashes off a translation of Virgil.[92] On 11 August 1807, he writes from London with breathless yet ironic nonchalance of being about to undertake an expedition through the Highlands and islands by Shetland pony: 'I mean to collect all the Erse traditions, poems, & & c. & translate, or expand the subjects, to fill a volume, which may appear next Spring, under the Denomination of "*the Highland Harp*" or some title equally *picturesque*.'[93] It comes as no great surprise that ten days later Byron has gone no further than Cambridge. His magnificent and corrosive irony (which produced that provocatively wrong-way-round title *English Bards and Scotch Reviewers*) sets in as soon as his Ossianic fervour takes off. But the knowing sophistication mixed with primitive enthusiasm is itself an Ossianic combination. Byron manifests from his earliest minstrel raptures just that 'antithetical mind' at which he marvelled when he reacted to Burns's poetry.[94] Eventually he would find a different key in which to play the music of the modern poet, archaic sensibility meeting modern, erudite impatience—'Hail Muse! et cetera'—but the Romantic primitivist in Byron would persist throughout the bookish cleverness.[95] Like Wordsworth, Scott, and other near contemporaries, Byron experimented on occasion with the Ossianic tone, fingered the bardic harp, but hardly went on sounding like Ossian throughout his career. Each of these early nineteenth-century poets found a voice to which that of Ossian contributed, but all perfected individual styles. However, what so many of the Romantic poets did maintain and develop were versions of the primitive-sophisticated role. They inhabited that cultural space which the work of Ossian had brought to prominence. While Ossian as form, style, and tone was richly productive for Romanticism, for poets Ossian as a cultural phenomenon was ultimately more important. Later chapters of this book will show how the primitive-sophisticated stance which Ossian delineated would be recast after Romanticism as the role

[91] Byron, *Poetical Works*, 38–40 ('The Death of Calmar and Orla: An Imitation of Macpherson's Ossian'), 43 ('When I Roved a Young Highlander'), 29 ('Lachin Y Gair').

[92] Ibid. 19 ('The Episode of Nisus and Euryalus: A Paraphrase from the Aeneid, Lib. IX'). Byron's first book acquired the title *Hours of Idleness*.

[93] Lord Byron, letter to [Elizabeth Bridget Pigot], London, 11 Aug. 1807, published in Leslie A. Marchand (ed.), *In my Hot Youth: Byron's Letters and Journals*, i: *1798–1810* (London: John Murray, 1973), 132.

[94] Byron, quoted ibid. 19.

[95] Lord Byron, *Don Juan*, ed. T. G. Steffan, E. Steffan, and W. W. Pratt (Harmondsworth: Penguin, 1977), 157 (Canto III. 1).

of the 'scholar-gypsy', then in the modernist period in T. S. Eliot's formulation of the poet as 'more *primitive*, as well as more civilized, than his contemporaries, his experience is deeper than civilization, and he only uses the phenomena of civilization in expressing it'.[96] As the conclusion of this book will argue, such a formulation remains influential today.

Though constantly referred to by Blair, Macpherson, and their readers as 'poems', the Ossianic works are presented in English prose. Moreover, the first published fragments are short prose passages, as, for instance, are the extracts translated in Goethe's *The Sorrows of Young Werther* (1774). In many ways, it is as such brief pieces that the Ossianic works are most powerful. From the very start, with the publication of the 1760 *Fragments* Blair makes us aware of the compositions as slightly distanced from normal English prose in their attempt to catch the poetical cadence, the music of the Gaelic original:

> They are not set to music, nor sung. The versification in the original is simple; and to such as understand the language, very smooth and beautiful. Rhyme is seldom used: but the cadence, and the length of the line varied, so as to suit the sense. The translation is extremely literal. Even the arrangement of the words in the original has been imitated; to which must be imputed some inversions in the style, that otherwise would not have been chosen.[97]

Macpherson too, in his 'Dissertation concerning the Antiquity, &c. of the Poems of Ossian', which accompanied Ossian's works, emphasizes the literalness of the translation. He alerts readers to the gap between the prose pieces which follow and their verse original, and makes an aesthetic virtue out of this. He 'wishes that the imperfect semblance he draws, may not prejudice the world against an original, which contains what is beautiful in simplicity, and grand in the sublime'.[98] The effect here is to float Macpherson's prose away from prose as normally read, and towards poetry, encouraging the reader to receive it in a special way. This, like assuring his audience that the Ossianic material is truly ancient, is an empowering and ambitious strategy on the part of Macpherson, who bonded invented and translated materials.[99] The works' very slipperiness gives them a dual status, as prose translations

---

[96] T. S. Eliot, 'Tarr', *Egoist*, Sept. 1918, 106.   [97] *Poems of Ossian*, ed. Gaskill, 6.
[98] Ibid. 52.
[99] See D. S. Thomson, *The Gaelic Sources of Macpherson's Ossian* (Edinburgh: Oliver & Boyd, 1952).

of poetry and as prose poems in their own right, linking them not just to the later development of prose poetry, but also to *vers libre*.[100] The sometimes biblical cadenced prose of Ossian is a latent source of power within Whitman's lines which sometimes extend to the length of short prose paragraphs. Blair's description of a poetry in which 'the cadence, and the length of the line varied, so as to suit the sense' might function as a description of the free verse tradition.[101] Emerging fully-fledged in Whitman and nineteenth-century French writing (where prose poetry was so important), this has become crucial to so many modern poets operating in the spirit of Pound's injunction 'to compose in the sequence of the musical phrase, not in sequence of a metronome'.

'The Romantic awakening dates from the production of Ossian,' wrote Pound. He was right, and, however indirectly, he benefited from Ossian's legacy.[102] While the Ossianic corpus is important as the first fully-fledged presentation of the role of the modern poet, and matters in the development of *vers libre* and the prose poem, it is also highly significant to later poets in another way. One of the things modernism inherited from Romanticism in poetry was the fragment. What in earlier literature had carried a largely factual meaning acquired in Romantic writing a powerful aesthetic patina. '*Desunt nonnulla*' ends the Second Sestiad in my edition of Marlowe's *Hero and Leander*: 'the rest is missing.'[103] There is nothing enormously alluring about this statement; nor is there allure attached to the word 'fragmentum' which was used since the Renaissance by editors of classical texts to denote part-works.[104] By the mid-eighteenth century the term was familiar to anyone with a classical education. The classically trained Macpherson had used the word 'fragment' in his elegy 'On the Death of Marshal Keith', an exiled former Jacobite hero, which was published in the *Scots Magazine* in October 1758:

> See! the proud halls they once possess'd decay'd,
> The spiral tow'rs depend the lofty head;

[100] See Jonathan Monroe, *A Poverty of Objects* (Ithaca, NY: Cornell University Press, 1987); Suzanne Bernard, *Le Poème en prose de Baudelaire jusqu'à nos jours* (Paris: Nizet, 1959), 25–37; Kirby-Smith, *The Origins of Free Verse*.
[101] *Poems of Ossian*, ed. Gaskill, 6.
[102] Ezra Pound, *Literary Essays*, ed. T. S. Eliot (1954; repr. London: Faber & Faber, 1974), 3 ('A Retrospect'), and 215 ('The Renaissance').
[103] Christopher Marlowe, *The Poems*, ed. Millar Maclure (London: Methuen, 1968), 41.
[104] See A. C. Dionisotti, 'On Fragments in Classical Scholarship', in G. Mort, (ed.), *Collecting Fragments* (Göttingen: Aporemata Vali, 1997), 1–33.

> Wild ivy creeps along the mould'ring walls,
> And with each gust of wind a fragment falls.[105]

Here 'fragment' may be related to the smashed Highland culture which Macpherson knew. However, more generally the word *Fragment* had begun to be used in the titles of English books, or, to be more exact, pamphlets. Usually these pamphlets had a satirical bent.

Perhaps the most interesting such usage is in the title of *A Fragment of the Chronicles of Zimri the Refiner*, a political satire in imitation of the scriptural parodies of Nathan Ben Saddi, that is, Robert Dodsley, published in Edinburgh in 1753. In the title of this work, which proclaims itself 'Nearly translated from the original Hebrew', the words 'A Fragment' are there to reinforce a sense of scholarly and textual antiquity. It is exactly such a nuance that James Macpherson sought when his *Fragments* appeared in Edinburgh in 1760, and he may have been aware that the Foulis Press at Glasgow University had published Lady Elizabeth Wardlaw's *Hardyknute: A Fragment of an Antient Scots Poem* in 1748.[106] Though there are several major discussions of the fragment and Romantic poetry, they omit Ossian entirely, or mention the work only in passing.[107] A notable exception to this grotesque exclusion of Ossian from critical discussions of Romantic form is Marjorie Levinson's *The Romantic Fragment Poem: A Critique of a Form* (1986), which sees something of the importance of Macpherson's *œuvre*, yet condescends to it as a mere hoax. More limited in scope, though more attuned to Ossian, are Ian Haywood in *The Making of History* (1986), Fiona Stafford in her fine study *The Sublime Savage* (1988), as well as the contributors to three essay collections: Howard Gaskill's *Ossian Revisited* (1991), Terence Brown's *Celticism* (1996), and Gaskill and Stafford's *From Gaelic to Romantic* (1998). Katie Trumpener has emphasized Ossian's importance for the novel in her study *Bardic Nationalism* (1997).

Nevertheless, none of these writers seems to appreciate to the full the importance of Macpherson's use of the term 'fragment' and of the

---

[105] [James Macpherson], 'On the Death of Marshal Keith', *Scots Magazine*, 20 (1758), 551.

[106] See Philip Gaskell, *A Bibliography of the Foulis Press*, 2nd edn. (London: St Paul's Bibliographies, 1986), 129.

[107] Thomas McFarland, *Romanticism and the Forms of Ruin* (Princeton: Princeton University Press, 1981); Balchandra Rajan, *The Form of the Unfinished* (Princeton: Princeton University Press, 1985); Anne Janowitz, *England's Ruins* (Cambridge: Cambridge University Press, 1990); for an older, more just view, see Paul Van Tieghem, *Ossian en France*, 2 vols. (Paris: F. Rieder, 1917) and 'Ossian et l'ossianisme' in his *Le Préromanticisme*, 3 vols. (Paris: Librairie Félix Alcan, 1924), i. 195–285.

fragmentary form. Macpherson's fragments pre-date and nourish the use of the fragment form by such continental writers as the great German theorist of Romanticism Friedrich Schlegel (who also wrote an essay on Ossian in 1812), as well as the poets Novalis in Germany and André Chénier in France.[108] Some of Ossian's appeal to such a wide European audience may be bound up with the fact that the origins of the Ossianic corpus lie partly in the researches of Blackwell, Stones, Blair, Macpherson, and others into Celtic and epic elements which they saw as shared among the foundations of several modern European cultures.

After Macpherson and Blair had produced their *Fragments*, the title came to be much more widely used in English writings. It was deployed not least to help works of English literature to claim for themselves the importance attached to classical texts. So Thorkelin in 1788 publishes his *Fragment of English and Irish History in the Ninth and Tenth Century… Translated from the Original Icelandic.* By the 1790s, when he is writing moony imitations of Ossian in such poems as 'The Complaint of Ninathoma', Coleridge is also the poet of 'A Fragment Found in a Lecture Room'. In this piece the words 'A Fragment' which begin the title carry as suitably classical and academic connotations as the words '[caetera desunt.]' which come at the end of the poem.[109] Over the centuries the fragment as a form has tended to attract poets with an academic bent. Byron, a decade later, in his first book, *Hours of Idleness* (1807), includes not only poetry about a college examination, and his prose 'Imitation of Macpherson's Ossian', but also poems with the word 'Fragment' in their title. Among these the most Ossianic is surely 'A Fragment', which begins

> WHEN, to their airy hall my father's voice
> Shall call my spirit, joyful in their choice;
> When, poised upon the gale, my form shall ride,
> Or, dark in mist, descend the mountain's side…[110]

Editing her late husband's poems, Mary Shelley included entire sections of 'Fragments'.[111] This was in the 1820s, by which time the fragment

---

[108] Friedrich Schlegel, *Charakteristiken und Kritiken II (1802–1829)*, ed. Hans Eichner (Munich: Verlag Ferdinand Schoningh, 1975), 221–36 ('Über nordische Dichtkunst').
[109] Coleridge, *Poetical Works*, 39 ('The Complaint of Ninathoma') and 35 ('A Fragment Found in a Lecture Room').
[110] Byron, *Poetical Works*, 24 ('Thoughts Suggested by a College Examination'), 38 ('The Death of Calmar and Orla: An Imitation of Macpherson's Ossian'), 3 ('A Fragment').
[111] See P. B. Shelley, *Poetical Works*, ed. Thomas Hutchinson, new edn. (London: Oxford University Press, 1970), 424, 444, 482, 535, 569, 584, 633, 659, etc.

and the fragmentary were aesthetically highly desirable, and the works of Ossian hardly forgotten. Thus Tennyson, long before he produced his own ancient epic, was versifying Ossian in the 1820s. His conversion of Macpherson's cadenced prose into the splendid, maturing movement and vowel music of his own 'Midnight' with its 'water-falls in various cadence chiming' and its 'swelling river' that 'Winds his broad stream majestic, deep, and slow' is a masterly piece of transmutation.[112]

We take it for granted that modern, scholarly editions of poets' works will include sections of fragments, but one of the continuities linking Ossian and Romantic to modernist poetry is the way academically trained poets have harnessed the word 'fragment' to their own work. As for Blair and Macpherson, so for later poets, the use of this word suggests that beyond what is present there may be the flicker of a greater, absent possible structure. It also signals ambition. Browning's first book is *Pauline: A Fragment of a Confession* (1833). Arnold, most academic of Victorian poets, published early work under the title 'Fragment of an "Antigone"' and 'Fragment of Chorus of a "Dejaneira"'. Reviewing the latter, Swinburne remarked that 'that must be a noble statue which could match this massive fragment', so reminding us (as if we needed reminding) that stone fragments like the 'shattered visage' of Shelley's Ozymandias and fragmentary buildings from the Parthenon to medieval abbeys, from Michael's unfinished sheepfold to Margaret's ruined cottage, are, along with texts, part of this Romantic aesthetic drive towards the fragmentary.[113]

In moving from Romanticism to modernism, we pass from an era where one may reasonably talk of Macpherson as influential, to a field where one may more fruitfully consider analogies with his work. The word 'fragment' was very long established in the titles of English-language works by 1926 when Eliot published his 'Fragment of a Prologue', later to be collected with a 'Fragment of an Agon' in *Sweeney Agonistes: Fragments of an Aristophanic Melodrama* (1932), or when Pound published his *Drafts and Fragments of Cantos CX–CXVII* (1969). Like

---

[112] See *The Poems of Tennyson*, ed. Christopher Ricks (London: Longman, 1969), 111 ('Midnight') and 141 ('Oh! ye wild winds, that roar and rave'); compare Macpherson's 'Croma: A Poem', in *Poems of Ossian*, ed. Gaskill, 187–92.

[113] Swinburne, quoted in *The Poems of Matthew Arnold*, ed. Kenneth Allott, 2nd., ed. Miriam Allott (London: Longman, 1979), 66 (headnote to 'Fragment of a Chorus of a "Dejaneira"').

Macpherson, Eliot and Pound were trained classicists. If Pound thought that Romanticism began with Ossian, then, as his early work makes clear, Pound had inherited Romanticism's later accessories along with his university textual training. It is a Romantic sense of loss and ruin, along with the academic's awareness of textuality, that produces the fragmentary 1916 poem 'Papyrus', which, with its many dots denoting ellipses, imitates a textual edition in which parts of the original are missing; read aloud, its silence is as important as its sound.[114] For its meaning, the poem depends on some knowledge of the conventions of textual editing. Pound may be the wild 'Idaho kid' who rejoiced in London in being, as he excitedly put it, 'like a painted pict with a stone war club', but he is also the former college professor and textual editor.[115] Like the translatorese of *Cathay*, a volume whose genesis in some striking ways parallels that of Macpherson's epics, 'Papyrus' relies on our realization that we are reading something brought over from a foreign culture, one where an unfamiliar noun, presumably a proper name, might have more meaning. The poem is not quite allusive, but it matters for what can be imagined round it. In this, it is akin to many a Romantic fragment (Shelley's 'Ozymandias' again springs to mind), and similar to Macpherson's *Fragments of Ancient Poetry*. Though she confines her reflections to the visual arts, Linda Nochlin in *The Body in Pieces: The Fragment as a Metaphor for Modernity* sees modernity as figured repeatedly through actual fragments which speak of the 'social, psychological, even metaphysical fragmentation that so seems to mark modern experience'.[116] The appeal of the Ossianic fragment, like that of the modernist one, is that it conjures around itself a culture, a civilization that may be lost.

This is apparent if we consider the best-known use of the word 'fragments' in twentieth-century poetry. In the babel that is the concluding lines of Eliot's *Waste Land*, where we hear of 'fragments I have shored against my ruins', the word 'fragments' carries the connotation of Ozymandias-like stone fragments—bits of ruins such as those, perhaps, of the collapsing London Bridge.[117] Yet its primary meaning is 'textual fragments'. In this passage spliced together from

[114] Ezra Pound, *Collected Shorter Poems*, 2nd edn. (London: Faber & Faber, 1968), 122 ('Papyrus').

[115] Rex Lampman, 'Epitaph', in Ezra Pound, *Pavannes and Divagations* (London: Peter Owen, 1960), p. vii; Omar Pound and A. Walton Litz (ed.), *Ezra Pound and Dorothy Shakespear: Their Letters 1909–1914* (London: Faber & Faber, 1985), 46.

[116] Linda Nochlin, *The Body in Pieces* (London: Thames & Hudson, 1994), 23.

[117] T. S. Eliot, *The Complete Poems and Plays* (London: Faber & Faber, 1969), 75.

various poetic sources we hear at its most intense a distinctive feature of the modernist acoustic: the sound of the fragmentary. It is not simply that as early as the prose poem 'Hysteria' Eliot was preoccupied with how 'fragments... might be collected'.[118] Nor is it just that modernist poems, like 'The Hollow Men' or *The Waste Land* or *The Cantos*, are put together out of bits of text, are made of breakage. It is much more than that, for the language, the English language in which these texts are written, is constantly and demandingly interrupted by other tongues, as if a subterranean presence erupted to disrupt the surface acoustic.

> Ἴδμεν γάρ τοι πάνθ' ὅσ' ἐνὶ Τροίη
> Caught in the unstopped ear;[119]

says Pound in *Hugh Selwyn Mauberley*, a work which makes considerable use of splinters of Greek, indicative of the classical cultural inheritance. Yet in the same poem Pound articulates a worry that civilization may now be 'botched', the sacrifices of the First World War made only for its fragments,

> For two gross of broken statues,
> For a few thousand battered books.[120]

The First World War saw the invention of the fragmentation bomb and fragmentation grenade, but it also marked the growth of that linguistic splintering so audible in the High Modernist poetry of Pound and Eliot. The fragment here becomes a unit of composition, the poem a shoring together of fragments that raises and exploits questions of cultural unity and, let's be honest, of linguistic coherence. For there are moments when the poet's native language seems overwhelmed, as happens at the end of *The Waste Land* or in a Poundian Canto such as XCIII. How many readers know Italian, Latin, English, *and* Sanskrit?—or Egyptian hieroglyphs, Chinese characters, *and* Greek and Latin? The poet here is using not so much a language as a linguistic spectrum that, for some moments at least, problematizes (as does the Ossianic *œuvre*) the notion of a 'native language'.[121] Something similar happens in a more extended prose fashion in *Finnegans Wake* and might be characteristic of much modernist discourse, that writing produced on the whole by un-English

---

[118] T. S. Eliot, *The Complete Poems and Plays* (London: Faber & Faber, 1969), 32.

[119] Pound, *Collected Shorter Poems*, 205 ('Hugh Selwyn Mauberley, I, E. P. Ode pour l'élection de son sépulchre').   [120] Ibid. 208 ('Hugh Selwyn Mauberley, V').

[121] See Robert Crawford, 'Native Language', *Comparative Criticism*, 18 (1996), 71–90.

writers. Yet perhaps the circular *Finnegans Wake*, with its tail in its mouth, is in obvious ways less fragmented than the poems I have just been discussing. In its spacing and typography, for instance, it does not send, as *The Waste Land* and *The Cantos* do, constant signals of breakage.

One might relate the impulse to move beyond the normal bounds of English in these modernist writers to the wish to get beyond ordinary language in Mallarmé, in the calligrammatic play of Apollinaire, in the *zaum* of early twentieth-century Russian poets, or in Dada. But I would like to stay with the word 'fragments', and suggest that the linguistic fragmentation of these Pound and Eliot poems may have to do not only with the poets' academic training but also with World War I. If in Apollinaire's 'Visée' (from *Calligrammes* (1918)) and in Italian Futurism's typographical explosions such as Marinetti's *Zang Tumb Tuum* (1914) poets and artists produced verbal fragments that were linked to militarism and the artillery blasts of the First World War, then in London it is surely no accident that the most arresting magazine in which Pound and Eliot published was called *Blast*. With its 'laugh like a bomb', *Blast* appeared in June 1914, following up with a 'War Number' in July 1915.[122] In its title, its pugilism, and its blasting and bombadiering editor, *Blast* is only one of several developments (Futurist poems and paintings as well as Vorticist ones) that link an explosive aesthetic to the shell-bursts of World War I. In this climate it may be perfectly reasonable to link the use of linguistic and typographical fragments to such an invention as the fragmentation bomb. In the twentieth century it is not only the Nobel Prize that connects literature with high explosives.

Eliot's literary response to the First World War was oblique but obsessive. It can be seen surely in his essay 'Tradition and the Individual Talent' (1919), where, just after Europe had been tearing itself to bits, he set out his ideas of 'the mind of Europe' as a unified, unifying entity.[123] We can see him employing a similar strategy immediately after the Second World War in a series of 'Reflections on the Unity of European Culture' and in an address given at London's Czechoslovak Institute in 1945 on 'Cultural Diversity and European Unity'.[124] Such attempts to

---

[122] Wyndham Lewis, 'Manifesto', *Blast* (June 1914), 31.

[123] T. S. Eliot, *Selected Essays*, 3rd enlarged edn. (London: Faber & Faber, 1951), 16.

[124] T. S. Eliot, 'Reflections on the Unity of European Culture', *Adam*, 14 (May 1946), 1–3; (June/July 1946), 1–3; (Aug. 1946), 20–2; T. S. Eliot, 'Cultural Diversity and European Unity', *Review-45*, 2 (Summer 1945), 61–9.

bind Europe together at times of cultural conflict and fragmentation are heard also in his poetry, not least in *The Waste Land*. Yet, in many ways, that poem is the dark underside of 'Tradition and the Individual Talent'. It seems far more aware of fragmentation than of coherence. If unity is envisaged, it remains elusive and perhaps absent. The same might be said of Pound's *Cantos*. Those attempt to gather the limbs of an Osiris, to pile up cultural fragments against societal and personal ruin, only to worry that 'I cannot make it cohere'.[125] Though Eliot would later describe *The Waste Land* as a piece of mere 'grumbling', it is hard to avoid thinking of it as an attempt to write an epic of a civilization, constructed out of fragments.[126] Its method is allusive, so that many, even most readers may fail to see the full scope of the work, yet all will realize that the fragments gesture towards a larger structure beyond the poem, an architecture that could be called 'the mind of Europe', though it extends beyond the merely European.

The Cantos reach even further, but their method is not radically different. Pound's first 'Three Cantos' were published in 1917 in a form quite unlike their final version, but still made up of 'many fragments', as Canto I then put it.[127] As usual in their earlier poetry, Eliot and Pound seemed to learn from one another, spurring each other on. Eliot too at this time was preoccupied with the fragmentary (as 'Hysteria' demonstrates).[128] His early verse is littered with bits of things—grimy scraps, a broken spring, a bitten macaroon, a torn-off smile—but the snippets of other languages, the linguistic fragments come after his meeting with Pound and post-date the outbreak of war. Eliot's epic attempt in *The Waste Land* to shore up the ruins of a civilization through the assembling of fragments learns from Pound's attempt to do the same, or at least a similar thing.

What I want to suggest is that this use of linguistic fragments by modernist poets during and after the First World War is not simply something inherited from the general Romantic imagination. It is actually much closer than is most Romantic poetry to what, at the start of the

---

[125]   Ezra Pound, *The Cantos* (London: Faber & Faber, 1975), 796 (Canto CXVI).

[126]   T. S. Eliot, quoted in *The Waste Land: A Facsimile and Transcript*, ed. Valerie Eliot (London: Faber & Faber, 1971), 1.

[127]   Ronald Bush, *The Genesis of Ezra Pound's 'Cantos'* (Princeton: Princeton University Press, 1976), reprints the first printed versions of the early Cantos; the phrase 'many fragments' occurs on p. 54.

[128]   Eliot, *The Complete Poems and Plays*, 32.

Romantic movement in Europe, James Macpherson was attempting in his *Fragments of Ancient Poetry*. Like *The Waste Land* and *The Cantos*, Macpherson's *Fragments* emerge in important ways from a war threatening a civilization. They are an attempt on the part of the modern poet to carry forward something of that civilization into new, changed conditions, so that it may continue to underpin modern culture. They are fragments that gesture towards a larger epic structure, one that lies beyond the English language. Macpherson's fragments are a literary consequence of Culloden and the Jacobite Rebellions, an attempt to salvage a culture with whose destruction the poet (who grew up in Ruthven, site of a vast British Army barracks) was intimately familiar. Gaelic culture was shattered on the battlefield, as well as being threatened by new commercial, linguistic, and educational pressures. Not only *The Waste Land* and *The Cantos*, but also the other work of Eliot and Pound, from Eliot's lectures on 'The Aims of Education' to Pound's strictures on economics, show that they too saw themselves as defenders of a civilization whose roots were in the classical world and which was under threat by modern commercial, linguistic, and educational forces. In each of these cases—Macpherson, Eliot, Pound—the danger of cultural fragmentation leads to the self-conscious use of the fragment (not least the ancient fragment) by the classically trained poet as a way of speaking out of this position of break-up and attempting to address or gesture towards a cultural wholeness whose loss the poet fears. The fragment as a remnant of the earlier civilization is an emblem both of destruction and continuity. To assemble fragments may be a way of salvaging something of creative worth in the midst of fragmentation, of making a healing gesture to a snapped culture. *The Waste Land* and *The Cantos*, through quotation and allusion, attempt to preserve a poetic canon in a climate which threatens destruction. Eliot and Pound, like Macpherson before them, edit and anthologize as well as create. Where Macpherson, following Jerome Stones, aimed to collect and remake Gaelic in a sort of translatorese, Eliot and Pound tried largely to collect the fragments of imperial tongues, fixing their fragments in a slightly barbarous English that lies open to the remote and ancient. In their use of language as in other ways, all these poets strove to be 'archaically new'.

To seek a closed, standard, correct language, as Hugh Blair often did in his teaching, and as eighteenth-century and too many modern anthologists seem to have wished to do, is to thrust a death mask on words.

Yet if Blair may stand as the modern poet's enemy, he is also the modern poet's friend and begetter as the critic who joined with James Macpherson to produce the Ossianic texts which were launched with the *Fragments*. The fragment, written in another tongue, hints at something beyond itself and/or beyond the language in which it is embedded. In the past the fragment has gestured towards a lost aboriginal wholeness, and has been associated with tragedy or loss. But in our postmodern weather the fragment may be the condition of speech, signalling from the English language access to a wider linguistic spectrum. Following Bakhtin and other theorists we may be happier to accept that 'one's own language is never a single language'; to write in such a way that this is either implicit or explicit may be a good thing.[129] For the fragmented, never complete and so never finished, points not just to loss, but always towards the possibility of building, growth, and renewal. Whatever the truth about its 'forged' status, the Ossianic corpus does not just speak of lack; it also articulates invention or reinvention. Therein lies its ultimate imaginative worth. Postmodern buildings are made of fragments. The fragment, such ideas suggest to us, may be viewed not as the shattered remnant of something old but as the small beginning around which may accrete something unexpected. The fragment may turn from tragedy to new combination and joyful initiation, part of a continuing process rather than simply a lost shard. In the long run, given the course of poetry, that is what the fragments of Macpherson, Eliot, and Pound have proved to be. Complicating and teasing us beyond the normal texture of English, they have alerted us to fresh possibilities, hinting at new ways of being a modern poet. Self-consciously sophisticated and primitive at once, the *Fragments* set out not only a style which would be crucial to Romantic writing, but also a model of poetic identity which continues to evolve to this day.

Jerome Stones, James Macpherson, Hugh Blair, and other eighteenth-century Scots shared a fascination with the 'primitive' and the civilized, with Highland wilderness and Lowland university classroom. That conditioned their legacy to us, one linked to the formation of the modern poet. Yet other aspects of their bequest also continue to haunt us. If Stones's collecting of Gaelic poetry was bound up with his vision of a canon, as expressed in his dream of Minerva, then Blair's encouraging and championing of Macpherson's Ossianic works through his

---

[129] Mikhail Bakhtin, *The Dialogic Imagination*, ed. Michael Holquist, trans. Caryl Emerson and Michael Holquist (Austin: University of Texas Press, 1981), 66.

own professorial lectures and publications was also part and parcel of the construction of a literary canon by the university teachers of Rhetoric and Belles-Lettres.[130] The corpus of writings which their lectures praised and expounded may be different from that of more recent canonical formations—whether of Arnold or of Eliot. For Blair, one suspects, Alexander Pope outshone Shakespeare. Yet in choosing to commend some texts such as Ossian, and to censure or ignore others, the literary academics of Blair's era were establishing a preferred body of poetic work—what we would now call a canon. This argument has been presented, and sometimes contested, a good deal of late, as will be made clear in the next chapter. However, instead of concentrating on the poetic canon solely in the university classroom, I shall focus in what follows on the way that Professor Blair helped develop the canon in the wider literary marketplace. Jerome Stones's vision centred on a (largely poetic) canonical body of texts housed in an otherworld, a select gathering of poems, accessible only in dreams. In Chapter 2, I shall consider another body of chosen poets emerging around the same time as Stones's striking vision. This grouping of writers also evolved as part of the development of the modern poet. It belonged not to the realms of pastoral vision, but to the streets of commerce. It was no ethereal canon of the greatest verse. Rather, it was very much a *de facto* canon of poets for sale. Just as this chapter argues that the Ossianic figuration of the modern poet, however transmuted, is of relevance to much more recent poetry, so the next will contend that the commercial national poetic canon of the mid-eighteenth century continues to shape our conception of who and what is a poet.

---

[130] See Price, 'Ossian and the Canon in the Scottish Enlightenment', 109–28.

CHAPTER 2

Acts of Judgement: Making a National Body of Poetry

The preceding chapter drew attention to several lines of connection between eighteenth-century poets and academics on the one hand, and more recent conceptions of the modern poet on the other. In this second chapter I shall begin by returning to the Scotland of Jerome Stones, Hugh Blair, and their fellow Enlightenment literati in order to look at how assumptions about the construction of national poetic anthologies and canons were linked to the way poetry and academia interacted. The results of this association helped to shape the cultural space occupied by the modern poet from the eighteenth century to the present. Moreover, it allowed Hugh Blair, following his championing of James 'Ossian' Macpherson, to set his stamp on a developing canon into which was grafted another of his associates, James 'Minstrel' Beattie. As in the last chapter, I shall be alert to Scottish–English rivalries which are bound up with literary production. Chapter 1 looked at material from lecture notes, letters, and manuscripts. Chapter 2 involves some examination of law cases and publishing practices which may seem remote from the business of poetry. Together, though, both chapters demonstrate that there are ways in which for the modern poet, poetry, academia, and business are insistently bound together. This chapter shows how since the mid-eighteenth century the acts of judgement made by anthologists in their gathering of a national body of poetry are constantly shaped by legal, aesthetic, economic, and nationally inflected considerations. These in turn condition the canonical background against which the modern poet is perceived, and in which he works.

If Jerome Stones's vision of 'The Immortality of Authors' imagined a future in which Gaelic literature would be treated with excited respect, then it also presented a broader vision of a literary canon. There has been considerable scholarly debate about the extent to which there was a concept of 'literature' in the eighteenth century, and how far it might relate to our modern understanding of the word. Richard Terry and others have helped clarify the ways in which terms such as 'belles-lettres' set up the arena which we now designate as 'literary'.[1] Again, it is arguable how far the modern sense of the word 'canon' might be applied to the eighteenth-century conception of literature. Though I shall return to this point later in the present chapter, the rediscovery of a document like Stones's vision makes it clear that a conceptual zone existed which corresponds to what we would now call a 'canon'.

Stones never published a book. He knew, however, as he imagined his own proposed 'two octavo Volumes' and sought Thomas Tullideph's advice about them, that such a project would involve particular kinds of apparatus and machinery. He planned 'explanatory Notes, Illustrations, Passages from ancient Authors, &c.' He was in touch with a local bookseller who had trade contacts with 'the Shops in London, and Edinburgh'. His aim was to draw up an abstract of the work and to seek advice about it from Tullideph and his other mentors. He was concerned about access to libraries, and had discussed with his bookseller friend how to use 'the publick Libraries' to further his project.[2] In other words, Stones was alert to the conditions of operating in a literary and scholarly marketplace. His work was conducted out of a love of literature and of learning, yet as an ambitious writer he was also interested in how to reach potential readers. He was conscious of the processes of circulation which would allow him to get access to the texts which he wanted. Stones would not have put it like that, but his own early careers as an itinerant bookseller, then later as an intimate student friend of Andrew Angus, the young Keeper of the University Library at St Andrews, and as an aspiring author, would have made him well aware that books as a business involved complex systems of imaginative (or 'sympathetic'), critical (or judgemental), and financial (or trade) circulation.[3]

---

[1] Richard Terry, 'The Eighteenth-Century Invention of English Literature: A Truism Revisited', *British Journal for Eighteenth-Century Studies*, 19 (1996), 47–62. See also the various articles on this topic in the Feb. and Nov. 1997 issues of *Eighteenth Century Life*; also Douglas Lane Patey, 'The Eighteenth Century Invents the Canon', *Modern Language Studies*, 18 (1988), 17–37.
[2] Stones, fair copy of letter to [Tullideph], Dunkeld, 6 May 1756, EUL MS La.III.251, pp. 23–4.
[3] Stones, 'On the Death of a Friend Written in the Year 1749' (the friend was Andrew Angus), EUL MS La.III.251*, p. 1.

In this awareness, Stones is close to another ambitious young literary figure of the 1750s. Early that decade a London Irishman produced an account of a dream vision of Parnassus in some ways strikingly similar to that of the Highland schoolmaster. This Parnassus is divided so that each poet lives on his own estate:

> The great *Shakespeare* sat upon a cliff, looking abroad through all creation. His possessions were very near as extensive as *Homer's*, but in some places, had not received sufficient culture. But even there spontaneous flowers shot up, and in the *unweeded garden, which grows to seed*, you might cull lavender, myrtle, and wild thyme. Craggy rocks, hills, and dales, the woodland and open country, struck the eye with wild variety. Over our heads rolled thunder, deep and awful. The lightning's flash darted athwart the solemn scene, while on the blasted heath, witches, elves, and fairies, with their own *Queen Mab*, played in frolick gambol. Mean time the immortal bard sat with his *eyes in a fine phrenzy rolling*, and writers both in the tragic and comic stile were gathered round him. *Aristotle* seemed to lament that *Shakespear* had not studied his Art of Poetry, but *Longinus* admired him to a degree of enthusiasm. *Otway*, *Rowe*, and *Congreve* had him constantly in their eye. Even *Milton* was looking for flowers to transplant into his own Paradise.[4]

Arthur Murphy's 1752 account of walking on the slopes of Parnassus is more worldly-wise, less awestruck than that of Stones. As one might expect of the editor of the *Gray's-Inn Journal* and future copyright lawyer, Murphy is alert to questions of originality in the canon. He also presents, as Mark Rose puts it, 'a spectacular example of the attempt to represent literary property as analogous to real estate'.[5] Murphy was a merchant's clerk, banker's bookkeeper, journalist, dramatist, editor, translator, lawyer, biographer, and critic. Used both to producing literary work and to dealing with it as a commodity, he was as much 'on the make' as James Macpherson.[6]

However, Murphy's vision of Parnassus is not just a piece of property speculation. It is also a vision of the canon in terms of a landscape in which the culture is at least as much horticulture as literary culture—full of 'grounds . . . laid out in the most exquisite taste . . . hot-beds . . . spon-

---

[4] Arthur Murphy, *Gray's-Inn Journal*, 4 (11 Nov. 1752), in Arthur Murphy, *Works*, 6 vols. (London: n.p., 1786), v. 31–6.

[5] Mark Rose, *Authors and Owners: The Invention of Copyright* (Cambridge, Mass.: Harvard University Press, 1993), 7.

[6] See George Taylor (ed.), *Plays by Samuel Foote and Arthur Murphy* (Cambridge: Cambridge University Press, 1984), 36–40; also Donald W. Nichol, 'Arthur Murphy's Law', *TLS* 19 Apr. 1996, 15.

taneous flowers . . . lavender, myrtle, and wild thyme . . . flowers to trans-
plant'.[7] This language, attentive to a mixture of the wild and the
cultured, is highly significant. Combining ideas of horticulture and
literary culture, it derives from the classical idea of the 'anthology', a
word made by combining the Greek words for 'flower' (*anthos*) and
'word' (*logos*). The anthology is a garden of flowers. Samuel Johnson's
1755 *Dictionary* defines 'anthology' primarily as 'A collection of flowers',
and only lastly as 'A collection of poems', now the principal sense of the
term.[8] Murphy's Parnassus is a great anthology in which we are aware of
the classical Greek and Roman gardeners, and the modern British ones.
This anthology is hedged about by legal and financial terms increasingly
the subject of judicial and authorial scrutiny in the eighteenth century
('possessions . . . let on lease . . . hereditary estate . . . held *by copy*').[9] It is a
work of calculation; but it is also simply beautiful. This present chapter
is about such anthologies.

The emergence of the modern poet, Jerome Stones's short career,
and Arthur Murphy's long one all date from a period when the subjects
of institutional literary criticism and political economy developed as
two related responses to the growth of free-market capitalism in the
British trading arena. Works like *The Wealth of Nations* were designed to
identify for a wide public the best in commercial practices, codifying
them with a view to national growth. At the same time proliferating and
codifying treatises on belles-lettres were aimed at making clear to a
growing literary market which were the best literary practices, those
which would most fully articulate and develop the nation. There was an
awareness not least among the ambitious Scottish literati that successes
in these areas were linked, and that literature could be viewed as a
commodity. This is evident in the university lectures of such teachers
of Rhetoric and Belles-Lettres as Adam Smith at Glasgow, William
Barron at St Andrews, and Hugh Blair at Edinburgh.[10] Though
his editorship is now disputed, it is significant that in the eighteenth
century Blair was thought to have been the critic who opens 'The Scots
Editor's Preface' to a 1753 edition of *The Works of Shakespear* with the
words

---

[7] Murphy, *Works*, v. 32–6.

[8] See Barbara M. Benedict, in *Making the Modern Reader: Cultural Mediation in Early Modern Literary Anthologies* (Princeton: Princeton University Press, 1996), 9 n. 11.

[9] Murphy, *Works*, v. 31–6.

[10] Robert Crawford (ed.), *The Scottish Invention of English Literature* (Cambridge: Cambridge University Press, 1998) and *Launch-Site for English Studies* (St Andrews: Verse, 1997).

The distinguished character of SHAKESPEAR as a dramatic writer, the great demand for his works among the learned and polite, and a laudable zeal for promoting home manufactures, were the principal motives for undertaking an edition of his works in *Scotland*.[11]

For this writer, Shakespeare's 'works' were not only literary works in the modern sense; they were also 'works' in the sense of 'manufactures', a commodity that would improve Scottish trade, as well as Scottish education, if manufactured as part of the home economy rather than imported from London booksellers. The Scottish editor draws variously on the textual and critical labours of Rowe, Pope, Theobald, Hanmer, and Warburton. He adorns his text with various sets of inverted commas to denote passages of special beauty. He is building on the most modern techniques of Shakespeare manufacture.

His edition came to be known as the 'Scottish Shakespeare', a provocative nickname which serves to remind us Shakespeare was scarcely Scottish. Whether or not Blair was that 1753 editor, it is clear from his later career that the Professor would develop as a champion of more obviously native 'home manufactures'. Hence his later support for John Home's *Douglas*, Macpherson's Ossian, the verse of Robert Burns, and other literary productions. The poetry of Macpherson and Burns became spectacularly successful Scottish exports in European and North American, not to mention British, markets. Promoting these two bards, Blair exemplifies the united functions of literary critic and patriotic entrepreneur. He knew the taste of the market.

While the Shakespeare preface was being composed, the future author of *The Wealth of Nations* was lecturing on Rhetoric and Belles-Lettres at Glasgow University. Adam Smith made the point in his lectures that, though poetry was found in primitive societies, it was only improved, commercial societies which attended to the refinement of prose. His words make it clear that Commerce nurtures the arts in general and prose in particular. Smith also argues that good prose nurtures commercial society and so quickens the quest for poetic pleasure. The pursuit of refined literary delight and commercial success are bound together as part of a system of circulation:

---

[11] 'The Scots Editors Preface' to *The Works of Shakespeare*, vol. i (Edinburgh: Kincaid & Bell, et al., 1753), p. i. See Robert Morell Schmitz, *Hugh Blair* (New York: King's Crown Press, 1948), 140, and Warren McDougall, 'Copyright Litigation in the Court of Session, 1738–49, and the Rise of the Scottish Book Trade', *Edinburgh Bibliography Society Transactions*, 5 (1988), 2–31.

Tis the Introduction of Commerce or at least of opulence which is commonly the attendent of Commerce which first brings on the improvement of Prose.— Opulence and Commerce commonly precede the improvement of arts, and refinement of every sort...—Prose is naturally the Language of Business; as Poetry is of pleasure and amusement.[12]

This passage occurs as part of a lecture on judicial and deliberative eloquence. Such forceful fluency will be of use to rising lawyers, ministers, academics, politicians, and public figures in the nation—men whose speech will be crucial to acts of judgement. For them a knowledge of the regularized codes of eloquence will be a commercial asset. It will help them towards the opulence in which, Smith argues, literature can be most fully enjoyed. As he is training his audience in an approved standard of literary judgement Smith is also educating them in commercial ability. Refined, codified taste and an improved codified market are bound together. Even if the era is one dominated by prose (such as that of Smith's own Rhetoric lectures), this is the environment in which the modern poet would develop.

However, while Adam Smith would defend the benefits of free trade, there were great fears in the eighteenth century that an unrestricted literary market would lead to a crash occasioned by the limitless proliferation of books and writers. Fielding opens chapter 1 of book IX of *Tom Jones* (1749) with a revealing sentence:

Among other good uses for which I have thought proper to institute these several introductory chapters, I have considered them as a kind of mark or stamp, which may hereafter enable a very indifferent reader to distinguish what is true and genuine in this historic kind of writing, from what is false and counterfeit.

This passage, in common with so many others in eighteenth-century writing, reminds us that books, like money, are a standardized medium of exchange. The most obvious validating 'stamp' setting genuine apart from counterfeit currency was the monarch's image. For teachers of Rhetoric and Belles-Lettres it was the royal court which set the standard for genuinely refined language. Yet in his wish to avoid 'a swarm of foolish novels', Fielding demands also that those of 'our profession', i.e. writers, have 'a competent knowledge of history and of the belles-lettres'. In *Tom Jones* he looks towards the developing court of 'belles-lettres' to

---

[12] Adam Smith, *Lectures on Rhetoric and Belles-Lettres*, ed. J. C. Bryce (Oxford: Clarendon Press, 1983), 137.

help regulate 'THOSE WHO LAWFULLY MAY...WRITE SUCH HIS-
TORIES AS THIS' (I. ix) and so guard against the 'swarms' of the
'counterfeit'. The notion of literature, like money and commerce, being
subject to lawful regulation is one which grows in the eighteenth
century. The laws of criticism as codified and set forth by academics
like Smith and Blair provide an institutional framework for the regulation of writing alongside the laws of copyright which control literary
production through the law courts. The period develops the institutions
of literary judgement as part of a wider apparatus of commercial, legal,
and artistic management. The institutions through which all this develops are predominantly, often exclusively, male.

Crucially, this phrase 'literary judgement' covers the courtroom, the
academic classroom, and the wider world of business, as well as the
private acts of selection carried out by the writer with pen and paper.
The regulatory process of literary judgement is confined to no one
venue. It goes on in all at once. Emblematic of this linkage is a figure
such as Henry Home, Lord Kames, who first persuaded Adam Smith to
lecture on Rhetoric and Belles-Lettres and who published in 1762 *The
Elements of Criticism*. Blair recommended that his students read this book
along with Rollin on the Belles-Lettres.[13] Kames sought to examine and
articulate principles of literary judgement. Like his friends Smith and
Blair he was a judge of literature in the everyday sense of that expression. But he was also an arbiter of writing as a judge in the Scottish
Court of Session who pronounced on 'the commerce of...books' as
part of a series of literary lawsuits which defined the conditions of
authorship and of the modern literary market.[14]

Spurred in part by Foucault's essay 'What Is an Author?' which draws
attention to 'the moment at which he [the author] was placed in the
system of property that characterizes our society', a good deal of recent
academic work has looked at the development of eighteenth-century
copyright law.[15] In Britain this legislation defined the legal rights of the
author by viewing literary works as a form of property. It also opened up
the market for books by defeating the monopolistic claims of London
booksellers to perpetual copyright. The growth of the New Historicism

[13] John Bruce, notes from Blair's *Lectures on Rhetoric and the Belles-Letters* (1765), EUL MS
Dc.10.6, p. 14.
[14] Lord Kames (1774) cited in Trevor Ross, 'Copyright and the Invention of Tradition',
Eighteenth-Century Studies, 26 (1992), 11.
[15] Michel Foucault, 'What is an Author', in Josue V. Harari (ed.), *Textual Strategies* (London:
Methuen, 1980), 149.

in literary studies and the impinging of literary concerns on legal scholarship has encouraged the work of Carla Hesse, Mark Rose, Trevor Ross, Brad Sherman, Alan Strowel, Martha Woodmansee, and others looking at ideas of a 'Genealogy of Modern Authorship' (to use Rose's Foucauldian terminology) or of 'Copyright and the Invention of Tradition' (Ross).[16] This scholarship demonstrates how developing ideas of intellectual and literary property in the eighteenth century governed the literary market and defined modern ideas about authorship. The complementary work of John Feather on the literary and political ramifications of copyright law is also relevant.[17]

Rather than repeat the arguments of these writers, I would like to suggest that we view the law cases about copyright as examples of 'literary judgement'. This allows us to perceive how they interact with other forms of literary judgement to lead to the growth of what we would now call (anachronistically but helpfully) a national canon. That body of texts was very much both the product of 'literary judgement' in the most inclusive sense of that term and of entrepreneurial judgements about the commercial marketplace. Given the subject of *The Modern Poet*, the canon discussed in the present chapter is one of verse, the kind of literature most highly valued by all centuries until the twentieth. However, canons of drama and prose were also being formed in the period through largely analogous processes.

The first, crucial act of literary judgement was the 1710 Copyright Act which, Trevor Ross argues, 'inadvertently created the public domain'.[18] This 'Act for the Encouragement of Learning' was created as a piece of market regulation designed to remedy a particular situation:

Printers, Booksellers, and other Persons have of late frequently taken the Liberty of Printing, Reprinting, and Publishing, or causing to be Printed,

---

[16] Carla Hesse, 'Enlightenment Epistemology and the Laws of Authorship in Revolutionary France, 1777–1793', *Representations*, 30 (1990), 108–37; Mark Rose, 'The Author as Proprietor: *Donaldson v. Becket* and the Genealogy of Modern Authorship', *Representations*, 23 (1988), 51–85; Rose, *Authors and Owners*; Ross, 'Copyright and the Invention of Tradition'; Brad Sherman and Alan Strowel (eds.), *Of Authors and Origins* (Oxford: Clarendon Press, 1994); Martha Woodmansee, 'The Genius and the Copyright: Economic and Legal Conditions of the Emergence of the "Author"', *Eighteenth-Century Studies*, 17 (1984), 425–88; Martha Woodmansee, *The Author, Art, and the Market* (New York: Columbia University Press, 1994); Martha Woodmansee and Peter Jaszi (eds.), *The Construction of Authorship* (Durham, NC: Duke University Press, 1994).

[17] See John Feather, 'The Book Trade in Politics: The Making of the Copyright Act of 1710', *Publishing History*, 8 (1980), 19–44.

[18] Ross, 'Copyright and the Invention of Tradition', 2.

Reprinted and Republished Books, and other Writings, without the Consent of the Authors or Proprietors of such Books and Writings, to their very great Detriment, and too often to the Ruin of them and their Families.[19]

As Feather summarizes it, this Act (sometimes referred to as 'the Statute of Queen Anne') set out that 'From 10 April 1710 all existing books shall be copyrighted to their present owners for 21 years; and all new books for 14 years, with the possibility of a second 14-year term.'[20] In the ensuing decades, however, London booksellers continually attempted to use legal means (including the Court of Chancery) to prevent in particular provincial and Scottish booksellers marketing specific works. The copyrights of these, the London firms contended, had been assigned to them and were their perpetual property under common law, quite apart from the jurisdiction of the Statute of Queen Anne. Argument over this issue lasted for much of the century. It came to a head in a number of law cases, several involving Thomson's *Seasons.* The 1753 edition of Shakespeare, supporting Scottish 'home manufactures', should be seen as a contribution to the struggle of the Scottish and provincial booksellers against a London-centred monopoly. Blair's friend Kames, giving judgement at a 1773 decision of the Scottish Court of Session, argued that the Statute of Queen Anne 'excites men of genius to exert their talents for composition; and it multiplies books both of instruction and amusement. And when, upon expiration of the monopoly, the commerce of these books is laid open to all, their cheapness, from a concurrence of many editors, is singularly beneficial to the public.' Kames was against the idea of perpetual copyright because it would 'unavoidably raise the price of good books beyond the reach of ordinary readers. They will be sold like so many valuable pictures. The sale will be confined to a few rich men who buy out of vanity as they buy a diamond or a fine coat.'[21]

Lord Kames's legal judgement, therefore, favours the expansion of the literary marketplace which was made possible by the judgement of the House of Lords in the celebrated 1774 case of *Donaldson* v. *Becket.* In this wrangle the Edinburgh bookseller Alexander Donaldson (whose legal team included the Scot James Boswell and the Irish lawyer-playwright Arthur Murphy) defeated a group of London booksellers headed by Thomas Becket. The latter had accused Donaldson of

---

[19]   Cited in Feather, 'The Book Trade in Politics', 19.   [20]   Ibid.
[21]   Kames (1774), cited in Ross, 'Copyright and the Invention of Tradition', 11.

breach of copyright for publishing an edition of Thomson's *Seasons* over which the Londoners claimed perpetual copyright.[22] The 1774 judgement effectively ended London booksellers' claims to perpetual copyright, and hugely opened up the literary marketplace. Mark Rose has pointed out how a growing interest in what constituted authorial identity, and in treating authors as brand names, led to proliferating studies of writers, their biographies, and their characteristics.[23] In this sense the legal developments reinforced the growth of English literary studies such as those in the Scottish universities. Yet in a sharp and stimulating article, Trevor Ross points out that a consequence of this case was that in some ways the balance of power shifted from the author (whose original genius secured him or his assignees perpetual copyright), to the reader, whose ability to buy, to pick and choose between books for sale, was greatly increased.

If authors and booksellers were the apparent losers in the decision of 1774, the clear winners were English readers, who could now look forward to multiple cheap editions of canonical works... Pamphlets and monographs on the art of reading began to appear for the first time, and reading for comprehension and appreciation becomes a subject of pedagogical concern. In criticism, practical considerations about the utility of literature and the norms for writing are being eclipsed by elaborate discourses on the faculties of taste and judgement. The upshot of all this is that the value of literature is being redefined to reflect a change from production to consumption, writing to reading, rhetoric to reception. Or, in the terms of the copyright debate, literary works, once vehicles for ideological instruction and hegemonic control, become instead cultural items to be broadly circulated in society. Emancipated from the forceful codes of rhetoric, readers may purchase books to suit their taste, pleasure, and self-image. And with this commodification of writing, canons become something for a consuming public to make... On February 22nd, 1774, literature in its modern sense began.[24]

I have quoted from Ross at length because I believe his insights to be extremely helpful and subtly wrong. They are of use because they focus attention on the importance of the opening-up of the market initiated by the 1774 House of Lords judgement. At the same time, though, Ross ignores the way in which the Lords' decision, instead of releasing the

---

[22] See Rose, *Authors and Owners*, 92–7; W. Forbes Gray, 'Alexander Donaldson and his Fight for Cheap Books', *Juridical Review*, 38 (1926), 180–202; Nichol, 'Arthur Murphy's Law', 15–16.
[23] Rose, *Authors and Owners*, 113–29.
[24] Ross, 'Copyright and the Invention of Tradition', 14–16.

public from 'the forceful codes of rhetoric', may have given those 'forceful codes' access to a much wider market. For the pronouncement of their lordships opened the way to the wider dissemination of the judgement of Hugh Blair.

Like the Ossianic controversy, the 1774 judgement involved Scottish–English tensions. It was given in a case fought by an Edinburgh against a London bookseller over a poem by a Scottish poet much of whose life had been lived in the south of England and some of whose poetry had been preoccupied with Britishness and with liberty. As well as writing a poem called *Liberty*, Thomson hoped in *The Seasons* that Britain might be 'in Soul united as in Name' – a common aspiration of eighteenth-century Scots who felt that the English thought of 'England', even if at times they paid lip-service to 'Britain'.[25] The 1774 judgement opened up British markets to all British booksellers, not just to London ones jealous of their supposed monopolies. It cleared the way for literature as a truly national *British* possession.

So it was that at the same time as the London literati were fascinated by the *Donaldson* v. *Becket* trial the Edinburgh publishers Kincaid and Creech employed Hugh Blair to edit a multivolume set of *The British Poets*. What this meant was that the literary judgement of the House of Lords was working along with the literary judgement of the Professor of Rhetoric and Belles-Lettres at Edinburgh University and with his publisher's commercial *nous* to regulate the production of a corpus of poetry which could be seen as a national property. This property, *The British Poets*, was again the product of 'a laudable zeal for promoting home manufactures' and of a refined taste attuned to the developing literary market.

In his helpful book *The Making of the Modern Canon* Jan Gorak argues that 'eighteenth-century usage does not support any unqualified extension of *canon* to a context outside Scripture or antiquity'.[26] This may appear a salutary reminder since it is very tempting for me to talk of Blair's *British Poets* as the first physical embodiment of a consciously formed and marketed British poetic canon. At the same time, though, visions such as those of Stones and Murphy demonstrate that the mid-eighteenth century could easily conceive of what we would now recognize as a canon. Moreover, the term 'canon' in the sense of 'law,

[25] See Robert Crawford, *Devolving English Literature*, 2nd edn. (Edinburgh: Edinburgh University Press, 2000), 45–110.

[26] Jan Gorak, *The Making of the Modern Canon* (London: Athlone Press, 1991), 46.

rule, edict' or 'standard of judgement' was familiar in English from the sixteenth century (*OED*). What we may (with some awareness of anachronism) call Blair's canon was itself the product of law—its production was stimulated by the law cases over copyright in the eighteenth century that culminated in the judgement given in *Donaldson* v. *Becket*. The modern literary canon is the product of the regulatory canons of the law, and of the regularizing 'canons of criticism' as Warburton called them in his 1747 edition of Shakespeare.[27] The canon is the product of the canons. It is the result of intersecting acts of judgement.

Just as the judges in the eighteenth-century law cases had their eyes directed towards the marketplace for books and the effects which their legislation would have there, so Blair's edition of *The British Poets* was very much commercially oriented. Designed to take advantage of the extension of the British literary market, it appropriated from the London booksellers the most significant English-language poets. It may have drawn inspiration from a series of volumes of 'English Poets' produced by the Foulis Press at Glasgow University from 1765, though this does not appear to have been presented from its inception as a gathering of the most important national poets.[28] Blair's collection marketed his poets not separately but as part of a uniform edition which could present for the first time a full national corpus appealing to those who treasured British commercial liberty as well as British literature. All that and more is signalled in the uniform format and in that title, *The British Poets*. Blair (who worked anonymously, as he had on earlier editorial projects) was the employee of the booksellers aiming to exploit a newly expanded market. As Professor of Rhetoric and Belles-Lettres, he also offered them his professional skills and judgement as to which works to include in *The British Poets*.[29] The edition, published in Edinburgh by Kincaid, Creech, and Balfour in forty-four volumes between 1773 and 1776, was the product of literary taste and of market forces. Like all anthologies, it is itself an act of literary and commercial judgement.

To appreciate the importance of Blair's *British Poets* we should set the work in the wider context of anthology-making in earlier

[27] Ibid. 47–8.

[28] See David Murray, *Robert and Andrew Foulis and the Glasgow Press* (Glasgow: James Maclehose, 1913), 48; Philip Gaskell, *A Bibliography of the Foulis Press*, 2nd edn. (London: St Paul's Bibliographies, 1986), 18 and 62; Thomas Bonnell, 'Speaking of Institutions and Canonicity, Don't Forget the Publishers', *Eighteenth Century Life*, 21/3 (Nov. 1997), 97.

[29] The best modern account of Blair's career is Schmitz, *Hugh Blair*.

eighteenth-century Scotland and England. Barbara Benedict, in the standard work on this topic, emphasizes how anthologies' 'format prompts the formation of a canon' and how historically arranged gatherings present 'the history of English literature as a patriotic and moral commodity', so that readers of national anthologies 'become part of the culture they absorb'.[30] In Scotland a number of anthologies with a national aspect had appeared, but these were smaller (often single-volume) productions aimed at maintaining a sense of the Scottish, rather than the British nation. Among them was James Watson's three-volume patriotic anthology *A Choice Collection of Comic and Serious Scots Poems* (1706, 1709, 1711) which aimed to supply the basics of a Scottish literary tradition. This was followed by Allan Ramsay's 1724 *The Ever Green* which assembled and celebrated '*these good old* Bards' such as Dunbar and Henryson whose 'Poetry *is the Product of their own Country, not pilfered and spoiled in the Transportation from abroad*'.[31] Though the Scots songs in Ramsay's *Tea-Table Miscellany* (1725, 1727, 1732, 1737) achieved, along with similar collections, substantial popularity beyond Scotland, it was a Scottish, rather than a wider British corpus which they gathered. The earlier eighteenth-century anthology which most clearly aims at collecting poetry as part of an assertion of British national prestige is Thomas Hayward's three-volume *The British Muse; or, A Collection of Thoughts Moral, Natural, and Sublime, of our English Poets: who Flourished in the Sixteenth and Seventeenth Centuries* (1738). Glancing back towards Edward Byshe's *The British Parnassus* (1714) which suggested in its title and contents that Britain might have its own classic poetry, Hayward's volumes suggested in their dedication to Lady Mary Wortley Montagu that support for poetry was a national service: 'It is an honour to the *British Nation*, that it has, from time to time, produced so many illustrious Patrons of the *British Muse*.' Cherishing and republishing work by the older British poets is seen here by Hayward as 'honourable to our Nation'.[32] His collection is made up of short poems and extracts arranged thematically under such headings as GAMING or LAW and includes work by poets and playwrights like Alexander Brome, Sir John Davies, Samuel Daniel, Donne, Herbert, Shakespeare, Spenser, Suckling, and others. Though the authors are almost all English, there is some Scottish representation. Work by Sir David Lindsay (from the 1709 Edinburgh edition) is

---

[30] Benedict, *Making the Modern Reader*, 4, 166, and 173.
[31] Allan Ramsay, 'Preface' to *The Ever Green*, 2 vols. (Edinburgh: Ruddiman, 1724), i, p. vii.
[32] Thomas Hayward (ed.), *The British Muse*, 3 vols. (London: F. Cogan, 1738), dedication.

included. Yet as a national commonplace book or collection of extracts, *The British Muse* falls far short of *The British Poets*, which included entire works such as *Paradise Lost*. In some ways closer to *The British Poets* was the six-volume anthology *The British Stage*, a 1750 reprint (with a new title page) of twenty-four plays originally printed separately between 1718 and 1730. A related, contemporary mustering of dramatic resources takes place in William Rufus Chetwood's anonymous *The British Theatre* (first published in Dublin in 1750). Chetwood presents in one volume the lives of the English dramatic poets, an account of their plays, along with the lives of principal actors, and what his work's title page calls 'a short view of the rise and progress of the English stage'. Yet, however popular the theatre, it was poetry which was viewed as the most important literary genre, particularly by such emerging critical authorities as Blair. *The British Poets* marked not only a bold Scottish step beyond the anthologizing of Caledonian national collections. It was also a project that proceeded on a more elevated cultural level than *The British Stage*. It moved on this higher plane because both the authority of poetry and the judgemental authority of Blair as the anthology's supervisor lent dignity to the commercial judgement of its backers as they attempted to produce and sell a national corpus to the British market.

The way the men behind *The British Poets* worked as a commercial team is emphasized by Blair's biographer R. M. Schmitz. He points out the several connections between Blair and the businessmen producing the edition, Alexander Kincaid, John Balfour, and William Creech.

Kincaid, H.M. Printer for Scotland, had already published several sermons by Blair, had issued the *Heads of the Lectures* [*on Rhetoric and Belles-Lettres*], and had been one of the many booksellers concerned in the *Shakespeare*, in which Balfour also had an interest. Balfour, in partnership with Gavin Hamilton, had published the [Ossianic] *Fragments of Ancient Poetry*.

Of the three men, William Creech was closest to Blair ... Later, the shop of Kincaid and Creech, booksellers, became the chief informal gathering place for the literary great of the city, and stood cheek-by-jowl with St. Giles where Blair was minister. Creech was later to publish Blair's *Sermons* and *Lectures*. It was probably he who suggested Blair as literary supervisor for *The British Poets*.[33]

It is essential to realize how closely Blair was working as part of an economic venture. He has been called both 'editor' and 'supervisor' of the edition. We cannot be sure how far he selected the poets for *The*

---

[33] Schmitz, *Hugh Blair*, 70.

British Poets, and how far they were the choice of the publishers. What this means is that the perception of a distinction between aesthetic and commercial judgement is impossible: the two are at one. Even if we knew for certain that Blair chose the poets for inclusion, we could be sure too that he would be constrained by what was still in copyright under the Statute of Queen Anne, and by what the publishers judged the market could stand. Schmitz concludes that Blair

> may well have indicated the poets and poems to be included, but he certainly placed his *imprimatur* upon every page of the proposed text. The Edinburgh publishers had, in fact, come to depend upon him . . . for all manner of advice and promotion dealing with books.[34]

What this makes clear is that in his supervision of *The British Poets* as in his wider literary work as academic and as publisher's adviser Blair was part of a regulatory system. Through this the work of poets had to pass in order to be included as part of the modern canon. During this period there emerged what Clifford Siskin terms 'the modern system of letters we call Literature'.[35] Books were, and are, disseminated according to acts of judgement, legal, commercial, and aesthetic. The different aspects of these acts should be viewed not as independent but as interdependent. *The British Poets* is a striking product of this interdependence and of the cultural momentum seen in such works as *The British Muse* and *The British Stage*. All these are attempts to produce what can be regarded as national anthologies, whose patriotic aspect will be part of their appeal.

Working within the institutions of eighteenth-century Scotland and Britain, Professor Blair, the champion of Ossian, is an originating model of how the academic literary critic in the centuries that follow operates as part of a wider economy and set of institutions which combine to regulate through acts of judgement the circulation of ideas. But Blair is also responsible for the supervision of a new institution: the multi-volume anthology which rallies and disseminates a national corpus. Alert to their unusual importance, Thomas Bonnell has suggested that 'These collections and series . . . did nothing if not dictate versions of the canon to a wide public'.[36] Before Blair's edition you could buy and sell work by British poets, but not *the* British Poets. With *The British Poets*

---

[34] Schmitz, *Hugh Blair*, 71.
[35] Clifford Siskin, *The Work of Writing* (Baltimore: Johns Hopkins University Press, 1998), 111.
[36] Bonnell, 'Speaking of Institutions and Canonicity', 98.

there was a canonical body of work, uniform and clearly uniformed, which represented the modern nation and which anyone with enough money could buy and take home for the shelf.

The success of this new literary institution is evident when we look at the nationally signposted multivolume editions of the poets (and I mean '*the* poets') which followed in Blair's wake. Between 1778 and 1783 there appeared John Bell's *The Poets of Great Britain Complete from Chaucer to Churchill* in 109 volumes printed in Edinburgh at the Apollo Press. This provoked a large grouping of London booksellers to issue in response their *The Works of the English Poets with Prefaces Biographical and Critical by Samuel Johnson*. That demonstration of metropolitan authority in sixty-five volumes was published by an array of London booksellers between 1777 and 1781, then supplemented by eight additional volumes in 1790. It was followed by the thirteen fat tomes of Robert Anderson's *The Works of the British Poets* (London and Edinburgh, 1792–4). An 1805–9 edition of the *British Poets* produced in London by John Sharpe and Charles Whittingham, and edited by Thomas Park in forty-eight volumes, had no sooner appeared than the Scottish editor Alexander Chalmers produced for a group of London booksellers *The Works of the English Poets from Chaucer to Cowper*. This included in twenty-one volumes everything in the series for which Johnson had written his *Lives*, plus much more besides. At the Chiswick Press in 1822 the Charles Whittinghams, uncle and nephew, unleashed the 100-volume *British Poets*, 500 sets published simultaneously as 50,000 volumes.[37] The Whittinghams' friend William Pickering marshalled from 1830 to 1844 his uniform Aldine English Poets, several times reprinted before Pickering's bankruptcy, then (after the bankruptcy) reprinted in 1866 and supplemented until 1889 when the series reached sixty-three volumes.[38] The mid-nineteenth century had already seen several publishers with periodically published multivolume anthologies of the national poets competing in an expanding marketplace. A Dundee minister, George Gilfillan, edited *The British Poets* for Edinburgh publisher James Nichol in forty-eight volumes between 1853 and 1860 in competition with Routledge's *British Poets* (London; 24 vols., 1853–8) and the Irishman Robert Bell's *Annotated Edition of the English Poets*, published in London by John W. Parker and Son between 1854 and 1857 in twenty-nine volumes.

[37] See Arthur Warren, *The Charles Whittinghams, Printers* (New York: Grolier Club, 1896), 79.
[38] See Sir Geoffrey Keynes, *William Pickering, Publisher*, rev. edn. (London: Galahad Press, n.d.), 27.

In late nineteenth-century America huge, popularly priced editions of *The British Poets* went on selling. By 1887 Little Brown's multivolume edition of that title, edited by Professor Francis James Child of Harvard, passed its hundredth 75-cent volume in a reissue of an earlier (1865–6) 130-volume set. In Britain, though, such vast national assemblies seem to have been going out of fashion, not least because there were now significant American poets such as Longfellow who demanded to be part of a standard edition but who could not be contained in the title 'British' or 'English'. Later nineteenth-century British and English national awareness continued to be articulated through smaller, more selective anthologies such as T. H. Ward's 1880 four-volume *The English Poets*, while larger multivolume sets of canonical authors tended to bear the title of a publisher's imprint rather than of the nation. So we have The Lansdowne Poets, the Chandos Classics (including not just poetry), and the Oxford Standard Authors. The word 'British' or 'English' has ceased to contain all the English-language poetry seen to be suitable for inclusion in such editions; the 'body' of important verse has been recognized as a multinational body. Yet for over a century that institution of a uniform national poetic corpus, instigated with Blair's edition of *The British Poets*, played an important role in the literary life of the nation and in the articulation of modern national literary character. The identity of the modern poet was developed alongside, and through, these great anthologies. Though a continuous history of the smaller-scale anthology in English is only beginning to be written, far too little attention has been paid to these massive and influential multivolume, canon-stating gatherings.[39] Their influence (this chapter will argue) extends to today's anthologies, such as those published by Penguin, Oxford, and Norton. It would be foolish to contend that the collections mentioned in this chapter shared the same audience. Obviously their eighteenth-century readers were not all students, and were long dead before the Norton anthologies appeared! But from Hugh Blair's editing of *The British Poets* through Matthew Arnold's involvement with *The English Poets* to the modern *Norton Anthology* as developed by M. H. Abrams, David Daiches, and others, the links between poetry and academia have become increasingly pronounced and potent, reinforcing the development of what this book calls 'the modern

---

[39] On anthologizing, see the works by Barbara Benedict and Thomas Bonnell mentioned in this chapter, along with Barbara Korte, Ralf Schneider, and Stefanie Lethbridge (eds.), *Anthologies of British Poetry: Critical Perspectives from Literary and cultural studies* (Amsterdam: Rodopi, 2000).

poet'. These links shape the background against which the modern poet is perceived as well as the literary environment in which he works. As with the genesis of the Ossianic poems, so with the growth of vast multivolume anthologies, the crucial early protagonist is Hugh Blair.

If it was Blair's *British Poets* which began this movement, then the importance of such an edition was soon grasped in London. What followed in the wake of the 1773–6 Edinburgh edition was a sort of 'canon warfare' which saw repeated literary-entrepreneurial formations of a uniform national body of verse. John Bell, the lively English entrepreneur whose *Poets of Great Britain,* printed in Edinburgh, so upset the other London booksellers, knew well the value of a national corpus that would appeal to national sentiment. So in the 1790s his advertisements 'respectfully intreated' 'THE BRITISH AND IRISH NATIONS' to patronize such works as his weekly published 'new and splendid edition of *The British Theatre*' (comprising 110 plays, available in editions of varying luxury ranging from sixpence to five shillings in cost), *The British Album,* and *The Poets of Great Britain,* a republication of his earlier edition which was 'to include all the BRITISH CLASSICS'. In the century which saw the establishment of such organizations as the British Museum, whose statutes were published in 1757, Bell, like Blair and his publishers but with greater entrepreneurial flair, knew the value of setting up and marketing a patriotic-sounding British institution. He called his base in the Strand 'The British Library'. That title again stresses the unity of the literary and the commercial, as does Bell's exhortation to booksellers to allow his *British Theatre* 'a free circulation, as a means of convincing the World, that the Productions of the BRITISH PRESS are not at present to be excelled by the Artists of any Country upon Earth'.[40]

Bell's business card announced him as 'BOOKSELLER and PUBLISHER of the POETS OF GREAT BRITAIN from CHAUCER to CHURCHILL,' and advertised his wares to 'Gentlemen *for their Libraries,* Merchants *and* Captains *of* Ships *for Exportation,* Booksellers *and* Shopkeepers *to sell again*'.[41] Among modern commentators only Thomas Bonnell perceives the full importance of what Bell called his 'vendible

---

[40] Bell's documents are reproduced and cited in Stanley Morison, *John Bell, 1745–1832* (London: The First Edition Club, 1930), illustrations following p. 36; see also pp. 39–40; other information about Bell is also taken from this work.

[41] Ibid., illustration following p. 36.

poetry'. Bonnell argues that it is the bookseller who invented 'a broadly disseminated poetical canon'.[42] One of the first literary retailers to publish a comprehensive catalogue, Bell with his corpus of British Classics, and in league with an Edinburgh printer, was such a commercial threat that the rest of the London booksellers had to band together against him, and rapidly produce their own, opposing corpus. This thirty-six of them did, approaching Johnson to write his *Prefaces Biographical and Critical* (or *Lives of the Poets*) for the edition. The bookseller Dilly described Bell's edition scornfully as a 'little trifling' one, but Bonnell points out that this is persiflage, since in less than a decade Bell's *Poets of Great Britain* involved the printing of nearly 400,000 copies, with further, frequent reprints going on into the early nineteenth century.[43] Bell's commercial success had to be countered by the economic weight of the London booksellers and the critical *gravitas* of Johnson.[44] The booksellers' input was also critical—they chose most of the poets—while Johnson's cultural clout was an asset in the marketplace. His *Prefaces* and the use of his name on the title page of each volume would be a unique marketing advantage. Just as Johnson's *Dictionary* had become a standard market-leader, so might an edition of the poets endorsed by him. His 'Advertisement' to the edition makes clear the booksellers' intention to establish a national corpus or, as Johnson puts it, 'a Body of English Poetry'. He writes of how he has gone far beyond his original design of giving 'every Poet an Advertisement, like those which we find in the French Miscellanies'.[45] Instead he has furnished something much more thorough. Implicit here is the suggestion that this patriotic 'Body of English Poetry' comes in a format superior to any foreign rival.

Robert Anderson, prefacing his *Works of the British Poets*, looks back to Johnson and the earlier *Works of the English Poets* as a collecting of 'classics' in 'a work which bore so close a relation to the national honour'.[46] Setting out in his own collection 'to extend the honour of

---

[42] Thomas F. Bonnell, 'Bookselling and Canon-Making: The Trade Rivalry over the English Poets, 1776–1783', *Studies in Eighteenth-Century Culture*, 19 (1989), 63 and 65.

[43] Thomas F. Bonnell, 'John Bell's *Poets of Great Britain*: The "Little Trifling Edition" Revisited', *Modern Philology*, 85/2 (Nov. 1987), 147 and 152.

[44] Charles Knight, *Shadows of the Old Booksellers* (London: Bell & Daldy, 1865), 250.

[45] Samuel Johnson, 'Advertisement' to *Prefaces Biographical and Critical to the Works of the English Poets*, 10 vols. (London: C. Bathurst, et al., 1779–81), i, pp. v–vi.

[46] Robert Anderson, 'Preface' to *The Works of the British Poets*, 13 vols. (Edinburgh: Mundell & Son, 1792–4), i. 3. Unless otherwise indicated, all other Anderson quotations in this chapter are from the preface, with page references given in my text after the abbreviation 'A.'

our national poetry, as far as possible both abroad and at home', Anderson shows an increased literary-commercial self-consciousness. His preface carefully differentiates this new gathering from previous models. Having reviewed earlier, smaller collections from Tottell to Ritson, he calls attention to the virtue of the more modern compilers of multivolume national anthologies 'who, uniting industry with taste, have presented the public with uniform and elegant editions of the British Poets, in the manner of those of Italy, Spain, and France' (A. 1). He pays tribute to that moulder of the modern poet, 'Dr Blair', as the originator of such collections, but censures the incompleteness of *The British Poets*; then he laments how hard it is to find full sets of Bell's *Poets of Great Britain*, and what a pity it is that several poets were excluded from or included in Johnson's edition. Johnson is seen as a national hero who 'gave up his life to the literature of his country' (A. 3), yet Anderson makes it quite clear that his own edition excels in containing '*one hundred and fourteen* authors, of whome *forty-nine* are not to be found in the last edition of the "Works of the English Poets," commonly called Dr Johnson's edition; and *forty-five* are now, for the first time, received into an edition of English poetry' (A. 5). What Anderson's production constitutes, its editor explains, is

a collection, upon an enlarged plan, which might unite the works of the ancient and modern poets in one comprehensive view, and exhibit the progress of our national poetry, corresponding with the gradual refinement of language and of manners, from the rudeness and simplicity of a remote period, to the polish and elegance of modern times. (A. 4)

This ancient as well as recent body of work articulates a country's progress, setting 'our national poetry' alongside Britain's other great achievements, and beside the output of comparable nations. Reading Anderson's preface, one is aware of both his pride in the edition and his sense of how strongly it has been driven by economic demands. So he denies any responsibility for the correctness of the text, and writes embarrassedly that 'The engraved title-page, bearing to be "A *Complete* Edition of the Poets of Great Britain," was improperly copied by the proprietors, in the *first* volume, from Mr Bell's edition, and retained in the subsequent volumes, for the sake of uniformity' (A. 5). Again, to preserve regularity in volume size, chronological order has been departed from, while some of the lives of the poets have been written by other hands, and 'were solicited and obtained by the proprietors, to expedite the publication, and never seen by the editor till they were printed' (A. 7). Anderson sounds at times like the literary man complaining about commercial pressures. Yet his own, subtler devaluing of competing products and his appropriation of their contents are equally commercial as well as literary acts of judgement. While he was not an academic, Anderson like Blair shows the literary and the economic as inseparable. Indeed, though a graduate of St Andrews, Anderson did his studying in Edinburgh and, if he is content to expose the shortcomings of Blair's *British Poets* in his preface, then in the body of his collection he makes it clear that he owes 'the learned and amiable Dr Blair' a great debt as 'the venerable director of his youthful studies'. Anderson offers 'the testimony of a grateful pupil, to the merit of his [Blair's] "Academical prelections," which constitute an aera in the history of Scottish literature'.[47] In other words, Blair as supervisor of *The British Poets* is Anderson's model, but Blair the Professor of Rhetoric and Belles-Lettres is also the moulder of Anderson's taste. So in various ways Blair's acts of judgement continue to shape the developing British poetic canon into the nineteenth century. Blair's 'Taste for the Belles-Lettres' would continue to be propounded by later influential anthologists such as Vicesimus Knox, whose *Elegant Extracts* meant much to Jane Austen.[48] This is yet another example of the way in which the cultural space occupied by the modern poet (and by those older poets admitted to the modern canon) is shaped by the mid-eighteenth-century convergence of poetry and academia.

Viewing the later uniform multivolume editions, one can see their editors' sense of moulding what Alexander Chalmers in 1810 calls 'a work professing to be a BODY OF THE STANDARD ENGLISH POETS', and what George Gilfillan's publisher (whose brother was John Nichol, the first Professor of English Literature at Glasgow University) fifty years later describes as a collection of 'those authors whose names stand most prominent on the list of British Poets, keeping in view, at the same time, that the series as a whole, should present historically a view of our poetic literature from the time of Chaucer'.[49] In the later collections, as in the earlier, eighteenth-century ones, there are obvious commercial

---

[47] Anderson, 'The Life of Blair', *The Works of the British Poets*, viii. 851.

[48] See Benedict, *Making the Modern Reader*, 215–16; also Leah Price, *The Anthology and the Rise of the Novel, from Richardson to George Eliot* (Cambridge: Cambridge University Press, 2000), ch. 2.

[49] Alexander Chalmers, 'Preface' to *The Works of the English Poets from Chaucer to Cowper* (London: J. Johnson, et al., 1810), i, p. v; Anon., *Announcement of the Seventh Year's Issue of the Library Edition of the British Poets* (Edinburgh: James Nichol, 1859), 4.

as well as academic forces moulding the corpus. Yet at the same time
these economic pressures demand that the edition increasingly articulates a confident sense that it contains the full body of the national
poetry in a balanced way. Though modern academics are attached to the
idea of the canon as a metaphysical entity, a *notional* body of work, it is
important to see how these eighteenth-and nineteenth-century uniform
editions produced a physical, *national* body of work which approximated
to an actual canon that anyone with enough money could go into a shop
and buy.

   The impact of such vast productions is not always easy to gauge. It
does, however, appear to have been widespread. After his initial 400,000
volumes, Bell, for instance, was prepared to invest a further £20,000 in
the early 1790s, reprinting his *Poets of Great Britain* in a variety of formats.
When Walter Scott in his introduction to the *Chronicles of the Canongate*
mentions that he invented epigraphs because 'I found it too trouble-
some to turn to the collection of the British poets to discover apposite
mottoes', this is surely a light-hearted indication that for him Blair's *The
British Poets* (or possibly later gatherings by Anderson or Thomas Campbell) represented the modern canonical standard.[50] Wordsworth corresponded with Robert Anderson about poets to be included in an
enlarged edition of the latter's multivolume anthology.[51] These sets of
volumes not only included but were also used by modern poets, as well
as a wide variety of other readers and writers for whom in practical
terms they formed a canon. In many early libraries a uniform multivolume edition may have constituted the available poetry. In 1795, for
instance, with the exception of the poems of Ossian, all the verse
contained in the Edinburgh Subscription Library took the form of
ninety-two volumes of Bell's *Poets of Great Britain*. This library's catalogue provides a stark example of the way various regulatory systems
might intersect to promote institutional control over poetry reading. For
not only were its poetry holdings governed by the contents of Bell's
Poets, it was also stocked with the increasingly fashionable academic
criticism, such as George Campbell's *Philosophy of Rhetoric* and Blair's
Lectures on Rhetoric and Belles-Lettres. The only other secondary materials
on poetry on the library's shelves were four volumes of 'Johnstons [*sic*]

---

[50] Scott quoted in Gérard Genette, *Paratexts*, trans. Jane E. Lewin (Cambridge: Cambridge
University Press, 1997), 147.
[51] Duncan Wu, *Wordsworth's Reading 1800–1815*, (Cambridge: Cambridge University Press,
1995), 136.

Lives of the poets'—whose contents were again, of course, determined by a booksellers' series.[52]

One library's stock does not prove a norm. Yet it is important to bear in mind how far these anthologies constituted a national poetic core. Johnson's books presented lives not of poets but of 'the Poets'. The definite article in such titles as Blair's *The British Poets* or Bell's *The Poets of Great Britain* signals that these are *the* poets, the ones who are essential to the nation. Bell's edition, Bonnell points out, was the first to settle on 'a simple uniform phrase, "The Life of ..."' prefacing an account of each poet.[53] The editions' uniformity also makes for a sense of national unity. All the poets' works in their regular series format share a physical identity. There they are—the British poets—drawn up together as a regular body, as much a representation of national strength and honour as the uniformed services who fought on the battlefields of Europe. Several of these series appeared while Britain was at war with other European nations. When Johnson or Anderson subtly aligns the mustered and regularized rows of the English or British poets with their less well-presented continental counterparts, such acts have a clear national and nationalist resonance. Their eighteenth-century and nineteenth-century promoters knew that to support the British poets, setting them like a standing army on one's shelves, might be an exploitable patriotic gesture.

For the 'national body' of poetry was in some ways analogous to the national army, regimented and uniform. This uniformity is also part of a much wider eighteenth-century drive for regulation. Just as it was a judgement of the British House of Lords, the highest regulatory body in the land, which reformed copyright law and made possible *The British Poets*, so the production of that series mirrors other acts of national regularization. Several of these are part of the Scottish Enlightenment. *The Statistical Account of Scotland*, edited by the lawyer Sir John Sinclair and completed in 1799, presented for the first time in Europe a parish-by-parish national survey providing uniform information in a standardized multivolume format. Gathered through identical questionnaires and issued in matching volumes, *The Statistical Account*, like *The British Poets* and the sciences of politial economy and literary criticism, is designed to

---

[52] 'Catalogue of the Books Belonging to the Edinburgh Subscription Library', transcribed in Paul Kaufman, 'The Rise of Community Libraries in Scotland', *Papers of the Bibliographical Society of America*, 59 (1965), 281–3.

[53] Thomas F. Bonnell, 'Patchwork and Piracy: John Bell's "Connected System of Biography" and the Use of Johnson's *Prefaces*', *Studies in Bibliography*, 48 (1995), 211.

facilitate the circulation of accurate, regularly formatted materials which will be acceptable currency in the market. These phenomena are all part of the industrial revolution's drive to standardize mechanically production processes. After the *Statistical Account*, Sinclair published his *Code of Agriculture*; as well as forming his British poets Blair concerned himself with moral and literary codes in his *Sermons* and *Lectures*. The standardized *British Poets*, the standard-sized proto-computer cards of a Jacquard loom, the invention of tinned food, and the drive to codify and regularize both trade and language are all aspects of the same phenomenon. Where centuries earlier the Domesday Book had made possible a body of knowledge available for limited circulation, *The Statistical Account* and *The British Poets* provided constantly replicable bodies which could populate the nation, spreading national images throughout Britain and allowing the export of a modern British 'body' abroad. We take for granted in our modern work and leisure practices a huge degree of uniformity produced by systems as various as questionnaires, auditing, containerization, the highway code, and prefabricated industrial construction. Such regularized mass systems did exist before the eighteenth century—in language, and in movable type for instance. But it is the Enlightenment and the industrial revolution which give rise to the immense proliferation of the ideal of the regularized unit, suitable for high-volume production, standard transmission, and widespread consumption. Like Adam Smith's pins, *The British Poets* in their serried, vendible ranks are part of this great cultural shift.

What is important is not that these standardized multivolume sets were read entire (for surely they were not) but that they established themselves as embodying a desirable national body of work. Their success is evident from the sheer number of the different sets produced, and from the fact that many of these went through several reprints, as certainly did Bell's, Johnson's, Anderson's, and the Aldine series. They also appeared in varying formats (each uniform within itself), being available to subscribers on a weekly, monthly, or quarterly basis, as well as to those who wished to purchase a whole set. In 1791 Bell reissued his *Poets of Great Britain* in weekly volumes at 1*s*. 6*d*. a week, though the lot were also on offer at £8 3*s*. 6*d*. unbound for all 109 volumes. Just over sixty years later George Gilfillan's Library Edition of the British Poets was issued at the rate of six volumes per annum, each six volumes costing a guinea. Robert Bell's contemporary 1850s Annotated Edition of the English Poets sold at 2*s*. 6*d*. per volume. These, like the mass-market edition of Routledge's British Poets, were clearly aimed at a large public. They represent an appeal to a wider readership beyond those people who might have afforded the hefty tomes of the editions by Anderson or Chalmers. Nevertheless, the sense of the poets as a national body persists. The standard preface to the volumes in Robert Bell's series stresses the innovatory importance of the annotations and is directed to 'the Students of our National Literature', again marking the powerful convergence of poetry and institutionalized education.[54] The poet presented to students and other readers is increasingly offered as a *national* figure, or at least one to be seen in a national context. Such recent scholars as Chris Baldick and Franklin E. Court have demonstrated how students studied poetry in national and even nationalistic terms.[55] That literary scholarship should have developed in this way was surely encouraged by those vast anthologies which in the eighteenth and nineteenth centuries assembled a body of national poetry. Opposite the preface to Bell's Annotated Edition there appeared an epigraph from 'Sir James Stephen on Desultory and Systematic Reading' which began 'I hold that no man can have any just conception of the History of England who has not often read, and meditated, and learnt to love the great Poets of England.' It was the work of these writers—'the great Poets of England'—which Robert Bell's volumes, in common with all the other series, sought to present.

Or was it? For one of the most interesting aspects of these anthologies is that not all of them were English, and that some used the word British, others the word English in their titles. Several of the editors—Blair, Anderson, Chalmers, and Gilfillan—were Scots. There are certainly interesting variations in the construction of the national body of poetry which often have to do with Scottishness/Englishness/Britishness, and which relate (like aspects of the Ossianic debate) to issues of national pride and linguistic anxiety already touched on in Chapter 1. The Scots were keen to market the poets, but felt vulnerable about their own poetry.

So it is that the earliest of these British national bodies was constructed from Scotland, and was almost completely English in its make-up. As I have demonstrated in *Devolving English Literature*, this is

[54] 'Annotated Edition of the English Poets', prefatory pages to Robert Bell (ed.), *The Annotated Edition of the English Poets*, 24 vols. (London: John W. Parker, 1854–7), i.

[55] Chris Baldick, *The Social Mission of English Criticism, 1848–1932* (Oxford: Clarendon Press, 1983); Franklin E. Court, *Institutionalizing English Literature* (Stanford, Calif: Stanford University Press, 1992).

entirely in keeping with the Anglocentric nature of eighteenth-century Scottish Rhetoric and Belles-Lettres teaching.[56] But the only two Scottish poets included in Blair's *British Poets* are significant. The first is James Thomson, the first Scottish poet who as a self-consciously British writer had won wide acceptance among English audiences. The presence of Thomson reminds alert English readers that *The British Poets* are more than English. So does the presence of the poems of the most recent writer to be included in the series, a man whose credentials and subject matter announced him to be very much the modern poet. This author was James Beattie, a close friend of Blair's, a fellow Church of Scotland minister and academic. Beattie taught at Aberdeen, and found new ways of fusing his activities as poet and as academic. In 1768 he edited Thomas Gray's *Poems*.[57] That book, produced as a result of a considerable correspondence with the author of 'The Bard', is probably the first instance of a volume by a living poet being edited by an academic. Beattie's own career illustrates the convergence of poetry and academia in areas of eighteenth-century Scotland, while his widely read verse went on to shape Romantic taste.

Added to *The British Poets* in 1776, Beattie's poems by their presence reinforce the idea that modern British literature can be of Scottish origin, though regularly presented in proper English diction. When his works became part of the series Beattie was under 40, his verse still in copyright. It is probably friendship with Blair which cemented his inclusion, an act of daring that hints at an awareness of the body of national work as shaping and being shaped by the present. Just as he had done with Ossian, so with Beattie Blair used his academic position and kudos to advance the work of modern poets whose writings he admired. Beattie too was an enthusiastic supporter of the Ossianic corpus. His own finest poem (important to Wordsworth, Scott and others) was *The Minstrel* (1771). Written in Ossian's wake, it celebrates the life of Edwin, a poet who lived in a primitive age, yet displayed a remarkable sophistication and a modern temperament. Here is another 'modern poet' who can be judged suitable for immediate admission to the canon. On the one hand, Edwin has a soul which is (in a phrase that would be applied to Robert Burns) 'heaven-taught'; he anticipates Wordsworth as a 'visionary boy' at one with a nature which, with its 'solitary tree, | Or mossy stone', is suspended between the Ossianic and the Words-

---

[56] Crawford, *Devolving English Literature*, 16–44.
[57] See Gaskell, *A Bibliography of the Foulis Press*, 475–6.

worthian; Ossianically, he dreams of 'long-robed minstrels' in the midst of 'loud lament' and 'lonely gale' while 'lighted by the evening star'. This is a poem dealing with what Wordsworth would call 'the growth of a poet's mind'. Edwin is a figure of poetic wildness:

> Song was his favourite and first pursuit.
> The wild harp rang to his adventurous hand,
> And languished to his breath the plaintive flute.
> His infant Muse, though artless, was not mute:
> Of elegance as yet he took no care;
> For this of time and culture is the fruit;
> And Edwin gained at last this fruit so rare

To gain that 'fruit' of culture which will mature him as a poet, Edwin is urged 'To curb Imagination's lawless rage' and develop 'comprehensive mind' through some philosophical learning and 'science' or, as we would now say, knowledge. So it is that wild young poet is advised,

> Flee to the shade of Academus' grove.
> Where cares molest not, discord melts away
> In harmony, and the pure passions prove
> How sweet the words of Truth breathed from the lips of Love.[58]

Beattie's idyllic picture of academia as the perfect destination for the wild young poet was published when he was Professor of Moral Philosophy at the University of Aberdeen. It complements nicely the figure of the modern poet as developed by his friend Hugh Blair, who presents Beattie's new poem and figuration of the bard as the last word in his British poets.

Blair was using his work as an anthologist not only to develop a modern form of national canon, but also to further ensconce the figure of the modern poet as a sophisticated primitive. Yet the presence of Beattie's work at the chronological culmination of *The British Poets* also highlights the lack of any of the sort of earlier Scottish writing anthologized by Allan Ramsay. In Bell's *Poets of Great Britain* as in the London booksellers' edition for which Johnson wrote the *Lives*, Thomson is the first Scottish poet, and Johnson even had to persuade the London booksellers to include him. James Engell in *Forming the Critical Mind* suggests that 'The omission may have been because Thomson was a

---

[58] James Beattie, *The Minstrel*, in *The Poetical Works of Gray, Beattie and Collins* (London: Warne, n.d.), 188, 203, and 206.

Scot and the publishers were competing for the poetry market against the Apollo Press of Edinburgh'—Bell's printers.[59] Certainly the choice of title *The Works of the English Poets* is one which differentiates the London edition from the Edinburgh-printed ones of Blair and Bell by stressing England rather than Britain. The clearly different title makes sound commercial sense and emphasizes that even if this is a collection which includes Thomson and Mallet, it is essentially *English*.

Such were the pressures, the acts of mixed commercial, legal, literary, and political judgement which governed these anthologies of national poetry, that a Scottish tradition was bound to be insecure. The poetry of Ossian may have been aimed at reducing such insecurity, but it did so only partially, if at all. Schmitz reminds us that Blair, for all his Ossianic enthusiasm, thought in general of medieval (then called 'Gothic') literature as the product of a time of 'gross ignorance'; his *British Poets* does not contain Chaucer, let alone Dunbar or Henryson.[60] Bell's *Poets of Great Britain* includes only Chaucer from the entire Middle Ages, while Johnson failed to persuade the London booksellers to have even Chaucer in their *Works of the English Poets*. Clearly they were worried he would not sell. The first poet in the editions associated with both Blair and Johnson is Waller; the second is Milton. Bell is braver in including Chaucer, Spenser, and Donne, but his entrepreneurial good sense drew the line at medieval Scottish verse of the sort included in Ramsay's less than popular *Ever Green*. The London Scots Thomson, Mallet, and Armstrong are the only Scottish poets among Bell's 109 volumes. Ossian's best-selling work was still in copyright when Blair made his anthology, and by the date of the later multivolume collections the question of Ossian's authenticity was so controversial that inclusion of Ossianic material could have been seen as compromising, particularly by an English audience. So the representation of Scottish and medieval work in these multivolume anthologies remained outstandingly low.

Such a predicament seems to have struck Robert Anderson when he discussed his edition with the Edinburgh printers Mundell & Son in 1792. Mundell had originally intended simply republishing in part 'the Collection of English poetry, which goes under the name of Dr Johnson', but Anderson argued for something more ambitious (A. 4). His own edition has a much stronger Scottish presence—ten poets

[59] James Engell, *Forming the Critical Mind* (Cambridge, Mass.: Harvard University Press, 1989), 163.
[60] Schmitz, *Hugh Blair*, 70.

beginning with William Drummond and ending with Anderson's friend James Graeme. Anderson's is the first of these multivolume editions to contain a detailed preface describing the project as well as relating it to its predecessors and to ideas about a national body of verse. He laments his inability to persuade his publishers to include Langland, Gower, and other medieval writers (A. 4). With reference to the medieval and Elizabethan work, Anderson clearly wished 'to allure curiosity into this unfrequented track of reading'. However, Mundell consented to include only 'the works of those authors, who, though not universally read or understood, . . . are notwithstanding familiar to us in conversation, and constantly appealed to in controverted points of poetical taste' (A. 4). We can see here a developing strain between literary-antiquarian and commercial judgement which had to be resolved in order to produce the anthology. At least as important, though, is that Anderson feels obliged to make an explanatory apology that 'The classical compositions of Barbour, James I, Henry the Minstrel, Dunbar, Douglas and Lindsay, being written in the Scottish language, could not be received into an edition of English poetry' (A. 4). Economics and language-politics here combine. In an English-dominated British market, these barbarous Scottish poets will not make their way linguistically or commercially. A little Middle English can be admitted, but no Middle Scots. What this makes clear is that, though the anthology is titled *The Works of the British Poets*, the language of Britain and of her national poetic body must be exclusively English. The only Scots poem in Anderson's entire collection is by William Wilkie, the country-born St Andrews Professor, and highlights Scots as an anthropological curiosity. The work of Wilkie's St Andrews student Robert Fergusson, who was not only arguably the eighteenth century's finest university-trained vernacular poet but who had also been a friend of Robert Anderson, is excluded, though it was out of copyright.[61] A better known acquaintance of Anderson is mentioned in passing in the 'Life of Thomson' as 'Mr Burns, whose poems in the Scottish dialect are well known among his countrymen, and universally admired'. Several stanzas of Burns's English 'Address to the Shade of Thomson' are quoted, but the language of Burns's best poetry is firmly excluded from the anthology.[62] As Anderson explains in his 'Life of Drummond',

---

[61] See David Daiches, *Robert Fergusson* (Edinburgh: Scottish Academic Press, 1982), 33.

[62] Robert Anderson, 'The Life of Thomson', in Anderson (ed.), *The Works of the British Poets*, ix. 180.

AFTER the accession of James VI of Scotland to the Crown of England, the Scottish Language, in which the classical compositions of Barbour, James I, Henry the Minstrel, Dunbar, Douglas, and Lindsay, were written, yielded by a necessary contingency, to the English, to which it was collaterally allied; and the poets of Scotland, from that period, wrote in the language of the greater and more polite nation.[63]

Professor Blair could not have put it better. Anderson is clearly aware of the heritage of medieval Scottish verse, and of modern vernacular writing, but, in keeping with his mentor Blair, and with the linguistically Anglocentric polite Scotland of his day, he nods towards that tradition only to exclude it. Again he pays tribute to anthologies such as Pinkerton's *Ancient Scottish Poems* but he leaves their contents to circulate only in a Scottish, not a British arena.[64] Anderson and his publishers knew that, to compete in the British literary marketplace, their poetry required to wear the correct, polite linguistic dress. Otherwise it could not be 'received'. Consequently, he sought to establish William Drummond of Hawthornden as the originator of a modern Scottish tradition, being 'the first Scottish poet who wrote in English with purity and elegance'.[65] As in the case of the Ossianic 'translations', English, it seems clear, must be the price of admission to the modern canon of poetry, and the language of the modern poet.

Anderson's strategy as an anthologist would be repeated by his fellow Scot Alexander Chalmers in his *Works of the English Poets from Chaucer to Cowper*, a production which not only contains Johnson's *Lives* and the poets in the earlier *Works of the English Poets*, but also recalls in its title Bell's edition which ran 'from Chaucer to Churchill'. Though Chalmers clearly hesitates over older poetry, finds Chaucer hard-going, and sees his 'barbarous' age as lacking 'refinement', he addresses his volumes to 'students of poetry, a class which seems to be increasing', and he does try to extend the Scottish tradition within his volumes.[66] So his first Scottish poet is not Drummond but William Alexander, Earl of Stirling. Alexander, one feels, is present more because he wrote in approximately the right language than because of his poetic merit:

His style is certainly neither pure nor correct, which may perhaps be attributed to his long familiarity with the Scotch language, but his versification is in general

---

[63] Anderson, 'The Life of Drummond', in Anderson (ed.), *The Works of the British Poets*, iv.
621.   [64] Ibid. 624.
[65] Ibid. 621.
[66] Chalmers (ed.), *The Works of the English Poets*, i, pp. xiii and viii.

very superior to that of his contemporaries, and approaches nearer to the elegance of modern times than could have been expected of one who wrote so much.[67]

About Drummond Chalmers is more enthusiastic ('the neglect with which he has been treated would appear unaccountable'), and he does include more Scottish poets than any of the other multivolume anthologists.[68] But his collection simply confirms the policy set by Anderson, i.e., that even when a Scottish editor is presenting a national body of British work or English work with a substantial Scottish presence, the language must be monoglot English. What happens in these pioneering anthologies which establish a national body of work has repercussions that persist even today when it is so often assumed that collections of British poetry will exclude Gaelic, Welsh, and (almost always) Scots work. Historically, however, these other languages of Britain were allowed literary circulation within the smaller, internal markets of Scotland and Wales, but were kept out of any wider national corpus. While it might be objected that most English-speaking readers in Britain would simply refuse to buy even a small quantity of verse not in the English language, it was standard practice for these books' producers to mix up less popular with more popular work so as to increase the amount of material for sale. The reason for the exclusively monoglot nature of the anthologies was by no means a purely commercial one. It was also political-aesthetic considerations which determined that the Scots should censor their own heritage and that what was perceived as the British national body should (supposedly naturally) have only one tongue. Even in twentieth-century Scotland, England, and elsewhere, these linguistic attitudes towards poetry continued to inhibit many anthologists.

The issues raised by multivolume, canonical anthologies whose origins are contemporary with the origins of the modern poet, and which helped shape the presentation of poets in the modern era, remain very much with us. It might appear that these vast works are mere relics from the library stack, but it is from them rather than from better-known Victorian anthologies such as Palgrave's *Golden Treasury* that some of the major collections and anthologists' assumptions in the last century spring. To understand this, we can examine a fertile offshoot of the earlier multivolume series, and one which is again a product of the

---

[67] Chalmers (ed.), *The Works of the English Poets*, v. 292 ('The Life of William Alexander, Earl of Stirling').   [68] Ibid. 641 ('The Life of William Drummond').

convergence of poetry and academia. This smaller anthology is the work of the academically trained poet Thomas Campbell, a student of 'the philosophic' Professor George Jardine's Rhetoric class at Glasgow University, where many of Campbell's poetic tastes were formed. Campbell went on to found London University and to be Lord Rector at Glasgow as well as lecturing widely to student and public audiences about poetry.[69]

Campbell too was a 'modern poet' according to the model suggested in my first chapter: bard of 'Morven and Fillan' and a youthful admirer of Ossian, he enjoyed posing as one of the 'savages' of Mull at the same time as using his time in the Highlands to translate Greek.[70] His own poetry enjoys blending the wild and the sophisticated. Though his once-popular *œuvre* has been in eclipse for some time, works such as *The Pleasures of Hope* (1799), the Ossianic 'Lord Ullin's Daughter' (1809), and *Gertrude of Wyoming* (1809) were an important contribution to Romantic verse. His writings were frequently republished and his *Poetical Works* was part of the Oxford Edition of the poets as late as 1907. Campbell's work is being rediscovered now by literary historians interested not least in his writing about and impact in America.[71] Few recall, though, that in 1819 he produced the seven important volumes of his *Specimens of the British Poets; with Biographical and Critical Notices, and An Essay on English Poetry*. The word '*Specimens*' in the title introduces a note of classroom rigour. This scientific-sounding collection of poetry will benefit students, though it might also improve those excluded from the universities. In 1819 J. G. Lockhart's Peter Morris notices in a bijou Edinburgh shop a 'haughty bluestocking, with a volume of Campbell's Specimens'.[72] Here was a multivolume anthology which aimed to cover the course of poetry in English, with a slight Scots admixture, from Chaucer to the end of the eighteenth century. Campbell shares his fellow Scots' embarrassment about their literary heritage. Separate from his principal (book-length) *Essay on English Poetry* is a brief account of 'Scottish Poetry' which prefaces a short selection from the medieval Makars (whom Campbell significantly Englishes as '*Makers*') in volume ii. As

---

[69] William Beattie (ed.), *Life and Letters of Thomas Campbell*, 3 vols. (London: Moxon, 1847), i. 56–7, 60–1, 80–1, 113; Mary Ruth Miller, *Thomas Campbell* (Boston: Twayne, 1978), 13–46, 122–39.

[70] Beattie (ed.), *Life and Letters of Thomas Campbell*, i. 134–5.

[71] See, e.g., Crawford, *Devolving English Literature*, 179–82.

[72] John Gibson Lockhart, *Peter's Letters to his Kinsfolk*, ed. William Ruddick (Edinburgh: Scottish Academic Press, 1977), 94.

in the cursory mention of poets like Dunbar in his *Essay on English Poetry*, Campbell tends to damn with faint praise, worrying about 'false ornament' and 'frequent coarseness'.[73] In later volumes, though, he breaks new ground by including work by Allan Ramsay and Robert Fergusson as well as Burns, whose verse he admires greatly, claiming that he has given 'the elixir of life to his native dialect'.[74]

The presence of a number of these Scottish and Scots-language poets gives Campbell's *Specimens of the British Poets* a flavour subtly different from most of the multivolume anthologies described earlier. However the overall effect is still that these Scots-writing poets are seen as curious exceptions to an English rule. Campbell is innovative in disregarding his title to the extent of including at least one American (Timothy Dwight) among his 'British Poets'. One may see this either as an effortless act of intellectual recolonization, or as a sign that for the editor, who was in contact with several American correspondents, poetry in the English language is beginning to outgrow the British canon. Where compilers of other, larger multivolume collections included the complete works of each poet, Campbell included only a few poems by each of the 250 or so authors whom he chose and whose biographies he supplied. His work therefore is a crucial link mediating between the huge gatherings of Professor Blair and his followers, and the modern, often academically tinged, single-volume anthologies of poetry with which we are more familiar. Indeed, in 1841 the writer Peter Cunningham (son of the Scottish poet Allan Cunningham) produced with Campbell's approval a one-volume edition of the *Specimens* which included in its 700 double-column pages all the poets and biographies previously available in seven volumes, along with further annotation, elaboration, and corrections. In his opening 'Advertisement' Cunningham points out that the *Specimens* 'have been corrected and appealed to by Lord Byron, applaudingly quoted by Sir Walter Scott, and frequently cited and referred to by Mr. Hallam'.[75] So some of the greatest modern poets are presented as contributing to this production which seems increasingly aimed at a large market comprised not least of students. Its title page carries an engraving of Chaucer's tomb in Westminster Abbey, and so links

[73] Thomas Campbell (ed.), *Specimens of the British Poets*, 7 vols. (London: John Murray, 1819), i. 93 and ii. 67, 69.
[74] Ibid. vii. 240.
[75] Peter Cunningham, 'Advertisement' to Thomas Campbell (ed.), *Specimens of the British Poets*, new edn. (London: John Murray, 1841), p. [i].

Campbell's *Specimens* with that other influential, national canon-forming institution, Poets' Corner. With its crammed pages, annotations, and headnotes, this edition of Campbell's *Specimens* is a clear forerunner of such modern academic collections as the *Norton Anthology of Poetry*. It signals a shift towards the rapidly expanding educational milieu which will more and more surround the modern poet.

Certainly when Oxonian academia, in the persons of Thomas Humphry Ward and Matthew Arnold, turns its attention towards the production of a comprehensive anthology of *The English Poets*, it is to the examples of the multivolume anthologies edited by Scots such as Alexander Chalmers and to Campbell that they turn for instances of British predecessors. Ward's *The English Poets* would achieve an influential, global circulation, and is still used in some academic quarters today.[76] It would serve as a benchmark for future academically produced anthologies of poetry. While claiming novelty, Ward's 'Preface' makes clear an awareness of antecedents produced by the earlier converging of academia and poetry that can be traced back to Blair:

> The aim of this book is to supply an admitted want—that of an anthology which may adequately represent the vast and varied field of English Poetry.
> Nothing of the kind at present exists. There are great collections of the whole works of the poets, like that of Chalmers; there are innumerable volumes of 'Beauties' of a more or less unsatisfactory kind; there are Selections from single poets; there are a few admirable volumes, like that of Mr. Palgrave, which deal with special departments of our poetical literature. The only book which attempts to cover the whole ground and to select on a large scale is Campbell's; and Campbell's, though the work of a true poet and, according to the standard of his time, a critic of authority, can no longer be regarded as sufficient. It is indeed impossible that a selection of the kind should be really well done, should be done with an approach to finality, if it is the work of one critic alone.[77]

Here we hear the tones of academic specialization. Ward parcels out his selections to individual experts and poetry is brought deeper into the labyrinth of the modern university. His poets have been 'chosen and judged by those whose tastes and studies specially qualify them for the several tasks they have undertaken'.[78] The accent on 'studies' is

---

[76] J. R. Watson told me recently that this work was still used in some Indian universities.

[77] Thomas Humphry Ward (ed.), *The English Poets: Selections with Critical Introductions* by Various Writers and a General Introduction by Matthew Arnold, 4 vols. (London: Macmillan, 1880), i, p. v ('Preface').

[78] Ibid., p. vi.

significant. Of the thirty-four specialist editors commissioned by Ward for the original edition, only half a dozen are identified in the table of contents as professors. Yet even this is significant since clearly their professorial titles (like the titles of the 'Dean of St. Pauls' and the 'Dean of Westminster') are there to add to the anthology's authority. Moreover, we now recognize them as pioneers in Victorian university English studies: Edward Dowden (whose relations with Yeats will be examined in the following chapter) was the first Professor of English at Trinity College, Dublin; J. W. Hales was Professor of English Language and Literature at King's College, London; William Minto was Professor of Logic and Rhetoric at Aberdeen; John Nichol was the first Professor of English Literature at Glasgow; Henry Skeat was Professor of Anglo-Saxon at Cambridge; A. W. Ward held a chair at Manchester. Among the other contributors, future professors are in evidence, notably John Churchton Collins (then a campaigner for an English School at Oxford, and later Professor of English at Birmingham), A. C. Bradley (then teaching at Glasgow), and George Saintsbury (the future holder of Hugh Blair's chair at Edinburgh). Further dons abound. Their numbers include Walter Pater, Mark Pattison, and T. H. Ward himself, a Fellow of Brasenose College, Oxford. The rest of Ward's impressive team was made up of poets and writers, including Austin Dobson, Andrew Lang (a former don), and A. C. Swinburne. At their head was Matthew Arnold, the figure who most represents for the Victorian period the fusion of poetry and academia. Arnold was the former Oxford Professor of Poetry as well as the distinguished poet. His introduction to Ward's anthology was later republished in the second series of Arnold's *Essays in Criticism* (1888) under the highly significant title 'The Study of Poetry'. Increasingly in the Victorian period, study was one of the important things that poetry was for. Though his four volumes may have addressed a general readership, rather than exclusively a student one, in the 1870s Ward had a background in University Extension lecturing. The strongly academic flavour of his editorial team is an indication of the way an increasingly institutionalized study of poetry in the universities is governing its dissemination and reception.[79] If Hugh Blair had started this tendency with *The British Poets* in the 1770s, then just over a century later Ward and his men consolidated it with *The English Poets*. By now some of the leading English poets, such as Arnold and

---

[79] John Sutherland, *Mrs Humphry Ward* (Oxford: Oxford University Press, 1991), 44 and 56.

Swinburne, were co-workers in this classroom-led exercise in canon-formation and the institutional academic processing of verse.

Arnold in his introductory essay approvingly quoted Wordsworth's description of poetry as 'the breath and finer spirit of all knowledge'.[80] Such an emphasis on the presentation of poetry as 'knowledge' brings it into alliance with the mission of the universities. It aligns poets with academics as figures whose careers involve the manipulation, acquiring, and disseminating of learning. In a sense this is a Victorian reformulation of the old idea of the poet as teacher, a concept familiar to the classicist Arnold, and dear to his friend A. H. Clough. Yet Arnold's additional insistence that poetry is 'a criticism of life' defines it in terms of criticism. This sets the poet beside multiplying numbers of professional academic critics some of whose work, along with that of the poets themselves, Arnold is introducing. 'The best poetry is what we want,' maintains Arnold.[81] That is what the anthology he was prefacing was designed to supply. His essay heads up a national poetic canon, but it is as much about criticism as it is about poetry. Arnold is present as the famous emeritus Professor of Poetry, one of a team of professors, as well as writing as a poet with insider's instinctual knowledge. Indeed, it is probably impossible to separate these two Arnolds, and that is one of the key factors which marks out Arnold as a Victorian development of the concept of the modern poet as outlined in this book.

Arnold's own work, along with that of his fellow poet and academic Arthur Hugh Clough, will be the subject of my third chapter. For the moment, though, we may note that Ward's anthology, prefaced by Arnold's essay and uniting poets and professors, would go through nineteen reprintings between 1883 and 1930, the years in which modernism emerged and reached its apogee.[82] At the head of this movement would be a number of poets whose quasi-professorial deployment of learning is one of the most distinctive features of their verse. Professionally trained, the young Extension Lecturer on English Literature T. Stearns Eliot would return obsessively to Arnoldian themes. Eliot argues in the cheekily titled 'The Function of Criticism' that Arnold, author of a famous essay of the same name, distinguished too bluntly between creation and criticism. The younger poet stressed 'the capital

---

[80] Matthew Arnold, 'The Study of Poetry' (1880), repr. in *Essays in Criticism, First and Second Series* (London: Dent, 1964), 236.

[81] Arnold, 'Introduction' to Ward (ed.), *The English Poets*, i, pp. xviii–xix.

[82] See successive editions of Ward (ed.), *The English Poets*.

importance of criticism in the work of creation itself' and maintained that the bulk of an author's compositional labour was critical labour.[83] This is surely a development of Arnold's own position as poet-critic/ critic-poet operating in an English culture where criticism of English texts was moving more and more into the institutional foreground. Eliot, as an American, came from a country where the university teaching of English had a much longer history, and one by which he had been moulded. His early essays show how much his eye was on academia. However, as later chapters of this book will argue, he is in fact very much the inheritor and modifier of Arnold's version of what it is to be a modern poet. That account is powerfully articulated in the manifesto piece which is Arnold's introduction to Ward's major Victorian amalgamation of the rapidly growing power of academia and the English poetic canon.

One other fact about Arnold's prefatory prose is unusually striking. In an essay introducing an anthology which runs from the Middle Ages to modern times and which includes in its original edition over 160 poets, Arnold allots more than a quarter of his space to just one of these. The culminating pages of his essay are devoted to an author who was neither English nor, as Arnold admits, wrote his best verse in the English tongue. This poet is not the Caledonian bard Ossian, but his successor Robert Burns. If Ossian, emerging from a fusion of Highland orality and Edinburgh scholarly refinement, had annoyed the John Bull of eighteenth-century London print culture, Samuel Johnson, then a century later the gabby Lowlander Burns appeared to Matthew Arnold similarly and awkwardly challenging. Burns features so prominently in the introduction to *The English Poets* because his work insists on disrupting the Oxonian patterns which Arnold is trying to establish. This oddly disproportionate attention paid to Burns is in part a result of Arnold's long-standing argument with his friend J. C. Shairp (later Principal of St Andrews University), and shows Arnold's awkwardness with Burns and Scottish poetry.[84] It is also a legacy of the anthologies discussed throughout this chapter—collections often edited by Scots, yet with a complex embarrassment or cultural cringe about Scots work. The Oxford don Ward is happy to call his anthology *The English Poets*, yet it is noticeable that he is more generous than any of his predecessors in

[83]   Eliot, *Selected Essays*, 30.
[84]   See Mary W. Schneider, 'The Real Burns and "The Study of Poetry"', *Victorian Poetry*, 26 (1988), 135–40.

his inclusion of Scottish verse. As Ward's volumes grew in later editions, Australian and Canadian poets would be co-opted for England, though, probably for reasons of copyright and cultural power, Americans would be allowed to get away. The imperial mentality manifest here is of a piece with the close relationship between Oxford and empire in the later nineteenth century, a connection particularly evident in the early development of Oxonian English studies.[85] It is clear too in the way in which Arthur Quiller-Couch, editor of the hugely popular *Oxford Book of English Verse* first published in 1900, would not only co-opt poetry written in other parts of the British Isles as 'English' but would also include poetry from overseas which his preface proudly describes as 'spoil' to be brought home.[86] The connections between anthologizing and cultural imperialism do not end in the eighteenth or the nineteenth century. They are part of the conditions in which the modern poet writes and through which his or her work is disseminated.

A cursory glance at more recent mainstream Oxford anthologies of poetry shows that it is constantly taken for granted that their editors will be eminent academics. So we have such works as Alastair Fowler's *New Oxford Book of Seventeenth-Century Verse*, Roger Lonsdale's *New Oxford Book of Eighteenth-Century Verse*, Jerome McGann's *New Oxford Book of Romantic Period Verse*, and Christopher Ricks's *New Oxford Book of Victorian Verse*, followed by the same professor's *Oxford Book of English Verse*. An exception is Philip Larkin's *Oxford Book of Twentieth-Century Verse*, but this inconsistency may be explained in part by the reluctance of Oxford University to teach modern verse until relatively recently, so that contemporary poetry would not be regarded as an area of the most respectable academic specialization. In Britain, one may contrast the Oxford Books with the anthologies of poetry produced by Penguin and by Faber, which are more often edited by practising poets. So the Penguin anthologies include volumes edited by Brendan Kennelly, George Macbeth, Blake Morrison, Andrew Motion, Simon Armitage, and others, while the Faber anthologies have such editors as Douglas Dunn, Seamus Heaney, Ted Hughes, and Tom Paulin. Specialist poetry houses in Britain such as Bloodaxe, Carcanet, and others also produce major anthologies, usually edited by poets, though these incline not to

---

[85] See Chris Baldick, *The Social Mission of English Criticism* (Oxford: Clarendon Press, 1983), 70–2.

[86] Arthur Quiller-Couch (ed.), *The Oxford Book of English Verse*, new edn. (Oxford: Clarendon Press, 1939), vii ('Preface to the First Edition').

command the same widespread distribution as the anthologies published by Oxford University Press, Penguin, and Faber. In some ways,
then, though the vast, multivolume anthologies of the eighteenth and
nineteenth centuries are no longer with us, certain patterns which they
helped set up remain current. Editors are likely to be male, and the
gatekeepers to the poetry of the past will tend to be a mixture of
academics and poets, though the prevailing trend is for older poetry
to be more and more the province of the academic editor. Anthologies
continue in many cases to present a national body of work—*The New
Penguin Book of Scottish Verse*, *The Oxford Book of Irish Verse*—and where
the word 'English' is part of the title this often involves a co-opting of at
least some other national traditions around a clearly English national
core, as happens a little awkwardly in Ricks's *Oxford Book of English Verse*.
Only America, presumably because of its economic and cultural power
and since it is not part of the British and Commonwealth copyright area,
tends to escape being subsumed under the word 'English'. In Britain the
mixture of academics and poets who are editors of anthologies shows
the anthology itself as a genre which emphasizes the links between
poetry and universities which have developed in the wake of T. H.
Ward. Yet the fact that Penguin, Oxford, and Faber anthologies normally come with introductions but without much annotation (what Les
Murray calls 'a dense barbed wire of commentary and exegesis') suggests
that while the academic market is certainly important, the volumes are
packaged in ways that signal appeal to the general reader as much as to
the classroom user.[87]

In contemporary America the situation is strikingly different, and has
been so for some decades. There the standard poetry anthology is likely
to be a descendant of the 1962 *Norton Anthology of English Literature*,
produced under the general editorship of M. H. Abrams and wholly
edited by professional academics aiming at a campus audience, though
one whose members might be inclined to read 'in one's own private
room, in the classroom, or under a tree'.[88] Though the *Norton Anthology*
includes much prose and drama as well as poetry, one of its main
functions is to supply students with a studiable corpus of verse. This
anthology's origins plainly lie in the classroom. David Daiches recalls
that it grew out of a Cornell University survey course which he and

---

[87] Les Murray, *Blocks and Tackles* (North Ryde: Angus & Robertson, 1990), 156.
[88] M. H. Abrams (gen. ed.), *The Norton Anthology of English Literature*, 2 vols. (New York:
W. W. Norton, 1962), ii, p. xxx ('Preface').

M. H. Abrams taught in the 1940s, and was produced in a historicizing spirit of reaction against the New Criticism championed by Ransom and others. Daiches suggested to Norton that Abrams act as general editor, and the two professors used their Cornell course as a model.[89] Abrams's original preface makes it clear that

> The editors of this anthology were selected on the basis of their expertness in their individual areas, and also because they combine respect for the best that has been thought and said about literature in the past with an alertness (as participants, as well as observers) to the altering interests, procedures, and evaluations in contemporary scholarship and criticism. Each editor was given ultimate responsibility for his own period, but all collaborated in the total enterprise, from the establishment of general principles and selection of contents to decisions about the details of editing the various texts.[90]

Abrams takes it for granted that involving 'participants' as editors means bringing together participants in contemporary criticism, not practising poets. He had been educated at Harvard where the custom of using such anthologies in teaching was well established. While his scholarship in works like *The Mirror and the Lamp: Romantic Theory and the Critical Tradition* (1953) shows an encyclopedic knowledge of the way in which poetry was shaped in the eighteenth and nineteenth centuries, as well as a specific awareness of such figures as Blair and Campbell, Abrams remembers with regard to the *Norton Anthology* that 'The only earlier anthology that I can recall checking, when we developed a Table of Contents, was one I had used as an undergraduate at Harvard—edited, I believe, by a Professor Robert Shafer.'[91] This was *From Beowulf to Thomas Hardy*, a two-volume anthology of poetic 'texts' first published in the 1920s, but reprinted on a grand scale for the American military in 1944–5 along with an *Instructor's Course Outline*.[92] Backed by the power of the US Armed Forces Institute, this work supplied a template for the *Norton Anthology*. If Blair's *British Poets* and other collections influenced by it recruited a standing army of poets in support of Britannia's imperial mission, then by the mid-twentieth century these same British poets (with an added medieval cohort) were being

---

[89] David Daiches, letter to the present writer, 17 Mar. 1997.

[90] Abrams (gen. ed.), *The Norton Anthology*, ii, p. xxxi ('Preface').

[91] M. H. Abrams, letter to the present writer, 28 Apr. 1997.

[92] Robert Shafer (ed.), *From Beowulf to Thomas Hardy*, 2 vols. (Garden City, NY: Doubleday, Page, 1924). The work grew in 1930s reprints to include substantial period introductions and annotation.

regimented under professorial command in support of the United States of America.

Where T. H. Ward in the 1880s had sought the endorsement and imprimatur of Arnold, the poet-professor, and had signalled the professors among his editorial team by mentioning their titles in the table of contents, the 1962 *Norton Anthology* (like its successors) lists the academic titles and affiliations of its editorial team as part of the title page of the book. A similar format is followed in the volumes of the *Oxford Anthology of English Literature* launched by the New York arm of Oxford University Press in 1973 under the general editorship of Professors Frank Kermode and John Hollander. Obviously competing with the Norton products, its aim is nonetheless reminiscent of Ward's almost a century before. Kermode and Hollander plan 'to provide students with a selective canon of the entire range of English Literature from the beginnings to recent times'.[93] Arnold's introduction, his 'Study of Poetry' essay, was an editorial coup for Ward. Yet one suspects that for the *Norton Anthology* having an introduction by a modern poet-critic might have been a liability, suggesting that the anthology was tied to one poetic movement or camp. The *Norton* and competing products which followed in its wake were linked instead to academia. They took it for granted that twentieth-century poetry as well as the poetry of the past belonged there, as their annotation makes clear. The general preface of the *Norton* addresses not the general reader but the 'student'. The publication of this anthology, so widely used throughout America and, increasingly, the English-speaking world, marks a cultural shift in the situation of the poet. The significant poet, it assumes, becomes the possession of academia. The poem becomes the text. The *Norton Anthology* dates from the period in which American poets were more and more the inhabitants of academe, drawn there by the proliferation of Creative Writing programmes on which they might be employed as teachers. This cultural shift took place before the birth of the youngest generation of American authors. It is not unusual to meet poets whose first significant encounter with poetry came through the *Norton Anthology*, and who went on to 'study poetry' not only in departments of literature but also in departments of Creative Writing. This academicization of verse in English which began with Hugh Blair and his contemporaries has been crucial to the formation of the modern poet.

---

[93] Frank Kermode and John Hollander (gen. eds.), *The Oxford Anthology of English Literature*, 6 vols. (New York: Oxford University Press, 1973), iv, p. v ('General Editors' Preface').

What is happening on a linguistic level throughout the pages of so many of these anthologies is very much part of the wider phenomenon of the anthologies as cultural artefacts. For in their language as in their physical format such collections are shaped by the eighteenth-century drive for regularization and uniformity. While Chaucer (and, later, in the nineteenth century, Burns) may be seen as part of a regular national body, they are exceptions that prove the rule. The House of Lords judgement which initiates the multivolume anthologies seems to open the market as a free for all, yet leads to an increased regularization that affects both form and content. While our own intellectual climate, with its emphasis (particularly in North America) on pluralism and diversity, may alert us to the regularizing limitation of the eighteenth-century acts of judgement which make and market this national body of literature, we must realize that the consequences of these *British Poets* collections have shaped representations of national poetry not only in the nineteenth century but also throughout the last hundred years. For all our protestations of poetic variety there are precious few volumes of British 'national anthologies' of contemporary poetry, for instance, which contain Gaelic, Welsh, and Scots work in parallel text alongside work produced in varieties of English. That this is so suggests that the legacy of Hugh Blair, *Donaldson* v. *Becket*, and the various results of eighteenth-century acts of judgement has been longer lasting and more profound than we might like to think. Our task today is to find a more appropriate balance between the standardized techniques applied to the tasks of book creation and our wish for and enjoyment of conditions of diversity within our artistic and everyday culture. Only once we have done this will we have a subtler and more mature sense of what it means to be a modern poet.

As a poet who writes in English and Scots, I relish a wide linguistic spectrum, a verbal sharawaggi. As an editor of *The Penguin Book of Poetry from Britain and Ireland since 1945* (1998) and of *The New Penguin Book of Scottish Verse* (2000), I have attempted to challenge linguistic assumptions which, deriving from the era of Blair, continue to govern the making of many recent anthologies. In some ways remarkably little has changed since the early decades which saw under the Edinburgh professor's guidance the emergence of the modern poet and anthologies that further bonded the presentation of poetry to the growing influence of academia. Such a linkage continued in the Arnoldian era. Yet as the authorial role of the poet developed in the nineteenth century it did not simply replicate the attitudes of a Romanticism fuelled by Ossian. Rather, while drawing on cultural presuppositions rooted in the age of Blair, Macpherson, Beattie, and their Romantic successors as writers and anthologists, Victorian authors reinvented the conception of the poet as primitive-sophisticate. The preceding chapters have pointed out some of the ways in which the figure of the modern poet evolved in later eighteenth- and early nineteenth-century writing, and have shown how such a development accompanied the formation of a modern canon. Chapter 3 looks at the recasting of the modern poet as the figure of the scholar-gypsy.

CHAPTER 3

Scholar-Gypsies

Arnold and Clough were doomed to become eminent Victorians. A patina of worthiness clings to their names. In Arnold's case this process happened quickly. Writing more and more social reflections, less and less poetry, he seems to have felt it himself. The dashing, youthful poet and brilliant Professor of Poetry was gradually immured in a mausoleum of committees. By the start of the twentieth century the young T. S. Eliot heard Arnold's Christian name as inextricably linked to 'The army of unalterable law'.[1] Eliot plotted that army's defeat. Yet, ironically, he went on to become the most Arnoldian of twentieth-century voices. Arnold, this chapter will argue, is not only the dour Victorian Sage. He is also, in his guise of scholar-gypsy, very much the modern poet.

His friend Arthur Clough is even more so. Clough, largely forgotten and unread, his most spirited poem out of print as I write, exemplifies better than any other Victorian writer that coming together of the regulated academic career and the wild poetic fling. Clough's work has excitement, overflow, *furor poeticus*; its author is also a responsible don. In 1848, that year of European revolutions in which he publishes his most effervescent poem, the one which makes his name in America, he also applies for a Chair of English Language and Literature. Two years later he is teaching the subject to University College London undergraduates.[2] Clough is the first really significant poet to become a university teacher of English. He is good at the job, yet uncertain if he likes it. Soon he leaves, in search of other employment. Yet this period of his interest in the academic teaching of English is also the time of Clough's finest poetry. The verse he wrote then is enthusiastically concerned with a fusion of knowledge and wildness. The professor who spoke eagerly in

[1] T. S. Eliot, *The Complete Poems and Plays* (London: Faber & Faber, 1969), 30 ('Cousin Nancy').
[2] Katharine Chorley, *Arthur Hugh Clough: The Uncommitted Mind* (Oxford: Clarendon Press, 1962), 212.

the classroom of 'a democratic revolution' in language was also the pre-eminent English-language poet of the events of 1848. Even a decade later we catch him drafting part of his adventurous poem *Amours de voyage* on the back of an examination paper headed 'English Literature and Composition...27 June 1857'.[3] No poet exemplifies better than Arthur Hugh Clough the way in which poetry and academia can intermingle. No poet is more wrongheadedly condemned to neglect.

What is most important in Clough's work for a modern audience is the panache with which from early in his career he self-consciously attempted to write a poetry of knowledge. He made sparkling use of his intellect within a modern world of proliferating communications and information networks. At the same time, he supplied the reader with poetic excitement, strong emotion, dazzle. In so doing Clough was instrumental in remaking for the Victorian and later periods the cultural space occupied by the modern poet. He did this both through his own verse and by his poetic example. If the only acute recent criticism of him is an essay by Tom Paulin, that is probably because Clough's position resonates so strongly with that of this contemporary poet, a barbarian-voiced, vernacular don.[4] Clough as a teenager belonged to a clique of poets and scholars who met as students at Balliol College, Oxford. The most notable other members included the poet-professors John Campbell Shairp and Matthew Arnold, through whose work was articulated the ideal of 'The Scholar-Gypsy'. Much later, in 'Thyrsis', his memorial poem to Clough, Arnold connects his friend with this iconic figure in whom the 'natural' Romantic pursuit of Wordsworthian delights is linked to an awareness of scholarship and the world of learning. The most refreshing and revealing expression of such an ideal came in Clough's first major poem *The Bothie of Toper-na-fuosich* (1848). Born out of the academic high culture of Homeric scholarship and out of a wish to counter or outflank the rarefied atmosphere of Oxford, *The Bothie* embraces the popular and the 'primitive', represented by the milieu and landscape of the Scottish Highlands. There is more than a hint of the Ossianic about such a literary manœuvre. With amusing poetic justice the original title page of Clough's poem carries the name of an Oxford printer named Macpherson.[5]

---

[3] *The Poems of Arthur Hugh Clough*, ed. F. L. Mulhauser, 2nd edn. (Oxford: Clarendon Press, 1974), 617.

[4] Tom Paulin, 'Citizen Clough', in *Minotaur* (London: Faber & Faber, 1992), 56–76.

[5] See the facsimile title page in Arthur Hugh Clough, *The Bothie*, ed. Patrick Scott (St Lucia: University of Queensland Press, 1976). All references in my text are to this edition of the original version of Clough's poem.

To suggest a link between the early poetry of Clough, heir to Byron's proto-modernist slangy-academic tone, and the Ossianic work of Macpherson is heretical. Yet the impulses behind Clough's champagne poem, *The Bothie*, are significantly similar to the underlying drives which led Blair and Macpherson to their production of the 1760 *Fragments* and the ensuing Ossianic corpus. Like Macpherson, Clough and his circle were university-trained classicists. All shared an interest in Homer. Clough's Hellenist pals were also fascinated by Highland culture which they tended to see as increasingly marginalized, alluring, and possessing quasi-classical virtues. Clough set his first major poem in the Highlands. Compulsively, he revisited that deeply loved landscape in work written just days before he died.[6] Arnold lectured not only on Homer but also on the Celtic spirit in literature. Shairp as the first (and only) Scottish Professor of Poetry at Oxford spoke on Ossianic and Gaelic poetry, while his own verse is permeated by Highland subject matter.[7] He went on to become Principal of the University of St Andrews, running his careers as academic and as pro-Highland poet in tandem. Where Hugh Blair and his circle in eighteenth-century Scotland were initiating the study of English literary texts within university institutions, these Oxonian Victorians were among the pioneers of English literary studies in England's nineteenth-century universities. They combined scholarly and poetic preoccupations as their careers developed. It was the 'primitive' Highlands which served as a poetic laboratory from which the modern poet emerged in works that were the fragmented literary aftermath of Culloden. A century later it was again the Highlands which functioned as the marginal territory crucial to the mid-Victorian re-articulation of the concept of the modern poet.

Liverpool-born, Clough spent his early childhood in Charleston, South Carolina. Educated at Dr Arnold's Rugby, he was known there as 'Yankee' Clough. At 17 an enthusiast for 'Tocqueville on the American democracy', and later a friend and admirer of Emerson, Clough was both an insider and an outsider in upper-class Victorian England.[8] This position was subtly matured during his time at Oxford. In the university worry about subscribing to the Church of England's

---

[6] *Poems of Arthur Hugh Clough*, 426–39, and 767.

[7] John Campbell Shairp, *Aspects of Poetry* (Oxford: Clarendon Press, 1881), 256–315; John Campbell Shairp, *Kilmahoe: A Highland Pastoral* (London: Macmillan, 1864).

[8] *The Correspondence of Arthur Hugh Clough*, ed. Frederick L. Mulhauser, 2 vols. (Oxford: Clarendon Press, 1957), i. 49 (Clough to J. N. Simpkinson, Liverpool, 16 July 1836).

Thirty-Nine Articles (then necessary for all dons) went side by side with the radical political interests which led to his being nicknamed 'Citizen Clough'.[9] Where Matthew Arnold's ultimate loyalties lay clearly with the Oxonian 'dreaming spires', Clough, though moulded by his Oxford education, always had a longing for an environment which he felt was closer to the grain of modern, everyday life. As an undergraduate he joked about establishing a 'Platonic Republic' in Van Diemen's Land; he preferred the peasant poet Robert Burns to the High Tory Walter Scott as presented by J. G. Lockhart.[10] In part, such sympathies may have been a Romantic dream, but it was one which underpinned much of Clough's work and allowed the sophisticated don access to territories far from the college garden. It also led him to achieve poetic effects alien and virtually incomprehensible to his less adventurous friend Matthew Arnold.

The Bothie was composed in the autumn of 1848 when the 29-year-old Clough was a Fellow of Oriel College. Oxford at this time was convulsed by wrangles about access to knowledge and the dissemination of learning through the academic curriculum. In the spring of 1848 over 80 per cent of the tutors in the University made representations to the Vice-Chancellor and Heads of Houses over the issue of reform of the examination system.[11] As Benjamin Jowett, Master of Clough's undergraduate College, Balliol, put it that March, the question was, 'Are we doing enough for the cause of sound and useful learning?' There was anxiety in Oxford about how the University could best cope with the increasing professionalization of academia and with 'the new methods of investigation which criticism has opened in so many different branches of knowledge, of the sciences which have been absolutely created during the last half century'. Jowett worried that in 'the richest University in the world' standards were slipping, and that an old-fashioned attitude prevailed according to which dons behaved like parish priests rather than modern scholars. Oxford's examination system demanded simply 'drilling undergraduates...in Aldrich's Logic or Aristotle's Ethics' rather than giving them a deeper understanding or love of their subject. Troubling too was how to

---

[9] See *New Zealand Letters of Thomas Arnold the Younger*, ed. James Bertram (London: Oxford University Press, 1966), 220–1.

[10] *Correspondence*, i. 91 (Clough to J. P. Gell, Balliol, [19 May 1839]) and 96 (Clough to T. Burbridge, Oxford, 16 Oct. [1839]).

[11] [Benjamin Jowett and Arthur P. Stanley], *Suggestions for an Improvement of the Examination Statute* (Oxford: Francis Macpherson, 1848), 15–16.

balance 'the Academical course, as well as time for general knowledge'.[12]

A flurry of pamphlets in the early part of 1848, the year of European revolutions and radical discontent in Britain, indicates that Oxford seemed caught up in its own worries over learning. Some of the dons, indeed, discussed Oxford as if it were a state—'our Academical Republic'—and Clough's lifelong friend Arthur Stanley pointed out that Oxford's resources were 'equal it has been said to the revenues of most of the smaller states of Europe'. Nevertheless, with nervous arrogance, Stanley wondered, 'Can we say that Oxford has assumed that lofty position, at the head of the whole Academical world of Christendom, to which these resources, properly applied, must almost inevitably entitle her?'[13] In 1848 Clough, though breakfasting with one of the pamphleteers in this Oxford debate, was impatiently annoyed by it: 'Up here in Oxford . . . I could sometimes be provoked to send out a flood of lava boiling-hot amidst their flowery ecclesiastical fields and parterres. Very likely living in this state of suppressed volcanic action makes one more exasperated than one should be.'[14] Clough was about to set out for continental Europe where he would see for himself the social upheavals in Paris. He had made his own Oxonian intervention the previous year when he called the 'young men of Oxford, who gallop your horses over Bullingdon, and ventilate your fopperies arm-in-arm up the High-street' to pay attention to the gap between themselves and the poor or uneducated. Clough's pamphlet reminded members of the university that they and their learning depended for their existence on the labour of those whom they too readily ignored or scorned: 'As ignorant and unrefined parents stint themselves to secure knowledge and refinement for their children, so the laborious poor of the land support, at their painful cost, the aristocracy of the rich and educated.' Like others before and since, Clough was both sympathetic to the world of knowledge represented by Oxford's intellectual aristocracy and disturbed by its self-indulgence. Ironically and reluctantly, he reached the conclusion that

the welfare of the nation does undoubtedly require the existence of a class free for the most part to follow their own devices; that it is right that there should be men with time at their disposal, and money in their purses, and large liberty in

[12] Ibid. 5, 7, 10. [13] Ibid. 29, 32.
[14] Clough, *Correspondence*, i. 203 (Clough to Anne Clough, [18 Apr. 1848]).

public opinion; men who, though thousands and tens of thousands perish by starvation, stoically meanwhile in books and in study, in reading, and thinking, and travelling, and—it would seem too, enjoying, in hunting, videlicet, and shooting, in duets, and dancing, by ball-going and grousing, by dejeuners and deer-stalking, by foie-gras and Johannisberger, by February strawberries and December green peas, by turbot, and turtle, and venison, should pioneer the route of the armies of mankind.[15]

Since he had participated in not a few of these pursuits, Clough is engaged partly in acute self-examination. Later in 1848 he would not only write *The Bothie*, in which many of these issues are returned to, but would also resign his Oxford fellowship, and apply for a chair of English at the more egalitarian University College London (which he successfully obtained in 1850). That he and his circle were alert to links between the politics of Oxford and those of Europe is signalled graphically by a broadsheet circulated in the University on the fourth of July 1848. Even if Clough, fresh from Paris, is not the author, it shows a clear awareness of his position:

LIBERTY! EQUALITY!
FRATERNITY!

CITIZEN ACADEMICIANS,

The cry of reform has been too long unheard. OUR INFATUATED RULERS refused to listen to it. The term of their Tyranny is at length accomplished.

The VICE-CHANCELLOR has fled on horseback. The PROCTORS have resigned their Usurped Authority. The SCOUTS have fraternized with the Friends of Liberty.

The UNIVERSITY is no more. A REPUBLICAN LYCEUM will henceforth diffuse light and civilization.

The Hebdomadal Board is abolished. The Legislative Powers will be entrusted to a GENERAL CONVENTION of the whole Lyceum.

A PROVISIONAL GOVERNMENT has been established. The undersigned Citizens have nobly devoted themselves to the task of Administration.

(Signed) Citizen CLOUGH
President of the Executive Committee.
SEWELL.

---

[15] A. H. Clough, *A Consideration of Objections against the Retrenchment Association* (Oxford: Francis Macpherson, 1847), 10, 13, and 14–15.

BOSSOM, (Operative.)
JOHN CONINGTON.
WRIGHTSON, (Queen's)
FLOREAT LYCEUM.[16]

At the end of the year in which this proclamation appeared, Citizen Clough resigned his Oriel fellowship. His reason was his difficulty in subscribing to the Thirty-Nine Articles of the Church of England, which his employer, Oriel College, required him to do. Clough's problems here related to his religious faith, but also to questions of the nature of knowledge and access to it which were very much part of contemporary Oxford debates. We see this in his passionate engagement in a controversy of 1847 sparked off by an introductory lecture given at London's new University Hall by its first Principal, Francis Newman. Newman, brother of the celebrated and execrated Oxonian John Henry Newman, had been a Fellow of Balliol, but had resigned because he could not subscribe to the Thirty-Nine Articles.[17] His London address was entitled 'On the Relations of Free Knowledge to Moral Sentiment' and took as its starting point Francis Bacon's maxim 'Knowledge is Power'.

Newman argued that 'the appropriation or monopoly of it [knowledge] by a few' was an evil. In the university context in which they were delivered, his words were a clear attack on the way Oxford excluded from the academic powerhouse of England's ruling elite Catholics, Jews, Dissenters, members of the established Church of Scotland, and others who were not in the Anglican fold. Newman attempted to negotiate between modern ideas of systematized knowledge as bound up with 'Royal Institutions, British Associations, Academies, Colleges, Universities' on the one hand and, on the other, older, more primitive ideas of 'sages' who 'by solitary musings courted truth' often 'in the depths of the wilderness'. His lecture ended as a paean to 'free knowledge',

break down the walls of exclusiveness; let the wind of heaven play through the dark chambers of pretension; pour the natural light into the desks and drawers of official technicality; and a healthier, sweeter breath soon comes forth from professional halls, when scholastic and traditionary lore is forced to endure the gaze of strong native intelligence.

[16] Reproduced in Arnold, *New Zealand Letters*, 221.
[17] 'Newman, Francis William', *DNB*.

Newman's lecture, having started with Bacon's 'Knowledge is Power,' concludes by trying to envisage utopian conditions under which 'Knowledge is Love'; in such circumstances education might be pursued freely in a way that mixes 'self-education in the world' with 'a regeneration of university and college instruction ... of great moment for the welfare of England'.[18]

Newman's paean to 'Free Knowledge' links academic instruction to wider issues of knowledge and to politics and the nation. We know that Clough responded enthusiastically to this lecture in letters to the *Spectator* in late 1847.[19] Newman was also writing about the need for political reform in April 1848, when he feared a violent revolution would break out in England.[20] Clough's own contributions to this debate about the cost and nature of knowledge and access to it should be seen in relation to both the narrow Oxford arguments about university reform and the wider social unrest of 1848. William Young Sellar, who succeeded Clough at Oriel in 1848 and who had been his friend at Balliol, possessed at this time a volume which had the 1847–8 pamphlets of Jowett, Clough, and Francis Newman bound together.[21] Late in 1848, after unsuccessfully applying for the post of Professor of English Language and Literature at University College London, the poet of *The Bothie of Toper-na-fuosich* was being considered for Newman's job at University Hall, to which he was soon appointed.[22] By 1850 he was University College London's Professor of English. Clough's effervescent poem of knowledge, *The Bothie of Toper-na-fuosich*, is an outgrowth of these debates about learning, politics, and convictions. Yet its setting, as the title makes clear, is not Oxford, nor even England. The reasons for this lie again, though, in Clough's Oxford background, not least his experience and friends as a student at Balliol College.

Balliol, where both Clough and Arnold were undergraduates, is often thought of as a centre of later nineteenth-century imperialism. Its famous head, the classicist and philosopher Benjamin Jowett (who became Master in 1870), had intimate access to the levers of power

[18] Francis W. Newman, *On the Relations of Free Knowledge to Moral Sentiment* (London: Taylor & Walton, 1847), 1, 11, 13, 12, 24, 12, 23.

[19] See Chorley, *Arthur Hugh Clough*, 124.

[20] Francis W. Newman, *An Appeal to the Middle Classes on the Urgent Necessity of Numerous Radical Reforms, Financial and Organic* (London: Taylor & Walton, 1848).

[21] This volume of pamphlets, inscribed 'William Y Sellar, Oriel Coll.', is now in St Andrews University Library (classmark AC.900.P239).

[22] Chorley, *Arthur Hugh Clough*, 212 and 170–4.

and looked to encourage close links between Balliol and such arms of the British establishment as the India Civil Service.[23] However, another aspect of Balliol made an impact on Clough. This was the College's Scottish connections. Founded in the fourteenth century by the parents of a Scottish king, Balliol had for centuries drawn Scots to Oxford.[24] Since the seventeenth century among its principal attractions were the Snell Exhibitions which brought graduates of Glasgow University southwards for further studies. The numbers of the Exhibitioners had included such figures as Adam Smith, J. G. Lockhart, and many distinguished public men.[25] Theodore Walrond, son of a Glasgow businessman, and one of the Balliol Scots, matriculated at the College in 1842, becoming a Fellow there 1850–7.[26] He was a member of the 'little interior company' of four men who met in Clough's rooms every Sunday morning after Clough had been elected a Fellow of Oriel College in 1842.[27] The other members were Matthew Arnold and his brother Tom. Walrond recalled the long walks in the Oxford countryside which followed breakfast with Clough; the poet would travel on the Continent with Walrond in the summer of 1843. He stayed at Walrond's father's house, Calder Park near Glasgow, in August 1845 when returning from one of the Highland reading parties which provided the subject matter of *The Bothie*.[28] Another close Scottish friend was John Campbell Shairp, Snell Exhibitioner of 1840, who arrived at Balliol fresh from undergraduate successes at Glasgow which included a prizewinning essay on Pope's translation of Homer. Shairp 'had Highland blood in his veins', and strong Highland interests (evident from his later poetry and criticism), as well as close friends from Gaelic-speaking areas.[29] Though he regretted not having studied Gaelic at Glasgow University when he was a student, it is clear that Shairp had a concern with the language from which he went on to publish some translations, and on whose behalf he would campaign.[30] He became a close and trusted friend of Clough,

---

[23] John Jones, *Balliol College: A History* (Oxford: Oxford University Press, 1988), 219–20.

[24] See William Innes Addison, *The Snell Exhibitions* (Glasgow: Maclehose, 1901).

[25] See Addison, *The Snell Exhibitions*, from which biographical information is drawn here.

[26] Jones, *Balliol College*, 204.   [27] Chorley, *Arthur Hugh Clough*, 114–19.

[28] David Williams, *Too Quick Despairer* (London: Hart-Davis, 1969), 51; Clough, *Correspondence*, i. 149–53 (Clough to T. Burbridge, Calder Park, 31 Aug. and [18 Sept. 1845]).

[29] Addison, *The Snell Exhibitions*, 125; Mathew Rodger, *John Campbell Shairp* (Edinburgh: David Douglas, 1885), 5; William Knight, *Principal Shairp and his Friends* (London: Murray, 1888), 23–6, and 298–301.

[30] Knight, *Principal Shairp*, 298–301; Shairp, *Kilmahoe*, 140; Shairp, 'Preface' to M. C. Clerk, *A Birthday Book: In Gaelic and English, Selected from 'Ossian'... and Other Sources* (Edinburgh: MacLachlan & Stewart, 1885), pp. ix–xii.

who called him 'my pupillus' in 1843. Later Clough sent a draft of *Amours de voyage* to Shairp and Walrond to read.[31] Highland experiences of Shairp and Tom Arnold helped shape *The Bothie*.[32] Other Scots in the Clough–Arnold circle included William Young Sellar, whose father Patrick Sellar (1780–1851) had been Factor for the Duke of Sutherland and the man behind some of the most vicious of the Highland Clearances.[33] Walrond, Shairp and his friend the Balliol classicist James Riddell were among the Scottish participants in the small Oxford debating society the Decade, of which Clough was an influential member.[34] It would be possible to exaggerate the importance of Clough's Scottish friends, but, taken together with the young poet's admiration for the writings of Carlyle (particularly Carlyle's essays on Burns and Boswell), they help explain why a Scotland viewed through classical lenses should form the subject of his first major poem.[35]

The classical education culture of mid-nineteenth-century Oxford, not least the pressures of the examination system which were occasioning so much debate in the early spring of 1848, also encouraged this Scottish focus through the peculiar phenomenon of the 'reading party'. In the 1840s reading parties were a familiar Oxford experience.[36] With a tutor parties of undergraduates would meet in Wales, the Lake District, or the Highlands (or sometimes in Continental locations such as Switzerland) in order to undertake intensive study as well as recreational activities. In effect the students read classical Latin and Greek texts in the landscapes made admirable by Romanticism. On one reading party, Clough stayed with his fellow Wordsworth devotee Shairp and with the Walronds at Calder Park. From there he travelled to the Falls of Clyde (famously painted by Turner), where he heard J. G. Lockhart's daughter singing, before going on to discuss Burns with her celebrated father, the son-in-law and biographer of Walter Scott.[37] Bonding the Latin and Greek canon to the terrain of the modern British classics, reading

[31] Clough, *Correspondence*, i. 126 (Clough to J. P. Gell, Liverpool, 8–13 Oct. 1843) and 274 (Clough to J. C. Shairp, U[niversity] H[all], 31 Oct. [1849]).

[32] Clough, *The Bothie*, 4–7; Knight, *Principal Shairp*, 73–5 and 103–14; Arnold, *New Zealand Letters*, 164–6.

[33] Scott in his edition of *The Bothie* suggests a reference to the Clearances (Explanatory Notes, 30); Shairp's *Kilmahoe* treats them directly.

[34] Chorley, *Arthur Hugh Clough*, 138–9.

[35] Clough, *Correspondence*, i. 96 (Clough to J. N. Simpkinson, Oxford, [20 Oct. 1839]).

[36] Clough, *The Bothie*, 11 (introduction).

[37] Clough, *Correspondence*, i. 150–1 (Clough to T. Burbidge, Calder Park, 5 Sept. [1845]); Knight, *Principal Shairp*, 75 and 88.

parties may also be seen in terms of a certain assured Oxonian cultural imperialism. They brought students with leisure and money to travel into areas where those commodities were often scarce among the local population. Like Queen Victoria at Balmoral, these students were debonair cultural trippers, attracted in the wake of Macpherson and Scott to the more 'primitive' areas of Britain, their mountain sublimity and their charming local customs. Something of this cultural tourism is often bound up with Romantic poetry more generally. For a moment in 'Michael' when Wordsworth speaks of 'men | Whom I already loved;— not verily | For their own sakes, but for the fields and hills | Where was their occupation and abode' one senses that landscape is being valued more highly than its inhabitants.[38] Byron may have 'roved a young Highlander', but he grew up to be a lord who grand-toured Europe's mountains and cities.[39] Though poets such as Burns, Hogg, and Clare had emerged from the lower classes, it was the upper-class and often Oxbridge-educated Romantic vision which did most to school perception of the British mountains.

Reading parties were a product of Oxford culture, but also an escape from it, a spirited spilling over. Lively acoustic excess characterizes Clough's hexameters. Aural extravagance may typify the English hexameter in general, but Clough encourages it with gusto. If the iambic pentameter (whose metronomic dominance of English poetry Ezra Pound would later attempt to break) is the ground of English verse and the staple of English native epic, then, for the classicist in particular, that metre is challenged by the possibility of quite different sound-patterns, not least those of the Homeric epic in the original Greek. Homer's hexametric lines are based on quantity rather than stress. That means they depend not on heavily accented syllables but on the lengths—long or short—of vowels. There is much argument about how best to represent Homer's word-music in English verse translation. The problem is that if iambic pentameter is the assumed norm for English epic, having been used most famously for that purpose in *Paradise Lost*, then hexameters, even iambic ones, seem too long to the English ear, giving a sense of overload. More than that, if not all the feet in the English hexameter are iambic, but some are, say, dactylic, then the

[38] William Wordsworth and S. T. Coleridge, *Lyrical Ballads 1805*, 2nd edn., ed. Derek Roper (London: MacDonald & Evans, 1976), 238 ('Michael: A Pastoral Poem').
[39] Lord Byron, *Poetical Works* (London: Henry Frowde, 1904), 43 ('When I Roved a Young Highlander').

line gets even more syllable-crammed and sounds oddly extended. Longfellow's *Evangeline* (1847), which Clough read aloud to his mother shortly before composing *The Bothie*, makes splendid use of this sense of acoustic overbrimming in its opening lines:

> This is the forest primeval. The murmuring pines and the hemlocks,
> Bearded with moss, and in garments green, indistinct in the twilight,
> Stand like Druids of eld, with voices sad and prophetic,
> Stand like harpers hoar, with beards that rest on their bosoms.[40]

Lasting a little longer than the anglophone ear expects, the aural extendedness of these lines matches the plenitude of the American wilderness. Those harpers are there because, as in Ossian, they go with the primal terrain. Written by a man who would become a university professor, *Evangeline* is a modern poem, but also one that seeks attunement with 'the forest primeval'. If it celebrates a landscape 'Spreading afar and unfenced', then it does so not only in its images, but also through its acoustic. Just a little later, the long, 'unfenced' lines of Whitman will take the process further. More immediately, though, Longfellow's music will infect Clough in the writing of his own poem of the wilderness. Clough chooses not a forest, but the barer, if more poetically consecrated landscape of the Scottish Highlands. There he travelled with his students as a university teacher, but also as a writer of verse. Where Longfellow in *Evangeline* had headed hexametrically for Maine, Clough strode out in the same lanky, long-stepping metre for the wild northern shores of Loch Ness. For him the excesses of modern hexameter would re-echo the political brimmings-over in Britain and Europe in the late 1840s. Clough, in the footsteps of Ossian and the Romantics, went north as a modern poet. His sometimes apparently uncontainable hexameters sound for us the music of democracy.

As a don at Oriel College who was publishing work on classical metres in the periodical the *Classical Museum*, and who was applying to classical translation the theories of Edinburgh's Professor J. S. Blackie, Clough organized three summer reading parties in the mid-1840s.[41] The first was to Grasmere in 1843; the others, which form the basis for *The Bothie*, were to Castleton, near Braemar, in 1846, and to Drumnadrochit by Loch Ness in 1847. Clough was the typical cultural tourist, participating in upper-class entertainments and escaping from his homosocial

---

[40] Henry Wadsworth Longfellow, *Poetical Works* (London: Collins, n.d.), 70 (*Evangeline*).
[41] Clough, *The Bothie*, 4–6 (introduction).

Oxonian environment to sport with local girls. Yet there are also other
ways in which he shows himself remarkably sensitive to the Scottish
milieu. He produces a poem both Romantic and characteristically
modern in its attempt to blend the extreme sophistication of his
academic knowledge with his attraction to the comparatively under-
developed conditions of the Highland environment. Delighting in kinds
of primitive simplicity at the same time as deploying a formidable store
of learning, *The Bothie* is the product both of donnishness and the desire
to escape it. Such a combination makes it crucially modern, though it is
too easily overlooked by recent commentators.[42] Today Clough is
treated almost exclusively as the poet of the later *Amours de voyage* and
Dipsychus. In an attempt to redress the balance, and to pay deserved
attention to a passed-over work, I shall concentrate here on the Clough
of *The Bothie*, though I would wish to make the point that the textual
self-consciousness of that poem becomes the obsessive self-consciousness of the same poet's later verse.

　The Bothie of Toper-na-fuosich is a poem about knowledge and delight. It
wishes to connect the two as part of an ethical vision, sees each as
reinforcing the other. Its framework signals knowledge from the start,
since the poem focuses on an Oxford reading party, studying their
classical texts in the Scottish Highlands. Yet the setting indicates also
joie de vivre. Clough relishes the beauties of the landscape, not least its
waterfalls and lochs in a poem full of erotic liquidity. The work of
knowing carried out by the reading party extends to getting to know this
Highland environment which is portrayed in terms of the classical
literature studied. Spurred by Longfellow's *Evangeline*, the poem's hexameters also imitate classical precedents, while Clough's events and
settings are pushed in the direction of epic and pastoral texts, especially
those of Homer, Theocritus, and Virgil. At the same time, though,
Clough builds in an enlivening resistance to mere antiquarianism by
elastically springing his form into the modern world of cities, student
slang, postal technology, railways, tourism, and other contemporary
phenomena. The poem negotiates between ancient and up-to-the-
minute. Its Highland environment (as had happened in the Ossianic
poems) mediates between these two. This is a work aimed at a highly
self-aware, knowledgeable audience such as the reading party with

---

[42] *Clough: Selected Poems*, ed. J. P. Whelan (London: Longman, 1995) omits the poem entirely;
more sympathetic was Walter E. Houghton, in *The Poetry of Clough* (New Haven: Yale
University Press, 1963), 92–118.

which it deals, and it is dedicated to the students whom Clough had taught on his own long-vacation excursions.

Yet *The Bothie* is about sexual knowledge also. Its radical protagonist 'Philip Hewson the poet' finds that in addition to his college labours he has to 'Study the question of sex in the Bothie of What-did-he-call-it' (II. 333). If sex for Hewson the student cramming for his finals sounds here a bit like another exam, then that is the case only ironically. What Hewson learns in the Highlands to some extent undoes and in other ways complements the knowledge which he gains through academia. As he passes through several infatuations, leading him eventually to the site of 'The Bothie of Toper-na-fuosich' and to the Highland girl Elspie Mackaye, Hewson is educated not only by Adam, his Oxford tutor ('the teacher'), but also by Elspie and her Highlander father Davie, an admirer of the democratic verse of Robert Burns, that writer who among other things scorned 'Colledge-classes'.[43] The poet Hewson does not despise such learning, but seeks both intuitively and deliberately to give it life beyond academia by combining it with other kinds of sexual and practical knowledge, as well as book-learning from arcane sources. In so doing, Hewson functions very much as the modern poet.

Clough knew that knowledge was protean, and never more so than in modernity. In 1849, the year after writing *The Bothie*, he returned to the work of Francis Newman. Clough was fascinated by Newman's investigation of inner knowledge; Newman operated, the poet points out, in the spirit of '*gnothi seauton*' ('know thyself'). Clough also realizes that just as 'the mystic inscription of the soul' may seem 'variable, shifting', so may scientific knowledge when 'We approach, and behold, leagues away, and receding and receding yet again beyond each new limit of the horizon, a new visible unknown'.[44] This sense of unending deferral, and of knowledge as extending beyond our horizons of knowing, characterizes not just the science but also a good deal of the poetry of the last two centuries. Clough possessed a superb alertness to fluidity and flux—in knowledge, religion, language, politics, and, not least, in verse form. In *The Bothie* he likes his hexameters as irregular as possible, constantly variegated, changeful, surprising, disappearing beyond the

---

[43] Robert Burns, *Poems and Songs*, ed. James Kinsley (Oxford: Oxford University Press, 1969), 67 ('Epistle to J. L*****k, an Old Scotch Bard').

[44] *The Poems and Prose Remains of Arthur Hugh Clough*, ed. his wife, 2 vols. (London: Macmillan, 1869), i. 302.

horizon of expectation. Around 1850, as Professor of English Language and Literature at University College London, he lectured on 'The Formation of Classical English' and told his students that 'Our language before the Restoration certainly was for the most part bookish, academical, and stiff.'[45] He heard in Dryden's verse an interest in 'Political agitations—the plot and the new plot' which was bound up with 'a democratic movement in the language'.[46] More than once he relates Dryden's recasting of English in a freer, more fluent mode to parallel reconfigurations in scientific and political knowledge:

Dryden, a true litterateur, simply reflects his epoch; the revolution he was intent upon, and which we are especially bound to consider, was that of English verse composition. While Newton was balancing the earth, and Locke was weighing the intellect, Dryden was measuring syllables. While Penn and Locke were venturing experiments in government, he was making them in prosody.[47]

Clough the scholar of classical metres and the practising hexametrist of *The Bothie* was doing something very similar for his own era. As a lecturer he told his audience that 'A democratic revolution' was 'effecting itself' in the language of their own time, and alerted them to the need for new forms of expression. 'We have something new to say, but do not know how to say it.'[48] *The Bothie* tries to articulate that new thing. Its lines are alert to the jostle, rush, and breathlessness of modernity. 'Have we any one who speaks for our day as justly and appropriately as Dryden did for his?' Professor Clough asked his students; yet that question also came from Clough the admirably excitable young author.[49] Poet and academic were fused in Clough in a characteristically modern way. He argued in his lectures that 'A democratic revolution' in language required an 'aristocratic reconstruction'.[50] Clough was no blue-blooded aristocrat but he was a member of England's upper-class intellectual aristocracy. In *The Bothie* he sought to balance that polished, privileged, and sophisticated position with his awareness of a need for something partaking more of the 'vernacular' and of 'living instincts' as exemplified by the lower-class poet Burns.[51] Lecturing on 'The Development of English Literature' at the heart of imperial Britain's capital city, Clough the academic, like Clough the poet, signals a significant attraction to something wilder than his customary milieu, something 'plebeian,

---

[45] Ibid. 330. [46] Ibid. 329 and 331. [47] Ibid. 329. [48] Ibid. 333.
[49] Ibid. [50] Ibid. [51] Ibid. 353.

unintellectual, unrefined', and 'barbarian', such as those forces which brought new energy to ancient Rome or modern England, to give 'back life to the world'.[52] His UCL students responded warmly to this lively combination of elements in their teacher, noting in him both 'an almost Olympian air' and an ability to be 'quite uncouth... now and then, when the light shone in his eyes, there was something, in spite of the air of fine scholarship and culture, which reminded one of the best likeness of Burns'.[53] It was just such a union of elements that the Professor of English Language and Literature had sought to achieve a few years earlier when, still an Oxford don, he wrote his first major poem.

The Bothie of Toper-na-fuosich is a marriage poem which deals not simply with personal union but with the bonding and interpenetration of worlds—of class, nation, sex, learning, and modes of knowledge. Light-hearted and sophisticated, but also profound, it is a manifesto for modern verse. Drawing on 'fragments' (IX. 101), conversations, documents; allusive, aware of its own 'irregularity' ('Note'); peppered with classical epigraphs; fascinated by, yet also in flight from academic knowledge; displaying a complex torque that bonds contemporary life to classical literature; at once flippant and profound, it is from its title onwards a poem whose allure seems bound up with a certain sometimes playful obscurity. Some awareness of the work's immediate genesis is helpful here, not least if we are to comprehend the significance of the title. In 1847 John Campbell Shairp, Theodore Walrond, and Thomas Arnold (who was planning to emigrate to New Zealand) paid a visit to Clough's reading party at Drumnadrochit on Loch Ness. Finding themselves stranded beside 'wildest' Loch Ericht where Shairp was keen to find Jacobite sites, they spent the night in a remote bothie. It is worth quoting Shairp's recollection at length:

It was one of the loveliest, most primitive places I ever saw even in the most out-of-the-way parts of the Highlands. We told Clough of it, and when his reading party was over, later in autumn, he went on our track. He spent a night at the inn at the west end of Loch Rannoch called Tighnaline, where he met with some of the incidents which appeared in *The Bothie*. He also visited the house by the side of Loch Ericht, a small heather-thatched hut, occupied by one of the foresters of the Ben Alder forest. He found one of the children lying sick of a fever, the father, I think, from home, and the mother without any medicines or aid for her child. He immediately set off, and walked to Fort William, about two days' journey from the place, but where the nearest

<hr>

[52]   Ibid.   [53]   R. H. Hutton, quoted in Chorley, *Arthur Hugh Clough*, 220.

medicines and other supplies were to be had. These he got at Fort William, and
returned on his two days' journey, and left them with the mother. He had four
days' walk, over a rough country, to bring medicines to this little child, and the
people did not even know his name. On these occasions in Scotland he told me
that he used to tell the people he was a 'Teacher,' and they were at once at ease
with him then.[54]

What Clough the Oxford tutor manages to do at the conclusion of the
classical reading party is to translate himself culturally into the role of
the practical 'Teacher' who can use his knowledge (and income) in a way
immediately vital to the community in that 'most primitive' place.
Clough's walk along Loch Ericht, which underlies *The Bothie*, illustrates
the importance of being a kind of 'Teacher' whose work goes beyond
the academic knowledge of the reading party. This story, one suspects,
appealed to the Christian Shairp because in it Clough acts as the great
Rabbi or Teacher, Christ. An alert modern audience may recall William
Dyce's impressive Victorian painting *The Man of Sorrows* (1860), where
Christ sits on a boulder in a deserted Highland landscape.[55] Shairp's
narrative, though, is also about a Teacherly knowledge and wisdom that
transcends the classroom, having an emotional, not simply an intellectual appeal. This is an important aspect of *The Bothie* in which Shairp
among others recognized Adam the tutor, who is also known to the
Highlanders as 'the teacher' (VII. 55), as Clough himself. Yet his poem
of 1848 focuses more on the student than his teacher. Its protagonist is
the poet-pupil Hewson who gains his knowledge as a modern poet in an
environment where the Oxford reading party is joined to the culture of
the Highland bothie.

Mixing academic slang, 'whatever was recherché and racy' (I. 30) with
the repeated acoustic allure of foreign, not quite digested Gaelic vocabulary—'Knoydart, Croydart, Moydart, Morrer and Ardnamurchan'
(IV. 16, 24, 32)—the poem wears its eclecticism, its cultural *mélange*, on
its sleeve. Beginning with a description of a Highland games which is
patterned on Homeric accounts, it soon moves on to dinner-jacketed
aristocrats. It flaunts academic learning, introducing one of the students,
for instance, as 'Skilful in Ethics and Logic, in Pindar and Poets
unrivalled; | *Shady* in Latin, said Lindsay, but *topping* in Plays and Aldrich,'
(I. 23–4). Its diction is Byronically supercharged, with expressions such

[54] Knight, *Principal Shairp*, 113.
[55] See Duncan Macmillan, *Scottish Art 1460–1990* (Edinburgh: Mainstream, 1990), 210 (plate
171).

as 'plusquam-thucydidean' (I. 94) and 'unnatural up-in-the-air balloon-work' (II. 70). Like Byron before him, Clough delights in elasticating his poetic form so that it will hold any verbal item he chooses to land in it. Tom Paulin detects in this a note of 'camp', even of 'inauthenticity'; but I hear in the lines a developing new acoustic able to take in anything, vernacular yet fully intellectual, felt and dreamed as well as spiced with wit.[56] If aspects of the technique re-echo Byron, they also pre-echo T. S. Eliot, W. H. Auden, and many poets to come. In the immediate, reading-party context, a slangy-academic note reinforces the literary games set up by the use of classically oriented hexameters and quasi-Homeric language. The latter's post-Ossian inversions produce an English well on its way to translatorese: 'Turned to them Hewson, the chartist, the poet, the eloquent speaker' (II. 19). Yet countering allusive knowledge-games are other kinds of homelier, more down-to-earth matters such as digging potatoes and gardening, which form part of an argument about gender and female beauty. Quoting a part of this debate among the students illustrates the range which Clough can cover in a relatively small space:

Or—high-kilted perhaps, cried Lindsay, at last successful,
Lindsay, this long time swelling with scorn and pent-up fury,
Or high-kilted perhaps, as once at Dundee I saw them,
Petticoats up to the knees, or, it might be, a little bit higher,
Matching their lily-white legs with the clothes that they trod in the wash-tub!
Laughter loud ensued; and seeing the Tutor embarrassed,
It was from then, I suppose, said Arthur, smiling sedately,
Lindsay learnt the tune we all have learnt from Lindsay,
For oh, he was a roguey, the Piper o' Dundee.
Laughter ensued again; and the Tutor still slightly embarrassed
Picked at the fallen thread, and commenced a reply to Hewson.
There's truth in what you say, though truly much distorted;
These, I think, no less than other agaceries, cloy one;
Still, there's truth, I own, I perfectly understand you.
While the Tutor was gathering his thoughts, continued Arthur,
Is not all this just the same as one hears at common-room breakfasts,
Or perhaps Trinity wines, about Gothic buildings and Beauty? (II. 122–38)

A clue to the remarkable acoustic variety of these (all hexametric) lines lies in the internal punctuation of each. Almost no two are alike in their exact emphases, or the location and nature of the pause(s), whether

<hr>

[56] Paulin, *Minotaur*, 70.

denoted by comma, semicolon, or full stop. Perched between quantitative and stressed metre, sometimes the verse tune slows down, as in the close-spaced stresses of 'Laughter loud ensued'; at other moments it frisks ahead at the speed of accelerating speech, skittering across short and unstressed syllables ('Is not all this just the same as one hears at common-room breakfasts?'). Clough seems less concerned with syllable-counting than with constant modulations of a six-stress pattern from which some ears might perceive he departs on occasion. The word-music is fizzingly lively, constantly mobile, wedded to the shifts in subject matter. If use of the hexameter can run the risk of monotony, then Clough (more than Longfellow) fights this in the spirit of stylish irregularity. Matching the politics to which it alludes, the poem is a metrical and linguistic uprising. So, in the less than twenty lines just quoted, we speed from the scornful voyeurism of the leisured student peeking at the thighs of working-class washerwomen to the nonplussed embarrassment of the older tutor. Sex, gender, and class are made to clash as they do throughout a poem where 'knowledge' involves an attempt to juggle gendered, class-bound, and nation-bound perspectives as well as classical texts and resonances. The latter come under pressure too as Homeric conventions are amusingly stretched by the situations of modern life: one might catch a Homeric hero 'swelling with scorn and pent-up fury' but not 'still slightly embarrassed'. Clough's vocabulary moves from the Scots '*roguey*' to the High Table 'agaceries', and the settings from Dundee to Trinity College, Oxford, from 'the wash-tub' to 'common-room breakfasts'. Telescoping different dictions and environments, this passage also compacts kinds of learning. The presence of the tutor and mention of Trinity summons up English academia, yet the verb 'learnt', repeated in line 129, refers to learning a vernacular and implicitly bawdy Scots song. In its lively tonal and contextual shifts, this passage encapsulates some of the larger ploys and topics of a poem which often enjoys debating techniques, at the same time as finding such debates ultimately wanting. The way in which, cleverly, mockingly, and immaturely, the homosocial society of students turns its argument about female beauty towards the production of a mock-Pugin thesis on *The Laws of Architectural Beauty in Application to Women* is a piece of academic bookishness, not nearly sufficient for the real world as Philip Hewson comes to know it. Tomes are to be learned from, but also to be renounced. Yet, even in describing their renunciation, the high-spirited knowledge-poet Clough supplies through his character Hope a scholarly bibliography featuring Greek dictionaries, allusions, quotation, classical texts and topics:

> Four weeks here have we read; four weeks will we read hereafter;
> Three weeks hence will return and revisit our dismal classics,
> Three weeks hence re-adjust our visions of classes and classics.
> Fare ye well, meantime, forgotten, unnamed, undreamt of,
> History, Science, and Poets! lo, deep in dustiest cupboard,
> Thookydid, Oloros' son, Halimoosian, here lieth buried!
> Slumber in Liddell-and-Scott, O musical chaff of Old Athens,
> Dishes, and fishes, bird, beast, and sesquipedalian blackguard!
> Sleep, weary Ghosts, be at peace, and abide in your lexicon-limbo!
> Sleep, as in lava for ages your Herculanean kindred,
> Sleep, and for ought that I care, 'the sleep that knows no waking,'
> Æschylus, Sophocles, Homer, Herodotus, Pindar, and Plato. (II. 278–89)

In such lines we hear, perhaps, in the clash of stressed syllables ('bird, beast', for example) an anticipation of Hopkins, another learned poet who shares Clough's delight in verbal cascades and Highland waterfalls. As some of the students leave their books while others go on reading, Philip progresses to 'Study the question of sex' as he heads, more unconsciously than consciously, for 'the Bothie of What-did-he-call-it' (II. 333). Moving emphatically into the Highland landscape, the poem also details the pleasures of bathing in secluded mountain pools where

> You are shut in, left alone with yourself and perfection of water,
> Hid on all sides, left alone with yourself and the goddess of bathing.
> Here, the pride of the plunger, you stride the fall and clear it;
> Here, the delight of the bather, you roll in beaded sparklings,
> Here into pure green depth drop down from lofty ledges. (III. 44–8)

The repeated passages on bathing in *The Bothie* may function in part as a translation into the wilder Highland landscape of the Oxford nude bathing practices carried out at the men-only area of the river Isis called Parson's Pleasure. However, the presence of the 'goddess of bathing' introduces a more female aspect, and may be one of the factors which leads the critic Paul Turner to draw attention to Clough's heterosexual anxieties about his own masturbation.[57] Water in the poem, though, represents female as well as male sexuality, and symbolizes the mixing of the two. So when Philip and Elspie begin to embrace before their

[57] Paul Turner, *English Literature 1832–1890* (Oxford: Clarendon Press, 1989), 60 and 65.

marriage, she is imaged as a burn and he as the sea. The sea plays the traditional male, active role, 'Forcing and flooding the silvery stream' (VII. 160), while the stream is more passive; yet, though some readers may wish to dismiss it simply in terms of male quasi-pornographic fantasy, the passage that follows contains also considerable awareness of female sexual desire:

> That great water withdrawn, receding here and passive,
> Felt she in myriad springs, her sources, far in the mountains,
> Stirring, collecting, rising, upheaving, forth-out-flowing,
> Taking and joining... (VII. 161–4)

Post-Freudian audiences may feel uneasily fascinated, even amused by the writing here. Its syntactic and imaginative energy are clear, perhaps a bit over the top, but, in lines about exuberance, this is appropriate. What the modern reader needs to be reminded is how much such passages are also, in Victorian terms, about 'knowledge'. The form and content of Clough's poem, as well as his extra-poetic participation in the contemporary debates about 'Free Knowledge', show his acute awareness that the mid-nineteenth century was a time in which knowledge (scientific, textual, historical, cosmological, biological, archaeological) was proliferating at a rapidly accelerating speed. As Clough understood, the grounds of knowledge were under increasing philosophical scrutiny. Though the St Andrews philosopher James Frederick Ferrier did not coin the term 'epistemology' until early in the following decade, philosophical questions of knowledge and consciousness were much discussed in the 1840s, not only in specialist academic textbooks of the sort familiar to Oxford students, but also in wider circulation periodicals such as the *Spectator*, in whose columns Clough joined in the knowledge debate. So, for instance, during Clough's student days Ferrier himself had contributed to *Blackwood's Magazine* a series of articles on the philosophy of consciousness. In these he laid out foundations on which he later built his epistemological work in the *Institutes of Metaphysics* and he strove to find a position from which philosophy and knowledge might include the practical as well as the abstract, a standpoint from which philosophy

loses her merely theoretical complexion, and becomes identified with all the best practical interests of our living selves. She no longer stands aloof from humanity, but, descending into this world's arena, she takes an active part in the ongoings of busy life... Her sleeping waters become the bursting fountainhead from whence flows all the activity which sets in motion the currents of human practice and of human progression.[58]

There is no need to suggest that the acutely self-conscious Clough ever read this paragraph, which goes on to praise the maxim '*gnothi seauton*' ('Know thyself'). It does, though, form a useful commentary on his first major poem, and alerts us to the way in which its theme of knowledge relates to a contemporary ideal union of practical and theoretical *nous*. Transforming what Ferrier calls 'inert tutorage' into 'actual life', *The Bothie* is a work attempting to unite 'science' (that word whose older meaning is simply 'knowledge') with 'verdure'.[59] Furthermore, in using imagery of waters breaking and of female sexuality, Ferrier's paean to knowledge subliminally signals, as does the frequent erotic liquidity of Clough's poem, a way in which knowing, particularly for mid-Victorians such as Clough and Ferrier who struggled to reconcile Christian teaching with the modern world, was linked to sexuality. The connection, familiar to readers of Shakespeare or the Authorized Version of the Book of Genesis, was clearer to nineteenth-century audiences than it is today. For the verb to 'know' for anyone brought up on the Authorized Version was a word with strong sexual connotations. So, for instance, in Genesis 24: 16 we read of 'a virgin, neither had any man known her'. Though the *Oxford English Dictionary* indicates that the noun 'knowledge' in the sense of sexual intimacy was archaic or confined to legal use by the nineteenth century, it survived in this sense (as it still does) in the expression 'carnal knowledge'. In the case of an academically trained classicist like Clough, whose education was a schooling not least in etymology and linguistic usage, and who had a poet's sense of verbal resonance, it is hard to argue that the term 'knowledge' could have been free from sexual connotations. Though *The Bothie of Toper-na-fuosich* avoids making explicit links between the sexual and intellectual senses of the term 'knowledge', it relies on this subliminal connection.

Such dependence is present not only in the jokey, parodically academic systematization of sexual attraction (*The Laws of Architectural Beauty in Application to Women*), but also in the continuous paralleling of nudity and erotic liquidity with academic subject matter, in the overall bringing together of scholarly and sexual knowledge, and in specific juxtapositions. So at the start of the eighth section of the poem, as a

[58] James Frederick Ferrier, *Philosophical Works*, ed. Alexander Grant and E. L. Lushington, 2nd edn., 3 vols. (Edinburgh: Blackwood, 1875), iii. 204–5.
[59] Ibid.

bride approaches, the Catullan epigraph excitedly invokes Hymen, god of marriage, and introduces Elspie's fears about the extent and nature of Philip's knowledge:

> But the many things that he knew, and the ease of a practised
> Intellect's motion, and all those indefinable graces
> (Were they not hers too, Philip?) to speech and manner, and movement,
> Lent by the knowledge of self, and wisely instructed feeling,—
> When she thought of all these, and these contemplated daily,
> Daily appreciating more, and more exactly appraising,—
> With these thoughts, and the terror withal of a thing she could not
> Estimate, and of a step (such a step!) in the dark to be taken... (VIII. 7–14)

Ostensibly Elspie's fears are about Philip's intellectual knowledge being so much greater than any she has acquired in what she has just called her 'ignorant Highlands' (VII. 178). This section goes on to discuss 'true education'. Yet it is hard to uncouple Elspie's trepidation about knowledge from the worry about sex felt by Elspie and Philip elsewhere in the poem (as in Philip's dream of modern urban prostitutes, or Elspie's shock and terror at the suddenness and strength of her attraction to Philip). Elspie goes on to be schooled by 'the teacher' (VIII. 55, 61) Adam, Philip's university tutor, whose very name signals a link between various connotations of the word 'knowledge'. As Adam the Oxford academic educates Elspie, so David Mackaye, Elspie's Highland father, mentors Philip. Such parallelism may remind us of another submerged pun in the text, that on 'class'. For the poem is about classes in the sense of university classes and education, but it is also about classes in the sense of upper-class undergraduates meeting lower-class Highlanders. If Elspie wants to read Philip's books (VIII. 111), as a Highland girl craving an Oxford education, then Philip, 'sick of our books' (VIII. 117), is also eager both for a Highland schooling in practical learning and for the intuitive knowledge he associates with Elspie and the feminine ('Women must read,—as if they didn't know all beforehand' (VIII. 114)). Their marriage represents a union of individuals, temperaments, sexes, classes, nations, and kinds of knowing. This linking of erotic and book knowledge may call to mind a poem published the year before *The Bothie*, Tennyson's narrative about an attempt to set up a female university in *The Princess* (1847). To that the Victorian Poet Laureate later added some of his most stunningly erotic lyrics. But where the bulk of *The Princess* is now very hard to read, Clough's poem retains a shimmer and buoyancy as well as an intellectual ambition. Nor should it be thought simply that he settles for a presentation of Elspie as passive earth-mother or water spirit. When Clough has her tell Philip that she feels 'Like the Peruvian Indians I read about last winter, | Out in America there, in somebody's life of Pizarro' (VIII. 84–5), he presents Elspie on the one hand as being like a 'primitive', yet on the other hand as familiar with up-to-date, sophisticated texts. Her retort to Philip about reading demonstrates her spirit, at the same time as reconstellating the view of the Highlands which the poem presents:

> What, she said, and if I have let you become my sweetheart,
> I am to read no books! but you may go your ways then,
> And I will read, she said, with my father at home as I used to.
> If you must have it, he said, I myself will read them to you.
> Well, she said, but no, I will read to myself, when I choose it;
> What, you suppose we never read anything here in our Highlands,
> Bella and I with the father in all our winter evenings. (VIII. 120–6)

In this Victorian poem so anticipatory of modern society and literature, Elspie's is the subservient role, but she has spirit, intellect, and determination. The Highlands may function primarily as a repository of the primitive through which the thoroughly English poet Hewson may acquire kinds of knowledge different from and complementing those of academia. Yet the same Highlands are also shown as textually developed, with their own books, technologies of communication, and modern tourists, not to mention their own language and historical wounds. Balanced with farouche irony, at once knowing and preoccupied with bringing together kinds of knowledge, *The Bothie of Toper-na-fuosich* sends its Oxonian poet hero with his Highland bride off to a new life powered by the chartist's awareness of 'the old democratic fervour'. 'Philip, the poet, the speaker, the chartist, | Delving at Highland soil, and railing at Highland landlords' (IX. 153–4) sets out with his new wife and their wedding presents (including books and plough) to 'Democracy' and 'New Zealand'. The result is that, as the last line of the poem puts it, 'the Antipodes too have a Bothie of Toper-na-fuosich'.

That Gaelic name which is the poem's title and conclusion brings us to the final sense in which this is a poem of knowing. Clough appears to have selected the title almost at random, having spotted it on a map and half-heard an explanation of its meaning. Yet eyebrows were soon raised by some of his early reviewers, and Clough himself wrote an awkward postscript to Thomas Arnold who was now, like the poem's chartist poet Philip, in New Zealand:

At the risk of destroying the effect of my pastoral which somehow or other is to reach you I must tell you what has turned up.

You remember *Toper-na-fuosich*, in the Map, on Loch Ericht—and how I made out afterwards that Dallungart was the present name. Good reason why! for now that I from tender recollections of you and Shairp under the blanket together and of that Madonna like Mother and two children—now that I, I say, have published the name to all the drawing-rooms and boudoirs (of course) of all the world—What think you?—it turns out, they tell me, to mean what Horace calls 'teterrima belli causa'—O Mercy!—It is too ludicrous not to tell some one, but too appallingly awkward to tell any one on this side of the globe:—in the Gath and Ascalon of the Antipodes you may talk of it, and laugh at your pleasure. Do you know too that in the boat on Loch Ericht I asked the boatman 1st where it was, and 2d what it meant. He replied, the bairds' well, which I could not understand. Did he mean the *bairns'* well, homunculorum fons et origo.[60]

Indicative of erotic anxiety, this is a confused, embarrassedly oblique response. No one knows just how or when Clough learned the meaning, but later in 1849 a reviewer in the *Literary Gazette* was pointing out that the poem's Gaelic title corresponded to 'an ancient Highland toast to the female genital organs' and in the following year W. M. Rossetti in the *Germ* wrote that ' "The Bothie of Toper-na-fuosich" means "the hut of the bearded well", a somewhat singular title, to say the least.'[61] It was as if Tennyson had published a poem called *Vagina*.

Clough appears horrified, yet he is prepared to allow Tom Arnold 'to laugh at your pleasure' in that far-off New Zealand to which Clough's poem consigns his hopes for a better future and where 'The Antipodes now have a Bothie of Toper-na-fuosich'. For all Clough's awkwardness, it is surely the poem's title and what goes with it which provide the answer to Philip Hewson's study of 'the question of sex in the Bothie of What-did-he-call-it'. In this work so full of gushing waters, the Bothie stands as the rather mysterious goal of the quest being undertaken by the student poet searching for knowledge. Here is a poem which deals with the translation of knowledge as power into knowledge as love. Clough the intellectual poet of knowledge was carried beyond direct

---

[60] Arnold, *New Zealand Letters* (Clough to T. Arnold, 24 Feb. [1849]), 139.   [61] Ibid.

cerebral awareness by his poet's dream-mind. What he produced is not least a homage to the bearded well. Once the full meaning of the poem's title became public property, Clough had to bowdlerize it, altering it to the meaningless 'Bothie of Tober-na-Vuolich'. Yet in its energetic and splendid first edition, it demands republication. This poem stands as a brilliantly developed combination of kinds of intellectual and intuitive knowledge, a work whose modernity of form and content remains both anticipatory and exciting.

Formally the very irregularity of the long, hexametric lines, and the way in which they blur the distinction between prose and poetry, loosened the rhythms of English verse even as they applied oddly poetic quasi-Homeric, Ossian-like terms and inversions. Tom Paulin has argued that they may have encouraged the process of metrical development which led to free verse, not least to the long lines of Walt Whitman's *Leaves of Grass* in the following decade.[62] If Paulin is right, then 'Yankee' Clough's greatest legacy was to American poetry. Tellingly, Whitman's admirer Ralph Waldo Emerson was Clough's friend, and one of his leading American champions. A much-lauded visitor to the North Eastern United States in the early 1850s, Clough was lionized there, where he was seen primarily as the author of *The Bothie*. His influence was particularly strong in Boston, and he pronounced himself 'an established Bostonian' in 1852, meeting not only Emerson, but also Thoreau, Hawthorne, Longfellow, and Channing. He became a friend of two leading Bostonians who greatly praised his writing, the poet James Russell Lowell and the young Charles Eliot Norton, later an influential American editor and Harvard professor who would edit Clough's poetical works for an American audience in 1862.[63] In the *North American Review* of 1853 Clough wrote in favour of a poetry of modernity. There is a sense in which his interests, even perhaps his sound-world, linked him to the young Bostonian T. S. Eliot, born thirty-five years later. If Clough could write of 'Morning and Evening and Noonday and Night', then Eliot would intone in the early twentieth century, '*Morning Evening Noontime Night.*'[64] An academically nurtured, self-conscious poet fascinated by the primitive, Eliot (as my next

[62] Paulin, *Minotaur*, 59–60.

[63] Clough, *Correspondence*, ii. 329–30 (Clough to Blanche Smith, Tremont House, Boston, 15 Nov. 1852), 329–30; *Poems of Arthur Hugh Clough*, 653.

[64] *Poems of Arthur Hugh Clough*, 332 ('Four black steamers plying on the Thames'); Eliot, *The Complete Poems and Plays*, 123 (*Sweeney Agonistes*).

chapter will argue) was one of Clough's descendants as a modern poet. In Victorian England, though, Clough went on to be viewed very much in terms of his crisis of religious belief and early death, being turned into the somewhat insubstantial, melancholy 'Thyrsis' by Matthew Arnold. For citizens of the United States Clough's name conjured up the vigour and modernity of his verse, particularly of *The Bothie*. What the Americans saw and heard was Clough the modern poet.

The Bothie marries Oxford to the Highlands and then ends in a democratic New Zealand, its poet Philip and his clever wife fortified with tools, picture, and books. Matthew Arnold's vision of perfected poetic knowledge, though, heads from Oxford into an ethereal never-never land. Clough's poetic ideal, linking the knowledges of two cultures, one suavely sophisticated and the other primitively noble, remains in the modern world. It demonstrates acute intuition, if not quite second sight; Elspie, in a work about equality, emigrates to the country which, some decades after Clough's death, will be the first nation on earth to give women the vote. Arnold, though, is uneasy about both modernity and democracy. He is unable to break loose from what his elegy for Clough calls the 'dreaming spires' of Oxford, and consigns his poetic ideal to dreamland. Arnold complains to Clough in a letter of December 1852 about the 'modern situation in its true *blankness* and *barrenness*, and *unpoetrylessness*'.[65] Clough is trying to counter such attitudes not only in his poetry but also in his celebrated 1853 *North American Review* essay. Surveying Arnold's *Empedocles on Etna* and Alexander Smith's *A Life-Drama*, he asks of contemporary verse,

> Could it not attempt to convert into beauty and thankfulness, or at least into some form and shape, some feeling, at any rate, of content—the actual, palpable things with which our every-day life is concerned; introduce into business and weary task-work a character and a soul of purpose and reality; intimate to us relations which, in our unchosen, peremptorily-appointed posts, in our grievously narrow and limited spheres of action, we still, in and through all, retain to some central, celestial fact?[66]

Though Clough's questions betray the doubt which would become increasingly apparent in his later poetry, they also constitute a defence of his earlier achievements. For *The Bothie* is a poem built out of the

---

[65] *The Letters of Matthew Arnold to Arthur Hugh Clough*, ed. Howard Foster Lowry (Oxford: Clarendon Press, 1962), 126 (Battersea, 14 Dec. 1852).

[66] Clough, *Poems and Prose Remains*, i. 361.

'weary task-work' of the business of academic knowledge. Moreover, it is full of everyday events—postal deliveries, political arguments, flirtations, drudgery, and delight—giving to these a shape and a significance. It accomplishes what Arnold thought impossible. Though Clough sees Alexander Smith's poetry as having substantial faults, he is also excited by its efforts to deal with modernity. This leads him to make a striking speculation about the need for an up-to-date urban poetry, one attuned to that 'democratic revolution' of which he had spoken to his English students:

There are moods when one is prone to believe that, in these last days, no longer by 'clear spring or shady grove,' no more upon any Pindus or Parnassus, or by the side of any Castaly, are the true and lawful haunts of the poetic powers; but, we could believe it, if anywhere, in the blank and desolate streets, and upon the solitary bridges of the midnight city . . . there walks the discrowned Apollo, with unstrung lyre . . .[67]

While this is partly triggered by the rather lurid tone of Smith's poem, it is also an acute response to the Glaswegian's handling of modern urban material. When Smith perceives 'Another beauty' in contemporary Glasgow with its apocalyptic furnaces making the urban industrial landscape both 'Terror!' and 'Dream!' he anticipates the later *City of Dreadful Night* and the Eliotic 'Unreal City'.[68] Clough, though, is also concerned with championing his own earlier work against Arnold's poetics. For, while *The Bothie* is certainly, as its subtitle calls it, 'A Long-Vacation Pastoral', it also contains moments which come close to the later visions of Smith. The most striking of these is Philip's anxious dream about urban prostitutes:

Tell me then, why as I sleep amid hill tops high in the moorland,
Still in my dreams I am pacing the streets of the dissolute city,
Where dressy girls slithering-by upon pavements give sign for accosting,
Paint on their beautiless cheeks, and hunger and shame in their bosoms;
Hunger by drink and by that which they shudder yet burn for, appeasing,—
Hiding their shame—ah God, in the glare of the public gas lights? (IV. 174–9)

This is close in tone to the poetry of the Spasmodic School, and far from Matthew Arnold. It is a reminder that in reviewing Alexander Smith in 1853 Clough was again defending the modernity of his own work, in

[67] Ibid. 362–3.
[68] Alexander Smith, 'Glasgow' (1857), repr. in Hamish Whyte (ed.), *Noise and Smoky Breath* (Glasgow: Third Eye Centre and Glasgow District Libraries, 1983), 8.

which concerns with knowledge of various kinds are mixed, against the archaizing voice of Arnold.

Nowhere is that voice heard more clearly than in Arnold's poetic paean to the kind of learning he regarded as essential for the poet, 'The Scholar-Gipsy'. Like Clough, Arnold tries to fuse academic learning and primitive *nous*, but he does so with much more of a dying fall. However contrastingly accented, the poetic ideals of Arnold and Clough develop in the Victorian period that figuration of the modern poet which through Romanticism grew from the eighteenth century of Jerome Stones, Ossian, and Beattie's *Minstrel*. Professing Poetry and English Literature from their university chairs, these Victorian poets also furthered the institutionalization of the modern poet and of the poetic canon shaped by earlier 'acts of judgement'. Yet, for all their similarities, the two men were temperamentally different. Both left a legacy to the twentieth century, but where Clough's was at its best an inheritance of energy, Arnold's too readily shaded into a heritage of alluringly plangent nostalgia.

What lies behind Arnold's Scholar-Gypsy belongs once more to that concern with learning which was so central to the careers of both these two poet-professors. Significantly, Arnold's plans to write a poem about this emblematic individual date from around the time of the publication of Clough's *Bothie*. 'Thyrsis' suggests that the figure of the Scholar-Gypsy was important to both Clough and Arnold in their Oxford youth when he was, as Arnold put it, 'Our friend'.[69] The story of the Scholar-Gypsy comes from a book which Arnold purchased in 1844, Joseph Glanvill's 1661 *The Vanity of Dogmatizing*, whose subtitle pronounces it to be *A Discourse of the Shortness and Uncertainty of our Knowledge*. Glanvill's *Discourse* examines the grounds and limitations of knowledge, making it clear how hard it is to be sure what kinds are genuine or valuable. For one thing, as he puts it in his 'Preface',

We lay us down, to sleep away our diurnal cares; night shuts up the Senses windows, the mind contracts into the Brains *centre*. We *live* in *death*, and lye as in the *grave*... What is't then that prevents our Sensations; or if we do perceive, how is't, that we *know it not?* But we Dream, see Visions, converse with *Chimaera's*, the one half of our lives is a *Romance*, a fiction.[70]

[69] *The Poems of Matthew Arnold*, ed. Kenneth Allott, 2nd edn., ed. Miriam Allott (London: Longman, 1979), 355–6 and 540 ('Thyrsis', line 29).

[70] Joseph Glanvill, *The Vanity of Dogmatizing* (1661), repr. with introd. by Stephen Medcalf (Hove: Harvester, 1970), preface.

Glanvill's book is a critique of knowledge with a frequently sceptical tone; it was later revised by him under the title *Scepsis Scientifica* (1675). Glanvill's interest in 'The Disease of our *Intellectuals*' encourages Arnold's emphasis in 'The Scholar-Gipsy' on 'this strange disease of modern life'.[71] While, harking back to Plato, Glanvill sees 'the evil conduct of our *Imaginations*' as a source of frequent error, he is also suspicious of claims to knowledge that emanate from '*Pedantick Adoration*'.[72] He sympathizes with modes of knowing that may extend beyond those of official education systems. Nowhere is this seen more clearly than in his presentation of the account of the Scholar-Gypsy. Basing his summary of it on Glanvill's own words, Arnold supplies a version of this tale to accompany his poem:

There was very lately a lad in the University at Oxford, who was by his poverty forced to leave his studies there; and at last to join himself to a company of vagabond gipsies. Among these extravagant people, by the insinuating subtilty of his carriage, he quickly got so much of their love and esteem as that they discovered to him their mystery. After he had been a pretty while well exercised in the trade, there chanced to ride by a couple of scholars, who had formerly been of his acquaintance. They quickly spied out their old friend among the gipsies; and he gave them an account of the necessity which drove him to that kind of life, and told them that the people he went with were not such impostors as they had been taken for, but that they had a traditional kind of learning among them, and could do wonders by the power of imagination, their fancy binding that of others: that he himself had learned much of their art, and when he had compassed the whole secret, he intended, he said, to leave their company, and give the world an account of what he had learned.[73]

Like Philip in *The Bothie*, the Scholar-Gypsy represents a poetic combination of academic and non-academic, more primitive, even scandalous knowledge. Though gypsy-like travellers had been an object of fascination for Wordsworth, among Arnold's circle there was still an awareness of the gypsy as connected with the sinister or forbidden. When J. C. Shairp won Oxford's Newdigate Prize for poetry in 1842, William Knight, a close friend of Shairp and Walrond, recalled that Shairp's entry 'was justly regarded as the poem of the most original power which had appeared since Stanley's *Gipsies*'.[74] This 1837 poem whose impact was still recalled among Arnold's circle was by a celebrated predecessor

[71]   Ibid. 62; *Poems of Matthew Arnold*, 366.
[72]   Glanvill, *The Vanity of Dogmatizing*, 95, 136.   [73]   *Poems of Matthew Arnold*, 357.
[74]   Knight, *Principal Shairp*, 39.

of Arnold at Rugby and Balliol in the 1830s, Clough's friend Arthur Penrhyn Stanley. Entering for the Newdigate in 1843, Arnold would certainly have known it. Opening with its 'Fond dreamer' in a 'quiet lane' among 'wild hawthorn bowers', 'rose-clad cottages', and 'flowery ground', Stanley's sylvan poem is set in a pastoral English landscape similar to those of 'The Scholar-Gipsy' and 'Thyrsis'. Yet Stanley's gypsies with their 'savage court' are threateningly unEnglish. They are at once 'Children of Nature' linked to 'ethereal freshness' and cursed 'Children of the night' doomed to wander the modern world as a penance for ancient sin, 'In lonely woe, themselves without a home!' Their name links them to ancient Egypt with its 'wisdom' and 'priestly lore', but these have now degenerated.[75] Arnold's later poem 'The Scholar-Gipsy' picks up this theme of endless wandering, while using Glanvill's story to play up the aspect of the gypsies' secret wisdom. For Arnold the Scholar-Gypsy is a figure who combines academic and other forms of knowledge. The poem opens in the luxuriantly attractive August countryside outside Oxford where Arnold, Clough, Walrond, Tom Arnold, and sometimes Sellar or other friends and acquaintances walked together in the 1840s:

> . . . near me on the grass lies Glanvil's book—
> Come, let me read the oft-read tale again!
> The story of the Oxford scholar poor,
> Of pregnant parts and quick inventive brain,
> Who, tired of knocking at preferment's door,
> One summer-morn forsook
> His friends and went to learn the gipsy-lore,
> And roamed the world with that wild brotherhood,
> And came, as most men deemed, to little good,
> But came to Oxford and his friends no more.[76]

This wanderer renounces academia, yet takes with him (as the poem's title reminds us) his scholarship, adding to it the wilder 'gipsy-lore', what Glanvill had called the gypsies' 'traditional kind of learning.' When the runaway scholar meets two other Oxford students, he tells them that

> the gipsy-crew,
> His mates, had arts to rule as they desired
> The workings of men's brains,

---

[75] *Letters and Verses of Arthur Penrhyn Stanley, D.D.*, ed. Rowland E. Prothero (London: John Murray, 1895), 29–38. [76] *Poems of Matthew Arnold*, 359.

And they can bind them to what thoughts they will.
'And I,' he said, 'the secret of their art,
When fully learned, will to the world impart;
But it needs heaven-sent moments for this skill.'[77]

The Scholar-Gypsy is not explicitly presented as a poet, but as Arnold's headnote points out, his special skill involves 'the power of imagination'. He surely functions as an ideal for Arnold, the former Scholar of Balliol, who is now attempting to influence an audience by his own imaginative-scholarly productions. The Scholar-Gypsy never fully reappears in the poem. Instead, he is glimpsed fleetingly as he 'haunt[s]' the countryside around Oxford, visiting such sites as Bagley Wood, where Arnold, Clough, and their circle had walked and which was a gypsy campsite.[78] The work ends with an exclamatory and regretful realization that, as the speaker puts it, 'I dream!' The Scholar-Gypsy has been 'gone' for centuries, and 'grave Glanvil' whose volume underpins this bookish poem, wrote his account 200 years earlier. No sooner is this asserted than a note of determined denial is sounded '—No, no, thou hast not felt the lapse of hours!' The concluding lines inveigh against the 'repeated shocks' which 'Exhaust the energy of strongest souls', and beyond which the Scholar-Gypsy still in some sense appears to exist.[79] We are left with the sense of a poetic ideal, fusing different kinds of knowledge, yet one beyond attainment in this world.

It is on to this Scholar-Gypsy that Arnold grafts the author of *The Bothie*. Arnold's 1866 poem 'Thyrsis' is subtitled 'A Monody, *to commemorate the author's friend* Arthur Hugh Clough, *who died at Florence*, 1861'. In 1867 Arnold points out how 'Throughout this Poem there is reference to another piece, *The Scholar-Gipsy*' and the stanza form repeats that of the earlier work.[80] Aware of his own precursor poem, Arnold also seems haunted by Clough's *Bothie*, that 'Long-vacation Pastoral', since it is as a pastoral figure, the Theocritan 'Thyrsis', that he memorializes Clough. Yet instead of siding with Clough's attempt to break out of Oxonian academe and combine scholarly with other knowledge, Arnold's poem is enraptured by 'that sweet city with her dreaming spires'. Clough, who was 'irked...to be here' in the Oxford countryside is judged a 'Too quick despairer'. However, the sight of a tree associated with the Scholar-Gypsy recalls that earlier ideal, and Arnold, contrasting himself

[77] *Poems of Matthew Arnold*, 359.   [78] Ibid. 360, 362.
[79] Ibid. 363.   [80] Ibid. 538.

with Clough, pledges himself to it afresh. He hymns his fleeting Scholar-
Gypsy who 'by his own heart inspired' seeks 'A fugitive and gracious
light' that is removed from 'the world's market'. Having just separated
himself from the subject of this elegiac poem, Arnold goes on to co-opt
Clough as a fellow Scholar-Gypsy: 'Thou too, O Thyrsis, on like quest
wast bound.' He regrets that his friend's 'rustic flute | Kept not for long
its happy, country tone'. The poem concludes with Arnold putting
words into Clough's mouth, making his dead companion the guarantor
of Arnold's faith in the Scholar-Gypsy as a rural spirit of imaginative
faith:

> Too rare, too rare, grow now my visits here!
>   'Mid city noise, not, as with thee of yore,
>   Thyrsis! in reach of sheep-bells is my home.
>   —Then through the great town's harsh, heart-wearying roar,
>   Let in thy voice a whisper often come,
>   To chase fatigue and fear:
> *Why faintest thou? I wandered till I died.*
> *Roam on! The light we sought is shining still.*
> *Dost thou ask proof? Our tree yet crowns the hill,*
> *Our Scholar travels yet the loved hill-side.*[81]

Arnold's poem is beautiful not least in the way in which it continues to
argue with his friend. It also takes the unfair step of posthumously
recruiting him to Arnold's own cause. For to hear in the music of
Clough's 'Long-Vacation Pastoral' simply the 'country tone' of a 'rustic
flute' is to distort that work hugely. *The Bothie* is sunny, yet agitated; it is a
poem of knowledge and modernity, highly alert to democratic, sexual,
and intellectual pressures that Arnold's poem attempts to suppress and
oppose. For all its reliance on Homeric scholarship and techniques, the
energetic up-to-dateness of *The Bothie* removes it from Arnold's own
classicizings. Philip may be Homeric and Theocritan, but he wears
spiritedly Victorian dress. Arnold's heroes too often sport an archaizing
and dubious toga. 'Thyrsis' remakes Clough in their mould. The
poet Philip Hewson blended knowledges in a much more modern,
here-and-now, practical, and democratic way than either the wispy
scholar-gypsy or the even more etherealized Thyrsis in whose voice all
the energy of Clough's is reduced to a '*whisper*'. The relationship
between Clough and Arnold was a quarrelsome one, and in trying to

---

[81] Ibid. 548–50.

hush that quarrel Arnold continues it in ways that have been damaging for Clough's reputation.

Certainly Clough's later poetry shows increasing 'despair' as it develops many of the techniques first essayed in *The Bothie*; but in that poem of knowledge we see a much more vigorous fusion of scholarship and imagination, academic and other forms of learning than Arnold's more wraithlike attempts would suggest. Surely this is why Shairp, in the opening words of his elegy for Clough, takes strong issue with Arnold's portrayal:

> No Thyrsis thou, for old Idyllic lays,
>> But a broad-browed, deep-souled, much suffering man,
> Within whose veins, thrilled by these latter days,
>> The ruddy lifeblood ran.[82]

Shairp is not as good a poet as Arnold, but in his resistance to the Theocritizing of Clough, and his insistence on strong intellect ('broad-browed') coupled with physical excitement quickened by modernity, he shows a critical honesty towards qualities of Clough's creative power that Arnold wished simply to airbrush away. Rather than accepting Arnoldian notions of a rarefied Clough or modern conceptions of him which pay little or no attention to his first major work, we should see *The Bothie* for what it is. This excited and exciting knowledge-poem presents the figure of the modern poet as drawing on yet outflanking the merely academic in ways that parallel and anticipate but also surpass in energy the emblematic figure of the Scholar-Gypsy.

Though Clough, not Arnold, offered a more promising model for the modern poet in a world of rapidly proliferating modes of knowledge, it was Arnold's which became the dominant voice. Professor Clough had urged his London students of English Literature to be alert to the need for a contemporary idiom, pointing out to them that 'We have had a good deal of new experience, both in study and in action—new books and new events have come before us. But we have not yet in England, I imagine, had any one to give us a manner suitable for our new matter.'[83] Clough admired the way Dryden had made available to his own time a language for modernity, and Clough's lectures (though they deny that the new developments of Victorian England have found

---

[82] Shairp's elegy is quoted in Knight, *Principal Shairp*, 89.
[83] Clough, *Poems and Prose Remains*, i. 332.

their poetic voice) hint at what he wanted for his own poetry. Only fragments of these lectures, however, found their way into print. Professor Arnold's public pronouncements were better known, and far more widely published. Yet increasingly he sought in academia an escape, rather than the launch-site it had been for Clough's poet Philip in *The Bothie*. Contemporary with the composition of 'Thyrsis' is Arnold's preface to the first series of his *Essays in Criticism* with its praise of Oxford as 'home of lost causes'.[84] What Arnold is doing in his influential writing of this period reverses Clough's achievements in his finest early poetry. For if in *The Bothie* Oxford was taken to the Highlands in a way that amplified and revivified academic knowledge, projecting the two to a New Zealand of the future in the persons of the poet Philip Hewson and his bride, then in the 1860s Arnold brought Celtic culture to Oxford in such a way that a sense of loss permeated both. The result was not a development of that poetry of knowledge incipient in the Ossianic texts but rather a melancholy anti-modernity out of which grew the later nineteenth century Celtic Twilight and a view of academia as refuge.

Though published separately, the contents of Arnold's 1867 volume *On the Study of Celtic Literature* were delivered as part of his lectures when he was Oxford's Professor of Poetry between 1857 and 1867. As the only major poet to hold the chair in the nineteenth century, Arnold was able to develop it as a vehicle for his own poetics in addition to his ideas on literature and society. In some senses, his occupation of the professorship did for nineteenth-century Oxford what Blair's holding his Chair of Belles-Lettres had done for Edinburgh in the century preceding. Certainly if Blair can be seen as one of the founders of the worldwide university study of English literary texts, then Arnold's time in the Chair of Poetry marks the belated start of the pressure for English literary studies in Oxford. True, many of Arnold's addresses dealt with classical literature; it may be characteristic of his mind, a significantly different intellect from that of Clough, that his lecture 'On the Modern Element in Literature' deals entirely with classical texts. Yet Arnold also considered recent writing, including Clough's, and it is clear that, just like his friend, he was using the platform of his academic chair to expound his poetics. Two of the leading English poets of their generation, Clough and Arnold were appointed to influential literary

[84] Matthew Arnold, *Essays in Criticism, First Series* (1865; repr. London: Dent, 1964), 6.

professorships in the same decade. Though neither occupied his chair for a lengthy period, each combined his tenure with the writing of his own poetry and the presentation of his poetics. In so doing, they set a pattern which later poets would adopt or adapt. Together, though in significantly different ways, they played a key part in the evolution of the modern poet.

Arnold's *On the Study of Celtic Literature* (1867) is contemporary with 'Thyrsis' (1866), with Arnold's most famous descriptions of Oxford in that poem and in the preface to the first series of *Essays in Criticism* (1865), and with the publication of 'Dover Beach' (1867). When we align these texts we can see how far Arnold in this time was considering the kinds of cultural pattern set up by Clough in *The Bothie*. That work (part of whose action takes place near Loch Ossian) was set in a Homeric Highlands, the most convincing such since Ossian. Clough's poetic northern landscape was academicized not by being linked with the learning of Enlightenment Aberdeen or Edinburgh, but by being married to that of Oxford. Arnold essays a similar connection. He had been reading James Macpherson's work in 1865. His Oxford addresses on Celtic literature begin with an epigraph misquoted from Ossian, '*They went forth to the war, but they always fell.*'[85] While Arnold's lectures deal more with Welsh literature than Scottish, it is what he regards as this Ossianic spirit which pervades his view of those peoples and literatures which he designates 'Celtic'. The work from which his epigraph is taken, Duan Second of 'Cath-Loda', is typically Ossianic in being an account of heroic warfare set in a 'grassy...mossy...rocky' upland environment of 'mist', 'streams', 'Bards', 'the darkened moon', and 'clouds of hail', where 'The traveller sees...thro' the twilight, from his lonely path...the ghosts of the aged.' Here between 'streamy hill' and 'silent vale', by 'rolling ocean' under 'heaven's bow in showers', are Romantic landscape and moodiness in concentrated form.[86] The professor-poet Arnold turns a blind eye to all the scholarly apparatus which was part of the Ossianic texts. Yet it is surely as a classicist with particular interests in Homer that he comes to Ossian, and he does see Ossian as an essential foundation for the Romantic imagination of which his own work forms a belated part. Claiming that 'the sense

---

[85] Matthew Arnold, *Lectures and Essays in Criticism*, ed. R. H. Super (Michigan: Ann Arbor, 1962), 291 and 498.

[86] *The Poems of Ossian and Related Works*, ed. H. Gaskill (Edinburgh: Edinburgh University Press, 1996), 313–15.

for style which modern English poetry shows' may plausibly be derived 'from a root of the poetical Celtic nature in us', Arnold continues,

Its chord of penetrating passion and melancholy, again, its *Titanism* as we see it in Byron,—what other European poetry possesses that like the English, and where do we get it from? . . . A famous book, Macpherson's *Ossian*, carried in the last century this vein like a flood of lava through Europe. I am not going to criticise Macpherson's *Ossian* here. Make the part of what is forged, modern, tawdry, spurious, in the book, as large as you please; strip Scotland, if you like, of every feather of borrowed plumes which on the strength of Macpherson's *Ossian* she may have stolen from that *vetus et major Scotia*, the true home of the Ossianic poetry, Ireland; I make no objection. But there will still be left in the book a residue with the very soul of the Celtic genius in it, and which has the proud distinction of having brought this soul of the Celtic genius into contact with the genius of the nations of modern Europe, and enriched all our poetry by it. Woody Morven, and echoing Lora, and Selma with its silent halls!—we all owe them a debt of gratitude, and when we are unjust enough to forget it, may the Muse forget us![87]

Seeing Ossian as essential to the spirit of English poetic inspiration, Arnold goes on to quote a passage from Macpherson's 'Carthon' about the desolate walls of Balclutha and to show how the Ossianic poems and a Celtic note made its impact on 'All Europe' from Goethe to Napoleon to Byron.[88] His perception is both acute and courageous, at a time when English prejudice against Ossian and things Celtic was strong (a fact demonstrated not least by hostile reactions to Arnold's lectures on the Celtic).[89] However, Arnold is also using his view of Ossian to produce a picture of Celtic culture which would be influential, fruitful, and op-pressive. He sees it as characterized by 'the eternal softness and mild light of the west' in such places as 'Wales, where the past still lives', though the Celtic languages are 'going in Brittany and the Scotch High-lands'.[90] The Celts are 'lively', showing 'something of the Greek in them, something spiritual, something humane' which removes them from 'the outward and visible world of material life' and gives them special access to 'the inward world of thought and science' (Arnold appears to be using the word 'science' in its classical sense to mean 'knowledge').[91]

---

[87] Arnold, *Lectures and Essays*, 370–1.   [88] Ibid. 371–3.

[89] See Carl Dawson and John Pfordresher (eds.), *Matthew Arnold, Prose Writings: The Critical Heritage* (London: Routledge & Kegan Paul, 1979), 153–70.

[90] Arnold, *Lectures and Essays*, 291, 293.   [91] Ibid. 295, 296, 298.

Though calling himself 'an unlearned belletristic trifler', Arnold uses the authority of his Oxford chair to develop a view of Celtic literature which is he claims 'disinterested' in its portrayal of the Celt as representing a kind of endlessly deferred note of extinction:

And as in material civilisation he has been ineffectual, so has the Celt been ineffectual in politics. This colossus, impetuous, adventurous wanderer, the Titan of the early world, who in primitive times fills so large a place on earth's scene, dwindles and dwindles as history goes on, and at last is shrunk to what we now see him. For ages and ages the world has been constantly slipping, ever more and more, out of the Celt's grasp. 'They went forth to the war,' Ossian says most truly, '*but they always fell.*'[92]

Arnold's paeans to Oxford should be seen in this context. For if the 'beauty, charm, and spirituality' of the Celt were also bound up gloriously with 'ineffectualness', then it is just such a combination which he sees as characterizing Oxford. This pairing permeates the Oxford of the 'dreaming spires' in 'Thyrsis', as it does that of the 'Preface' to the first series of *Essays in Criticism*, or of the opening section of *Culture and Anarchy*—all pieces of writing contemporary with the lectures on Celtic literature. *Culture and Anarchy*, in whose 1869 'Preface' Arnold quoted Ossian to describe modern Eton, has as its first part the celebrated 'Sweetness and Light', delivered after the Celtic literature lectures as the culmination of Arnold's Poetry Professorship. Here he presented an Ossianic vision of Oxford whose

sentiment against hideousness and rawness, has been at the bottom of our attachment of so many beaten causes, of our opposition to so many triumphant movements. And the sentiment is true, and has never been wholly defeated, and has shown its power even in its defeat. We have not won our political battles, we have not carried our main points, we have not stopped our adversaries' advance, we have not marched victoriously with the modern world; but we have told silently upon the mind of the country, we have prepared currents of feeling which sap our adversaries' position when it seems gained, we have kept up our own communications with the future.[93]

Arnold's Oxford, continually on the losing side, yet making possible the chance of spiritual victory, is at one with those Ossianic strugglers who 'went forth to the war, but they always fell'. As he had done with Celtic

---

[92]   Arnold, *Lectures and Essays*, 305, 328, 346.
[93]   Matthew Arnold, *Culture and Anarchy*, ed. John Dover Wilson (Cambridge: Cambridge University Press, 1966), 9 and 61–2.

literature, so with Oxford, Arnold celebrates its role among the defeated in modern civilization, but also holds open the possibility of spiritual triumph. If a Celtic *numen* is seen as underpinning the English literary imagination, then so an Oxonian spirit may bring 'sweetness and light' to vulgar modernity making possible a kind of ethereal victory in the midst of actual defeat. This is the same phenomenon which Arnold had celebrated in 'The Scholar-Gipsy' and 'Thyrsis'. However, sentimental and moonlit Oxford is also, like the pathos-clouded, lunar poetry of Ossian, essentially of the romantic and feminized past as it fuses the learned and the barbarous:

Beautiful city! so venerable, so lovely, so unravaged by the fierce intellectual life of our century, so serene!

There are our young barbarians, all at play!

And yet, steeped in sentiment as she lies, spreading her gardens to the moonlight, and whispering from her towers the last enchantments of the Middle Ages, who will deny that Oxford, by her ineffable charm, keeps ever calling us nearer to the true goal of all of us, to the ideal, to perfection,—to beauty, in a word, which is only truth seen from another side?—nearer, perhaps, than all the science of Tübingen. Adorable dreamer, whose heart has been so romantic! who hast given thyself so prodigally, given thyself to sides and to heroes not mine, only never to the Philistines! home of lost causes, and forsaken beliefs, and unpopular names, and impossible loyalties![94]

Such a realm is an appropriate location for Arnold's Celtic spirit. He places the essential academic home of his own poetry of knowledge in an Oxford which is exiled in dreams, a 'queen of romance' whose mission is to rescue the planet from 'DAS GEMEINE' (the commonplace).[95] He cannot connect his labours in the modern world of education in London and throughout England (where he worked as a Schools Inspector) with the Oxford which he associates with poetry as well as with the highest forms of academic endeavour. So, as he becomes more and more of a social critic, writer on universities, and on educational or cultural matters, Arnold leaves poetry behind. Ironically, the words 'spire' and 'Dream' are brought together in those lines about industrial Glasgow by Clough's admired Alexander Smith.[96] When Arnold praises Oxford's 'dreaming spires' it is because they offer an otherworld to that of contemporary life.

---

[94] Arnold, *Essays in Criticism*, 6.   [95] Ibid. 7.

[96] Smith, 'Glasgow' (1857), in Whyte (ed.), *Noise and Smoky Breath*, 8.

In his paean, Arnold produces an ideal paralleling that of the 'ivory tower'. Such a structure was described by his admired French master, Sainte-Beuve, whom Arnold regarded as 'the most notable critic of our time' and whom he had visited in Paris most recently in 1866. Sainte-Beuve had written of the poet Alfred de Vigny as 'plus secret, | Comme en sa tour d'ivoire' ('more secret | As in his ivory tower').[97] Widely used in mid-nineteenth-century France, the phrase 'ivory tower' does not seem to have entered English until around the turn of the century. Since then it has been used of both poets and academics.[98] In France it remained associated with poets, featuring for instance in Paul Valéry's essay 'Existence du Symbolisme' which concludes, 'Jamais plus haute n'a paru la Tour d'ivoire' ('The Ivory Tower has never seemed higher').[99] While French Symbolism would influence the development of modernist poetry in English, it was the ivory towers of academe in which the great modernist poetry of knowledge would find its most nourishing soil. That the making as well as the reception of contemporary poetry should more and more be bound up with the universities was part of the legacy of the poet-professors Clough and Arnold. But the increasingly self-conscious modernists' task would be to find a way of fusing academic learning with other kinds of knowledge and with the concerns of a wider society without betraying their intellectual allegiances. In this, though they had no wish to confess it, they would follow at least as much the pattern of the young Clough as that of the more formidable Victorian sage Arnold.

If academia was crucial to the careers of those modern poets Clough and Arnold, it was comparatively tangential to their great contemporaries Tennyson and Browning. Yet the angle of the tangent is revealing. Browning, more learned a poet than most of his contemporaries, and one who 'spent a lifetime turning encyclopaedias into poetry', was wary of campus culture.[100] Despite the quasi-academic filiations of his verse—his early hero Paracelsus wants nothing less than comprehen-

---

[97] Matthew Arnold, *The Last Word*, ed. R. H. Super (Ann Arbor: University of Michigan Press, 1977), 106 and 413; Charles-Augustine Sainte-Beuve, *Poésies complètes* (Paris: Charpentier, 1845), 374 ('A M. Villemain').

[98] *OED Supplement*; Ivor Evans, *Brewer's Dictionary of Phrase and Fable*, 2nd rev. edn. (London: Cassell, 1981), 599.

[99] Paul Valéry, *Œuvres*, ed. Jean Hytier, 2 vols. (Paris: Gallimard, 1957), i. 707 ('Existence du Symbolisme').

[100] William Irvine and Park Honan, *The Book, the Ring, and the Poet* (London: The Bodley Head, 1974), 6–7.

sively 'to KNOW'—Browning had dropped out of University College London after only a few months as a student.[101] Albeit obliquely, his view of academic life may be summed up in 'A Grammarian's Funeral'. In that poem the scholar sees 'the bard and sage' as linked since both have 'most studied man'. Yet the grammarian is also presented as 'bald', with 'eyes like lead', and is eventually dismissed as someone who 'Gave us the doctrine of the enclitic *De*, | Dead from the waist down'.[102] Browning is on the attack, though these lines themselves are bound to beckon academic footnoters ready to assist an audience whose biblio-holic poet recognizes (or at least relishes the phrase) 'the enclitic *De*'. The grammarian, lifeless long before his funeral, both fascinates and repels this learned poet. Browning's attitude towards scholars would be repeated at times by Yeats and Pound. Admiring Burns, Byron, and the Shelley whom Oxford had expelled, Browning loved vivacity and dash. Yet, almost despite himself, his career hints at the way academia and poetry were converging.

Browning was gladdened to have his often obscurely learned books devoured by students at Oxford and Cambridge. Though the offer was withdrawn, he was approached to become a candidate for the Oxford Chair of Poetry when it was vacated by Arnold. The thought of writing lectures made him anxious—he would later turn down an invitation to take up a professorship at Johns Hopkins—yet he was excited enough to be given an honorary Oxford MA and to be elected 'Honorary Fellow of Balliol!!!'[103] Not long after, in 1881, the Victorian educationalist Dr Frederick Furnivall founded the Browning Society to aid 'the Browning student' in reading '*the* most thought-full' living poet.[104] Like it or not, Browning was being positioned in the academic arena. Meeting, ironic-ally enough, at University College London, 300 adherents of the early Browning Society saw their association burgeon, with branches being set up throughout Britain and America. The poet chatted with admiring Oxbridge dons and students, lauded as a 'thinker and philosopher'; all this was meat and drink to the *Journal of Education*.[105] Only two years after Browning's death he was the subject of literature lectures given

---

[101] Robert Browning, *The Poems*, ed. John Pettigrew, supplemented and completed by Thomas J. Collins, 2 vols. (Harmondsworth: Penguin, 1981), i. 44 (*Paracelsus*, I, line 282).

[102] Ibid. 733.

[103] Irvine and Honan, *The Book, the Ring*, 411 and 418; D. G. Myers, *The Elephants Teach* (Englewood Cliffs, NJ: Prentice Hall, 1996), 22.

[104] Irvine and Honan, *The Book, the Ring*, 500–1.   [105] Ibid. 502.

as part of the curriculum at St Andrews University by Professor
Henry Jones, author of the monograph *Browning as a Philosophical and
Religious Teacher* (1891).[106] Several decades earlier, Balliol's Benjamin
Jowett had warmed to Browning not just as a poet of 'great ability and
knowledge' but also as one who, rather to Jowett's astonishment,
was 'perfectly sensible'.[107] Browning may have been on his best
behaviour, but his conduct encouraged academia's overtures to living
poets. In love with the verb 'to KNOW', he was exactly the right poet for
the Master of Balliol, of whom that college's Victorian undergraduates
joked,

> First come I. My name is J-W-TT.
> There's no knowledge but I know it.
> I am Master of this College,
> What I don't know isn't knowledge.[108]

For Browning, popularity came relatively late in his career. As a poet
of knowledge, so fond of recondite words and themes, he appealed to the
academic mind-set. University employees promoted his work. Alfred,
Lord Tennyson, had been a Cambridge undergraduate, but as Poet
Laureate was able to rely on both royal patronage and huge popular
sales, rather than appearing dependent on students or professors. Politely, the Laureate accepted Jowett's suggestions for poetic themes; he
became the first living author to have his marble bust purchased for
display among the pantheon in Trinity College Library, Cambridge.
Having made clear his interest in the topic of education in *The Princess*,
which deals with a college for ladies, Tennyson gave over the best parts
of that work to those beautiful erotic lyrics which fly completely free of
worthiness: 'Now slides the silent meteor on, and leaves | A shining
furrow, as thy thoughts in me.'[109] A shy man, Tennyson four times
declined the award of an honorary degree from his *alma mater*. Philip
Larkin enjoyed telling a story which illustrates Tennyson's wariness
towards the academy. According to Larkin, on a visit to Balliol the
Victorian poet read an unpublished poem to the Master. When he had
finished, Jowett said, ' "I shouldn't publish that if I were you, Tennyson." Tennyson replied, "If it comes to that, Master, the sherry you gave

---

[106] See Robert Crawford (ed.), *Launch-Site for English Studies* (St Andrews: Verse, 1997), 72.
[107] Irvine and Honan, *The Book, the Ring*, 411.
[108] From *The Masque of B-ll-l* (1881), repr. in Jan Morris (ed.), *The Oxford Book of Oxford*
(Oxford: Oxford University Press, 1978), 315.
[109] *The Poems of Tennyson*, ed. Christopher Ricks (London: Longmans, 1969), 835.

us at lunch was downright filthy." '[110] Tennyson made a lot of money from his work, and did not need professorial patronage. At the same time, though, he acted as sponsor to the anthology produced by that great Victorian educationalist F. T. Palgrave, and eventually accepted an honorary fellowship of Trinity College, Cambridge.[111] Balliol got Browning, Trinity got Tennyson. Their fellowships indicate that the greatest Victorian poets and the elite English educational institutions were on terms of polite acquaintance, often reinforced by personal friendships. Unlike Arnold and Clough, however, neither Tennyson nor Browning gave lecture courses or taught classes. They remained uncorrupted by what Browning in *Paracelsus* (drawing, it has been argued, on his experiences at University College London) called the 'dry wells' of 'pedants'.[112] Yet the fact that Browning wrote those words in his knowledge-obsessed poem indicates that if not all poets were attuned to academic practice, then certainly academia was a topic with which they had to engage.

Browning's style and some of his poetic attitudes helped set the tone for modernist poets such as Pound and Eliot. In their linking of an interest in the primitive with a love of arcane learning, these modern poets were the heirs of Clough and Arnold. Yet there is also a sense in which Arnold's Celticism passed not to those High Modernists, but to the Celtic Twilight movement in Ireland, Scotland, and elsewhere, whose greatest exponent was William Butler Yeats. He, it might be claimed, was the last and greatest of the scholar-gypsies, though one particularly suspicious of academia. Before examining some achievements of twentieth-century modernism in the following chapter, it seems appropriate to conclude this one by looking at aspects of a poet who would find much strange lore in his own tower, built not of ivory but of Irish stone.

The young Yeats, albeit warily, followed in some of Matthew Arnold's footsteps. He even went to Oxford, but not as a student, and always felt something of an outsider in the place. As a mature writer he enjoyed staring at the Japanese Noh masks in the Pitt Rivers Museum.[113] When younger he had a taste for stravaiging the countryside:

[110] Philip Larkin, *Required Writing* (London: Faber & Faber, 1983), 59.

[111] Biographical details about Tennyson are taken from Robert Bernard Martin, *Tennyson* (Oxford: Oxford University Press with Faber & Faber, 1980), 424, 435–6, 467, 578.

[112] Browning, *The Poems*, i. 51 and 45 (*Paracelsus*, I, lines 581 and 357).

[113] I remember being told this by a curator in the 1980s.

This is a most beautiful country, about here—I walked sixteen miles on Sunday—going to the places in Matthew Arnolds poems—the ford in 'the Scholour Gipsey' being the furthest away & most interesting. How very unlike Ireland the whole place is—like a foreign land (as it is).[114]

In Oxfordshire the 24-year-old Yeats feels very alien. The Irish poet who had not gone to university has a little joke about the undergraduates, who may have 'scared' the local people into good behaviour.[115] All this may make it seem strange that he should be following in 1889 the trail of 'Thyrsis' and 'The Scholar-Gipsy', yet it was very much as a gypsy-scholar that Yeats began and developed his career. His first books included not only collections of his own poetry but also in 1893 would-be scholarly editions of William Blake. Yeats's learning was often dodgy (he claimed Blake's father was Irish).[116] Where Arnold's scholar had run off to find the secret knowledge of the gypsies, Yeats was interested in occult wisdom. Like Arnold, he attempted at a crucial point in his development to become a Professor of Poetry. Yeats went on to maintain throughout his career a precarious balance between mainstream and esoteric learning. To find him following in the footsteps of Professor Arnold and his Scholar-Gypsy is not as absurd as it seems.

Yeats's earliest Celticism is Ossianic and Arnoldian in tone. His first long poem, *The Wanderings of Oisin* (1889), draws substantially on the *Transactions of the Ossianic Society*.[117] Founded on St Patrick's Day, 1853, the Society was patriotically Irish and sought to preserve and publish the manuscripts of the Fionn cycle.[118] However, as its very title suggests, it was a reaction to Scottish Ossianic endeavours. Yeats was pleased when in 1889 Arthur Griffen wrote to him about the newly published *The Wanderings of Oisin*, saying that 'his father who knows well the old legends says my "Oisin" gave him a better idea of the mingled nobility and savagery of the ancient heroes than MacPherson's "Ossian"'.[119] Yeats's early Ossianic tone and interests are part of the movement now designated the Celtic Twilight. That label covers a number of late

---

[114] *The Collected Letters of W. B. Yeats*, i: *1865–1895*, ed. John Kelly and Eric Domville (Oxford: Clarendon Press, 1986), 181 (to Katharine Tynan, Oxford, [14 Aug. 1889]).

[115] Ibid.

[116] *Poems of William Blake*, ed. W. B. Yeats (London: Lawrence & Bullen, 1893), p. xv.

[117] Yeats, *Collected Letters*, i. 176 n. 2.

[118] Robert Welsh (ed.), *The Oxford Companion to Irish Literature* (Oxford: Clarendon Press, 1996), 458.

[119] Yeats, *Collected Letters*, i. 141 (to Katharine Tynan, Chiswick, 6 Feb. [1889]).

nineteenth-century Irish and Scottish writers, including William Sharp
('Fiona Macleod') and Elizabeth A. Sharp, editor of *Lyra Celtica: An
Anthology of Representative Celtic Poetry* (1896). This important anthology
features several poets who might be designated scholar-gypsies, and
who, alert to an inheritance from the two preceding centuries, continued
the development of the modern poet at the start of the twentieth
century. As well as work by Macpherson's Ossian himself, *Lyra Celtica*
includes poetry by Arnold's confederate J. C. Shairp, Yeats's friend
Katharine Tynan (to whom he wrote of Arnold's Scholar-Gypsy), Fiona
Macleod, and Yeats; it also contains verse by Bliss Carman, Villiers de
l'Isle-Adam, and the poet-professor Arthur Quiller-Couch. These in-
clusions signal something of the ambition of what Yeats, writing on
Fiona Macleod in 1898, called 'Le Mouvement Celtique'.[120] *Lyra Celtica*
was published in Edinburgh by John Grant during the year which
marked the centenary of James Macpherson's death. 1896 also saw
the publication by the proto-modernist Edinburgh polymath Patrick
Geddes of a new edition of Macpherson's *Poems of Ossian*. Its
preface was by William Sharp who, in the same year, championed Yeats
in the introduction to *Lyra Celtica*, assuring readers that 'no one is
more essentially Celtic'.[121] Nurturing post-Ossianic Celticism in
Scotland and Ireland, Sharp and Yeats were modern poets operating
cannily in the wake of the celebrated author of *On the Study of Celtic
Literature*.

Born in the Scottish Lowland industrial town of Paisley, but becoming 'Fiona Macleod' (the first name Ossianic, the second clearly Highland), William Sharp regendered himself as Matthew Arnold's feminized
Celt. Sharp was the contemporary Scottish writer in whom the young
Yeats was most interested. The Irishman reviewed several of Sharp's
1890s volumes, corresponded with their author, and met with him to
discuss the occult. Sharp was keen on Gaelic lore, the faery, and the
gypsy; his book *The Gypsy Christ* was published in America in 1895. He
was a poet, though Yeats preferred his prose.[122] Some of the most
interesting of this prose was treated by reviewers as prose poetry,

[120] *Uncollected Prose by W. B. Yeats*, vol. ii. ed. John Frayne and Colton Johnson (London:
Macmillan, 1975), 108.
[121] *The Poems of Ossian*, trans. James Macpherson, with notes, and with introd. by William
Sharp (Edinburgh: Patrick Geddes & Colleagues, 1896); Elizabeth A. Sharp (ed.), *Lyra Celtica*,
pp. xliv–xlvii ('Introduction' by William Sharp) and 427 ('Notes' by William Sharp).
[122] Elizabeth A. Sharp, *William Sharp (Fiona Macleod)* (London: Heinemann, 1910), 335.

though Sharp was wary of the term.[123] What his short 'prose rhythms' do is combine the diction of the Celtic Twilight with the Ossianic fragment form to produce brief paragraphs of cadenced prose. These are often over-jewelled. Sharp makes clear an awareness of Turgenev, Baudelaire, and of Whitman's 'free verse', but a much more manifest ancestor is the Macpherson of the *Fragments* and other Ossianic works.[124] As Macpherson's prose fragments crystallized the emergent voice of European Romanticism, so Sharp's 'prose rhythms' carry an Ossianic legacy as they encapsulate the notes of the international Celtic Twilight movement of which Yeats was a part:

THE TWILIT WATERS

Upon the dim seas in the twilight I hear the tide forging slowly through the still waters. There is not a sound else: neither the scream of a sea-mew, nor the harsh cry of the heron, nor the idle song of the wind: only the steadfast forging of the tide through the still waters of the twilit seas. O steadfast onward tide, O gloaming-hidden palpitating seas![125]

Though he made much of his intuitive knowledge of Gaelic lore, his childhood sacrifices to the sea-god Shony, his nature-mysticism, and his youthful associations with 'gipsies, wandering pipers, and other musicians', Sharp was every inch a self-conscious modern poet. He combined marketable Celtic primitivism with his university education in English Literature at Glasgow University (where he had been in the same English class as J. G. Frazer, author of *The Golden Bough*).[126] Sharp may have been something of a gypsy, eager to cultivate his own writerly primitivism, but he was a scholar-gypsy, slyly engaging in the world of modern academia.

Sharp's 1896 'Centenary Ossian', along with such publications as the periodical the *Evergreen*, was part of Patrick Geddes's campaign for a Scottish cultural renaissance, but can be seen as linked to the wider Celtic Twilight movement of the 1890s. Yeats's *The Celtic Twilight* (1893) is a work largely in prose, but takes its title from a final poem, 'Into the Twilight', which whispers of 'a time out-worn', and repeats the phrase 'the grey twilight' as it hopes for a rebirth of Ireland.[127] This

[123] William Sharp, *The Silence of Amor* (London: Heinemann, 1910), 32 ('Foreword to the Original [1896] Edition').
[124] Ibid.   [125] Ibid. 12.
[126] Sharp, *William Sharp*, 5–15; Class Catalogue for 1872–3, Glasgow University Archives.
[127] W. B. Yeats, *Early Poems and Stories* (London: Macmillan, 1925), 315.

emphasis on dimness and twilight is familiar to any reader of Macpherson's Ossianic works. It had conditioned Arnold's lectures *On the Study of Celtic Literature* which was a book Yeats knew, and which appeared in a popular edition in 1891.[128] By 1892 in *The Countess Kathleen and Various Legends and Lyrics* Yeats was publishing a poem about the 'defeated', full of 'dim tides' of 'the dim grey sea' and 'Beauty grown sad'. Yeats's poem's title was 'They went forth to the Battle, but they always fell', a version of the very words from Ossian which form the epigraph to Arnold's *On the Study of Celtic Literature*.[129] The climate of the Celtic Twilight period was one in which not only Arnold's lectures but also his poetry could be glimpsed through a Celtic glimmer. So William Sharp, editing a selection of Arnold's poetry in the same year as *Lyra Celtica* and the centenary Ossian, wrote in 1896 that of Arnold's

many critical and interpretative studies only those which deal with literature *per se*, and pre-eminently the Celtic Essay, will survive...The mainsprings of contemporary Celticism (apart from philology) are in Macpherson's Ossian and in the Mabinogion of Lady Charlotte Guest; but...Arnold's famous... Celtic Essay, however, is of particular interest: for here is the prose-bridge which leads us to the poetry of Matthew Arnold.[130]

Arnold's poetry could be read in the 1890s through his speculations about the Celtic; perhaps some of it still can. In the publication year of his lectures on the Celtic spirit, which open with talk of 'the eternal softness and mild light of the west', there also appeared Arnold's most famous poem, one which begins in a lyrical twilight:

> The sea is calm to-night.
> The tide is full, the moon lies fair
> Upon the straits; on the French coast the light
> Gleams and is gone; the cliffs of England stand,
> Glimmering and vast, out in the tranquil bay.
> Come to the window, sweet is the night-air!
> Only, from the long line of spray

---

[128] Richard Ellmann, *The Identity of Yeats* (1954; repr. London: Faber & Faber, 1983), 303 n. and 323 n.; Matthew Arnold, *The Study of Celtic Literature*, popular edn. (London: Smith, Elder, 1891).

[129] See *The Variorum Edition of the Poems of W. B. Yeats*, ed. Peter Allt and Russell K. Alspach (New York: Macmillan, 1957), 113; W. B. Yeats, *Collected Poems*, 2nd edn. (London: Macmillan, 1950), 42. Yeats later retitled this piece 'The Rose of Battle'.

[130] William Sharp, *Papers Critical and Reminiscent* (London: Heinemann, 1912), 3–5; see also p. 373.

> Where the sea meets the moon-blanched land,
> Listen! you hear the grating roar
> Of pebbles which the waves draw back, and fling,
> At their return, up the high strand,
> Begin, and cease, and then again begin,
> With tremulous cadence slow, and bring
> The eternal note of sadness in.[131]

Though it was written earlier, 'Dover Beach' has a beautiful gloaming quality, an emphasis on the fading and glimmering, on moony melancholy, and sad cadences of tides, which is all in keeping with Arnold's view of the Celtic world. Indeed, with its sense of twilit marginality, of being on the edge of a 'distant northern sea' ('distant' presumably from the Aegean centre of European civilization), 'Dover Beach' turns England into a remote periphery, dissolving into 'a land of dreams'. Arnold anticipates the landscapes and seascapes of those twilit zones which *Lyra Celtica* calls, in what would become an imperial put-down, 'the Celtic Fringe'.[132] The 'Glimmering' images, tone, and acoustic of Arnold's Celticism and of 'Dover Beach' provide a nourishing context for one of the most celebrated Celtic Twilight poems. 'The Lake Isle of Innisfree' from Yeats's 1893 collection *The Rose*, eagerly anthologized by Elizabeth Sharp in *Lyra Celtica*, seems fitted with a dimmer switch that reduces everything to a twilight where 'midnight's all a glimmer, and noon a purple glow'. The poem's verbal repetitions, pace, and imagery send a constant tidal pulse of 'water lapping with low sounds by the shore'. Where Arnold had contrasted Celtic spirituality with the pressures of modern urban society, Yeats sets up the ideal of Innisfree as a spiritual refuge attuned to the rhythms of the 'deep heart's core' rather than those of city life 'on the roadway, or on the pavements grey'.[133] Even as his later poetry reforms itself, Yeats does not abandon a love of twilit effects, whether in 'The light of evening, Lissadell' that opens 'In Memory of Eva Gore-Booth and Con Markiewicz' or, even later, in 'Byzantium' when 'The unpurged images of day recede'.[134] A love of twilight and environments that are 'shadowy' (as in 'The Shadowy Waters'), the idea of making a new poetry based on Gaelic

---

[131] Matthew Arnold, 'On the Study of Celtic Literature', in *Lectures and Essays in Criticism*, ed. R. H. Super (Ann Arbor: University of Michigan Press, 1962), 291; *Poems of Matthew Arnold*, 254–5 ('Dover Beach').

[132] Sharp (ed.), *Lyra Celtica*, p. xv.   [133] Yeats, *Collected Poems*, 44.

[134] Ibid. 263 and 280.

folklore, the combination of quasi-scholarly research with access to forms of arcane knowledge—all these are recognizably related to Macpherson's Ossian as well as to the Irish Oisin cycle, and to some of the preoccupations of Ossian's most powerful nineteenth-century defender, the poet of 'The Scholar-Gipsy'.[135] In 1898 Yeats responded to Arnold at some length in his essay 'The Celtic Element in Literature'. He makes it clear that he knows Arnold's arguments thoroughly, yet denies building on them—an assertion questioned by modern scholars.[136] While one might argue that Yeats's own gypsy-scholarship develops most strikingly in *A Vision* and the poetry which goes with that remarkable volume, it is not my intention here to do so. Rather, I wish to conclude this chapter by focusing on the particular circumstances and tensions surrounding Yeats's aspirations towards what he called, in the Arnoldian phrase, a 'Professorship of poetry'.[137] In Yeats's ill-fated attempt to obtain a chair, we see elements emblematic of the further development of the modern poet in the course of the last century.

For the Yeats family Edward Dowden, that contributing editor to Ward's *English Poets* for which Arnold had written 'The Study of Poetry', summed up the relationship between poetry and academia. As young men Dowden and his brother had been the closest friends of Yeats's father John. Born and educated in Cork, then at Trinity College, Dublin, in 1867 Dowden became the first ever Professor of English at his *alma mater* when he was only 24. He was a home-grown academic literary luminary. For John Yeats as, later, for his son William, Dowden was also a promising poet who had killed his gift by incarcerating himself in academia for reasons of financial security. William M. Murphy, in his eloquent biography, *Prodigal Father*, records how for John Butler Yeats 'the real Dowden was the poet, not the essayist', and was 'a man gifted with the tongue of an angel which he sold to a

[135] Ibid. 473.
[136] J. V. Kelleher, 'Matthew Arnold and the Celtic Revival', in Harry Levin (ed.), *Perspectives in Criticism* (Cambridge, Mass.: Harvard University Press, 1950), 197–221; Terence Brown, 'Cultural Nationalism, Celticism and the Occult', in Terence Brown (ed.), *Celticism* (Amsterdam: Rodopi, 1996), 226–30; George Watson, 'Yeats, Macpherson and the Cult of Defeat', in Fiona Stafford and Howard Gaskill (eds.), *From Gaelic to Romantic* (Amsterdam: Rodopi, 1998), 216–25; David Cairns and Shaun Richards, *Writing Ireland* (Manchester: Manchester University Press, 1988), 66–8; Murray G. H. Pittock, *Celtic Identity and the British Image* (Manchester: Manchester University Press, 1999), 64–71 and 79–80.
[137] *The Letters of W. B. Yeats*, ed. Allan Wade (London: Hart-Davis, 1954), 551 (to Sydney Cockerell, 22 Sept. 1910).

Philistine devil' in return for the respectability of a position at Trinity.[138] Other friends detected in Dowden a brilliance accompanied by much Arnoldian polish: 'Dowden, Dowden burning bright, | Full of sweetness, full of light'.[139] The young William Butler Yeats recalled Dowden's early encouragement with appreciation, and remembered that 'for perhaps a couple of years he was an image of romance'. Yet, aware of 'Dowden's prosperous house, where all was in good taste, where poetry was rightly valued', Yeats came to share his father's view of Dowden as someone who should have given himself to 'creative art' when young, rather than embracing the ironic and cerebral world of academic criticism.[140] With reference to Dowden, John Yeats later wrote to W. B. Yeats, warning him to keep himself free of 'those Trinity College people', otherwise he would erode his freedom as a writer, and become 'a poet lost'.[141] For the Yeatses Dowden represented the university as a poet-trap. Dowden was the quintessential 'poet lost'.

However, as so often with the Yeats family, there was a strong element of myth-making here. For it is highly questionable if Dowden was ever much of a poet. His *Poems* of 1876 (the only collection which appeared in his lifetime) seems to have been published only as a result of his very successful 1875 critical study *Shakspere: His Mind and Art*. Dowden's *Poems* appeared in a 'small edition' the following year from the same publisher, and came adorned with admiring reviews of the Shakespeare book.[142] The poems are almost all bad. A number of them suggest that Dowden was an alert enough critic to know this, on one level at least. 'Why do I write no poems?' begins a sonnet, while a longer piece, 'The Fountain', confesses,

> I dare not follow that broad flood
> Of Poesy, whose lustihood
> Nourishes mighty lands, and makes
> Resounding music for their sakes...[143]

[138] William M. Murphy, *Prodigal Father* (Ithaca, NY: Cornell University Press, 1978), 121.
[139] John Todhunter, quoted ibid. 70.
[140] W. B. Yeats, *Autobiographies* (London: Macmillan, 1955), 86.
[141] John B. Yeats, quoted in Murphy, *Prodigal Father*, 378.
[142] Elizabeth Dickinson Dowden, 'Preface' to Edward Dowden, *Poems* (London: Dent, 1914), p. xii; Edward Dowden, *Poems* (London: Henry S. King, 1876), advertisement opposite title page.
[143] Dowden, *Poems* (1876), 159 and 3.

Echoes of Keats, Blake, Arnold, and others can be heard from time
to time in Dowden's verse, but they are always faint, unconvincing.
Dowden's earliest poems, written before he became a professor,
are neither better nor worse than his later. In the late 1860s, as a
young academic, Dowden delivered a Dublin public lecture on
Tennyson and Browning. Tennyson he saw as fascinated by 'protracted
self-control', Browning by 'the lightning of sudden passion'.[144] A
tension between these two underlies 'Renunciants', which Yeats
remembered his father quoting 'to prove what Dowden might have
written':

> Ah, stranger, lay aside
>   Cold prudence! I divine
> The secret you would hide,
>   And you conjecture mine.
>
> You too have temperate eyes,
>   Have put your heart to school,
> Are proved. I recognize
>   A brother of the rule.
>
> I knew it by your lip,
>   A something when you smiled,
> Which meant, 'close scholarship,
>   A master of the guild.'[145]

'Renunciants', though, is Dowden's only sustained poem. It surely came
to epitomize him for Yeats's father because Dowden was seen by the
Yeatses as having renounced creative art for 'the rule' of 'close scholarship' at Trinity College. This view of Dowden as 'renunciant' is reinforced by his widow's recollection that 'In the early seventies he felt the
urge very strongly towards making verse his vocation in life, and he
probably would have yielded to it, but for the necessity to be bread-
winner for a much-loved household.' So it was, she recalls, he committed himself to 'College lecturing'.[146] Here again, a strong element of
romanticizing is involved. With perhaps two exceptions, there are no
real indications in Dowden's *Poems* that he had much poetic talent. In his
heart of hearts, Yeats knew Dowden had never been much of a poet. He
omitted him from his 1895 *Book of Irish Verse*. Dowden was more useful

[144] John P. Mahaffy et al., *The Afternoon Lectures on Literature and Art* (Dublin: William
McGee, 1869), 172 and 173.
[145] Yeats, *Autobiographies*, 86; Dowden, *Poems* (1876), 176–7.
[146] E. D. Dowden, 'Preface' to Edward Dowden, *Poems* (1914), pp. xii and xiii.

as a 'might have been'. He could be displayed as a fearful warning about the academicization of poetry.

Yeats picked a public quarrel with Dowden on more than one occasion. In 1886 he used the Professor as a stalking horse in his articulation of what has been called Yeats's 'first major statement of his literary philosophy'.[147] Writing about 'The Poetry of Sir Samuel Ferguson', a celebrated English-language Irish poet and antiquary who, drawing on the texts of the Irish Ossianic Society, had attempted to rival or replace Macpherson's *Fingal* with works such as his own epic *Congal* (1872), Yeats complains that Irish critics have ignored native literature and listened instead 'for the faintest echo of English thought'. His explicit target here is 'the most distinguished of our critics, Professor Dowden', whom he sees as oppressive to Irish literature since he has helped develop a climate in which 'The most cultivated of Irish readers are only anxious to be academic, and to be servile to English notions.'[148] Linking the idea of being 'academic' to that of being 'servile to English notions', Yeats is pinpointing an aspect of Dowden's unionist tone. Writing on 'The Interpretation of Literature', Dowden made it clear that he had 'said nothing of the historical study of literature and its interpretation through the general movements of the life and mind of nations'.[149] Dowden's *Poems*, for all their mentions of 'Latmos' or 'Dover', never use a single Irish place name, while a sonnet written during his time as an undergraduate at Trinity College, Dublin, refers to 'our blessed English clime'.[150] For all his Irish education, Dowden the Professor of English is viewed by the young Irish nationalist poet as if he were an English professor of the most Anglocentric hue. Yeats had been an art-school student, not a student of Eng. Lit. His quarrel with Dowden the West Briton shades into his resentment of Dowden the academic. It can be related to many other nationalist poets' arguments with university English teachers who seemed to exemplify a stance which kept the natives and their culture servile.[151] If Robert Fergusson

---

[147] *Uncollected Prose by W. B. Yeats*, vol. i. ed. John P. Frayne (London: Macmillan, 1970), 87 (Editor's Note to 'The Poetry of Sir Samuel Ferguson').

[148] Yeats, 'The Poetry of Sir Samuel Ferguson—II', 88–9.

[149] Edward Dowden, *Transcripts and Studies* (London: Kegan Paul, Trench, 1888), 237.

[150] Dowden, *Poems* (1876), 34 and 100; Dowden's 'Dover' sonnet is dated to 1862 in *Poems* (1914), p. vi.

[151] See Robert Crawford, *Devolving English Literature*, 2nd edn. (Edinburgh: Edinburgh University Press, 2000) and Robert Crawford (ed.), *The Scottish Invention of English Literature* (Cambridge: Cambridge University Press, 1998).

was the first poet to hint at such a posture, then Yeats, MacDiarmid, Les
Murray, among many others, have developed it at one point or another
in their careers, and the issue remains urgent for younger poets. Yeats's
nationalism melds with his hostility to Dowden, representative of
Trinity College academia. The poet champions Sir Samuel Ferguson's
verse as 'truly bardic', and complains that 'Almost all the poetry of this
age is written by students, for students.'[152]

There are several ironies here. One is that Ferguson's work emerged
from as academic a background as that of Macpherson, Blair, and
Ossian. Ferguson's initial cultural campaigns were conducted in the
pages of the *Dublin University Magazine*, just as Yeats's own first publication would be in the *Dublin University Review*. Another irony is that, for all
his resentment of Dowden's power, Yeats was keen enough to have the
Professor's endorsement. He delights in communicating to several
correspondents Dowden's appreciation of his early verse. Dowden
was often generous to the Yeats family, but the poet returned to the
attack in 1895 when 'Prof Dowden expressed scorn for the Irish Lit
movement' and Yeats took part in a public argument with the 'Prof' in
the columns of the Dublin *Daily Express* and elsewhere.[153] Yeats's
quarrel was a nationalist one. It is also, though, bound up with his
suspicion of the academicization of poetry. In the 1890s Yeats spent
some time reading and writing among the Trinity students in Dublin's
National Library, yet felt oppressed by

the glacial weight of scholasticism ... over all the would-be intellectual life of
Dublin. Nobody in this great library is doing any disinterested reading, nobody
is poring over any book for the sake of the beauty of its words, for the glory of
its thought, but all are reading that they may pass an examination; no one is
trying to develop his personal taste, but all are endeavoring to force their minds
into the mould made for them by professors and examiners.[154]

Yeats's telltale use of the word 'disinterested' here signals that his own
ideal of reading is being shaped by Matthew Arnold. If Yeats resented
Dowden's supposedly cosmopolitan sweetness and light, then Arnold,
the Celticist, the poet whose scholar-gypsy's footsteps were retraced by
the young Irishman in Oxford, still mattered to him. Dowden struck, in

---

[152] Yeats, *Uncollected Prose* i. 101.
[153] Yeats, *Collected Letters*, i. 427 (to Susan Mary Yeats, 20 Jan. [1895]) and 435, 437, 440–5 (to
the Editor of the *Daily Express* (Dublin)).
[154] Yeats, *Uncollected Prose*, i. 232 ('Dublin Scholasticism and Trinity College').

John Yeats's words, 'the pose of an Irishman trying to be an Englishman'; his Trinity College was 'the most unimaginative, the least original place in the world'.[155] At least Arnold and Oxford were genuinely English, offering real stimulation. Clough and Arnold were poets nurtured by a university; Dowden, according to the myth at least, was a poet stifled by one. Yeats's prodigal father wrote to Dowden telling him that he wished the Professor had written more poetry, and saying he was convinced Dowden would have done so 'had it not been for the Professorship' at TCD.[156] Attacking Trinity, Yeats the poet flyted,

'She has given herself to many causes that have not been my causes, but never to the Philistines,' Matthew Arnold once wrote of Oxford. Alas, that we can but invert the sentences when we speak of our own University—'Never to any cause, but always to the Philistines,' is written over her chimneys . . . Let us not sentimentalize over her, but let us grant her all that she has, her mathematics, and her metaphysics, and then acknowledge that a tractarian movement, or a single poet of the rank of Arnold or Clough even, were more than all these things.[157]

Dowden must have smarted on reading these words, as surely as he was meant to do. Yeats liked to sting the supposed lost poet and his supporters, complaining in the first part of his essay 'Professor Dowden and Irish Literature' that 'Dublin is dominated by scholastic—perhaps, I should say school room—ideals.'[158] The poet maintained an awareness of academic politics. He took some pleasure in Dowden's 'crown of martyrdom' when the Dublin scholar failed to obtain 'the Scotch Proffessorship he tried for' at Glasgow University in 1889.[159] Though he was a veteran of readings and lectures on (not least American) campuses, Yeats liked to pose as an Irish wildman where professors were concerned. Writing later to the upright Professor William Knight (a Wordsworth scholar who taught English and Philosophy at St Andrews, who possessed Dowden's poems, and who had been a rival of Dowden's for the Glasgow chair), Yeats relished terming himself 'very much of an Irish "extremist"'.[160] Yet there was also among the intelli-

---

[155] John B. Yeats, quoted in Murphy, *Prodigal Father*, 121 and 372.   [156] Ibid. 372.
[157] Yeats, *Uncollected Prose*, i. 233 ('Dublin Scholasticism and Trinity College').
[158] Ibid. 349.
[159] Yeats, *Collected Letters*, i. 175 (to John O'Leary, [late July 1889]).
[160] *The Collected Letters of W. B. Yeats*, vol. iii, ed. John Kelly and Ronald Schuchard (Oxford: Clarendon Press, 1994), 207 (to William Angus Knight, 19 June 1903); Knight's initialled copy of Dowden's 1876 *Poems* is in St Andrews University Library.

gentsia an awareness of what might be accomplished in Dublin by 'a Nationalist Dowden', and for a time at least Yeats aspired to that mantle, attempting to put himself forward as a professorial poet.[161]

He tried more than once. In 1910, casting around for sources of additional income, he learned that Dowden might be about to retire from Trinity. Yeats wrote at once to the Vice Provost there, asking for an interview for the job. Notoriously, his letter of application misspelled the word 'proffesrship', but the poet adeptly cultivated some influential figures in the Trinity establishment.[162] In March 1910 he lectured at Trinity. Soon he was giving public addresses on literature in England, and in April he was elected to an English-based organization significantly titled the 'Academic Committee of English Letters'.[163] In the same year Yeats accepted a British Civil List pension. He seemed to be entering the British academic establishment. The poet relished the thought of inhabiting Dowden's splendid Georgian rooms, not to mention drawing a professor's £600 annual salary, though he worried that pressure to produce regular critical work might have an adverse effect on his imagination.[164] Yeats's father felt similar anxieties for his son, concerned that the young man might find himself 'swallowed up' in Trinity's prose, as (he said) the promising poet Dowden had been. Yet John Yeats was also excited, thinking the job would be 'a great gain' to the poet, as well as 'an honour to Old Trinity' which was a producer of 'quiet scholars, but no poets, no men of imagination'.[165] Yeats the gypsy hovered on the brink of becoming a scholar.

Dowden, however, ensured that this was not to be. Rallying himself, he told Yeats's father that the poet might make 'a very inspiring Professor of Poetry, such as they have in Oxford, who may choose his own themes, and give a few annual lectures', but that he would not make the sort of scholarly professor needed at Trinity.[166] Enjoying being able to trump his old and young adversaries, Dowden explained to the Yeatses that 'the process of appointment is usually to become first an assistant to some Professor & teach Anglo-Saxon, to publish some piece of scholarship, & show one's capacity in scientific research,

[161] The phrase is John Todhunter's, from a letter to Dowden of 4 Feb. 1889, quoted in Murphy, *Prodigal Father*, 169.

[162] Yeats, *Collected Letters*, i. p. xli.

[163] R. F. Foster, *W. B. Yeats: A Life* vol. i (Oxford: Oxford University Press, 1997), 424.

[164] Ibid. 430.   [165] John Butler Yeats, quoted in Murphy, *Prodigal Father*, 278.

[166] Dowden, quoted ibid. 383.

& then to climb to a Professorship'.[167] Dowden's notion of such a pedestrian ascent may signal his imaginative limitations (though it hardly describes how he got his own chair). It is a put-down aimed at an uppity author, one not untypical of the attitudes towards poets held by some functionaries of the academic system in the century that followed.

Dowden had not forgotten Yeats's attacks on him. In 1911 he delighted in emphasizing to the poet's father that being an academic was 'a difficult and laborious trade, requiring a special training'.[168] This was something young Willie did not have. Emphasizing the 'difficult', Dowden's letter was calculated to annoy the poet who, in the previous year, had published *The Green Helmet and Other Poems*, in which he memorably chafes against 'The fascination of what's difficult'.[169] Yet Dowden's application of the word 'trade' to his profession chimes with Yeats's later exhortation, 'Irish poets, learn your trade.'[170] Even as they flyte, professor and poet here converge, each asserting the demands and qualifications of his work in similar terms. It is clear that, for a time at least, Yeats did dream of entering academia. In 1910 he asked his friend Sydney Cockerell for details about the Oxford 'Professorship of Poetry', and he kept Cockerell aware of his continuing negotiations with Trinity in 1911.[171] Two years later, when Dowden died, there was a proposal (to which Yeats responded eagerly) that the poet should have a specially created Chair of Poetry at Trinity. While he liked this idea, Yeats was wary of having to involve himself with exams and marking. In the end, Dowden's chair went to another candidate.

Yeats was never to be an academic. He had been interested in the possibility, yet, as he had told Cockerell, 'I am beginning to think I had better keep to my wandering life.'[172] One of his first books had been called *The Wanderings of Oisin*. To wander was Romantic, as Wordsworth (poet of 'The Wanderer') had known. Yet it was also the fate of the scholar-gypsy, who is called 'wanderer' in Arnold's poem.[173] Yeats's attitude towards academia was complicated. In 'The Scholars', written later in the decade when he almost became a professor, university life is

---

[167] Dowden, quoted in Foster, *W. B. Yeats*, i. 430.

[168] Dowden, quoted in Murphy, *Prodigal Father*, 383.

[169] W. B. Yeats, *The Poems*, ed. Richard J. Finneran (London: Macmillan, 1983), 93 ('The Fascination of What's Difficult').

[170] Ibid. 327 ('Under Ben Bulben').

[171] *Letters of W. B. Yeats*, 551 and 557 (to Sydney Cockerell, 22 Sept. 1910 and 6 Mar. 1911).

[172] Ibid. 551.

[173] *Poems of Matthew Arnold*, 365 ('The Scholar-Gypsy').

presented as trapping poetry, as it appeared to have trapped Edward Dowden. That poem features 'learned, respectable bald heads' which are deeply unoriginal. In a milieu where all 'shuffle and cough', these scholars sit and annotate poems written by passionate young men whom they would not even recognize.[174] Yet there was another part of Yeats which was convinced 'Truth flourishes where the student's lamp has shone, | And there alone.'[175] If as a child, he loved Scott's Ossianic *Lay of the Last Minstrel* (a poem he also relished late in life), then as a mature man Yeats would style himself and his friends 'the last romantics'.[176] On the whole, his attitude towards academia, and towards Dowden (the academic whom he knew best), was romantic. Dowden was not really 'a poet lost'. He might have wanted to be a poet, but he lacked sufficient talent. Nor need modern academia be alien to the poet. The Yeats who looked with some favour on the idea of being a Professor of Poetry knew that. Romantically, though, he chose 'wandering' away. After that, his involvement with academia was at best fleeting, though he was no stranger to campus life. The younger poets who were Yeats's equals or near-equals in English-language poetry—people such as Pound, Eliot, Williams, or Auden—were almost all more thoroughly moulded by immersion in universities. As is well known, when Pound became Yeats's secretary he helped the older Irish poet achieve a crucial change of style. Yeats, though, never fully became a modernist; instead, in *A Vision* he produced a work of wandering, gypsy scholarship whose arcana belonged at least as much to the world of Fiona Macleod as to that of *The Waste Land*. It was Yeats the last romantic, the adversary of Dowden the 'poet lost', who reacted to Pound with both fascination and passionate disdain. For Yeats academia was inescapable as an adversary. In that sense at least he was a modern poet. He denounced Pound once as a 'sexless American professor'.[177] Each of these three words could be delivered with venom by the Irishman. Despite his fleeting dreams of a chair at Trinity or at Oxford, perhaps the most damning was the last.

---

[174] Yeats, *The Poems*, 140–1 ('The Scholars').
[175] Ibid. 184 ('The Leaders of the Crowd').
[176] Foster, *W. B. Yeats*, 17; Yeats, *The Poems*, 245 ('Coole and Ballylee, 1931').
[177] W. B. Yeats, *Letters on Poetry from W. B. Yeats to Dorothy Wellesley* (London: Oxford University Press, 1940), 25 (8 Sept. [1935]).

CHAPTER 4

Modernist Cybernetics and the Poetry of Knowledge

Yeats may have rejoiced in being a 'last romantic'; many of his younger contemporaries did not. This chapter is about the work of several poets whose work forms part of the artistic movement which Edwin Muir in 1919 pioneeringly called 'modernism'. Muir's view was that 'If modernism be a vital thing it must needs have roots in the past and be an essential expression of humanity: in short, it can only be a tradition.'[1] The sense of modernism as bound up with tradition would be developed thoroughly by T. S. Eliot. Where Muir, like Yeats, had avoided a university education, Eliot and his friend Ezra Pound arrived overbrimming with academic training. Their poetry registers longing, and a jagged sense of pain. It is also accompanied by a heavy load of postgraduate learning. Theirs, even more than the work of Browning or of Clough, is a thoroughgoing poetry of knowledge.

In one sense the young American who volunteered to act as Yeats's secretary at Stone Cottage, Sussex, from 1913 until 1916 knew well that the Irish poet embodied both the scholar-gypsy and the modern poet. Ambitious and pushy, still unsure of the direction of his own writing, Pound at 28 wanted to learn from the older man; at the same time, he saw Yeats as a member of a Rhymers Club generation which belonged to an earlier age. With an undergraduate degree from Hamilton College, a postgraduate degree from the University of Pennsylvania, and experience of being a college professor behind him, Pound in England carried substantial academic baggage—soon after his arrival he was lecturing for the London Polytechnic. At the same time, however, he was able to trade on his exotic American wildness. He had come to London in 1908 with his eye on the main chance. When he wrote in 1913 that

---

[1] Edward Moore [Edwin Muir], *We Moderns* (London: Allen & Unwin, 1918), 128.

he had arrived 'knowing no one', that was a sly boast.[2] It was his way of saying that by 1913 (when he was about to set up house with Yeats) he knew everyone who mattered. Yet Pound remained aloof. Symptomatic of this is how in 1909, rewriting a famous celebration of 'The man of independent mind', he joked about himself in the style of Robert Burns:

> Ye see this birkie ca'ed a bard,
> Wi' cryptic eyes and a' that,
> Aesthetic phrases by the yard;
> It's but E.P. for a' that...[3]

Like Burns, Pound had travelled to the metropolitan centre and, like Burns, he negotiated with it carefully, turning it to his own advantage. He made use of its Polytechnic, and of the British Library, entering into the capital's clubs and societies, but remained of independent mind. No one called the ex-professor Pound a 'heaven-taught ploughman', but the English metropolitan world did caricature him as 'a son of the Arkansas soil'.[4] Pound was in search of cosmopolitan modernity in London. He also rejoiced exuberantly in his outsider's status, being 'like a painted pict with a stone war club', as he put it in 1912.[5] This is Pound the decorum-buster, making noises 'which sounded like Bantu clicks', speaking in his 'strong, odd accent, half American, half Irish', delighting in what *Poetry Review* in 1912 called 'Queer exotic hybridity!'[6] Pound's stage-managed outsider-ness and his combination of apparent primitivism with academically supercharged knowledge were essential to him. Clearly, when he signs himself 'Boaz' in a 1911 letter to his future wife Dorothy Shakespear, he is pleased to have been caricatured by *Punch* as 'Boaz Bobb', the exotic, polymathic outsider.[7] The following year he wrote that it would be about as easy for an American to become a Chinaman or a Hindu as for him to acquire an Englishness anything

---

[2] Ezra Pound, 'How I Began', *T.P.'s Weekly*, 21 (6 June 1913), 707.

[3] *Collected Early Poems of Ezra Pound*, ed. Michael L. King (London: Faber & Faber, 1977), 214–15.

[4] Omar Pound and A. Walton Litz (eds.), *Ezra Pound and Dorothy Shakespear: Their Letters 1909–1914* (London: Faber & Faber, 1985), 46 (editorial note).

[5] Ibid. 163 (Pound to Dorothy Shakespear, [Kensington, 1 Oct. 1912]).

[6] Ibid. 3 (Dorothy Shakespear's notebook, 16 Feb. 1909); Patricia Hutchins, *Ezra Pound's Kensington* (London: Faber & Faber, 1965), 56 and 77.

[7] Pound and Litz (eds.), *Ezra Pound and Dorothy Shakespear*, 45 (Pound to Shakespear, [24 or 31 Aug. 1911] and 46 (editorial note on 'Boaz').

more than half skin-deep.[8] *Cathay* (1915) holds the evidence that Pound tried harder to become a Chinaman than an Englishman; part of the poetry's appeal comes from his failure. The verse is neither Chinese nor English, but suspended between the two (as the poetry of Ossian is located between Gaelic and English), so that it seems written in that medium which, T. S. Eliot wrote in 1928, Pound had made his own: 'Throughout the work of Pound there is what we might call a steady effort towards the synthetic construction of a style of speech.'[9]

In his early London years, though, the stuff out of which Pound would synthesize his style of speech still lay about him. The materials are there as much in his awkwardly off-Whitmanian song of himself, 'Redondillas' ('I would sing the American people | God send them some civilization'), as they are in his Celtic Twilight echoes, strong before he left America.[10] In some of his earliest poems Pound was 'a hollow reed' and wandered 'Thru woodlands dim' or 'o'er silent waters' as he 'sought the wee wind'.[11] The London in which he arrived was one where Dorothy Shakespear in 1911 thought Fiona Macleod (a full edition of whose works appeared in 1910) 'very exquisite often', and the Celtic Twilight lingered on.[12] Robert Frost, in England in 1913, conversed with Macleod's widow about seeing a faun in an English lane, and worried 'how perilously near Yates [*sic*] comes to believing in fairies'.[13] In his first book, *A Lume Spento* (1908), Pound linked his own interest in fauns and dryads to the treatment of such by 'Mr. Yeats in his "Celtic Twilight"', and when Dorothy Shakespear saw the 'heather, & woods' near Stone Cottage in 1913 she reported the latter might be haunted; the lake in the woods she thought 'weird . . . —and possibly faerie'.[14] James Longenbach points out how lines in Pound's apprentice work such as 'Naught but the wind that flutters in the leaves' show borrowings from the Celtic Twilight Yeats.[15] This debt and the associated inheritance of

[8] Ezra Pound, 'Patria Mia, XI', *New Age*, 12 (14 Nov. 1912), 33.

[9] T. S. Eliot, 'Introduction' to Ezra Pound, *Selected Poems* (London: Faber & Faber, 1928), p. xiv.

[10] Pound, *Collected Early Poems*, 216 ('Redondillas, or Something of That Sort').

[11] Ibid. 46 ('Motif'); Pound, quoted in Humphrey Carpenter, *A Serious Character* (London: Faber & Faber, 1988), 37.

[12] Pound and Litz (eds.), *Ezra Pound and Dorothy Shakespear*, 50 (Shakespear to Pound, Southampton, [5 Sep. 1911]).

[13] See Robert Crawford, *Identifying Poets: Self and Territory in Twentieth-Century Poetry* (Edinburgh: Edinburgh University Press, 1993), 26.

[14] Pound, *Collected Early Poems*, 8 ('Note Precedent to "La Fraisne"'); Pound and Litz (eds.), *Ezra Pound and Dorothy Shakespear*, 249–50 (Shakespear to Pound, Sussex, [4 Sept. 1913]).

[15] James Longenbach, *Stone Cottage* (New York: Oxford University Press, 1988), 11.

apparitions and supernatural presences underpin not only the Yeats of the seances and *A Vision*, but also the Pound of some of the early poems, of *The Spirit of Romance* (1910), and of later supernatural visions in *The Cantos*. The bard Ezra liked those who had stared 'lang syne from shadowy castle towers'. The Pound who romanced about dwelling amid 'ancient boulders' which 'Gods had hewn and druids runed' became the poet who reinterpreted Provence and lingered among the chateaux of the Troubadours.[16]

In 1910, lecturing at London Polytechnic, his subject was not 'The Celtic Twilight' but 'The Phantom Dawn'. Hidden among the 'ante-lucanal glamor' are faint traces of Celtic awareness. Arguing that witches and magical fountains are not exclusive to the Romantic imagination, Pound pronounces a passage of Ovid 'as haunted as anything in Ossian'. He admires the way Ovid 'walks with the people of myth' and he links such encounters to 'the tales of Ywain and Ossian'.[17] Writing in the Chicago magazine *Poetry* in 1914 about his wish for a new American Renaissance, and looking for starting points, Pound points out that 'The Romantic awakening dates from the production of *Ossian*.'[18] As a poet, he was trying hard to exorcize his Celticism. One such attempt is an early, undated poem ' "It is a Shame"—with Apologies to the Modern Celtic School'. This mock elegy on 'the fairy dog' pokes fun at what Pound calls 'the impassioned rehash of the mystically beautiful celtic mythology'.[19] There was certainly something to exorcize. As far back as Cornelius Weygandt's 1907 University of Pennsylvania postgraduate class on Contemporary Poetry, Pound, that self-styled 'Master of Arts | And...man of parts', had been 'drunk with "Celticism"'.[20]

Much has been made of Pound's belief in 'a light from Eleusis', connecting the ancient cult of Demeter to Troubadour and more modern literature.[21] Yet the American poet who went to Provence and linked the rites of Demeter to the Troubadour cult of Amor was

[16] Pound, *Collected Early Poems*, 28 and 295 ('Li Bel Chasteus').

[17] Ezra Pound, *The Spirit of Romance* (1910; repr. London: Peter Owen, 1952), 12, 14, 16, and 17.

[18] *Literary Essays of Ezra Pound*, ed, T. S. Eliot (London: Faber & Faber, 1954), 215 ('The Renaissance').

[19] Pound, *Collected Early Poems*, 273.

[20] Pound, quoted in D. G. Myers, *The Elephants Teach* (Englewood Cliffs, NJ: Prentice Hall, 1996), 90; Emily Mitchell Wallace, 'Youthful Days and Costly Hours', in Daniel Hoffmann (ed.), *Ezra Pound and William Carlos Williams* (Philadelphia: University of Pennsylvania Press, 1983), 24.

[21] See especially Leon Surette, *A Light from Eleusis* (Oxford: Clarendon Press, 1979).

following in the Celtic footsteps of Fiona Macleod. That writer had gone to Provence at the turn of the century to write both a gypsy romance and a book on local culture. Alert to the way in which modern 'strange half pagan, half Christian ceremonies' contained survivals of ancient 'rites of the Demeter and the Persephone-Kore cult', Sharp published his mystical *The Silence of Amor* in 1902 with the American publisher Thomas Mosher, whom the young Pound would soon approach with a manuscript.[22] However much at Stone Cottage he helped Yeats to move beyond his earlier, Celtic Twilight self, Pound, like the Irish poet, was impelled on his own poetic course not least by a youthful Celtic intoxication. Though the Celtic Twilight produced no epic of its own, it inherited the epic of Ossian, whether in Irish or Scottish dress. Looking back on the earliest genesis of his *Cantos*, Pound once recalled his relationship with Joseph Ibbotson, his Professor of English at Hamilton College, with whom he had discussed Richard Bentley's eighteenth-century editing of and additions to *Paradise Lost*. Yet Ibbotson recollected that Pound's interest in epic at the time was not confined to Milton. One night the young student talked to his professor for over three hours about Ossian.[23] Present at the first glimmerings of Pound's own epic, Ossian and the Celtic Twilight were presences to be fiercely, but only partially repressed. Just as the hauntings of the twilight world were to return in Pound's mature poetry, so the notion of an epic both bardic and scholarly was to become his own life's work as a modern poet.

The search for primitive and supernatural knowledge pursued by both Pound and Yeats is a twentieth-century mutation of Arnold's idealization of the non-rational wisdom of the gypsy. Pound's hieratic view of art, developed and reinforced by his years at Stone Cottage, like Yeats's earlier 1898 statement that 'The arts are, I believe, about to take upon their shoulders the burdens that have fallen from the shoulders of priests,' is a restatement of Arnold's conviction that 'most of what now passes with us for religion and philosophy will be replaced by poetry'.[24]

[22] Elizabeth A. Sharp, *William Sharp* (London: Heinemann, 1910), 326–7, 342; Fiona Macleod, *The Silence of Amor* (Portland, Me.: Thomas Mosher, 1902); Noel Stock, *The Life of Ezra Pound* (Harmondsworth: Penguin Books, 1974), 57.

[23] Carpenter, *A Serious Character*, 51.

[24] W. B. Yeats, 'The Autumn of the Body' (1898), repr. in *Selected Criticism and Prose*, ed. A. Norman Jeffares (London: Pan, 1980), 41; Matthew Arnold, 'The Study of Poetry', in *Essays in Criticism, Second Series* (1888; repr. London: Dent, 1964), 235.

Yeats and Pound to different degrees are gypsy-scholars. Yeats, a poet of the nineteenth as well as the twentieth century, becomes increasingly given over to occult wisdom. Despite all his wishes for a fusion or more tolerant accommodation between the worlds of academia and poetry, as his poetic career develops it is increasingly the gypsy that leads the scholar. With Pound, though, the case is different. The American's earliest significant poetic quickenings are already bound up with the classroom, and with the academic presentation of literature by men like Ibbotson and Weygandt. Nicknamed 'Professor' at school, Pound developed his earlier poetry alongside his student and graduate student preoccupations.[25] Engaging with the philological tradition in which he was educated, he writes an article on 'Raphaelite Latin' (published in 1906) and a poem 'To the Raphaelite Latinists' (published in 1908).[26] His verse from and about Provençal or Troubadour poets in such collections as *Exultations* (1909) complements the London Polytechnic lectures published as *The Spirit of Romance* (1910). That latter book is presented as unburdened by the ' "scholarly" mind'. However, it seeks a new kind of 'literary scholarship', and its aim is 'to instruct'. Nothing could sound more pompously pedantic than the title of its introduction, 'Praefatio ad Lectorem Electum'.[27] Poet and professor, student and poet's secretary, Pound negotiates his way as a new kind of scholar-gypsy. His wish is not straightforwardly to link poetry and academia. He sought to preserve certain ideas of poetic truth and primitive wildness from the academic packaging which had surrounded poetry since his first reception of it. Pound was unsure where he was going. At the same time as he was denouncing the 'scholarly' he was trying to obtain his Ph.D. He maintained later that it was Yeats's presence which had drawn him to England so that he could 'learn what he knew'. When he first arrived, though, Pound was applying not to the Irish poet but to Balliol College, asking if he could complete his doctorate there.[28] In 1909 he was writing to his father to see if he could qualify for a Rhodes Scholarship to Oxford. During the same period he applied for an academic post at the University of Pennsylvania, enquired about another at Princeton, and put in for a third at Hobart College, New York State, equally

---

[25] Carpenter, *A Serious Character*, 26.
[26] Ezra Pound, 'Raphaelite Latin', *Book News Monthly* (Philadelphia), 25 (Sept. 1906), 31–4; Pound, *Collected Early Poems*, 205.
[27] Pound, *The Spirit of Romance*, 7–8.
[28] Carpenter, *A Serious Character*, 93.

without success.[29] For all his wildness, Pound, like Yeats and Arnold before him and like so many poets since, thought that he might work in academia.

The shrewdest study of Pound and Eliot as poets both formed by university life and in turn conditioning the development of academic literary studies is by Gail McDonald.[30] She draws attention to Pound and Eliot as moulded by campus culture at a time when American universities were transforming themselves from older patrician halls of culture into modern, quasi-industrial research institutions.[31] As part of this shift, these two poets present poetry using professional and scientific terminology.[32] Pound argued that intellectual culture needed a language no less efficient than that of 'the Amalgamated Pants-Button Co.'.[33] Eliot famously connected poetry to the chemistry of filiated platinum and elsewhere linked the poet to the scientist as contributing to the organic development of culture.[34] Emerging from the institutionalized study of literary texts and from their postgraduate training, both these poets knew from the inside the masculinized, professionalized world of academic research culture. Like their fellow modernists James Joyce and Charles Olson, they produced works of art which fed that. Yet there persisted also another aspect of Pound and Eliot that hankered after the older-style college which had been a part of their education. This was the Victorian generalism which had produced in Britain Thomas Carlyle's 'Professor of Things in General' and which, to a considerable degree, had been the knowledge-world of Arnold and Clough.[35] As noted in the preceding chapter, debates about free knowledge in mid-nineteenth-century Oxford were related not least to the growth of professionalism in European universities. Half a century later, that continuing expansion on several continents conditioned the emergence of modernist poetry. McDonald writes well about these aspects of both Pound and Eliot, but I wish to make points which are

[29] Carpenter, *A Serious Character*, 140–1.

[30] Gail McDonald, *Learning to be Modern* (Oxford: Clarendon Press, 1993).

[31] See also Louis Menand, *Discovering Modernism* (New York: Oxford University Press, 1987), 97–132.

[32] The fullest study of Pound's use of scientific terminology is Ian F. A. Bell, *Critic as Scientist* (London: Methuen, 1981).

[33] Pound (1918), quoted in McDonald, *Learning to be Modern*, 70.

[34] T. S. Eliot, *Selected Essays*, 3rd enlarged edn. (London: Faber & Faber, 1951), 17 ('Tradition and the Individual Talent'); T. S. Eliot, 'Contemporanea', *Egoist* (June–July 1918), 84.

[35] Thomas Carlyle, *Sartor Resartus* (1833–4), ed. Kerry McSweeney and Peter Sabor (Oxford: Oxford University Press, 1987), 14.

in some ways cruder than hers, in an attempt to draw a larger picture of the development of modern poetry.

First, if the young poets Pound and Eliot were moulded both by the older university tradition of generalism, and by the newer one of professionalism, then something similar can be said of the publication outlets available to them. Though Pound did publish early work in long-established magazines like the *Fortnightly Review* and the *North American Review*, while the fledgling Eliot, more successful in this regard, was a regular contributor to the *Athenaeum*, the nineteenth-century heyday of such wide-circulation clubman-oriented journals had passed. All are now extinct. Some other general intellectual periodicals have survived. The best known is the *Times Literary Supplement*, to which around 1920 the apparently orthodox Eliot, but not the more bohemian Pound, was a regular contributor. However, the pioneering poetics of modernism tended to be developed in small-circulation avant-garde journals such as *Blast* or the *Egoist* (in whose pages 'Tradition and the Individual Talent' crept into print). These small magazines, sometimes with Eliot or Pound or their friends as editors, were 'advanced', elite publications that enjoyed limited readerships. Even Eliot's *Criterion*, where *The Waste Land* first appeared, remained a small-circulation journal. On occasion, as with *Blast* or the *Egoist*, modernist magazines seemed designed to alienate the general public. In terms of publishing outlets as well as academic background, these modern poets found themselves caught between the older-style shared, upper-class, educated intellectual culture and a newer, specialized, minority professionalism. Though the poets hedged their bets, their inclinations tended towards the latter camp. If they were to establish a readership, then, like other modern poets before them from Macpherson to Wordsworth and Coleridge, they required to educate and nurture an audience. More immediately, they needed money. Given the increased institutional teaching of literature, one of the best ways both to earn a living and to cultivate a readership was by appealing simultaneously to an avant-garde literary audience and to an academic one. This instinct had been developed by the early careers of these graduate-student poets. It also suited the evolving market. So, in their first prose books, Pound and Eliot fly poetic and academic pennants side by side; indeed, so close that it is often hard to tell which flag is which.

The title page of Pound's *The Spirit of Romance* encapsulates this beautifully. The title itself sounds vaguely Celtic Twilighty, but the author, 'Ezra Pound, M.A.', appears brandishing his academic alongside his poetic credentials ('Author of "Personae" and "Exultations" '). The book's subtitle is a wonderful fudge between the precision of professional research academia with its anxiety to define and mark out fields, and old-style, Paterian vagueness, mesmerized by imprecise allure: *An Attempt to Define Somewhat the Charm of the Pre-Renaissance Literature of Latin Europe*.[36] Its 'Praefatio ad Lectorem Electum' announces of *The Spirit of Romance* that 'Only by courtesy can it be said to be a study in comparative literature', yet those words 'study' and 'comparative literature' carry the freight of US academia. Pound has his cake and eats it. He pronounces that 'There are a number of sciences connected with the study of literature', though on the other hand 'There is in literature itself the Art, which is not, and never will be, a science'. He goes on playing such games, drily reassuring the reader that he has worked in accordance with an early regulation of the University of Paris, and acknowledging the 'refined and sympathetic scholarship' of his mentor 'Dr. Wm. P. Shepherd of Hamilton College', though announcing too that 'This book treats only of such medieval works as still possess an interest other than archaeological for the contemporary reader who is not a specialist.'[37] Evolved from his own postgraduate work; developed in his London Polytechnic lectures; footnoted, yet cavalier, Pound's book holds out hands to poetic and to academic readers. It attempts to bring both groups together through a new kind of 'literary scholarship, which will weigh Theocritus and Yeats with one balance'.[38]

Eliot's *The Sacred Wood* (1920) does this in a subtler manner. Its author begins by engaging thoroughly and often disdainfully with Arnold, in important ways Eliot's precursor and master: 'In a society in which the arts were seriously studied, in which the art of writing was respected, Arnold might have become a critic.'[39] That phrase 'seriously studied' is a clear gesture towards Eliot's academic background and towards one of his volume's target audiences (*The Sacred Wood* would eventually become part of a library of 'University Paperbacks'). This book, like Pound's, aims to fuse the critical and the creative. It draws together academic and poetry-loving audiences, encouraging an overlap between the two. Writing in *The Sacred Wood* about the country he had left, Eliot stated that 'the culture of ideas has only been able to survive in America in the unfavourable atmosphere of the university'. In London he found a

---

[36] Pound, *The Spirit of Romance*, title page.   [37] Ibid. 7–9.   [38] Ibid. 8.
[39] T. S. Eliot, The Sacred Wood (1920; repr. London: Methuen, 1960), p. xiii.

culture beyond college walls, but he also wished to take academia with him. Educated by 'Mr. Babbitt', author of *Literature and the American College* (on which 'T. Stearns Eliot, M.A. (Harvard)' drew for his 1916 Oxford University Extension Lectures), and 'Mr. More', whom Eliot compared to Arnold's master Saint-Beuve, the author of *The Sacred Wood* berates the 'hobby' criticism of England. He is bringing to bear on his new homeland his substantial American academic training.[40] He may seem to be distancing himself somewhat from that 'American solemnity' which is unlike English solemnity, being 'more primitive, more academic, more like that of the German professor', but the tone of *The Sacred Wood*, hieratic, papal, and professorial, indicates that American solemnity has not been left far behind.[41] Eliot's volume appeared at the start of the decade which would see I. A. Richards's quasi-scientific *Practical Criticism: A Study of Literary Judgment* and many other academic works on criticism. His manner allowed him to appeal to those academics at the forefront of literary study as well as to readers of poetry. More than that, the fusion of the 'primitive' and the 'academic' which went with that 'American solemnity' was closely akin to Eliot's 1919 encapsulation of his poetic ideal of the artist as 'most competent to understand both civilized and primitive'.[42] It was what made Eliot a modern poet.

That these poets' project of writing their poetics in the form of academically tinged criticism was effective, indeed more commercially successful than their poetry, is indicated by the print runs of their early volumes. Until they had educated their audience through quasi-academic channels, making them trained readers of the new poetry, Eliot and Pound found a wider, mainstream circulation for their criticism than for their verse. Eliot's first book, *Prufrock and Other Observations* (1917), was published by his friends at the Egoist Press in a print run of 500 copies. It did not sell out until after the appearance of *The Sacred Wood* in 1920. In England Eliot's further early verse collections were published in editions of around 250 copies by other small presses. As his first critical book, however, *The Sacred Wood* was launched by the

[40] Ibid. 44; the syllabus for Eliot's Extension Lectures is reprinted in A. D. Moody, *Thomas Stearns Eliot, Poet*, paperback edn. (Cambridge: Cambridge University Press, 1980), 41–9. McDonald, *Learning to be Modern*, 56, links Babbitt's book to Eliot's lectures.

[41] Eliot, *The Sacred Wood*, 44.

[42] T. S. Eliot, 'War-Paint and Feathers', *Athenaeum*, 17 Oct. 1919, 1036; see Robert Crawford, *The Savage and the City in the Work of T. S. Eliot* (Oxford: Clarendon Press, 1987).

mainstream publisher Methuen.[43] Pound's early poetry volumes appeared from small presses in editions of around 100–150 copies. Though Elkin Matthews published *Personae* (1909) and *Exultations* (1909) in editions of 1,000, the sheets of around half of these were still available to be bound together in 1913. *The Spirit of Romance*, however, had a print run of 1,250 copies when it was produced by Dent and Dutton in London and New York in 1910.[44] Publishers were more confident in Pound and Eliot as critics than as poets. Alert to the developments of academia, the two Americans preached a fusion of the critical and creative intelligence. For them this combination was bound up with modern poetry to the extent that 'the critic and the creative artist should frequently be the same person'.[45] In the longer term this would lead the full assimilation of modernist poetry into the university canon and to poetry being seen by many as an academic property.

If Hugh Blair had used his scholarly mantle to evangelize on behalf of Ossian, then, as part of the attempted American Renaissance, Eliot used his own learning to stress that of Pound, marketing him as both exciting and professor-friendly in the anonymous, academic-sounding 'brochure' *Ezra Pound: His Metric and Poetry*. Amazingly, Knopf commissioned this work from Eliot and published it in 1920 in an edition of 1,000 copies.[46] Eliot stresses Pound's poetic merit and innovations, yet he also does a brilliant job of courting the academic audience. Emphasizing Pound's 'intensive study' and 'erudition' which make him too demanding for the 'casual reader', Eliot nonetheless insists that Pound's 'knowledge' is not 'pedantry'.

He is, it is true, one of the most learned of poets. In America he had taken up the study of Romance Languages with the intention of teaching. After work in Spain and Italy, after pursuing the Provençal verb from Milan to Freiburg, he deserted the thesis on Lope de Vega and the Ph.D. and the professorial chair, and elected to remain in Europe. Mr. Pound has spoken out his mind from time to time on the subject of scholarship in American universities, its deadness, its isolation from genuine appreciation, and the active life of literature. He has always been ready to battle against pedantry. As for his own learning, he has

[43] Donald Gallup, *T. S. Eliot: A Bibliography* (London: Faber & Faber, 1969), 23, 25, and 28.
[44] Donald Gallup, *Ezra Pound: A Bibliography* (Charlottesville: University of Virginia Press, 1983), 3–10.
[45] Eliot, *The Sacred Wood*, 16.
[46] *The Letters of T. S. Eliot*, i: *1898–1922*, ed. Valerie Eliot (London: Faber & Faber, 1988), 222 (to John Quinn, London, 4 Mar. 1918). Gallup, T. S. Eliot, 24.

studied poetry carefully, and has made use of his study in his own verse. *Personae* and *Exultations* show his talent for turning his studies to account.[47]

Here is a poet who engages in the debates of academia, whose academic training has developed his poetry, who has a dash of romance and anti-pedantic daring, yet is familiar with 'the professorial chair' and has been 'turning his studies to account'. With brilliant daring presented as scrupulous fairness, Eliot quotes from adverse reviews of *Canzoni*. Pound seems to one reviewer 'rather a scholar than a poet' and prompts another to wish the poet would 'walk out of the library'. Pound's work, moreover, has generated controversy at 'the University of Illinois'. Mockingly, Eliot cites the British critic William Archer who 'believes in the simple untaught muse'. Eliot's study concludes with mention of Pound's move to the epic in the *Cantos*. 'If the reader fails to like them, he has probably omitted some step in his progress, and had better go back and retrace his journey.'[48] This finger-wagging is obviously de-signed to get people to buy Pound's earlier poetry. It also makes that poetry sounds a bit like an exam where anyone who 'fails' can retake the course. As Pound wrote in the early 1930s, 'It would be hypocrisy to pretend that Eliot's essays are not aimed at professors and students.'[49] *Ezra Pound: His Metric and Poetry* is not directed solely at an academic audience, but it certainly works hard to pull them on board.

In the same year, 1920, Pound was making a further, unsuccessful attempt to get the University of Pennsylvania to award him a Ph.D. for *The Spirit of Romance*.[50] He wanted the validation and attention of academia, on his own terms; yet those very terms were a product of his academic training. It was that education which led him to begin his first major poetic manifesto with a nod to his late 'pastors and masters' and to call it a 'New Method in Scholarship', though its published title *I Gather the Limbs of Osiris* gives it a more esoterically Yeatsian ring. Pound discusses 'The aim of right education'. He maintains that his 'method' is one which 'has been intermittently used by all good scholars since the beginning of scholarship, the method of Luminous Detail'.[51] In summary, luminous details are literary diamonds plucked from the

---

[47] T. S. Eliot, *To Criticize the Critic and Other Writings* (London: Faber & Faber, 1965), 165–6.
[48] Ibid. 172, 174, 176, and 182.
[49] Ezra Pound, 'Praefatio Aut Cimicium Tumulus' (1933), in *Selected Prose, 1909–1965*, ed. W. Cookson (London: Faber & Faber, 1973), 364.
[50] McDonald, *Learning to be Modern*, 22.
[51] Pound, *Selected Prose*, 21.

surrounding mud that encrusts them; they are the vital material, the 'gists' to use another Poundian term. Modern readers might connect such talk with Arnold's notion of 'touchstones'. Pound puts the matter differently. As he summarizes it most interestingly in 1911, 'In my opening chapter I said that there were certain facts or points, or "luminous details", which governed knowledge as the switchboard the electric circuit.'[52] This scientifically expressed preoccupation with the governing of knowledge links Pound to the development of cybernetics (which literally means 'governing knowledge'), though that word would not be coined until 1948 when Norbert Wiener published his ground-breaking book on the subject. Modernist verse, so nurtured by and alert to academic channels as well as to the relationship between knowledge and power, is very much a poetry of the governing of knowledge.

More simply, Pound's preoccupation emerges from his student experience. For what the student (particularly the research student) constantly does is to sieve texts for their essential matter. Lectures are reconfigured as lecture notes, books are summarized, vital quotations transcribed. This is the way Pound and Eliot were trained. In the Houghton Library at Harvard are the index cards on which Eliot as a postgraduate transcribed the passages from his reading that mattered most to him, and in King's College, Cambridge, in the Hayward Bequest, are his student considerations of such topics as communication, classification, interpretation, and the nature of knowledge. The production of such materials does not make one a poet, but Pound and Eliot use their training to develop a poetic method. When the young Pound presents in a poem a query such as 'What are the kinds of knowledge?' he is asking the same question as Eliot the graduate student who wrote his thesis on *Experience and the Objects of Knowledge in the Philosophy of F. H. Bradley*.[53] This obsessive interest in knowledge on the part of both Pound and Eliot was nurtured by academia, and fed their poetry.

The 'New Method of Scholarship' christened by Pound that of the 'luminous detail' is not only a scholarly technique. It is at least as much a method of poetic composition. In *The Cantos* it produces a continual music of digested and excerpted knowledge where the sieved tomes of the library mix with studenty slang, so that within fifteen lines we can move from untransliterated Greek quotations through description of

[52] Pound, *Selected Prose*, 24.
[53] Ibid. 47 ('Religio'); T. S. Eliot, *Knowledge and Experience in the Philosophy of F. H. Bradley* (London: Faber & Faber, 1964), 11.

Homer in colloquial cliché ('blind as a bat') to Latin, English, Provençal, and Italian.[54] On the one hand, such *bricolage* harks back to the days when universities were more universal. It gestures towards an assumed golden age when a gentlemanly elite had a full education, allowing them to glide from language to language, before a stage was reached when 'departments do not communicate with one another'.[55] On the other hand, this poetry also points forward to the research university full of graduate students devoting all their time to a verse of labyrinthine difficulty. Either way, and whatever its lyrical flashes, the work is deliberately bookish and library fuelled. Yet there is too a curious sense in which this poetry is anti-academic. Pound, fascinated by learning and by government, attempts with his method of the luminous detail to have poetry, not academia, govern knowledge. So his verse is in accord with his 1914 prospectus for a College of Arts (no one enrolled) in which artists and poets, not academics, would run the curriculum; it is in tune with his later establishment of a one-man 'Ezuversity', a counter-university whose knowledge was at the service of poetry; it goes with his production of textbooks— the *Guide to Kulchur*, the *ABC of Reading* with its 'private word to students and professors . . . to save even them from unnecessary boredom in the classroom'.[56] Throughout a career inveighing against the wrongs of academia, Pound in his work constantly replicates its forms and procedures. Like Eliot, as he wrote to Eliot's conservative father in 1915, he is a scholar-poet.[57] But he is no product of and for the dreaming spires; his home, his place both of exile and return, is essentially the modern American university. He called Eliot in 1921 the 'Dean of English Letters'.[58] Pound was a one-man faculty.

Pound's poetry enacts a revenge on the academia which spurned him. It shows him as a poet out-professoring the professors, claiming not just access to, but governance of the knowledge he considers essential. So Pound, with a professorial arrogance which merges with his fascist leanings, tells people what to read, hectors them, dictates knowledge. From another point of view he simply continues the university model

[54] Ezra Pound, *The Cantos*, rev. collected edn. (London: Faber & Faber, 1975), 24 ('VII').

[55] Pound quoted in McDonald, *Learning to be Modern*, 109.

[56] See *The Selected Letters of Ezra Pound, 1907–1941*, ed. D. D. Page (London: Faber & Faber, 1950), 41–43, and Carpenter, *A Serious Character*, 518–32; Ezra Pound, *ABC of Reading* (London: Faber & Faber, 1951), 11.

[57] *Letters of T. S. Eliot*, i. 101 (Pound to Henry Ware Eliot, London, 28 June 1915).

[58] Ibid. 488 (Eliot to Richard Aldington, London, 17 Nov. 1921).

provided for him in his upbringing, and leads poetry into the seminar room. Just as he seemed to consider that his treason was a way of defending the essential virtues of his country (its good government), so his anti-philological betrayal of his own training was done in the spirit of preserving what really mattered in literature, and was carried out in a manner highly academic. In a phrase that again suggests not so much the scholarly as the military, Pound becomes a kind of 'double agent' towards both poetry and academia. His loyalties to each are impossibly complicated by his affiliation to the other, so that in the end his destiny as poet seems deeply implicated with the fate of academia itself. In this he foreshadows younger American poets who entered college life formally as teachers of poetry, men such as R. P. Blackmur, the title of whose 1935 volume, *The Double Agent: Essays in Craft and Elucidation*, summarizes the complex position of writers for whom knowledge was both academically and poetically structured.

Pound's career, much more bound up with the institutions of higher education than Yeats's, heralds a move beyond the position of the poet as 'scholar-gypsy'. Though Pound retains a mystical side that was nourished by the Celtic Twilight and by Yeatsian occultism, *The Cantos* mark the growth of that modernist poetry so involved with the government of knowledge that it can be called cybernetic. Eliot's career reinforces and complicates such a designation. Eliot exemplifies how the development of an academically conditioned twentieth-century poetry of knowledge emerged in important ways from a philosophical milieu shared with the pioneer of the science of cybernetics.

Like Pound, Eliot was an academic insider. He engaged in an argument with the system that produced him. His brilliant early poem 'Mr Apollinax' is based on Bertrand Russell's presence at Harvard. The speaker admires not only the 'dry and passionate talk' of Mr Apollinax, but also his 'submarine and profound' laughter which disconcerts his professorial host. Left behind by the alien visitor's brilliance, the wrong-footed professor can only manage the late retort, 'There is something he said that I might have challenged.'[59] Mixing imagery of the polite with symbols of the unconscious, Eliot's poem, with its Greek epigraph, announces its author as erudite, but also impatient with the usual trappings of academic learning. It rejoices in the outsmarting it describes. It has a sparring cleverness about it. Such a tone is detectable

---

[59] T. S. Eliot, *The Complete Poems and Plays* (London: Faber & Faber, 1969), 31.

in Eliot's correspondence with the future inventor of cybernetics, an exchange of letters dating from the same period as 'Mr Apollinax'.

It would be possible to make too much of the connection between Eliot and Norbert Wiener, who, like the poet, had fallen under Russell's spell, but the link is at least emblematic, and probably more than that.[60] The two men shared a common Harvard philosophical background. Both had taken part in the epistemological graduate course 'A Comparative Study of Various Types of Scientific Method' run by Professor Josiah Royce. Wiener was a member of Royce's seminar from 1911 until 1913, while Eliot participated in 1913–14.[61] Among other things, the two students shared interests in the foundations of knowledge and in the work of such philosophers as Leibniz, William James, Bradley, and Bergson. Wiener wrote on all three in his published philosophical papers of 1914. Eliot, who had read James at Harvard, published on Leibniz in 1916, was writing his doctoral thesis on Bradley between 1913 and 1916, and had earlier attended Bergson's lectures at the Collège de France.[62] In 1914–15 Eliot and Wiener were both in England, and in close contact. Much of the communication between the two took the form of conversations, but some correspondence has survived. This makes clear the detailed attention each was paying to the other's work. In particular, Eliot's January 1915 letter to Wiener demonstrates how strongly Eliot agreed with Wiener's recent paper on 'Relativism'. Eliot had received a copy of this essay from its author, and its subject was one which the two friends had discussed thoroughly in conversation.[63] Wiener, like Eliot, was interested in the basics of knowledge and experience. His 'Relativism' not only investigates whether or not there is 'self-sufficient knowledge', but also argues that 'we must experience in relation from the very beginning everything we ever know in relation' so that 'Our experience, if given at all, must be given as a system.' Wiener continues,

If each moment of our experience should be precisely what it is as if neither past nor future existed, then the experience of a moment would, to all intents and purposes, constitute my whole personality at that moment, and I would be

---

[60] Norbert Wiener, *Cybernetics*, 2nd edn. (New York: MIT Press and John Wiley, 1961), 13.

[61] Ibid. 1–2; Peter Ackroyd, *T. S. Eliot* (London: Hamish Hamilton, 1984), 48.

[62] See Norbert Wiener, 'The Highest Good', *Journal of Philosophy, Psychology and Scientific Methods*, 10 Sep. 1914, 512–20 and Norbert Wiener, 'Relativism', *Journal of Philosophy, Psychology and Scientific Methods*, 8 Oct. 1914, 561–77; Eliot, *Knowledge and Experience*, 177–207; Ackroyd, *T. S. Eliot*, 40–1.

[63] *Letters of T. S. Eliot*, i. 79 (to Norbert Wiener, London, 6 Jan. 1915).

undergoing a continual alteration of personality. It is indeed a logical possibility that our present is entirely dissociated from our past: that the I which writes this word is an entirely different person from the I which crosses this *t*. It is, however, a view which nobody will hold, for if it were true, our memory would be but an illusion, and our expectation a vain self-deception.[64]

This rather clotted passage of Wiener's 1914 prose is saturated with the issues that preoccupied the graduate student Eliot. The conclusion to Eliot's doctoral dissertation on knowledge and experience is missing, but the last words we have are 'all knowledge is relative'.[65] Wiener's 'Relativism', with which, wrote Eliot in 1915, he cordially agreed, presents experience and knowledge not only as relative but also as relational, as part of a system rather than as isolated in the present moment.[66] Writing about the experience and knowledge of literary creation in 'Tradition and the Individual Talent', Eliot would also emphasize a system (he calls it 'tradition') in which literature is relationally structured: 'No poet, no artist of any art, has his complete meaning alone. His significance, his appreciation is the appreciation of his relation to the dead poets and artists.'[67] Akin to Pound's wish for a literary scholarship which could 'weigh Theocritus and Yeats with one balance', Eliot's idea of literary tradition involves knowing, in Wiener's words, 'from the very beginning everything we ever know in relation'. So, for Eliot, the poet must 'write not merely with his own generation in his bones, but with a feeling that the whole literature of Europe from Homer and within it the whole of the literature of his own country has a simultaneous existence and composes a simultaneous order'.[68] This is Eliot's relational system. Where Wiener, interested (like the Eliot of Royce's seminar) in William James's notion of empirical egos, specialized selves—'a social, a professional, a business, a religious self, etc.'—speculates about 'a continual alteration of personality', Eliot, emerging from a similar philosophical background, wishes to separate the mundane self of 'the man who suffers' from the creative self 'the mind which creates', and so presents the artist's 'continual extinction of personality'.[69] In the same year that he wrote these words, Eliot related this idea of the poetic extinction of personality to the work of great

[64] Wiener, 'Relativism', 561 and 564.   [65] Eliot, *Knowledge and Experience*, 11.
[66] *Letters of T. S. Eliot*, i. 79 (to Norbert Wiener, London, 6 Jan. 1915).
[67] Eliot, *Selected Essays*, 15.   [68] Ibid. 14.
[69] Wiener, 'Relativism', 569; Eliot, *Selected Essays*, 18 and 17 ('Tradition and the Individual Talent').

scientists.[70] My intention is not to suggest that Eliot's thought derives from Wiener's, but to suggest points of contact between the ideas of the two philosophy students at this stage. Wiener's 'Relativism' paper concludes by looking towards a progressive view of science which, conscious of the relativity of its own knowledge, can still improve. His interest leads him eventually towards that concern with systems of knowledge which culminates in the publication of *Cybernetics* in 1948. Eliot's 1915 letter to Wiener makes it clear that for him the lesson of relativism was to avoid philosophy and give oneself over either to '*real* art' or to '*real* science'.[71] Eliot goes on to devote himself to real art.

Nonetheless, the point from which Wiener and Eliot diverge leads to connections between their later work. Wiener in his introduction to *Cybernetics* recalls as seminal his participation in Royce's seminar, and Manju Jain has demonstrated convincingly how important Royce's work was to Eliot as he evolved not only his philosophy but also his poetics.[72] Wiener's choice of Leibniz as 'patron saint for cybernetics', Leibniz being the last 'man who has had a full command of all the intellectual activity of his day', may be aligned with Eliot's celebration of Leibniz as uniquely important for modern thought—'No philosophy contains more various possibilities of development.'[73] Again, the way in which Wiener's first chapter of *Cybernetics* is entitled 'Newtonian and Bergsonian Time' reminds us of that obsession with time which was nurtured by Eliot's Bergsonian interests and which, having powered *The Waste Land*, culminates in *Four Quartets*. In his later chapter on 'Information, Language, and Society', Wiener gets to the heart of his theory of cybernetics, making it clear that, whether we are thinking of an organism, a brain, a body, a group of people, a machine or machines, 'the community extends only so far as there extends an effectual transmission of information'.[74] This emphasis on the vital part played by the transmission of information in structuring a community is rooted in the work of C. S. Peirce and William Royce, though for Royce the community was structured not simply by transmission but by interpretation of what was transmitted.[75] It is this process of mutual interpretation that

[70] T. S. Eliot, 'Modern Tendencies in Poetry,' *Shama'a*, 1 (Apr. 1920), 11.
[71] *Letters of T. S. Eliot*, i. 81 (to Norbert Wiener, London, 6 Jan. 1915).
[72] Wiener, *Cybernetics*, 1–2; Manju Jain, *T. S. Eliot and American Philosophy* (Cambridge: Cambridge University Press, 1992), 112–58.
[73] Wiener, *Cybernetics*, 12 and 2; Eliot, *Knowledge and Experience*, 197.
[74] Wiener, *Cybernetics*, 157–8.
[75] Jain, *T. S. Eliot and American Philosophy*, 133–7.

Eliot wrote about for Royce's seminar, though later as a poet-critic he would be obsessed by ideas of transmission, cultural, religious, educational, and poetic. He would contend in one extreme statement that 'there is no such thing as the interpretation of poetry; poetry can only be transmitted'.[76] Eliot's conception of poetry is cybernetic.

'Tradition and the Individual Talent' is about the passing on of poetry, a transmission that forms a community. Eliot himself was shaped by various communities, but crucial among them was the society of academia, that system through which knowledge was transmitted to him. We may think of Eliot as primarily a philosophy student, but in his first three years at Harvard he took nine courses in English and Comparative Literature. These included two on 'The Literary History of England and its Relations to that of the Continent'.[77] It is hard to argue that his view of literature was unaffected by his academic reception of it, or that his view of 'the mind of Europe' was not a product of the transmission of ideas through academia.[78] Arnold had insisted in 'The Function of Criticism' that

> The criticism which alone can much help us for the future, the criticism which, throughout Europe, is at the present day meant, when so much stress is laid on the importance of criticism and the critical spirit,—is a criticism which regards Europe as being, for intellectual and spiritual purposes, one great confederation...[79]

By the late nineteenth century these words were familiar to thousands of students as the epigraph to a series of twelve volumes on the 'Periods of European Literature' edited by George Saintsbury, Professor of Rhetoric and English Literature at Edinburgh University. Eliot later said that he 'greatly respected' Saintsbury, whom he invited to contribute to the first issue of his international magazine *The Criterion*, in 1922.[80] Work such as Saintsbury's underlay the sort of Comparative Literature courses taken by Eliot at Harvard. These presented English as related to European literature. The impact of this approach, and of this degree structure, was crucial for Eliot. Whether in literature or philosophy,

---

[76] T. S. Eliot, ' "The Duchess of Malfi" at the Lyric: and Poetic Drama', *Art and Letters*, 3 (Winter 1919/20), 39.

[77] For Eliot's courses see Jain, *T. S. Eliot and American Philosophy*, 252–6.

[78] Eliot, *Selected Essays*, 16 ('Tradition and the Individual Talent').

[79] Arnold, *Essays in Criticism*, 33.

[80] *Letters of T. S. Eliot*, i. 483 (to the Editor of the *TLS*, London [3 Nov. 1921]) and 550 (to E. R. Curtius, London, 21 July 1922).

Dante or Sanskrit, the pre-Socratics or Japanese Buddhism, his apparently atomistic Harvard education gave to him (and located him within) a proliferating system of knowledge-transmission and interpretation, a cybernetic community. That would provide the intellectual underpinning for *The Waste Land*.

Cybernetics emphasizes the transmission of information as crucial, and as constructing both the communities and the relational patterns on which knowledge depends. So does modernist poetry. Its constant use of textual and cultural allusion sets up a potentially endless knowledge and information flow, and seems designed to do so. Writing in his doctoral dissertation about 'The Epistemologist's Theory of Knowledge', Eliot stated that 'Epistemology, therefore, is simply the process by which what is at first knowledge is absorbed into another aspect: knowing becomes known, an activity becomes an object, and the process can be repeated *ad infinitum*.'[81] On one level this is about ever-increasing self-consciousness (a preoccupation of J. Alfred Prufrock), but it is also about how knowledge endlessly generates knowledge. This is the way allusion functions in *The Cantos* and *The Waste Land*. Those poems manifest a sometimes deliberate, sometimes subliminal awareness of other texts, so that they generate an infinitely proliferating set of relationships in which it becomes impossible ultimately to determine what is deliberate allusion and what is unplanned relationship. We have developed the term 'intertextuality' to help here, but that is a late twentieth-century word and can be applied to any text. What marks out modernist poems, and particularly *The Waste Land*, is the way in which the poetic production is undergirded by, and seeks to develop, a system of knowledge-government via institutional transmission through academia. These poems (like their poets) send their readers off endlessly to other texts which help construct a proliferating network of relationships. Spoof or not, the Notes to *The Waste Land* are aimed at the academic mind by an academic intelligence. The fact that this intelligence is in torment gives the poem an emotional feverishness whose excitement is highly contagious. *The Waste Land* avoids pedantic dustiness. It is a poem obsessed by the possibility of relationships, yet haunted by the fear that all relationships may be meaningless. This holds true for the level of personal liaisons as it does at the level of the relationships of intellectual and textual knowledge. Feral and

---

[81] Eliot, *Knowledge and Experience*, 86.

fragmentary, *The Waste Land*, like 'Mr Apollinax' before it, is Eliot's revenge on his own professors. It outsmarts them in its intellectual leaps and its encyclopedic frenzy. It transmits on a frequency they cannot quite catch. Crying out for understanding, its pain is bound up with its near incomprehensibility. If for Prufrock 'It is impossible to say just what I mean! | But as if a magic lantern threw the nerves in patterns on a screen', then *The Waste Land* projects a neural network that is a cybernetic system on the edge of running out of control.[82] It convinces us by its poetic music, yet we can understand it only with notes, guides, commentary. Drawing on all of Eliot's earlier knowledge and training, it is written out of these things. The details of Eliot's academic career are made luminous with pressure. In one light it is heartbreakingly human. In another, in terms of its ultimate textual and intellectual ramifications, it is a hypertext that only a computer could read.

This latter suggestion may sound insensitive, but the cybernetically developed computer systems of postmodernity allow us to comprehend better the poetry of literary modernism. They provide analogies that did not exist at the time. Modernist allusion functions as a hypertext system, taking the reader continually from one reference to another, setting up complex relationships among texts within texts. The older, manuscript-based analogy of the 'palimpsest' is too simple to express how a poem like *The Waste Land* works. It sets up so many simultaneous relationships, transmits such a multitude of messages, that it offers us a vast database, a growing library of texts, bridges between them, and connections between cultures. Its complexity is a cybernetic one which anticipates the computer age at least as much as it derives from earlier forms.

In saying this I am in no way attempting to deny the poem's emotional power, its sense of 'burning'. Nor am I trying to render it inaccessible. On the contrary, in various ways it became more accessible as the twentieth century and its technologies developed. As we look back on that epoch, we can see that modernist poetry is part of our evolving sense of ourselves as 'problem-solving' beings. The growth of the notion of people as problem-solvers runs across both popular and highbrow culture. Like the Sherlock Holmes stories Eliot loved, like the crossword puzzle, and the code-switching computer, the modernist poem is a deliberately coded work. Part of the reader's pleasure comes from 'solving' it.

---

[82] Eliot, *The Complete Poems and Plays*, 16 ('The Love Song of J. Alfred Prufrock').

Because they are complex literary productions, *The Waste Land* and *The Cantos* have no single solution. That does not stop them manifesting a 'problem-solving' allure to the reader. They are mounted as a challenge. They create round them interpretative communities. They transmit through allusion what appears to their authors and audiences important cultural information. Yet the degree to which they appear to do this self-consciously and seriously marks them out as modernist. Even if only from one aspect, it is important that they are exam-poems, testing the audience, and demanding in turn the attention of the reader as student. With them, magnificently and problematically, poetry becomes cybernetic. A long procession of examinees and examiners stretches in their wake.

Foremost among the students following *The Waste Land* is the young W. H. Auden, whose work *The Orators* is the most revealing and impressive early response to Eliot's poem. *The Orators* is one of Auden's less read pieces. It is also among his most entertaining in its near-surreal wit, formal adventurousness, and mixing of genres. At least one contemporary poet, Glyn Maxwell, has seen in it elements which have served to support and encourage his own work.[83] *The Orators* matters too in the context of academic English Studies at the time of the poem's composition. Appreciation of that fact may prompt a fuller consideration of the relationship between writers and academics at the present time, suggesting that while this connection may remain problematic, there may also be grounds for a slant of optimism when we think of today's modern poets.

The Orators carnivalizes concerns about the government of knowledge. Its 'Address for a Prize-Day' begins, 'Commemoration. Commemoration. What does it mean? What does it mean? Not what does it mean to them, there, then. What does it mean to us, here now? It's a facer, isn't it boys?' (*EA* 61)[84] Auden's 'Writing' essay, which dates from the same year (1932), ends like this: 'Its not only literature but our lives that are going to pot. We cant sit on the fence much longer. Well.'[85] These two voices are hard to tell apart. One parodies the haranguer of schoolboys, and we know from Christopher Isherwood that it is based

[83] Glyn Maxwell, 'Echoes of the Orators', *Verse*, 63 (1989), 25.

[84] The text of *The Orators* used is that in W. H. Auden, *The English Auden*, ed. Edward Mendelson (London: Faber & Faber, 1977), hereafter abbreviated in my text as *EA*.

[85] Quoted from the manuscript version of 'Writing' transcribed in *W. H. Auden: The Map of All my Youth*, ed. Katherine Bucknell and Nicholas Jenkins (Oxford: Clarendon Press, 1990), 54.

on a remembered sermon from Auden's own schooldays. The other voice is Auden himself, poet and schoolmaster, addressing the audience of Naomi Mitchison's *Outline for Boys and Girls and their Parents* for which his 'Writing' essay was commissioned. Both voices bumble a bit in their use of pally cliché—'It's a facer', 'going to pot'. In the first instance we laugh admiringly at an accurate spoof of the acoustics of authority; in the second we are a little taken aback when Auden unironically inhabits those acoustics, leaving his audience with that echoing, teachery 'Well.'

The coincidence of these voices is not random. If Isherwood liked to recall Auden's delight in the pseudo-sermonizing, oh-so-English voice—'Bert—whur does it mean to *ers, heah, nerw?*'—then it is startling to see the same words appearing six years before *The Orators* in one of Auden's early student poems, written just after he first read T. S. Eliot.

> What does it mean?
> After the hymn we sat, wiped sticky fingers,
> Thinking of home, What does it mean
> To us, here, now?[86]

Here the institutional voice is replayed as that of the lyric poet. The two are inseparable, and the bonding is emblematic. For Auden cannot ultimately detach his own voice from the institutional tone; nor, in the end, does he want to. What we always hear in his work is the voice of the master, not only in the sense of the great poetic craftsman, but also in the guise of the functionary of the academic system. Auden's is a voice which inhabits and is inhabited by the acoustics of authority, saying to young people the classroom-oriented, potentially intimidating 'Well.'

Auden was the first important British poet to study English at Oxford, then to go on to work in the educational system both at school and at university level. *The Orators*, subtitled *An English Study, sounds* like an academic volume. With its numbered diagrams, sets of instructions, alphabetically tabulated listings, and prose sections with such headings as 'Argument' and 'Statement', it also *looks* as much like a university textbook as a poem. Even if there was not already in existence a textbook called *The Orators*, that title suggests a student tome, one that might contain speeches by Demosthenes, or Cicero, or Burke. As Hugh Blair and Auden well knew, oratory is bound up with both knowledge and

---

[86] Christopher Isherwood cited in Edward Mendelson, *Early Auden* (London: Faber & Faber, 1981), 98; poem quoted in Humphrey Carpenter, *W. H. Auden* (London: Allen & Unwin, 1981), 57.

government. It is all about public control made possible by an admired voice; a respected voice belongs to an orator, a despised one to a demagogue.

Auden's book is about English schools and schooling. Part of the poem appeared in the St Andrews-based Scottish nationalist magazine the *Modern Scot*, and one might argue that it is because *The Orators* is written in Scotland, in the Clydeside town of Helensburgh, that the consciousness of Englishness and of nationalism is heightened. But we should remember that Auden had not only attended an English school as a pupil, he had also been part of a university School of English. His initial year at Oxford was the first year of the *Review of English Studies*, one of the very few academic journals then available to students in the School of English which Auden joined as a student in 1926. It is the job of the poet to be attuned to changes in language use; such alertness attracted Auden to Eliot's work, and Eliot to that of Auden. When the younger poet gave to *The Orators* the subtitle *An English Study* he was well aware of the existence of English Studies. His subtitle, like the poem which follows, directs us to the ways in which language, nation, and educational institutionalism are connected. Schooling in English and in Englishness go together in this English Study.

Though Auden was an undergraduate at Oxford, he was very interested in English Studies at Cambridge, particularly in the work of I. A. Richards. Auden complained to Stephen Spender that it was a scandal that the *TLS* had not devoted more attention to Richards's *Principles of Literary Criticism*, published in 1924, just before Auden went to Oxford.[87] Richards's 1926 essay *Science and Poetry* was also admired by Auden. It brought into conjunction poetry and psychology, as would *The Orators*. Valentine Cunningham has highlighted an immensely influential section of *Science and Poetry* which, drawing on Conrad's Stein in *Lord Jim*, told readers that 'The way is to the destructive element submit yourself, and with the exertions of your hands and feet in the water make the deep, deep sea keep you up.'[88] *The Orators* follows such advice. It gives itself over to institutional forms of discourse that it seeks to mock, yet from which it cannot keep itself separate. Half a century after Arnold's essay on 'The Study of Poetry', *An English Study* submits to English Studies.

[87] Carpenter, *W. H. Auden*, 55.
[88] Valentine Cunningham, *British Writers of the Thirties* (Oxford: Oxford University Press, 1988), 58.

We can see this most clearly if we align *The Orators* with Richards's 1929 *Practical Criticism*. Both works have poetry and prose, text and diagram, and are manifestly woven out a variety of opinionated voices, including ones that are clipped, numbered, and authoritative:

(1)   It is a sure sign of a busybody if he talks of *laissez-faire*. (*EA* 73)

snaps Auden.

6.32   The thought is worthless, and hopelessly muddled. (*PC* 85)[89]

snipes Richards.

Auden writes of 'the Enemy' in his *English Study*. Richards dedicates his book 'To My Collaborators', so that the literary shades into the military (as it so easily did for the knowledge-governor Ezra Pound), while he ends the work with 'Summary and Recommendations' as if it were an official institutional report from a government commission. Auden's poem too is a report, a 'school report' one might say, and a study of England—'Imagine to yourselves a picked body of angels, all qualified experts on the human heart, a Divine Commission, arriving suddenly one day at Dover' (*EA* 61). Poems appear in Richards's volume, but they are present far less to be read for fun than to be treated as educational material. They are specimens (to use Thomas Campbell's scientific-sounding term) that are of use in a process of analysis, testing, and judging, elements in the business of governing knowledge. Like Auden, Richards produces a book which is a huge examiner's report, a product of intense scrutiny (the founding of the Leavisite academic journal *Scrutiny* and *The Orators* date from the same year). Both Richards and Auden are preoccupied with the psychology of interpretation.

BETWEEN the bare apprehension of the literal sense of a passage and the full comprehension of all its meanings in every kind, a number of half-way houses intervene. To ascertain, even roughly, where failure has occurred is, in many cases beyond our power. Innumerable cat and mouse engagements between some investigator of the acumen and pertinacity of Freud and a string of hapless 'patients' would be needed to make plain even the outlines of the process that we so glibly call 'grasping or realising a meaning'. That the final stages are very sudden and surprising in their effects is nearly all that is known about it. (*PC* 43)

---

[89] I. A. Richards, *Practical Criticism* (1929; repr. London: Routledge & Kegan Paul, 1978), hereafter *PC* in my text.

This is Richards, for whom the business of examination becomes a kind of taunting fight ('cat and mouse engagements'), while the students or 'collaborators' become diseased 'patients' in need of Freudian cure. Richards's voice, the examiner's voice, is one of arrogant superiority, whose tone can be linked to that of the knowledge-governor Pound. Discussing 'inability to construe', 'inhibitions', and 'stupidity' in the next paragraph, he concludes, 'The most leaden-witted blockhead thereby becomes an object of interest.' The vicious, examiner's voice of the new discipline of English Studies is pushed further, but also carnivalized and subverted in Auden's *English Study*, a work of knowledge-government where fighters, patients, and students are also confused:

Conversion of hotels and boarding houses into private nursing-homes is carried out as rapidly as possible. Major operations without anaesthetics begin at noon. At 6 p.m. passages of unprepared translation from dead dialects are set to all non-combatants. The papers are collected at 6.10. All who fail to obtain 99% make the supreme sacrifice. Candidates must write on three sides of the paper. (*EA* 92)

Casting his eye on such matters as 'yet another queer interpretation' in a poem 'under examination' (*PC* 113), Richards exposes 'nervousness ... personal twists and accidents' and is worried by readers who produce 'private poems' (*PC* 160). Auden is preoccupied also with the surveillance that will detect the queer (though he is more alert than the po-faced Richards to gay slang): 'Self-regard is the treating of news as a private poem' (*EA* 73). If Richards's English students may become 'patients', Auden knows that he writes about 'England, this country of ours where nobody is well' (*EA* 62). Much of *The Orators* is preoccupied, like Richards's book, with examination of responses. Both authors present us with poetry in the context of testing. Richards seeks to combat 'the fixation of inappropriate responses' (*PC* 249). Auden, in the most memorable section of *The Orators*, puts it more bluntly when he offers us actual geometrical figures to which readers are invited to respond. Captioned 'A Sure Test', these diagrams are to be given to any person who is a 'suspect', and his reactions are to be closely observed. If the suspect picks the wrong diagram, 'it is wiser to shoot at once' (*EA* 74).

What *The Orators* shares with Richards and with the earlier twentieth-century development of English Studies is made clearest when we think of Michel Foucault's drawing attention to the 'examination' as something which links academia to medicine and to the discipline of social control.[90] All codify and institutionally classify us on the basis of our responses. Auden's school environment is also the world of bodily and sexual examination ('Poor little buggers. I'm afraid half of them won't get through the medical' (*EA* 88)) School is the classic locus of the test, and the final English exams Auden sat at Oxford were called 'Schools'. These precipitated in him psychological and physical illness— 'abject depression' and 'flu'. Just before the exams he wrote, 'Schools are becoming a nightmare...I shall start blood-spitting soon.'[91] Spitting blood makes Auden sound like a Keatsian tubercular poet. Whatever his condition, he broke down. A friend found him weeping in his rooms after the Anglo-Saxon paper. Famously, he got a Third. His responses were classified, judged, and the system found him wanting.

This suggests not just another reason for Auden's fascination with exams and illness. There is more at issue than minor verbal links between *The Orators* and *Practical Criticism*. What matters is that a lot of the poetry which appealed most to Auden—such as the Old and Middle English verse of which he makes frequent imaginative use in his early work—came to him through the institutional machinery of English Studies, of a university English degree with its systematic attempts to govern literary knowledge. For Auden, then, poetry was bound up with testing, judging, and examining within an educational system. *The Orators* sets verse in just that context, and does so with a vengeance. The ethos of school and education is all-pervasive, shading all too easily into military, sexual, and creative life. The acoustics of the work's internally rhymed verse epigraph play with the words 'private' and 'public' so as to suggest the two are intertwined. Intimate experience is openly declared: we sit round reading (and even discussing) a 'Letter to a Wound'. Poetry has become part of this intimate experience which is being made public through the workings of institutionalized literary study. Dante is not simply a superb poet for the reader to encounter; he has been recruited to the system: 'Some of the senior boys, I expect, will have heard of the great Italian poet Dante, who wrote that very difficult but wonderful poem, *The Divine Comedy*' (*EA* 62). The speaker, the orator, moves on from the study of Dante to urging the school to act as a fascist state. This is the world of 'The Liberal Fascist', to invoke the title of Auden's

---

[90] Michel Foucault, *Discipline and Punish*, trans. Alan Sheridan (New York: Pantheon Books, 1977), 184–5.
[91] Carpenter, *W. H. Auden*, 80.

essay on English public schools, the work that provides the best commentary on *The Orators* (*EA* 321–7). It is relatively easy to view this poem in political and sexual terms, but it is important also to see it in the light of the institutional processing of literature. Much of the poetry in *The Orators* celebrates English schooling. Auden's Odes are dedicated to a 'Captain of Sedbergh School XV', 'To Edward Upward, School-master', 'To My Pupils'. These are poems redolent of a world where 'The fags are flushed, would die at their heroes' feet' (*EA* 96) and where it is possible for acts to 'give you full marks' (*EA* 101). Auden is celebrating the educational machine from the inside at least as much as he is sending it up, and his 'English Study' is far from a simple attack on English Studies.

This poet wants both to enjoy and to subvert institutional organiza-tions. That is plain repeatedly in the form of *The Orators*. '*The Airman's Alphabet*' presents the most basic of learning systems, the alphabet, in words that range from ACE to ZERO, yet alongside each the gloss lays the emphasis always on another letter. So, instead of emphasizing the letter 'E', the verse for 'ENGINE' lays the stress on 'd' and 'r' sounds:

> ENGINE— Darling of designers
> and dirty dragon
> and revolving roarer (*EA* 79)

Something similar happens for each letter, except N; the system is set up and relished only to be violated. Codification and the governing of knowledge are replayed and mocked throughout: 'Three kinds of enemy face—the fucked hen—the favourite puss—the stone in the rain' (*EA* 81). Here we are being given instruction that is at once vivid and hard to respond to, except with puzzlement and laughter. Time after time the poem throws us back on our unsure reactions, like an exam paper or like I. A. Richards's exercises in practical criticism which deliberately re-moved context from their poems in order to focus on problems of response. Modernist poetry, so keen to be difficult and to problematize the reader's reactions, develops out of and is at one with institutional academia. If *The Waste Land* is in important ways the product of the Harvard elective system, and if *The Cantos* are lecture notes writ large, with Pound as his own Ezuversity, then in education in England things happened more slowly. In the English universities, English was a newer subject than it was in Scotland or America. It was not until Auden's generation that the academic institutionalization of poetry in England hit with full force. *The Orators* is the measure of its impact. In that work poetry and education infect each another, neither ever free of its counterpart. The poem is not just about Waterloo being won on the playing fields of Eton; it is also about the examinability of everything, about 'scrutiny'. School and 'Schools' loom omnipresent.

Auden is alert to the results of institutional pressures: 'The Oxford Don: "I don't feel quite happy about pleasure." ' . . . 'Renewal of work at my monograph on Professional Jealousy.' (*EA* 76, 90). But essentially he delights in the acoustics of command that emanate from the process of schooling, the accents of the Officer Training Corps which transfer the tone of authority from the government of knowledge in education to a more straightforwardly military environment:

> John Bull, John Bull, I understand well;
> I know, Bull, I know what you want me to tell.
> Calm, Bull, calm, news coming in time;
> News coming, Bull; calm Bull,
> Fight it down, fight it down,
> That terrible hunger; calm, Bull, first
> We must have a look round, we must know the worst. (*EA* 101)

In *The Orators* Auden inhabits, exploits, and sends up the speechify-ings of institutional authority. He becomes a class poet not by opposing the voices of one social class to another but by replaying to the officer class, the public-school class, the Oxford lecture-room class, its own tones, accents, and poetry at a slightly queered pitch and volume. In so doing he owes a debt to Clough, but where the Victorian 'class poet' looked to Homer, the Auden of the 1930s looks more to medieval English. So we hear, for example, a translated replay of part of *The Battle of Maldon* one of the cornerstones of the very Anglo-Saxon literature which, when examined, had reduced Auden the examinee to tears:

> What have we all been doing to have made from Fear
> That laconic war-bitten captain addressing them now
> 'Heart and head shall be keener, mood the more
>   As our might lessens':
> To have caused their shout 'We will fight till we lie down beside
>   The Lord we have loved'? (*EA* 108)

The passage Auden places between quotation marks is a modern English version of two lines from the Old English poem *The Battle of Maldon*, and Charles Wrenn, the philologically minded *Beowulf* editor who was Auden's Anglo-Saxon tutor, might just have okayed the translation. But what would he have made of finding this bit of translated work in a volume which also mentions ohms, menstruation, halitosis, and adhesive trousers? Very little, I suspect, or else he might have dismissed it as a student prank—and those, surely, are just the effects Auden was after. He has filled his poem with materials which would have seemed highly 'unpoetic' to the teachers of an English syllabus which ended in the nineteenth century. *The Orators* is probably the first poem to include diagrams, to mention 'Cyclostyle copies' or 'the screen of a television set' or the 'Vickers 163' (*EA* 84, 87). Its engagement with forms and technologies of information is part of its poetic excitement. Even the author of *Science and Poetry* and *Practical Criticism* might have been taken aback (it is salutary to compare the antique verse of I. A. Richards with the modernity of *The Orators*). When Oxford's David Nichol Smith (brother of Hugh MacDiarmid's admired G. Gregory Smith), who had been one of Auden's examiners, used to delight in saying of the famous poet, 'I gave him a Third', his hostility was justified, because Auden in *The Orators* hits back at the school mindset, the examination system, and the institution of English Studies with a poem that is in several ways as unpoemy as possible, and which will outsmart and bewilder the examiners.

   In this Auden is united with one of the other unquestionably great 1930s poets of the British islands, the MacDiarmid who crammed his poetry with so many scientific facts and examples that no reader, however learned, possessing however many degrees, would be likely to be familiar with them all. In Scotland MacDiarmid too sought to set himself up as an intimidating governor of knowledge, though one whose verse shows rather less humour than that of Auden. As I shall argue in what follows, MacDiarmid's poetry of knowledge, like *The Orators*, was a challenge to the institutional custodians of learning. *The Orators* and MacDiarmid's work similarly attempt to demonstrate that the poet is more intelligent than the headmaster or the don. Where the Scot's poems of the 1930s enact the autodidact's reprisal against the academia which had too often ignored him, *The Orators* constitutes the poet-student's revenge on the institutional system which had given Auden a third-class degree. Paul Muldoon (a brilliant poet with a third-class degree in English from Queen's University, Belfast) would do the same in *Madoc* some generations later. *The Orators* is more difficult than any exam. It makes us, like Richards's patient-students, feel inadequate as readers; it puzzles, though it also amuses; and it leaves us feeling bemused. Confronting the academic institutionalization of poetry, innumerable later modern poets have felt themselves to a greater or lesser degree in Auden's predicament. The 'Epilogue' to *The Orators* begins ' "O where are you going?" said reader to rider.' The word we expect there is 'writer', not 'rider', but the author has escaped into a plural world of voices and texts, and will not stay to reply. He has thrown down his challenge and formal manifesto to future readers and writers, all of whom—as insiders, outsiders, or people attempting to be both— will be affected directly or indirectly by the institution of English Studies,

As he left them there, as he left them there. (*EA* 110)

That is where we have all finished up, as writers and as readers. Today's poet is more often than not both inside and outside the institutional, academic literary machine, aware, even when like Auden he fights it, that frequently the most useful weapons are ones which bear the imprint of that system itself. Though in my native Scotland, where university education in English literature has gone on longer than anywhere else, several of our most distinguished writers from Burns through MacDiarmid to Don Paterson did not attend university, even those have had to confront the institution of Rhetoric and Belles-Lettres and its descendant, English Studies. Burns, like Macpherson, had his work edited by Hugh Blair; MacDiarmid attacked the Scottish universities, claimed to have attended one, and gave readings in them; Don Paterson has worked as writer-in-residence in the University of Dundee. In the nineteenth century several accomplished Scottish poets, including Thomas Campbell, Alexander Smith, and William Edmondstoune Aytoun, held university positions, sometimes as teachers of English. During the last century distinguished Scottish poets often worked in academia. Edwin Morgan was a Professor of English at Glasgow University; Norman MacCaig taught for years in Stirling University's English Studies Department. Now John Burnside, Douglas Dunn, and Kathleen Jamie are among my colleagues in the School of English at the University of St Andrews. Schoolteachers, writers-in-residence, writers in schools, teachers of creative writing—it is hard to name a modern poet in Scotland who has or has had no contact with English Studies in universities. This is true not only of Scotland, but of the wider world, especially North America.

At this point it is worth trying to articulate clearly the sort of problem which English Studies may pose for the writer, particularly the novice who finds himself or herself in its midst as a student. Though earlier poets, notably those regarded as great, are often intimidating for the poet outside academia, they may nonetheless be regarded as allies in acts of creative imagination. The aspiring writer may find inspiration and quickening in their example, may find some obscure connection between them and himself, even while attempting to move away from aspects of their practice. When these other authors are encountered as part of a degree in English Studies, however, their challenge to the young poet tends to be accentuated in particular ways. Instead of meeting precursors as allies, the fledgling author is pitted against them, having to master and subdue them in order to pass exams on their work. He or she is also made increasingly self-conscious about all acts of writing, both for good and ill. The student is expected to respond with critical essays, rather than other poems; learning *about* these earlier writers subtly predominates over and shapes learning *from* them. Diffi-cult work often provokes in the reader a mixture of challenge and intriguing attraction—we are lured on by what we partly but not yet entirely understand. However, under the pressures of institutional scrutiny and classificatory grading, the intimidating challenge can easily overcome the allure. Examinable works become hurdles to be cleared rather than structures to be inhabited, relished, and perhaps extended.

One could exaggerate the deforming rather than the formative pres-sures that the institutionalized study of English can have on young poets. Eliot, after all, pointed out that being critical was part of the business of writing verse. Yet it is noticeable that many poets are uneasy about the study of poetry at school. Even those who work, like Auden, as part of the educational community, feel a need to distance themselves from what they perceive as 'the system'. One poet in academia for whom Auden's early work—not least that of the Helens-burgh period—has been important is Edwin Morgan. No academics came to interview the young Auden at Larchfield School, but it is significant that by 1959, several years before Morgan published his first full collection, he was already being asked to state his position in the *Universities Quarterly* as part of a symposium on 'the don as poet, or the poet as don'.[92] Here he had to reconcile Morgan the contributor

---

[92] Edwin Morgan, untitled statement, *Universities Quarterly*, 13 (1959), 359–60.

to the *Review of English Studies* with Morgan the poet and translator of Anglo-Saxon poetry. His reaction will be discussed more fully in the following chapter. The immediate point is how frequently nowadays poets work in academia not just in America, but also, for instance, in Britain.

Perhaps for reasons of institutional history, leading female poet-academics may be harder to find, but many a lecturer must recognize the tensions present in *The Orators* and articulated by Morgan. In his book *English People*, Colin Evans examines the motives and practices of contemporary university teachers of English. It is noticeable that remarks such as this are not uncommon: 'There was always a sense that if I studied English I would learn how to write creatively. I learned that that was an inaccurate assessment of what I would get out of studying English...'[93] Here, again, as in *The Orators*, there is the sense of an institutional system which could too easily stifle literary imagination. As pointed out in my Introduction, such sentiments were expressed forcibly of late in the United States by Dana Gioia, inveighing in *Can Poetry Matter?* against the academicization of verse through the widespread university teaching of creative writing. Gioia urged poets to 'avoid the jargon of contemporary academic criticism and write in a public idiom' at the same time as arguing that 'Poetry needs to be liberated from literary criticism.'[94] In Australia, as we have seen, Les Murray's essay 'The Suspect Captivity of the Fisher King' contends that 'academic-led literature is a gentrified suburb' and warns about the exploitative rivalry between university teachers and creative writers.[95] Murray's own work has exhibited a wariness of academia that comes from his days as a student at Sydney University. There, like Judith Wright, he had to twist institutional curricula to his own ends in order to educate himself as a poet. Elsewhere, and for different reasons, James Kelman in 'English Literature and the Small Coterie' complains about the 'contemporary literary criticism' of our institutions as failing to be 'socially responsible'.[96] Professionalized and increasingly developing its own hieratic critical languages, 'advanced' English Studies may have tended to lose contact in its expression with the 'primitive' demotic to which literary

---

[93] Respondent 58 in Colin Evans, *English People* (Buckingham: Open University Press, 1993), 51.

[94] Dana Gioia, *Can Poetry Matter?* (St Paul, Minn.: Graywolf Press, 1992), 23.

[95] Les A. Murray, *The Paperbark Tree* (Manchester: Carcanet, 1992), 331.

[96] James Kelman, *Some Recent Attacks* (Stirling: AK Press, 1992), 23.

language must constantly return for nourishment. Many poets sense that strongly.

At home and abroad, then, for much of the last hundred years a multitude of modern poets in English have experienced the pressures of institutional English Studies encountered by Auden and so thoroughly presented in *The Orators*. Academics too are aware of these forces. In earlier stages of the development of English Studies this commonly resulted in a refusal to consider modern work. Even when I was an undergraduate in the late 1970s, the argument was heard frequently that it was good for students to encounter material (whether new writing or detective stories or texts from other parts of the world) which had not been institutionalized. The trend in literature departments to include more and more contemporary writing at the same time as extending the boundaries of courses far beyond traditional notions of a canon means that for today's students very little comes free of the inky fingerprints of the academy. Potentially almost all writing is fuel for English Studies, Cultural Studies, or a cognate subject. One consequence of this is that in an era already characterized by the self-referential games of postmodernism, poetry becomes more and more a remarkably self-conscious art.

The Orators suggests that society has become a great public school and Exam School rolled into one, and that there is no escape from this. What, then, are the results for today's modern poet, and, for that matter, for today's academic? One consequence is simply that we have to face up to the matter. We need to realize that while literature in no way belongs to the academy, academia has colonized it so thoroughly in subtle ways that even the apparently extra- or anti-academic writer is likely to be affected. In terms of simple economics, getting onto a syllabus is one of the surest bets for guaranteeing sales of less popular verse. Writers and publishers (particularly of poetry) often have an increased self-consciousness about canon-formation. We have seen this already in Eliot. 'Tradition and the Individual Talent' along with the rest of his criticism is in part strategically geared to furthering the reception of his own work, not least in those circles which were likely to applaud the notion that 'criticism is as inevitable as breathing'. By the time Eliot wrote these words in 1919 there was already a growing number of people eager to develop the idea of a critical sense that had to be worked for. This was exactly what kept them in salaried academic employment. Even Eliot, seized on with such eagerness by Richards,

Leavis, and Auden, felt obliged in 'Tradition and the Individual Talent' to warn that

> While, however, we persist in believing that a poet ought to know as much as will not encroach upon his necessary receptivity and necessary laziness, it is not desirable to confine knowledge into a useful shape for examinations...[97]

Yet the Eliot who taught at Harvard was not slow to see the promise of the potential audience for poetry in universities. Nowdays poets can be unhealthily aware of the implications of the academic syllabus or the school reading list. Some, like the contemporary Scottish poet Tom Leonard, even try to ensure that their books are unlikely ever to arrive in a package like the one which so discomfited Robert Frost—the parcel marked 'Educational Material'.

But there may be more positive implications associated with the expansion of English Studies and with contemporary trends. One of these has to do with a Bakhtinian emphasis on the impurity of language, as well as on pluralism and dialogue. To put it plainly, this has led to a sometimes tokenistic, but ultimately valid search for alternative accents which were previously excluded from the syllabus. These may be the voices of earlier women authors, of socially or racially 'marginalized' figures, or of other kinds of writing—unpublished diaries or journalism. One result is that today all anthologies are likely to pay heed to Tom Leonard's point in *Radical Renfrew*: 'Any society is a society in conflict, and any anthology of a society's poetry that does not reflect this, is a lie.'[98] Just as Auden hit back at his 'Schools' examiners in the way he constructed *The Orators*, so Leonard takes as his target the school system of English Studies, arguing that too often what we think of as poetry is something that 'above all contains nothing that will interfere with the lawful exercise of an English teacher going about his or her duty in a classroom'.[99] This view of English Studies, suggests that the best exam-passers 'will be the people best able to understand and to write po-etry'.[100] Whether or not this is an over simplification of popular atti-tudes, ironically it leads the anti-academic Leonard to discuss one of the most fashionable contemporary academic topics, canon-formation. Leonard and academia do not speak with one voice. Nor should they. But they certainly share enough common ground to have a lively

---

[97] Eliot, *Selected Essays*, 17.

[98] Tom Leonard (ed.), *Radical Renfrew* (Edinburgh: Polygon, 1990), introduction, p. xvii.

[99] Ibid.   [100] Ibid., pp. xvii–xviii.

dialogue. Versions of this argumentative conversation have developed since the mid-eighteenth century, and are very much part of being a modern poet.

Like Clough before him, Auden was a public schoolboy, an Oxonian, a littérateur. But he saw the limitations of the system he came from, and wished to investigate these. Coming from his very different background in working-class Glasgow, Tom Leonard has related targets. In their analysis and subversion of forms of cultural authority, *The Orators* and Leonard's work curiously converge, and meet up with the concerns of many recent academics. There may be ways in which the poetic and academic practice of our time could work together to encourage a plurality of voices that bursts out of the narrow range celebrated and undermined in *The Orators*. In terms of its effects on poetry, this is a healthy development. When we think about *The Orators* in relation to the subject of English Studies we raise questions which are very pertinent to the direction both of contemporary creative writing, and of an academic area where pressures for audited conformity may pose dangers as acute as those of military/OTC uniformity. That very phrase 'creative writing' is one which has achieved currency through the university teaching of it as a 'subject', particularly in the United States. If there is a useful common ground between parts of institutional Eng. Lit. and ongoing authorship, then it may be a good thing that Britain's universities are increasingly teaching creative writing. Poets, though, should have the right to work in academia as makers and critics, not just teachers of creative writing. There may even be poets who use an academic critical 'mask' to protect the deeper sources of their imaginative energy.

Alerting ourselves to the dangers of 'English Studies' highlighted in *The Orators* should be a reason for boldness in attempting not to homologize but to encourage more dialogue between modern poets and academics. We should try to find a way of teaching and examining which will allow for a system-busting or system-revising imaginative freedom such as that striven for by W. H. Auden and Tom Leonard. To do so is to encourage kinds of risk seen nowhere more strikingly than in some of the most impressively cybernetic poetry to emerge from the modernist period, the work of Hugh MacDiarmid. The concluding section of this chapter will look at how MacDiarmid, aware of (though tangential to) the knowledge-world of the modern universities, evolved in his prickly and restless fashion a cybernetic poetry attuned to the work of Eliot, Pound, and Auden, yet reaching beyond theirs in provocative and striking ways. Colluding or flyting with academia, MacDiarmid as a modern poet gravitated towards language that was tooled, artificial, and brilliant. Autodidactic, Teufelsdröckhian, and only partially if magnificently successful, what he sought to be was a poetic wildman who was also author of a poetry of knowledge.

MacDiarmid thrived on lexical vertigo. So many of his most impressive effects depend on access to areas of unusual vocabulary, whether using the Scots language or scientific terminology—'yow-trummle' or 'lithogenesis'.[101] If by 'vernacular' we mean the language 'naturally spoken by the people of a particular country or district' (*OED*), then MacDiarmid, whether in Scots or English, could certainly make use of the vernacular but would not be confined to it for long. So often in the Scots lyrics his move into Scots is a deliberate swerve into linguistic oddity—'Reuch Heuch Hauch', 'byspale', 'datchie sesames'.[102] In 1921, using such words as 'pedantic' and 'obsolete', MacDiarmid had attacked campaigners for the revival of the Scots language.[103] His vocabulary was often dredged from dictionaries, and he was intensely suspicious of the popularity and populism of Burns. His adoption of Scots in 1922 was a turning from the language of the Empire, the globally spoken English whose virtues had been extolled by Hugh Blair, to the language of some sections of a tiny country; it was at least as much a movement towards the unpopular as it was a gesture of identification with his own people. MacDiarmid's ambitious eyes were often 'in a fine frenzy rolling'. He liked always to operate out on the edge. He progressed through a calculated daftness.

Although many politely post-Burnsian members of the early twentieth-century Scots poetry-reading audience might enjoy MacDiarmid's lyrics 'The Bonnie Broukit Bairn' or 'Wheesht, Wheesht', those same readers were likely to be alienated by the blasphemy of 'I'm fu' o' a stickit God' or MacDiarmid's claim that the Doric might be 'no less ...uncontrollable, and utterly at variance with conventional morality than was Joyce's tremendous outpouring' in *Ulysses*.[104] When the 31-year-old Scot wrote these words in 1923 *Ulysses* was a banned book

[101] Hugh MacDiarmid, *The Complete Poems*, 2 vols. (London: Martin, Brian & O'Keeffe, 1978), 17 ('The Watergaw') and 422 ('On a Raised Beach').
[102] Ibid. 18 ('The Sauchs in the Reuch Heuch Hauch'), 31 ('O Jesu Parvule'), 74 ('Gairmscoile').
[103] See Alan Bold, *MacDiarmid* (London: John Murray, 1988), 116–17.
[104] Hugh MacDiarmid, *Selected Prose*, ed. Alan Riach (Manchester: Carcanet, 1992), 20–1 ('A Theory of Scots Letters').

which hardly anyone in Scotland had read. MacDiarmid's many uses of and references to *The Waste Land* in *A Drunk Man Looks at the Thistle* were most unlikely to appeal to a popular audience at a time when a good number of readers still regarded Eliot's poem as at best inscrutable, at worst a hoax. If MacDiarmid's entry to Scots produced a number of wonderful and (for some Scottish readers at least) accessible lyrics, for most English-language readers this was a move into inaccessibility. What most attracted him was vocabulary 'bound by desuetude' in the dictionary.[105] It was out of what he had so recently scorned as 'pedantic' that he wanted to make poetry. His singing school, his 'Gairmscoile', had a demanding entrance exam and still requires as much of its audience as does *The Orators*. 'Gairmscoile', the early MacDiarmid lyric most full of enthusiasm for the move into Scots, contains (like a good number of his other poems) words incomprehensible save to a few. In the 1920s, as today, most Scots did not read John Jamieson's four-volume *Etymological Dictionary of the Scottish Language*. Certainly no one else viewed those tomes in terms of *Ulysses*. MacDiarmid's doing so was a solar flare of genius, but also an unpopular or even anti-popular act.

I am emphasizing this point because it prevents any lingering illusion that this modern poet's immersion in Scots was a Kelmanesque gesture of popular identification while his swerve into scientific language was a contrasting elitist flourish. On the contrary, the motor for each of these moves is a similar linguistic strategy—a journey away from the most publicly accessible standard English language into productive but remoter acoustic and lexical corners. MacDiarmid attempted to manipulate the mass media in order to make a splash.[106] In trying to link his work to that of such writers as Joyce and Eliot, however, he was promoting himself as an unpopular, avant-garde artist. Writing to the *TLS* in 1927, replying to a review of his early Scots-language collection *Sangschaw*, he speculates penetratingly if a little whimsically that he 'might be indulging in "creative linguistics" like the Russian Khlebnikov or in forms of *skaz* or *zaumny*'.[107] In 1927 this combination of deep-dictionaried Scots and Russian Futurist poetics was likely to leave

[105] Ibid. 20.
[106] See Robert Crawford, 'MacDiarmid in Montrose', in Alex Davis and Lee Jenkins (eds.), *Locations of Literary Modernism* (Cambridge: Cambridge University Press, 2000), 33–56.
[107] *The Letters of Hugh MacDiarmid*, ed. Alan Bold (London: Hamish Hamilton, 1984), 765 (TLS, [Montrose, Sept. 1927]).

even most readers of the *TLS* as bamboozled as it would have left most of the folk in MacDiarmid's then home town of Montrose.

MacDiarmid loved to outsmart readers. His use of vocabulary is part of this. The experience of reading him is far less a convivial, sociable stroll in which reader accompanies writer than a car chase in which the reader has to steer for dear life in order to pursue the MacDiarmidian vehicle as it zig-zags, doubles back, and constantly exceeds the conventional verbal speed limit. Both excitement and exhaustion are produced by MacDiarmid's demanding poetry of knowledge. This is as true of 'Gairmscoile', that early language manifesto, as it is of 'The Kind of Poetry I Want'. These works reach for a linguistic nerve that carries 'undeemis jargons', whether in the line 'Ablachs, and scrats, and dorbels o' a' kinds' or the line 'Prose account of the endophragmal system of the crayfish'.[108] Such lines live because of their acoustic and referential strangeness. Each opens a road that is rarely taken, an unpopular and (for that very reason perhaps) exciting new direction.

It sometimes seems as if MacDiarmid had a crude, Romantic idea of genius—it had to be unpopular—and so he courted rejection, equating it with brilliance. Yet so many of the avant-garde figures whose work he discovered and praised with remarkable alacrity—Eliot, Stevens, Joyce to name only three non-Scots—have come to be seen as crucial voices in the poetic articulation of twentieth-century life. Erringly but remarkably prophetic, MacDiarmid combined acute taste with a desire to mark himself out as an oddity within his own society. Whatever judgement is passed on his wish to position himself as an avant-garde artist, it is clear not only that his interest in poetry and science is linguistically closer to his preoccupation with Scots than most critics would seem to believe, but also that his concern with poetry and science is developing at the very same time as he turns to Scots and matures as a modern poet.

1922, when MacDiarmid began his first Scots experiments, is also the year of his English-language poem 'Science and Poetry' whose speaker aligns himself with the scientific avant-garde in the person of the heretic Galileo, unpopular and right. Several of the lines in this English-language poem point towards MacDiarmid's contemporary Scots lyrics—not least the line 'Earth is a star, a star' (*CP* 1220), which sends us to 'The Innumerable Christ' with its 'Wha kens on whatna Bethlehems | Earth twinkles like a star the nicht' (*CP* 32). But the language of

---

[108] MacDiarmid, *Complete Poems*, 74 and 1006. Hereafter references to this work are supplied in the text, using the abbreviation *CP*.

'Science and Poetry' is a rather outmoded English. MacDiarmid learned to figure modernity in poetry first through Scots, partly at least because it allowed and encouraged a linguistic brinkmanship impossible in the conventional diction of his earlier English poems. This adventurousness centres round the decision to mine the dictionary in daring ways, but it extends from that in several directions, some of which are easy to miss. So, for instance, the word 'Bethlehems' in the lines just quoted is a very unusual verbal item: the Christmas story has usually and necessarily only one Bethlehem—to multiply it is daring perhaps to the point of blasphemy. This takes us to the heart of MacDiarmid's poem. Again, his noisy use of onomatopoeia brings a modernist clash of register and expectation. We do not expect 'The Last Trump', in the work of that title, to go

> Tootle-ootle-ootle-oo.
> Tootle-oo. (*CP* 29)

but MacDiarmid relishes the weirdness of the effect, just as he enjoys the line 'Hee-Haw! Click-Clack! And Cock-a-doodle-doo!' (*CP* 74). If we want, we can think of *The Waste Land*'s 'Co co rico' or Khlebnikov's 'Gau! gau! gau!', but however we hear these noises, it is evident that the freer palette of reconstructed language encourages other inventions and strange combinations.[109] As several critics have pointed out, MacDiarmid recombines whole citation entries from Jamieson, stealing extended pieces of text, rather than just single vocabulary items. A development of such modernist *bricolage* will also fuel his poetry of science.

In one sense, as he knew, MacDiarmid's leap into Scots and into Jamieson was a move away from the modern world in its metropolitan and technological manifestations. His alter ego C. M. Grieve was thinking about this even as he published 'The Watergaw' in 1922. In the same issue of *The Scottish Chapbook* he penned an editorial explaining that what MacDiarmid had to do was

to adapt an essentially rustic tongue to the very much more complex requirements of our urban civilization—to give it all the almost illimitable suggestionability it lacks (compared, say, with contemporary English or French), but *would have had if it had continued in general use in highly-cultured circles to the present day.*

---

[109] For an English translation of this noisy Khlebnikov poem see Edwin Morgan, *Sweeping out the Dark* (Manchester: Carcanet, 1994), 110.

That last reference to 'highly-cultured circles' again reveals the anti-popular strand in MacDiarmid's Scots. More interesting, though, is the problem of, 'What is the Doric for motor-car?'[110] MacDiarmid contends that for the modern consciousness to express itself in 'the Doric', poets must learn about the language's past, then imaginatively create its evolution. However, he continues throughout most of his Scots poetry to evade his question, 'What is the Doric for motor-car?', and his acknowledged demand for scientific and technological words. Yet the awareness of the need for such vocabulary is there at the very start of his decision to write in Scots. Here again is support for the idea that MacDiarmid's later poetry of science emerges not in contradistinction to but *out* of his poetry in Scots. Both are powered by a lexical and lexicographical acquisitiveness which is bound up with a drive for ever greater knowledge to provide '*names for nameless things*' (*CP* 74). In 1926, the year of publication of *A Drunk Man Looks at the Thistle*, MacDiarmid wrote with modernist arrogance that 'The highest art at any time can only be appreciated by an infinitesimal minority of the people—if by any' and that 'The ideal observer of art at work would be one conscious of all human experience up to the given moment.'[111] These two consecutive statements link an anti-popular stance to a drive for total knowledge, a combination present in *Annals of the Five Senses* (1923) and in *To Circumjack Cencrastus* (1930) with its assertion

> *It's no the purpose o' poetry to sing*
> *The beauty o' the dirt frae which we spring*
> *But to cairry us as faur as ever it can*
> *'Yont nature and the Common Man.*
>
> Like some puir spook that's no content in Heaven
> (A figure that's a variant o' the fau't)
> But needs maun haunt Earth still; and swear I've made
> My verses sic' a Noah's Ark—o' troot,
> Cormorants, ducklings, serpents, and losh kens what
> I might please W. H. Hamilton yet
> Wi a sang to a Hairy Oubit or Green Serene,
> Secondary sex characters in Asparagus Officinalis,
> Or buck-eye poisonin' o' the Honey Bee,
> Or Fungicidal Dusts for the Control o' Bunt,
> To fill the gaps in *Holyrood*. (*CP* 255)

---

[110] MacDiarmid, *Selected Prose* 10 ('Introducing "Hugh MacDiarmid" ').
[111] Ibid. 39 ('Art and the Unknown').

Here, mocking the minor Scottish critic W. H. Hamilton and his safe anthology *Holyrood: A Garland of Modern Scots Poems*, MacDiarmid produces a jokey doggerely manifesto for his own later poetry. It will be a 'Noah's Ark', taking in all comers, all strange shapes, all sizes. It will 'fill the gaps in *Holyrood*' by supplying material, tones, and effects that conventional poetry, not least couthy Scottish versifying, has not been able to include. It will do all this by heading in exactly the direction spelt out by the line 'Secondary sex characters in Asparagus Officinalis'—it will drive in the direction of scientific knowledge.

MacDiarmid's 1922 poem 'Science and Poetry' imaged the poet as Galileo-like beleaguered avant-garde scientist. Other writings from the short, great Scots sunburst of the mid-1920s also press towards a wish for a poetry of knowledge that will work *with* rather than against science. Such desires were hardly unique in the period. As has been noted, I. A. Richards, whose work MacDiarmid was to read with interest, published *Science and Poetry* in 1926. His writing in the 1920s attempted to move the reading of literature into a scientific framework. For Richards this involved the development of certain kinds of academic reading habits and a close attention to problems of interpretation which led him to develop with C. K. Ogden a special language, 'Basic English'. That attempt at formulating a world language eventually came to share its name with the computer language 'Basic'.

Producing his own 'Vision of World Language' in *In Memoriam James Joyce*, MacDiarmid takes issue with 'Professor Richards and his colleagues'. For them to claim that Basic English is freed from any taint of cultural imperialism 'displays', argues MacDiarmid, 'The magnificent insularity | Which is the pride of the Anglo-Saxon mind' (*CP* 789). Such a subtle yet naive concern with linguistic 'imperialism' here reminds us of MacDiarmid the poet in Scots (*CP* 790). More than that, the passage continues his obsession with vocabulary. If his best early poetry relies on mining the national lexis of Jamieson, the extraordinary later work mines the most impressive 'vast international vocabulary' of the twentieth century, that is, scientific language from books and journals. MacDiarmid's 1920s verse subverts Anglocentrism by turning to what most English speakers would regard as a minority 'dialect'; his later work outflanks the gravitational pull of England by turning towards international learning and scientific terms. Richards was interested from his youth in science and poetry, in what he called in a paper quoted by MacDiarmid 'An Agreement between Literary Criticism and Some of the Sciences' (*CP* 794). If the English critic moved from a microscopic scrutiny of responses to words, phrases, and lyric poems to a preoccupation with world language that pointed in the direction of computing, then the Scottish poet's career took a similar course. For MacDiarmid, obsessed in the 1920s with the qualities of individual Scots words and their lyric combinations, moved in the next decade towards a bigger-scale poetry whose vocabulary can be just as striking, yet which is literature and language on the edge of the computational. Tracts of the later poetry seem like nothing so much as material turned out by a computer database, bibliographical printout, cyber-text language that is far from 'Basic', yet does closely resemble the kinds of information today most commonly held in machine-readable form. MacDiarmid's use of Scots and of scientific terms can be viewed as self-conscious acts of linguistic barbarism which, coupled with his highly sophisticated encyclopedism, mark him out as a modern poet. The closeness of some aspects of MacDiarmid's late poetry to the cybernetic textures and forms of the modern computer is one of his poetry's splendours.

Before pursuing that point, I would like to encourage the reader to view MacDiarmid's later poetry, most of which was written in the 1930s, within the wider literary context established in the present chapter. This chapter argues that implicit or explicit in much modernist poetry is a contestation of knowledge. In particular there is a tussle with the increasing power of universities and their curricula in the systematization of learning and the control of its dissemination. Having seen this at work in the poetries of Yeats, Eliot, Pound, and Auden, it may seem odd to progress to MacDiarmid. Norman MacCaig pointed out on occasion that MacDiarmid (a postman's son) had once attended Edinburgh University—but only to deliver a parcel.[112] Such a joke is in some ways attuned to MacDiarmid's presentation of himself; yet if it masks his preoccupation with knowledge, its governing, and its institutionalization, then it is misleading in the extreme. MacDiarmid liked to stress the autodidactic nature of his own education with its origins in the laundry-baskets of books he carried from the Public Library in his native Scottish Border town of Langholm. Access to knowledge was an issue crucial to him. He was no university product, and he disliked, probably envied the attention given to the public-school Auden, for whom, MacDiarmid maintained, he had 'no use' (*CP* 1340). Yet there are

---

[112] Norman MacCaig, conversation with the present writer, early 1990s.

moments in MacDiarmid's verse when we can hear him trying on
Auden's poetic clothing, as in these lines from an Audenesquely titled
1934 poem 'The Frontier; or, The War with England', with its 'Nation-
alism whummled on Border moor. | Countries Indistinguishable in
Dark' (*CP* 1296).

In the early 1930s Auden and MacDiarmid are closer than we might
think. *The Orators* is Auden's determined outsmarting of the educational
system; *In Memoriam James Joyce* (largely written in the same decade) can
be read from a similar angle. MacDiarmid's hostility to the universities
of his own country is manifest in a celebrated passage in *To Circumjack
Cencrastus* (1930):

> *Oor four Universities*
> *Are Scots but in name;*
> *They wadna be here*
> *If ither folk did the same*
> *—Paid heed tae a' lear*
> *Exceptin their ain...* (*CP* 203)

The argument here is primarily about Scotland's 'ain' knowledge. The
sorts of tradition and learning so fundamental to MacDiarmid's Scots
poetry are those which, historically, were largely ignored or suppressed
by the Scottish university system, not least through the history of the
teaching of Rhetoric and Belles-Lettres.[113] MacDiarmid's Scots lyrics
are written against the Scottish educational system, even when, as in the
Scottish Educational Journal, he makes use of part of its apparatus. His
attacks on the universities as Anglicizing place him in a distinguished
line which includes not only the autodidact Burns but also the St
Andrews student Robert Fergusson in his address 'To the Principal
and Professors of the University of St Andrews, on their Superb Treat
to Dr Samuel Johnson'. MacDiarmid continues his fight against the
Anglocentric impetus of Scottish universities in such vitriolic pieces as
his 'Ode for the 350th Anniversary of Edinburgh University' (1933)
where as a 'poor aborigine' he inveighs against its '*careerists... toadies,
... distinguished lickspittles,* | *And Honours degree nobodies*' (*CP* 1286). In the
later 'Direadh II' he attacks 'The Fascist barracks of our universities | The
murder machine of our whole educational system' with its 'black-coated
workers' (*CP* 1183). These onslaughts, however, are directed not just at

[113] See Robert Crawford, *Devolving English Literature*, 2nd edn. (Edinburgh: Edinburgh
University Press, 2000), ch. 1.

the Scottish universities' failure to teach Scottish culture, but at the wider university control of knowledge. The poem against Edinburgh University attacks its various faculties, while 'Direadh II' complains about 'institutions of learning' which are 'designed for the depotentization of free intelligence' (*CP* 1183). Against this, MacDiarmid (like Pound) sets himself up as a one-man university,

I in myself a Cordoba, cultural centre of Europe,
A university town where intellectual tolerance
Scepticism and rationalism flourished when they
Were unheard of throughout the rest of Europe,
—A focal centre, where Persian, Babylonian,
Egyptian, Grecian, Roman, Byzantine and Christian cultures
Merged and fructified each other, the point where medicine and mathematics
(Arabic numerals, the zero, the local value of numbers, algebra)
Classical philosophy and jurisprudence and certain elements
Of poetry and rhetoric entered and re-entered Europe. (*CP* 1346)

Professor David Daiches once recalled in an interview that MacDiarmid had snapped at him, 'I'm more intelligent than you are, and I've read more books.' Daiches said to me incredulously, 'Well, what kind of poet says this to a literary critic?'[114] Ezra Pound, surely, was just such a poet. Eliot and Auden would never have said that to a literary critic, but their poetry implies the statement. Like MacDiarmid, these poets are trying to out-professor the professors in an effort to keep poetry and knowledge free, or at least partially free, from the total control of universities. MacDiarmid's late poetry seems so academic, so crammed with kinds of learning, precisely because it is concerned with refusing to academia a monopoly on knowledge. On behalf of poetry and non-institutional thinking it is a superb act of liberation and imagination whose cultural importance is hard to underestimate, even if, eventually, we see the attempt as flawed, and simply as part of the ongoing argument or dialogue with academia which has been vital to the development of the modern poet.

What MacDiarmid does is to appropriate from institutional processes areas of scientific knowledge and vocabulary, making these available for poetic access, for aesthetic contemplation and use. Pound's poetry of knowledge had its roots in his training as a medievalist; it was essentially

---

[114] David Daiches in 'Hugh MacDiarmid: A Disgrace to the Community' (transcript of 1992 BBC radio programme), *PN Review*, 89 (1993), 20.

palaeographical, relying on the recovery and comparison of historical documents. MacDiarmid's philological modernism was co-creation with the dictionary. It was more daring than Pound's palaeography, because MacDiarmid liked, as in the beginning of 'On a Raised Beach', to put the dictionary in the driving seat. If in the early poetry the dictionary helps shape the poem, then in the later the poem takes the form of the knowledge-base or dictionary:

> Or even as, in the Shetland Islands where I lived,
> I know, in the old Norn language, the various names
> Applied to all the restless movements of the sea
> —*Di*, a wave; *Da mother di*, the undulations
> That roll landward even in calm weather;
> *Soal*, swell occasioned by a breeze,
> *Trove*, a short, cross, heavy sea,
> *Hak*, broken water, *Burrik*, a sharp sea or 'tide lump',
> *Bod*, a heavy wave breaking on the shore. (*CP* 763–4)

This verse paragraph continues, beautifully presenting the dictionary as itself a poem, a minutely detailed encounter among linguistic differences. Language and the investigation of vocabulary go on to be at the heart of MacDiarmid's late poetry, as they are central to his delight in Scots. But in seeking for 'A language, a poetry, in keeping with the new quantum mechanics' (*CP* 782), MacDiarmid knows that it is necessary not least to recite and cavort with the vocabulary of science, whether relishing '"hohlraum" oscillators', or the internally alliterative 'Veiled allelomorphic transitions such as liquid helium' (*CP* 802). He produces arresting new combinations of lyrical and scientific beauty, letting each be seen in terms of the other as he alerts us to

> The endless joys of *Scripta Mathematica*,
> Recalling that when young ferns unfold in springtime
> They are seen as logarithmic spirals,
> When light is reflected under a teacup
> A catacaustic curve is spotted. (*CP*, 803)

Here a Romantic delight in organic nature is bonded to a modernist relishing of science and technology. MacDiarmid, more than any other major mid-twentieth-century poet, sees the opportunity offered by science and its terminology to make new poetic shapes and renovate old ones. His early work in Scots destabilizes Anglocentrism through deliberate ec-centricity, addressing itself to a minority audience. Yet the more time that passes, the more we sense his Scots reaching back to Ossian and Burns and out to Caribbean nation language and post-colonial dialects, to the predicament of Irish and Australian writers, for instance. Just as it is becoming easier for postcolonial audiences to appreciate something of the drive behind MacDiarmid's use of Scots vocabulary in the 1920s, so, I predict, this move towards science and scientific vocabulary will become clearer to a twenty-first-century audience to whom computing is second nature.

This is because MacDiarmid's late poetry anticipates and articulates for the first time in English the world of the computer with its databases and hypertext systems. That it does so is only partly accidental. For MacDiarmid, with his acute intuition for the new, was attempting to attune himself to modes of knowledge which in Nietzschean/Davidsonian fashion transcended the humanly possible. Such a desire gives rise to his lists of such works as ' . . . "Psychological Response to Unknown Proper Names," | Downey on "Individual Differences In Reaction to the Word-in-Itself "', and so on for another couple of pages (*CP* 805–6). This is MacDiarmid out-professoring the professors, setting up poetry's claims to knowledge in opposition to institutional academia's grip on it. He catalogues information sources, not ships, because he knows that information, knowledge, is the key to power in the modern world. In listing the innumerably varied studies of linguistic nuances he is celebrating the nuancing of language itself. Searching for a kind of superman-verse, MacDiarmid wants 'A poetry concerned with all that is needed | Of the sum of human knowledge and expression' (*CP* 1004). He seeks to programme his poetry with all available information, learning, vocabulary, that it may speak of these things in terms of one another. Language is seen as fundamental to thought and to knowledge, and the late poetry maintains MacDiarmid's obsession with linguistic variety—whether Leibniz's 'universal language' or Patrick Geddes's 'thinking graphics' (*CP* 801) or I. A. Richards's 'Basic English'.

This preoccupation with the subtleties of encoded information is something MacDiarmid shared with the pioneers of computing in the 1920s, 1930s, and later. One might point out that the perforated card technology used in many early computers derives directly from that of the Jacquard loom still used in factory weaving in MacDiarmid's day.[115]

---

[115] See *Pioneers of Computing* (London: Frederick Muller, 1983) and N. Metropolis, J. Howlett, and Gian-Carlo Rota (eds.), *A History of Computing in the Twentieth Century* (New York: Academic Press, 1980).

When he admires the production of a 'seamless garment' out of a 'machine' in which 'Hundreds to the inch the threids lie', MacDiarmid is admiring a process which is closely involved with the early development of computing technology (*CP* 311–13). Yet the way in which his later verse represents a braiding or weaving of scientific and other kinds of knowledge is far in advance of the hardware and software extant when that late poetry was composed. Even when he glimpsed directly the future of computing, MacDiarmid did so with contempt. He half-rhymes Norbert Wiener's term 'cybernetics' with 'electronic tricks' (*CP* 1062). Yet the experience of reading MacDiarmid's mature poetry of knowledge is often like surfing on the Internet or moving on impulse through a vast database or hypertext system. We are given aesthetic access to computational textures and the ever-reforming patterning of hypertext knowledge long before computers themselves reached such a level of sophistication, and before non-classified access was possible. The familiarity of the word-processor and the computer help us to make sense of and dispense with some of the questions of copyright and appropriation which have so dogged criticism of the late poetry, and see it instead as a prolonged paean to the knowledge base, to language and enquiry as the DNA of human thought. MacDiarmid's verse is enthusiastically cybernetic.

Our acquaintance with computer systems makes us readier to accept this work whose form seems in constant flux as it reconfigures repeatedly along new nodes of connection. MacDiarmid puts it explicitly in terms of weaving and the manipulation of papers:

> At this moment when braidbinding as never before,
> The creation of the seamless garment,
> Is the poet's task?
>
> (Even so we have seen a collection of papers
> Seemingly multifarious nevertheless connected with a system... (*CP* 876)

For us, though, it is probably easier to understand the kind of cybernetic poetry he wants in terms of a computing matrix whose underlying pattern may carry innumerable strands of information in a system which allows us to pass almost immediately from religious imagery to Hollywood moguls, from 'Kathakali dance-drama' to 'hedge-laying' in the way that MacDiarmid's late verse does (*CP* 1025). This is the way we move in the modern electronic information world. MacDiarmid's late poetry, more than any other written in his century, enacts our cybernetic mobility. Osip Mandelstam, in an acutely perceptive passage, set out his ideas about the movement of poetic imagery.

Dante's thinking in images, as is the case in all genuine poetry, exists with the aid of a peculiarity of poetic material which I propose to call its convertibility or transmutability. Only in accord with convention is the development of an image called its development. And indeed, just imagine an airplane (ignoring the technical impossibility) which in full flight constructs and launches another machine. Furthermore, in the same way, this flying machine, while fully absorbed in its own flight, still manages to assemble and launch yet a third machine. To make my proposed comparison more precise and helpful, I will add that the production and launching of these technically unthinkable new machines which are tossed off in mid-flight are not secondary or extraneous functions of the plane which is in motion, but rather comprise a most essential attribute and part of the flight itself, while assuring its feasibility and safety to no less a degree than its properly operating rudder or the regular functioning of its engine.[116]

This holds good for many, perhaps most poems, but it does not always work for MacDiarmid's verse unless we say that in the latter a jumbo jet may emerge from a small private plane, and that the direction may change suddenly and vertiginously. Mandelstam makes use of the new technology of his day to elucidate his ideal of poetry. To explain the kind of verse MacDiarmid wants and delivers, we need to turn to the technology of the future. It is surely no accident that one of the first critics to come close to understanding MacDiarmid's late poetry was the Edwin Morgan who produced poems apparently written by computer and who continued MacDiarmid's fascination with linguistic encoding. MacDiarmid helped give to Morgan the professional academic a space on which to stand as poet, and spurred him to use his knowledge for poetic rather than conventionally academic ends.[117]

MacDiarmid came to be a cyberpoet partly as a result of extreme isolation. The closest comparison is with the Thomas Carlyle who worked on *Sartor Resartus* at remote Craigenputtock, surrounded by reviews, journals, manuscripts, and built that sense of solitude and fragmentariness into his text as he developed, in opposition to conventional institutional wisdoms, the thought of his Professor

---

[116] Osip Mandelstam, 'Conversation about Dante' (trans. J. G. Harris), in *Collected Critical Prose and Letters* (London: Collins Harvill, 1991), 414.

[117] See the essays on MacDiarmid in Edwin Morgan, *Crossing the Border: Essays on Scottish Literature* (Manchester: Carcanet, 1990).

Teufelsdröckh. So MacDiarmid, embattled on Shetland, relying on uncertain long-distance communications, attempted in opposition to institutional academia to produce his own literature of knowledge constructed out of a tessellation of articles, appropriations, original pieces, insights. Even more effortfully than in the poetry of Ossian apparent cultural marginality and sophisticated, panoptic knowledge combine to produce the work of a modern poet. Often the strain shows. As MacDiarmid admitted in a letter written from Shetland to Ezra Pound,

I am, of course, a fraud as you will see from my address. I still contrive by a species of magic to maintain an appearance of being au fait with all that is happening in welt-literatur...But it must become increasingly difficult for me to produce these occasional effects of omniscience.[118]

The later poetry, though, shows just how MacDiarmid redoubled his efforts in this direction, aspiring, and frequently pretending, to a Godlike or machine-like omniscience. His 1922 poem 'Science and Poetry' had been dedicated to the Scottish scientist Sir Ronald Ross, some of whose undistinguished poems were included in the second series of MacDiarmid's anthology *Northern Numbers*. Ross's Nobel Prizewinning scientific work on malaria would have been of interest to Sergeant C. M. Grieve who had suffered from that disease in 1916. MacDiarmid was particularly attracted to Ross's statement that 'Science is the Differential calculus of the mind, Art the Integral Calculus; they may be beautiful when apart, but are greatest only when combined.' MacDiarmid cited this at the head of his poem 'Two Scottish Boys' (1950; *CP* 1360), but he also quoted (or misquoted) it as the epigraph to his 1930s poem 'Poetry and Science' where it appears as verse:

> *Science is the Differential Calculus of the mind,*
> *Art is the Integral Calculus; they may be*
> *Beautiful apart, but are great only when combined.* (*CP* 630)

This recurring reference to Ross emphasizes the continuing strength of MacDiarmid's wish to fuse poetry and science over several decades. More than that, MacDiarmid's versifying of Ross's prose is indicative of the larger compositional method of the later work, constantly appropriating prose for poetry. It raises (like the Ossianic texts) the question of the distinction between the two, and the issue of whether

---

[118] MacDiarmid, *Letters*, 845 (to Pound, 'Whalsay, Shetland Islands. 19/12/33').

MacDiarmid's later poetry matters simply as a magnificently impressive cultural phenomenon, or whether it is also fully achieved poetry.

I hope I have said enough to convince actual or potential readers of the cultural significance of this work. It is *the* twentieth-century poetry which most clearly anticipates the greatest revolutionary technological shift in our society— the development of the computer. Yet, as poetry, this may make it all the more rebarbative. MacDiarmid maintained that 'The rarity and value of scientific knowledge | Is little understood' (*CP* 630). He sought a poetry whose delight in this learning was likely to restrict its audience as much as his earlier choice of Scots would limit the immediate readership for his poetry of the 1920s. This diminution of audience may have appealed to MacDiarmid, who so often seems to have not simply accepted but courted isolation. Or he may have been playing a long game, hoping that just as the collapse of Anglocentrism might lead to a larger audience for his Scots work, so the increasing importance of science might win more readers for his poetry of knowledge. Whichever is the case, MacDiarmid's later verse had, he knew, nineteenth-century roots, not just in John Davidson but also in Whitman, whom he quotes enthusiastically in 'The Kind of Poetry I Want':

> 'In the beauty of poems', as Whitman said,
> 'Are henceforth the tuft and final applause of science
> …Facts showered over with light.' (*CP* 1028)

Yet MacDiarmid's attraction to science (including the science of language) is not least, like his love of Scots lexis, a movement towards the arcane. In his later poetry he tries constantly to upset ideas of the poetic. Does he do so to any purpose, and with any poetic success?

The answer to both those questions is surely 'Yes', though MacDiarmid's victory is sporadic. Often, even where gained, it teeters on the edge of failure. His breakthrough is audible frequently at the level of phrasing. In a line such as 'the glow-worm's 96 per cent efficiency' (*CP* 1016) he combines statistical and mechanistic vocabulary with the conventional Romantic gleam, renovating both. Like the Scots poetry, the later poetry is full of delicious lexical items and combinations— whether invented, or simply spotted and grabbed by MacDiarmid:

> A poetry full of *cynghanedd*, and hair-trigger relationships… (*CP* 1017)

> The thin pliancy of Galician… (*CP* 760)

> A sturdy Norsk-Murdoch spinning-rod, a 4-inch Silex reel… (*CP* 1008)

In such lines the new combinations of the modern world produce a mind-stretching, ear-bending music. As of old, MacDiarmid is captivated by lexical weirdness. After delivering the tongue-twister

> Shirokogoroff's *Psychomental Complex of the Tungus*

he comments in parenthesis,

> (If that line is not great poetry in itself
> Then I don't know what poetry is!) (*CP* 793)

This, for many readers, must be the nub of the question. Clearly such a line would appeal to the poet who had rooted through dictionaries and found 'rumgunshoch' and 'angle-titch'. There are bound to be readers for whom MacDiarmid's work, especially the late poetry, exists only at the level of spectacular freakishness, even if it is the oddity of writing a computer poem before the advent of modern computing. This late verse can be criticized as phallocentric, its sometimes electronic voice lacking in humour, humanity, and on occasion rhythmical interest. It may be that in future science in poetry will tend to take the form of lyric bytes. Perhaps MacDiarmid's project was often more alluring than his achievement. Certainly his most successful scientific poems, such as 'To a Friend and Fellow Poet' or 'On a Raised Beach', are of less than epic length. His extended late work annoys some readers by its overly willed modernist aesthetic.

Yet in claiming for poetry so much material, in refusing to surrender to academia the rights of the poet to traverse innumerable knowledge-terrains, MacDiarmid did poets who followed him an inestimable service. When Les Murray declares laughingly, 'I think a poet should know everything,' or when Ciaran Carson writes the chunky, clotted lines of *First Language*, each poet in a different way pays tribute to MacDiarmid's vision and sound-world, particularly that of his late verse.[119] In Scotland his example surely encouraged the later, more ludic experiments of Edwin Morgan and the fascination with informational textures present in some of the work of younger poets, among whom are W. N. Herbert, Don Paterson, and the present writer. Doing what very few poets ever do, MacDiarmid challenged and burst the horizons of poetry in his era. He did so sometimes uncertainly and lumberingly, in a manner which I still find easier to discuss in terms of science and knowledge than in

---

[119] Les Murray, talking with Robert Crawford, in Crawford et al. (eds.), *Talking Verse* (St Andrews: Verse, 1995), 169.

conventional poetic terms. His achievement does not lend itself to the restricted space of anthologies. In acknowledging those difficulties I am paying the highest tribute to MacDiarmid's success in challenging and expanding notions of what poetry can do. His breakthrough does not make it imperative that younger writers follow him. It may indeed have provoked more hostile reaction than sympathetic reading. But its existence extends the possibility of what poetry can say, how it can be textured, and where it can go. Challenging the monopoly of institutional academia, it extends poetry in the direction of our century's deepest preoccupations with science and with knowledge. It is the high water mark of cybernetic modernism, and initiates a poetry of the age of information which we now inhabit. For that future modern poets will owe to the later poetry of Hugh MacDiarmid an exciting and fundamental debt.

CHAPTER 5

Men, Women, and American Classrooms

Today the general assumption is that it is in twentieth-century American universities that creative writing emerges as part of the curriculum. In many ways this is entirely misleading.[1] For, as has been pointed out in an earlier chapter, the eighteenth-century Scottish teaching of Rhetoric and Belles-Lettres had been bound up not only with the appreciation of older literature but also with the production of new work. This had often led (most strikingly with the production of the Ossianic poems) to a close liaison or even fusion between the academic and the poet. Developments in America often followed that Scottish Belles-Lettres tradition whose echoes were heard for instance in the title of Princeton's nineteenth-century Holmes Chair of Belles-Lettres, English Language, and Literature.[2] Some have tended to lose sight of this history, perhaps because (in line with a late nineteenth-century Oxbridge model) they are accustomed to perceiving a strict distinction between the teaching of Rhetoric and Composition, instruction in ancient and modern literatures, and the development of creative writing. These, however, are uneasy modern divisions of what was once in universities a continuous spectrum. Now attempts are being made once more to reconfigure the relationship between the university teaching of reading and writing. In such efforts poets have a part to play.

At early nineteenth-century Yale Hugh Blair on Rhetoric was a standard text. Students were taught to recite, debate, and compose regularly.[3] From 1788 Harvard too used published versions of Blair's Rhetoric and Belles-Lettres lectures. In 1802 Professor Eliphalet

---

[1]   See Robert Crawford (ed.), *The Scottish Invention of English Literature* (Cambridge: Cambridge University Press, 1998).
[2]   See D. G. Myers, *The Elephants Teach* (Englewood Cliffs, NJ: Prentice Hall, 1996), 22.
[3]   Brooks Mather Kelley, *Yale* (New Haven: Yale University Press, 1974), 134 and 158.

Pearson, who had given addresses based on Blair's Rhetoric, published an abridgement of the Edinburgh academic's lectures (which would become an American academic best-seller), before drawing up the regulations for Harvard's new Boylston Professorship of Rhetoric and Oratory.[4] Furthermore, Harvard also had from the very early nineteenth century a Professorship of Belles-Lettres. This was linked to the Smith Chair in Modern Languages (originally French and Spanish). Nineteenth-century Harvard had a pronounced liking for having poets as holders of its Chair of Belles-Lettres. Successive incumbents included George Ticknor, Henry Wadsworth Longfellow, and James Russell Lowell, who among them held sway from 1835 until 1891.[5] They did not formally teach undergraduates how to make poetry, but were very much part of a local, close-knit, university writing community, with its Commencement Poems, Commemoration Odes, and literary clubs. Longfellow and Lowell, for instance, involved students in the development of their translations of Dante, while Longfellow's study became 'a Temple of the Muses for his own pupils, and for outsiders as well'.[6] Lowell made the Harvard Commemoration Ode the vehicle for a notable celebration of Lincoln and the American grain.[7] These poets were swept aside by their modernist successors. Today they may seem to us offputtingly tame, but they are significant writers. Aware not only of the Belles-Lettres heritage and of the traditions of Burns and Ossian, they looked towards a fusion of academic knowledge with that sense of the 'primitive' which both developed and underpinned the evolution of the modern poet.

Longfellow exemplifies this clearly. His education at Bowdoin College, Maine, involved reading 'Heckwelder's Account of the History, Manners, and Customs of the Indian Natives of Pennsylvania and the Neighbouring States'. That volume particularly impressed him as he prepared to play his part in a rhetorical 'Dialogue between a North American Indian and a European'. In this, Longfellow acted Miles

[4] Andrew Hook, *Scotland and America* (Glasgow: Blackie, 1975), 75; J. Tarver, 'Abridged Editions of Blair's *Lectures on Rhetoric and Belles-Lettres* in America: What Nineteenth-Century College Students really Learned about Blair on Rhetoric', *Bibliotheck*, 21 (1996), 58–9.

[5] Anon., *Quinquennial Catalogue of the Officers and Graduates of Harvard University* (Cambridge, Mass.: The University, 1905), 24 and 28–9.

[6] Samuel Eliot Morison, *Three Centuries of Harvard* (Cambridge, Mass.: Harvard University Press, 1937), 307 and 263.

[7] James Russell Lowell, *The Poetical Works*, ed. Thomas Hughes (London: Macmillan, 1896), 421 ('Ode Recited at the Harvard Commemoration, July 21, 1865').

Standish (who would become the subject of his poem *The Courtship of Miles Standish*), and soon determined to 'study belles-lettres' as part of his preparation for a literary career.[8] He wrote early work 'to the tune of [Burns's] "Bruce's Address"', and was involved in a student culture of orations and official poetic compositions similar to that of the Scottish universities. Longfellow became a professor at Bowdoin before taking up his Chair of Belles-Lettres at Harvard. His career was thoroughly nurtured by academia. Much of his best poetry, as in *Evangeline*, *The Song of Hiawatha*, and *The Courtship of Miles Standish*, involved a combination of classroom sophistication with an interest in societies then considered 'wild' or 'primitive'.[9] Brought up on poetic texts such as Anne Grant's 'The Highlanders' and maturing in the heyday of Scott (who influenced his verse), Longfellow mixed his academic learning with an interest not in the inhabitants of the Scottish Highlands, but in the customs of the native Americans.[10] Writing poems about academic colleagues such as Agassiz and Parker Cleaveland, interspersing his 'too flowery' lectures on Homer and on Anglo-Saxon with poems based on the same, he united his reading about Greek hexameters in *Blackwood's Magazine* with his attraction towards primitive societies. So he has the Acadian converse with the Shawnee in *Evangeline*, and relishes 'Aspinet, Samoset, Corbitant, Squanto, or Tokamahamon!' in *The Courtship of Miles Standish*.[11] Like the poetry of Ossian, *The Song of Hiawatha* has an immediately identifiable and infectiously powerful music ('Where the Falls of Minnehaha | Flash and gleam among the oak-trees'). Read in short sections, it soon communicates through cadence and tone, though today it is hard to enjoy at length.[12] The student Longfellow admired 'the sublime' in Gray's 'The Bard', but it is an American Ossian in particular who haunts the opening of *Evangeline* with its 'forest primeval' where great trees 'indistinct in the twilight | Stand like Druids of eld' or, even more Ossianically, 'like harpers hoar'.[13] When in the twentieth century 'The Love Song of J. Alfred Prufrock' swept aside *The Courtship of Miles Standish*, Professor Longfellow (whose statue in Cambridge, Mass.,

---

[8] Samuel Longfellow (ed.), *Life of Henry Wadsworth Longfellow*, 3 vols. (London: Kegan Paul, Trench & Co., 1886), i. 32 and 56.

[9] Ibid. 64–6.   [10] Ibid. 71.

[11] Ibid. 273, 251, and 281 and ii. 66; Henry Wadsworth Longfellow, *Poetical Works* (London: Collins, n.d.), 606–9 ('From the Anglo-Saxon'), 107 ('Evangeline'), 219 ('The Courtship of Miles Standish').

[12] Longfellow, *Poetical Works*, 169 ('The Song of Hiawatha').

[13] Ibid. 70 ('Evangeline'); Longfellow (ed.), *Life*, i. 29–30.

would have been all too familiar to the young T. S. Eliot) went into near-total eclipse. Yet his career as an author on campus anticipates the stance of many a later modern poet wild and tame en route to a creative writing class. In its combination of the 'savage' and the urbane, it even prefigures some of Eliot's most deeply held concerns.[14]

There is only one comprehensive history of the development of Creative Writing as an American university subject. D. G. Myers's *The Elephants Teach* is geared towards an account of classroom pedagogy at the expense of attention to poems or poets.[15] We need now a richer understanding of the developing symbiotic relationship between poets and academics (not just in the United States). For several generations, the teaching of creative writing has played its part in the making of many poets and readers. Emerging from departments of English, schools of Creative Writing furthered the assumption that poetry was at home in academia in a new way. Nonetheless, quarrels between poets in universities and their purely scholarly colleagues have often characterized the development of modern literary studies. One reason has been ignorance about the early development of university English, leading to the belief that the subject originated as a combination of philology and criticism, rather than philology, criticism, and creativity. Another reason is the post-1750s conception of the poet as not only sophisticated but also barbarous, and therefore by implication difficult to manage in an institutional framework. Ticknor, Longfellow, Lowell, and other nineteenth-century American poets who were Professors of Belles-Lettres appear, for all their interest in the primitive, to have been models of propriety. As the university teaching of verse evolves over the last hundred years, we can see the modern poet's tameness and wildness being remixed in differing proportions.

Nowhere is this clearer than in the case of Robert Frost. As one of the first twentieth-century poets brought onto campus to teach the writing of poetry to students as part of the work of a modern English Department, Frost at Amherst (as he did elsewhere) delighted in stirring things up. In a sense that was what he had been hired to do. Employed by the College's progressive President, Alexander Meiklejohn, in 1917, Frost was the second writer to be taken onto the faculty. He was preceded by the novelist, drama critic, and aspiring poet Stark Young, whom Meik-

---

[14] See Robert Crawford, *The Savage and the City in the Work of T. S. Eliot* (Oxford: Clarendon Press, 1987).

[15] Myers, *The Elephants Teach*.

lejohn had imported from the University of Texas.[16] Amherst was being reshaped by American arguments between those who favoured scientifically driven modern research universities and others championing a new version of general university training grounded on the classics. 'The Amherst Idea', accepted by the College's trustees in 1911, abolished the degree of Bachelor of Science. Amherst became what Meiklejohn called in the title of his 1920 educational manifesto *The Liberal College*. Here, before they might train in any more specialized way, students were given four years of general training in the classics, languages, history, and philosophy. They were also encouraged to develop their creativity through programmes of drama, music, and literary publications, as well as debates and oratorical contests strongly reminiscent of the Scottish Rhetoric and Belles-Lettres tradition.[17] Meiklejohn wanted his staff to be in touch with the world beyond academia: 'If a teacher is, within the classroom, practising beliefs which have no validity outside the classroom there cannot be much vitality or force in his instruction.' So, as part of his educational efforts to develop 'human growth and freedom', Meiklejohn employed Robert Frost.[18] Though he taught conventional English courses such as one on pre-Shakespearian drama, and part of the freshman composition course (in which he encouraged individual creativity), Frost was most interested in 'the special seminar devoted to the appreciation and writing of poetry'.[19] This met in a student fraternity house, and would appear to be the course later designated Advanced Composition ('Hours arranged at the convenience of the instructor and the students').[20] Frost's curricular waywardness annoyed some of his colleagues, who noted the writer's determination on his first arrival at Amherst 'not to appear either academic or literary'.[21] Frost presented himself as fresh from the soil; one topic he discussed at considerable length was horse-manure.[22]

In a sense this fits well with the Frost who had no university degree, having been thrown out of Dartmouth College where, posing as

---

[16] William H. Pritchard, *Frost* (Oxford: Oxford University Press, 1984), 123.

[17] Lawrance Thompson, *Robert Frost: The Years of Triumph* (London: Jonathan Cape, 1971), 83.

[18] Alexander Meiklejohn, 'Progressive Education in the Liberal College', in Paul Arthur Schilpp (ed.), *Higher Education Faces the Future* (New York: Horace Liveright, 1930), 301 and 307.

[19] Thompson, *Robert Frost: The Years of Triumph*, 98.

[20] Pritchard, *Frost*, 129.

[21] George F. Whicher, *Mornings at 8:50* (Northampton, Mass.: Hampshire Book Shop, 1950), 35.

[22] Ibid.

wildman, he had told fellow students that he went into the woods to 'Gnaw bark'. Here was a poet who, fed up with its English Department, had withdrawn from Harvard where he had enrolled as a mature student.[23] Yet Frost, for all his bark-gnawing revolt, had been formed by academic experience. It was in Dartmouth College Library that his poetic ambitions took shape; Richard Poirier and others have drawn attention to the connection between Frost's poetry and the philosophy of William James, with its emphasis on the individual's multiple selves, which Frost had studied at Harvard.[24] Elsewhere, writing about 'Robert Frosts' I have tried to demonstrate the importance of Frost as the child brought up by his Scottish mother to be familiar with the work of the farmer-poet Robert Burns, and have emphasized the significance of his time in Scotland and England in 1912–15 when the young Californian reinvented himself as a New England farmer-poet.[25] What I would stress here is that Frost's remaking of himself was very much in line with his reading of the piece of modern American academic criticism which he most admired around 1914, when publication of *North of Boston*, a collection written in Britain, established him as a New England regionalist. During the period of the book's composition this American in Europe was particularly close not only to Edward Thomas, but also to Lascelles Abercrombie, a Georgian poet and Manchester University graduate who was soon to become a university teacher of English at Liverpool, then Leeds and Oxford. In Abercrombie's library Frost read with attention and admiration a long article on American literature in the 1910 *Encyclopaedia Britannica* by the poet-critic George Edward Woodberry.[26] A professor at Columbia, and later Amherst, Woodberry preferred teaching to the pressures of the commercial world. Yet as a poet he was uneasy in the classroom, choosing to present himself (like Frost and many other poet-academics after him) as 'not a real professor'.[27] In the article which so impressed Frost, Woodberry contended that

The most obvious fact with regard to this literature is that—to adopt a convenient word—it has been regional. It has flourished in parts of the country,

[23] Lawrance Thompson, *Robert Frost: The Early Years* (London: Jonathan Cape, 1967), 141 and 234–5.

[24] Ibid. 143 and 238–40; Richard Poirier, *Robert Frost: The Work of Knowing* (1977; repr. Stanford, Calif.: Stanford University Press, 1990), pp. xxi–xxviii.

[25] Robert Crawford, *Identifying Poets* (Edinburgh: Edinburgh University Press, 1993), 17–41.

[26] Thompson, *Robert Frost: The Early Years*, 474–5.

[27] Harold Kellock, quoted in Myers, *The Elephants Teach*, 79.

very distinctly marked, and it is in each case affected by its environment and local culture; if it incorporates national elements at times, it seems to graft them on to its own stock.[28]

Though Frost's poetry may have shown some inclination in this direction, Woodberry's view of American literature came surely as spur and confirmation. To take a simple indicator, Frost's first book, *A Boy's Will* (1913), is set in a generalized landscape and uses no place names; but his second emphasizes locality from its title, *North of Boston*, onwards, happily dropping such names as 'Lunenburg', 'Lancaster', New Hampshire', 'Boston' in a way that makes American regionalism unignorable.[29] The poet whom Woodberry praises in particular as quintessentially American, William Cullen Bryant, also sounds like the emergent Robert Frost. Woodberry's Bryant is 'a man apart and he jealously guarded his talent in seclusion' so that

his poetry gives this deep impression of privacy...It is, too, an expression of something so purely American that it seems that it must be as uncomprehended by one not familiar with the scene as the beauty of Greece or Italian glows; it is poetry locked in its own land...the body and spirit of the true wild...he had freed from the landscape a Druidical nature-worship of singular purity, simple and grand, unbound by any conventional formulas of thought or feeling but deeply spiritual.[30]

Today such enthusiasm may sound over-the-top, but it is keyed to the kind of poetry Frost was composing in 'Mending Wall', with its strong sense of the necessity of privacy, and its 'old-stone savage' attunement to the American landscape which seems animated by 'not elves exactly', but some spiritual presence.[31] All this was shaped by Frost's Scottish tour where he admired the American-like people and their drystone walls.[32] It is also calibrated very closely to Woodberry's sense of what American literature was like. Frost wanted to sound and seem American. Calling his poem not 'Mending the Wall' or 'Mending a Wall' but 'Mending Wall', he caught a distinctive, vernacular accent. That acoustic, though, was learned before it was voiced.

---

[28]   George E. Woodberry, 'American Literature', in *Encyclopedia Britannica*, 11th edn., vol. i (Cambridge: Cambridge University Press, 1910), 833.

[29]   Robert Frost, *The Poetry of Robert Frost* (London: Cape, 1971), 41 ('The Mountain'), 44 ('A Hundred Dollars'), 73 ('The Generations of Men'), 96 ('The Self-Seeker').

[30]   Woodberry, 'American Literature', 834–5.

[31]   Frost, *The Poetry*, 33–4 ('Mending Wall').

[32]   Crawford, *Identifying Poets*, 26.

Concentrating much of his attention on New England writing, Woodberry stresses its 'academic quality', uniting religion and scholarship, yet
also views this 'academic' side, exemplified in James Russell Lowell, as
counterbalanced by Whittier's expression of 'the life of the farm'.
Woodberry hymned 'Harvard College, where Ticknor, Longfellow and
Lowell maintained a high ideal of literary knowledge and judgment in
the chair they successively filled'. Yet, while concluding by emphasizing
the importance of 'the colour of isolated communities and provincial
traditions' and the 'regional' strength of American literature 'always
much dependent on the culture of its localities', Woodberry felt there
had been a loss of energy in modern American writing. Today, he
lamented,

The universities have not, on the whole, been its sources or fosterers, and they
are now filled with research, useful for learning, but impotent for literature. The
intellectual life is now rather to be found in social, political and natural science
than elsewhere; the imaginative life is feeble, and when felt is crude; the poetic
pulse is imperceptible.[33]

In Britain Woodberry's reader Robert Frost was interested in the
relationship between poetry and academia. He had been discussing
Columbia (where Woodberry then taught) with his close friend and
American correspondent Sidney Cox, and wrote to him on 2 January
1915 about

the article on American literature by a Columbian, George Woodbury [*sic*], in
the Encyclopaedia Britannica. I wish you would read it or the last part of it just
to see that we are not alone in thinking that nothing literary can come from the
present ways of the professionally literary in American universities. It is much
the same in the Scottish.[34]

In 1915 Frost built bitterly on Woodberry's conclusion, calling the
modern American university approach 'the worst system of teaching
that ever endangered a nation's literature'.[35] Yet Woodberry's article had
also mentioned with admiration the Harvard of Longfellow. Frost in this
period, despite his hostility to academia, was not only manufacturing a
partly synthetic New England identity which was remarkably attuned
to Woodberry's contemporary academic view of American regionalist
literature. He was also dreaming of a possible accommodation between

[33] Woodberry, 'American Literature', 837, 838, 839, 841, 842.
[34] Frost to Cox, 2 Jan. 1915, quoted in Thompson, *Robert Frost: The Early Years*, 606.
[35] Ibid. 475.

poetry and academia: 'I should awfully like a quiet job in a small college somewhere where I should be allowed to teach something a little new on the technique of writing and where I should have some honor for what I suppose myself to have done in poetry.'[36] For Frost in the year of the publication of his second collection, this was ambitious, a 'dream' which was not least a financial flight of fancy—the poet knew he would require an income. Just such a vision of poetry, money, and respect led him back not so much to America's farms as to her universities.[37]

Frost toured various campuses as soon as he returned to the States. He read at Harvard in 1915 to the newly energetic Poetry Society, was Phi Beta Kappa poet there at the 1916 Commencement Time, and did a tour of colleges including Dartmouth and Mt. Holyoke.[38] When the Amherst job offer came to Frost, it found a poet who had been cultivating a university audience, as well as a 'farmer' deeply suspicious of academic 'Knowledge knowledge'.[39] Following in Woodberry's footsteps to Amherst, Frost is very different from the graduate-school poets Eliot and Pound. He had complained to Cox that in modern universities 'Everything is research for the sake of erudition,' and had written, 'I like the good old English way of muddling along in these things that we cant reduce to a science anyway such as literature love religion and friendship.'[40] Though Ezra Pound would soon hope that his friend Eliot 'might be granted "a professorship," as Robert Frost had recently been', Frost was out of tune with his erudite American modernist, academically supercharged contemporaries.[41] He distanced himself from the increasingly professionalized drive to turn literature into a science, the same thrust that assisted modernist poetry. Nonetheless, despite his protests, Frost is like these modern poets in his blending of the knowledgeably urbane with the deliberately barbarous. However much he posed as rough farmer, the ex-Dartmouth and Harvard poet teaching Heywood, Kyd, and Marlowe was well read and advanced in his education. In his own way, uniting the consciousness of the 'old-stone savage' with that of 'Professor Frost', he was as much a modern poet as

[36] Frost to Cox, Oct. 1914, quoted in Thompson, *Robert Frost: The Early Years*, 474.

[37] Ibid.

[38] Morison, *Three Centuries of Harvard*, 437; Thompson, *Robert Frost: The Years of Triumph*, 74–5 and 80.

[39] Frost to Cox, 2 Jan. 1915, quoted in Thompson, *Robert Frost: The Early Years*, 475.

[40] Ibid.

[41] Pound (1922), quoted in Lawrence Rainey, *Institutions of Modernism* (New Haven: Yale University Press, 1998), 83.

were Eliot and Pound. A note of primitivist rhetoric surfaces from time to time in his characterization of poetry, whether in his relishing of sentence sounds as 'real cave things', or his emphasis on the importance of 'wildness' in poetry.[42] 'Much of what I enjoyed at Dartmouth', he recalled, 'was acting like an Indian in a college founded for Indians.'[43] His primitivism may have been a pose evolved in part to cope with those who were 'bookish' and who did not pursue 'wildness pure'.[44] But it was a pose that mattered.

Frost's 'academic' and 'creative' teaching were fused. When he started at Amherst, using J. M. Manly's *Specimens of the Pre-Shakespearean Drama*, he referred students to the library for historical and scholarly background, preferring to concentrate in the classroom on how the plays worked: 'The first dramatic principle is to think in terms of situation; the second, to imagine tones of voice…Tones of emotion and voice are essential.'[45] This teaching is clearly developed from his own recent work. It draws not least on dramatic dialogues in *North of Boston* such as 'The Death of the Hired Man'. These function less through any naming or description of characters than through tones of voice.[46] Frost was evolving his theory of 'sentence sounds'. He taught students to develop their own appreciation of sound and rhythm, not only through critical listening, but also through an apprenticeship of creative participation. He assigned to volunteers on his pre-Shakespearian drama course part of a Heywood play with

instructions to modernize their lines by removing didactic passages and by rewriting archaic constructions. When ready to demonstrate, these four students stood before the class and read their parts with so much feeling for the dramatic tones of voice that the old interlude became 'surprisingly lively and entertaining.'[47]

Frost encouraged his classes to go on to do similar things with the other plays, including Kyd's *Spanish Tragedy* and *Othello*. This respeaking of texts is a creative-critical activity not a million miles removed from what

[42] Robert Frost, 'The Figure a Poem Makes', repr. in James Scully (ed.), *Modern Poets on Modern Poetry* (London: Collins, 1966), 54.

[43] Robert Frost, *Selected Letters*, ed. Lawrence Thompson (London: Jonathan Cape, 1965), 167.

[44] Robert Frost, 'Sentence Sounds', in Scully (ed.), *Modern Poets on Modern Poetry*, 53; Frost, 'The Figure a Poem Makes', 54.

[45] Owen S. White, quoted in Thompson, *Robert Frost: The Years of Triumph*, 99.

[46] Frost, *The Poems*, 34–40 ('The Death of the Hired Man').

[47] Thompson, *Robert Frost: The Years of Triumph*, 100.

happens when Eliot produces the great breaking-down and revoicing that is *The Waste Land*. However, few of Frost's colleagues appear to have had much sympathy with students rewriting *Othello*. Even Frost, though he prompted such stimulatingly innovative high-jinks at the time, in retrospect took a much crustier attitude. He recalled that the students 'had been made uncommonly interesting to themselves by Meiklejohn. They fancied themselves as thinkers.'[48] Initially, however, Frost responded to and encouraged that stance. Soon he was saddened by the students' wish to cite authorities rather than to think for themselves. In some ways he did what Meiklejohn had hired him to do. He stimulated and provoked members of his poetry class by asking questions like 'Why do they have classes anyway?'[49] In other ways, letting people play cards at the back of his lectures and urging a student in whom he saw literary potential to abandon his studies, Frost was harder to handle.[50] His own literary orientation had been nourished by the academic Woodberry. On campus, though, he honed that cussedness and dark anger which are crucial to his verse. He had thought that at Amherst he could be part of an experimental college community of rebels. Once there, he soon found that his own need for rebellion drove him to savage his colleagues and the institution.

Just before telling them that Frost was coming to teach at Amherst, Meiklejohn had read the students 'The Road Not Taken'. That poem with its diverging paths that embody a dividing self (the 'I— | I' of the poem) cannily prefigures the way Frost would pursue his academic career.[51] There was a professorial, teacherly aspect to him. He knew how to discuss A. C. Bradley over dinner, as well as how to stimulate students to get them thinking and writing.[52] But that had to be matched calculatingly by a savage side. Amherst students and colleagues soon noted his 'scorching anger... violent prejudices and hatreds', his strategic 'irritable anti-intellectualism' and cultivated 'all farmer' pose.[53] Soon he was trying to get his gay writer colleague Stark Young sacked, inveighing against the college, and cursing the students. Frost was

[48] Frost to Louis Untermeyer, 12 Aug. 1924, quoted in Pritchard, *Frost*, 123.

[49] Henry A. Ladd, quoted in Pritchard, *Frost*, 130.

[50] Thompson, *Robert Frost: The Years of Triumph*, 100 and 104–5.

[51] Pritchard, *Frost*, 125; Frost, *The Poetry*, 105 ('The Road Not Taken').

[52] Arnold Grade (ed.), *Family Letters of Robert and Elinor Frost* (Albany, NY: State University of New York Press, 1972), 43 (Elinor Frost to Lesley Frost, [Amherst, Nov. 1918]).

[53] Henry A. Ladd, quoted in Thompson, *Robert Frost: The Years of Triumph*, 103; Whicher, *Mornings at 8:50*, 35.

wild, yet, as his shrewd critic John C. Kemp pointed out in 1979, he was also tame enough to be poet-in-residence or hold official positions at Amherst (1917–20, 1923–6, 1926–38, 1949–63), the University of Michigan (1921–3, 1925–6), Harvard (1939–1943), and Dartmouth (1943–9) as well as being associated with the Bread Loaf School of English during summers from 1921.[54] Frost 'said he felt he had always fulfilled his academic obligations. But he admitted in himself what he called "a protective laziness." '[55] Such a necessary defence mechanism would be increasingly familiar in universities as the employment of poets grew apace. Kemp cites nice instances of Frost's struggle to present himself to his audience primarily as a farmer 'and keep them from realizing how much of his time was spent and how much of his income earned on college campuses'.[56] Yet one suspects Frost's need of academia was not simply financial. Universities also created a tame environment against which he could sharpen the wildness needed for his poetry. This is implicit in a celebrated prose piece 'The Figure a Poem Makes', which Frost included in his American *Complete Poems*. The essay makes clear a need for 'wildness' in a poem: 'If it is a wild tune, it is a poem.' Yet Frost goes on to link emotion in the poem to emotion in the poet, and then to inveigh against the educational system before contending that

Scholars and artists thrown together are often annoyed at the puzzle of where they differ. Both work from knowledge; but I suspect they differ most importantly in the way their knowledge is come by. Scholars get theirs with conscientious thoroughness along projected lines of logic; poets theirs cavalierly and as it happens in and out of books.[57]

This is of a piece with Eliot's contention that 'Shakespeare acquired more essential history from Plutarch than most men could from the whole British Museum', yet, like Eliot's statement, it masks a drive on the part of the poet to go to the centres of scholarship and knowledge in order to plunder and harry them.[58] Differently, though as emphatically as Eliot's, Frost's own career as campus poet demonstrates how far

---

[54] John C. Kemp, *Robert Frost and New England* (Princeton: Princeton University Press, 1979), 173.

[55] Robert Frost, *A Time to Talk*, recorded by Robert Francis (London: Robson Books, 1972), 35.

[56] Kemp, *Robert Frost and New England*, 174.

[57] Robert Frost, 'The Figure a Poem Makes', in Scully, (ed.), *Modern Poets on Modern Poetry*, 54 and 56.

[58] T. S. Eliot, *Selected Essays*, 3rd enlarged edn. (London: Faber & Faber, 1951), 17 ('Tradition and the Individual Talent').

poetry and academia have developed a symbiotic relationship. William Hughes Mearns's hugely influential books *Creative Youth* (1925) and *Creative Power* (1929) not only used the phrase 'creative writing' for the first time to refer to an academic course of learning, but also presented Frost as a model for the teaching of such a course. American schools began to form 'Robert Frost clubs', and, unsurprisingly, Frost praised *Creative Power* as 'the best story of a feat of teaching ever written'. Frost's calculated primitivism was in perfect harmony with Mearns's admiration for 'primitive art' and his championing of the child as 'a genuine primitive'. As D. G. Myers points out, such rhetoric was at one with the 1920s academic tracing of a 'contemporary vogue of primitivism to eighteenth-century critics like Hugh Blair'.[59] As in Blair's Edinburgh, so in Frost's American classrooms primitivism and sophistication blended. Poetry and academia grew more entwined.

By the decade of Frost's death their linkage was taken for granted on and off American campuses. For James Dickey in 1965 the poet touring the country to read at colleges and universities 'has been moving and speaking amongst his kind', while Theodore Roethke wrote that same year an essay on 'The Teaching Poet'. Dickey tries to make some attempt to distinguish between himself as 'a wandering singer, an American poet' and his host, 'a young professor who writes poems himself and is enthusiastic and companionable'; Roethke anti-intellectually maintains that 'Most teaching is visceral, and the genial uproar that constitutes a verse class, especially so'.[60] In such ways, efforts to preserve *furor poeticus* continue. After Frost virtually all American poets have a campus aspect, balancing in different proportions their tameness and wildness.

It is not my intention in this chapter to provide a comprehensive history of the link between poets and American universities. Instead, I have chosen some instructive instances. In later twentieth-century America one such is the career of Robert Lowell. Lowell's progress demonstrates how poets of the generations following Eliot, Frost, and Auden are increasingly formed by academic literary training. It shows too the continuing definition of the modern poet as both more sophisticated and more primitive than his contemporaries. Descended

[59] Myers, *The Elephants Teach*, 102–3 and 113.
[60] James Dickey, 'Barnstorming for Poetry', in *Babel to Byzantium* (New York: Farrar, Straus & Giroux, 1968), 251, 254, 256; Theodore Roethke, 'The Teaching Poet', in *On the Poet and his Craft* (Seattle: University of Washington Press, 1965), 51.

both from James Russell Lowell (the nineteenth-century American poet who had so admired Clough) and A. Lawrence Lowell, President of Harvard, Lowell in his own poetic career exemplifies the growing fusion of poetry and academia which, especially over the last century, has characterized modern poetry.

At high school, one of Lowell's most influential teachers was the young poet Richard Eberhart. He had studied at Cambridge, England, with I. A. Richards and William Empson. Ian Hamilton points out that Eberhart became a kind of 'senior adviser' to Lowell at this time—'a provider of booklists, and of books'.[61] Lowell submitted an early poetic manifesto to Eberhart for his approval, and his first published poetry dates from this period.[62] Starting his university career at Harvard in 1935, Lowell enrolled in an all-English course, though he gave up going to the classes. His poetic sensibility was academically formed, but like most poets on campus he wished also to preserve a sense of independence. While Harvard did not teach creative writing at this time, it did make a point of attracting poets to the Charles Eliot Norton Lectureship. Eliot, nodding respectfully to I. A. Richards, had held this post in 1932–3, and the lecturer during Lowell's student days was Frost, to whom Lowell showed a projected epic poem.[63] That apprentice work dealt with the theme of the crusades. The young poet's very desire to write an epic signals his affiliation with modernism; he was reading Eliot and Pound closely that year. One of Pound's mentors, Ford Madox Ford, whom Lowell met at Harvard, soon took the student poet to Vanderbilt University, launching him on a career even more self-consciously academically formed that of the author of *The Cantos*.[64]

With Ford, Lowell travelled south to attend some of the classes being given at Vanderbilt by the poet-professor John Crowe Ransom. Merrill Moore, whom Lowell had met at Harvard, had told him he 'ought to study with a man who was a poet', and Lowell had decided to do so.[65] That Arnoldian linkage of 'study' and 'poet' was important, and Ransom's example shows how closely the two had become interwoven. As well as writing his own poetry and teaching, Ransom had set up the magazine *Fugitive* with two of his students, the future poet-professors

---

[61] Ian Hamilton, *Robert Lowell* (London: Faber & Faber, 1983), 23.   [62] Ibid. 25–6.

[63] T. S. Eliot, *The Use of Poetry and the Use of Criticism* (1933; repr. London: Faber & Faber, 1964), 11; Robert Lowell in George Plimpton (ed.), *Poets at Work* (Harmondsworth: Penguin Books, 1989), 122.

[64] Hamilton, *Robert Lowell*, 35 and 42.

[65] Lowell in Plimpton (ed.), *Poets at Work*, 123.

Allen Tate and Robert Penn Warren. The latter's 1938 book *Under-standing Poetry*, co-authored with Cleanth Brooks, would be a further milestone in the growth of the notion that reading poetry went hand in hand with academic training. The Brooks—Warren collaboration has spawned many similar-sounding textbooks with titles such as *An Intro-duction to Poetry* ('written with the student in mind'), *How to Study a Poet*, or *The Poetry Handbook: A Guide to Reading Poetry for Pleasure and Practical Criticism*.[66] Lowell liked to recall that when he moved shortly afterwards, following Ransom to Kenyon College, he was something of a savage, 'abristle and untamed'. Such a self-image would remain important to him. Yet he was also enough of a modern poet to combine this with his university learning, and to acknowledge how much the latter had formed him: 'The kind of poet I am was largely determined by the fact that I grew up in the heyday of the New Criticism.'[67]

Lowell's early reading included the university poet William Empson's 1930 study *Seven Types of Ambiguity*.[68] A Cambridge student of I. A. Richards, who called him a 'semantic frontiersman', Empson had a reputation as a poet which was furthered by academics such as Leavis and Allen Tate. His work in verse and prose builds on Eliot's sense of the necessary difficulty of modern poetry. Lowell would regard Empson as the most intelligent poet writing in English, and would later teach with him alongside Ransom as part of the stellar Kenyon School of Letters.[69] What Lowell absorbed from the New Critical doctrines of Ransom, Empson, and others was a conviction that poetry should be clotted and difficult ('Thus outwardly, this inwardly the view; | loose paper blew about his voided eyes').[70] Kenyon College had a strong oratorical heritage, signalling the debt of American college English to the Scottish Rhetoric and Belles-Lettres tradition. This may have helped its development of the teaching of creative writing. Yet Lowell's time

[66] X. J. Kennedy and Dana Gioia, *An Introduction to Poetry*, 9th edn. (New York: Longman, 1998) (the quotation is from the book's entry in the Pearson Education *Literature 2000* catalogue); John Peck, *How to Study a Poet* (Basingstoke: Macmillan, 1988); John Lennard, *The Poetry Handbook: A Guide to Reading Poetry for Pleasure and Practical Criticism* (Oxford: Oxford University Press, 1996).
[67] Lowell, quoted in Hamilton, *Robert Lowell*, 57.
[68] Lowell in Plimpton (ed.), *Poets at Work*, 107.
[69] I. A. Richards, 'Semantic Frontiersman', in Roma Gill (ed.), *William Empson* (London: Routledge & Kegan Paul, 1974), 98–108; John Haffenden, 'Empson, William', in Ian Hamilton (ed.), *The Oxford Companion to Twentieth-Century Poetry* (Oxford: Oxford University Press, 1994), 151.
[70] Lowell, 'Walking in a Cornfield, after her Refusing Letter', quoted in Hamilton, *Robert Lowell*, 60.

there marked a clear bonding of his poetic career with the pursuit of knowledge in an academic context. By 1940 he hoped for a Harvard fellowship and was mixing what he then called 'the turbid waters of poetry and scholarship'. He was convinced that 'I must range about discovering the fundamentals of knowledge' as well as 'dipping into science, politics and other arcana'.[71] Lowell at this time was preoccupied with the sort of arguments advanced in Ransom's 1938 collection of essays *The World's Body*, that (as Lowell later put it) 'poetry was a form of knowledge'.[72] From one angle, this was a very academically sculpted idea of verse. Through various mutations, it remained with Lowell throughout his career. He immersed himself in teaching at Kenyon, Iowa, Boston University, Harvard, and elsewhere. He stood (unsuccessfully) as Professor of Poetry at Oxford, spending some unhappy time there as a Fellow of All Souls. 'Almost all the poets of my generation,' he maintained, 'all the best ones, teach.'[73]

Lowell's lectures and classes often appear to have had an *ad hoc* quality. Students such as Helen Vendler recall them as inspiring.[74] Certainly they seem to have been a way of exploring obsessions which nourished his own work. So, for instance, he lectured on Pound while teaching in Cincinnati in 1954. His performance apparently included a poem about Hitler of Lowell's own composition, written in the cybernetic modernist mode of *The Cantos*.[75] Such a piece relates to Lowell's lifelong obsession with power. It also anticipates the later style of *Notebook* and *History*. In those volumes the poet presents anthologies of allusion, knowledge, and experience, attempting, in the wake of Pound and Eliot, to produce poems or sequences containing history. Like *The Cantos*, they operate by relating history in a megalomaniac manner to the poet's autobiography. The works in which Lowell was schooled and in which he educated others were bound up with the making of his verse.

This is as true of Lowell's early poetry as of his late. Enthusiasm for the Metaphysical poets had taken off in the early twentieth century with Professor Herbert Grierson's 1921 anthology of their writings. It had grown with Eliot's essay-review of that collection. Eliot's linkage of Metaphysical verse with the modern need for a poetry of difficulty

---

[71]   Ibid. 69–70 (quoting Lowell's letter to Lawrence Lowell, [Feb. 1939]).
[72]   Ibid. 85 (quoting a *c*.1960 talk by Lowell).
[73]   Lowell in Plimpton (ed.), *Poets at Work*, 104.
[74]   Hamilton, *Robert Lowell*, 352.   [75]   Ibid. 209–12.

underpins alike Ransom's championing of Metaphysical poetry in *The World's Body* and Lowell's production of it in his early volumes which were shaped by the passions of the New Criticism. The remarkable fondness of twentieth-century poets and critics for Metaphysical poetry was largely a function of the academic mind, with its delight in cleverness and paradox. Probably pinching terminology from Lévi-Strauss's anthropological thought, Lowell had come to reject much of his own earlier verse as 'a poetry that can only be studied'. It was, he thought, too 'cooked', too tailor-made 'for graduate seminars'.[76] Yet, working on the more 'raw', open, eclectic style of *Notebook* and *History*, he still attempted a sonnet-epic in the wake of Pound and Eliot's epics of allusion. In *Life Studies*, his finest work, Lowell may be turning away from his ambitious early poetry of academia towards a tonally attentive, more humane poetry of family. However, he is still operating within the academic-poetic system. The impulse behind his move appears to have come from the familial poems in *Heart's Needle* (1959) by W. D. Snodgrass. Yet Snodgrass himself, as that book demonstrates, was very much the product of the academically fuelled modernist admiration of the Metaphysicals, and was fully part of poetry's academicization. Interviewed shortly after the publication of *Life Studies*, Lowell said of Snodgrass's work,

He did these things before I did, though he's younger than I am and has been my student. He may have influenced me, though people have suggested the opposite. He spent ten years at the University of Iowa, going to writing classes, being an instructor; rather unworldly, making little money, and specializing in talking to other people writing poetry, obsessed you might say with minute technical problems and rather provincial experience—and then he wrote about just that. I mean, the poems are about his child, his divorce, and Iowa City, and his child is a Dr. Spock child—all handled in expert little stanzas. I believe that's a new kind of poetry.[77]

Lowell sounds a little grudging at times in this interview. Despite that, no poet can pay another poet higher tribute than suggesting that he has brought into the world 'a new kind of poetry'. For many readers Lowell's own *Life Studies* followed his student Snodgrass in sounding a note not heard in the writing of the great, academically conditioned modernist poets.

The family had been absent from most modernist poetry. Eliot's parents, a religious poet and a businessman, produced between them a

[76] Ibid. 277 (quoting Lowell in 1960).   [77] Lowell in Plimpton (ed.), *Poets at Work*, 113.

businessman-religious poet, and meant an enormous amount to him. Yet they scarcely figure in his verse. Eliot's criticism, obsessed with issues of inheritance, usually suggests that the kind of tradition that matters comes from books, libraries, and universities, not parents. Often modernist poets seem embarrassed by Mum and Dad: Ezra Pound's father Homer is displaced by his namesake and by his son's academic-epic poem. Pound is his own hero, lonely, supermannish, and Ezuversical. One has to turn to MacDiarmid's biography to realize how much that Scottish poet's family sustained him as he produced such superb poems of isolation as 'On a Raised Beach'. In Auden, too, family can appear as weakness. Heredity, in various aspects of modernist culture from Freud to eugenics, is a source of worry that becomes, eventually, both a preoccupation with quasi-academic archives and a Nazi obsession.

Yet in Lowell's work of the late 1950s, heredity returned as something brighter. The voice of *Life Studies* grew out of a negotiation between European and American traditions (again something Lowell had learned from Pound and Eliot), with the balance of power tilting decisively towards America. Lowell, studenty and coming from an East Coast Wasp society, is entranced by, yet impatient with, his own family history. He gazes on the world of his grandparents, whose *ancien régime* may be represented by 'an *Illustrated London News*'.[78] From his study of the Metaphysical poet Henry Vaughan, Lowell takes one of the great lines of English poetry ('They are all gone into the world of light!') and impatiently speeds it up. Pragmatically, he recasts it in terms of his own inheritance: 'They're all gone into a world of light; the farm's my own.'[79] Encoded here is the transition from cybernetic modernism to a more personal and relaxed post-war style. The phrasing is allusive, conditioned by the academic enhancement of the Metaphysicals, yet also chattily familial, cutting away to daily life. For all the elite Bostonian whiff that comes off it (and, let's admit it, partly because of that whiff), *Life Studies* comes in 1959 as a refreshing book. Eliot, characteristically generous, recognizes the strength of Lowell's autobiographical poems.[80] In them the younger man has been able to write a kind of

---

[78] Robert Lowell, *Life Studies* (London: Faber & Faber, 1959), 83 ('Grandparents').

[79] Ibid. 82 ('Grandparents'); Henry Vaughan, *Poetry and Selected Prose*, ed. L. C. Martin (London: Oxford University Press, 1963), 318 ('They are all gone into the world of light!').

[80] T. S. Eliot, letter to Robert Lowell, London, 22 Oct. 1958 (Houghton Library, Harvard University, bMS Am 1905, 434).

verse that the author of *Four Quartets* could not manage, yet which Eliot's own family background had qualified him for. Suddenly, mother, father, and the grandparents come centre-stage. After the heroic, book-lined halls of modernist poetry, the family is back.

The first, unforgettable poem of the 'Life Studies' section of Lowell's collection opens with the pre-student, child-voice, 'I won't go with you. I want to stay with Grandpa!'[81] Many of the finest effects in this book come not from the Gothic or baroque parts of Lowell's imagination (which look towards his own early days as student and professor), but from a simplicity of emotion and diction. So, in 'For Sale', he pictures his newly widowed 80-year-old mother in the soon to be sold family home

> mooned in a window
> as if she had stayed on a train
> one stop past her destination.[82]

The irony of all this is that such an apparently new, familial, direct poetry, as Lowell's remarks on Snodgrass indicated, had actually emerged from the prolonged cogitations of academia.

Around the same time similar developments were taking place on both sides of the Atlantic. They are aspects of a reaction to what were perceived as modernist excesses. One might align with Lowell's *Life Studies* the poetry of Philip Larkin which Lowell then so admired. Just as Lowell's more straightforward manner springs from his academic back-ground, so does Larkin's apparently unlearned style. 'Books are a load of crap' concludes his academic-sounding 'A Study of Reading Habits'. That, however, as many readers know, is a poem produced by the Librarian of Hull University.[83] Larkin might have run a mile from a creative writing class, but was at least as much part of the academic system as was Lowell.

By this period, there had developed an assumption that such is the way things were and had to be. Interrogating Lowell for the *Paris Review* in 1961, Frederick Seidel begins immediately, 'What are you teaching now?' and progresses only later from academia to poetry.[84] In 1959 the

---

[81] Lowell, *Life Studies*, 73 ('My Last Afternoon with Uncle Devereux Winslow').

[82] Ibid. 90 ('For Sale').

[83] Philip Larkin, *The Whitsun Weddings* (London: Faber & Faber, 1964), 31 ('A Study of Reading Habits').

[84] Frederick Seidel in Plimpton (ed.), *Poets at Work*, 103.

English poet Charles Tomlinson stated simply that 'Poetry seems to have moved into the university. It is written there and it is there that the poet can count on some kind of attention being given to his work.'[85] Tomlinson, then a Lecturer in English at Bristol University, may have been one of the more internationally aware and American influenced of English poets. As a youngster he was enthusiastic about Pound. Yet he was also conscious that, as he put it in 1959, 'the extreme cultural provincialism of the recent Movement poets was a university product'.[86] In August of that year the British magazine *Universities Quarterly* produced a special feature on 'Poets as Dons'.

Carrying inside its front cover a Faber advertisement for the recently published *Life Studies* and works by Eliot, Berryman, and the Scottish poet-academic G. S. Fraser, this issue of *Universities Quarterly* is revealing in its form and attitudes. Its editor, Boris Ford, had read English at Cambridge before the Second World War, worked as an Information Officer for the United Nations in New York, then on his return to England in 1953 had served as 'Secretary of a national inquiry into the problem of providing a humane liberal education for people undergoing technical and professional training'. By the late 1950s he was Education Secretary at Cambridge University Press, editor of the *Journal of Education* and of the *Pelican Guide to English Literature*, a series published by Penguin Books in the late 1950s and early 1960s, often reprinted, and much used by generations of students.[87] Ford was thus deeply involved with modern educational thought and particularly interested in poetry. His editorial to the 'Poets as Dons' anthology makes it clear that such a topic may be suitable for the summer vacation because it is 'a less academic aspect of academic life', suggesting that in Britain poetry and the writing of it were still regarded in universities as a fringe activity.[88] Ford (who would commission Tomlinson to write the chapter on 'Poetry Today' for the last of his Pelican guides) notes that Tomlinson is the most American oriented of the poet-academics featured, and emphasizes that five out of the seven poets featured have Cambridge links. T. R. Henn, President of St Catharine's College, Cambridge, contributes an introduction to the work and some remarks about the

[85]   Charles Tomlinson, untitled statement, *Universities Quarterly*, 13 (1959), 373.

[86]   Ibid.; Charles Tomlinson, 'On First Reading Pound', in Michael Alexander and James McGonigal (eds.), *Sons of Ezra* (Amsterdam: Rodopi, 1995), 31–8.

[87]   Boris Ford (ed.), *The Pelican Guide to English Literature, 4* (Harmondsworth: Penguin Books, 1957), biographical note on back cover.

[88]   Boris Ford, 'Editorial', *Universities Quarterly*, 13 (1959), 331.

poets. Henn (a 'very vain' Yeats scholar who impressed his student Donald Davie) sounds stuffy and ill at ease.[89] He betrays no real awareness of the tradition of creative writing teaching in the American South, or in Scotland for that matter, and notes an awkwardness in academia towards poets:

When the more important universities, such as Leeds or Harvard, come to believe that the mere presence of a considerable poet might well disturb their young men with elevating thoughts, they must be imported, attached, for varying periods, and perhaps with varying success. The hand-reared product has not the same reputation or attraction.

Henn points out that Yeats and Eliot turned down famous chairs. He thinks Housman and Arnold were not helped by theirs. He lists as handicaps for the 'poet as don' pressures to behave respectably and to read vast amounts of material (essays, theses, critical works), leading to a state where the 'mind-cells' become 'covered with a kind of coating of silicate'. He is also worried that the academic poet will be impeded because 'he will *know* too much'. This is an interesting reversal of the impulse towards a poetry of knowledge so strong in the major modernists, and of the suggestion (in 'Tradition and the Individual Talent' and elsewhere) that the development of critical knowledge might enhance creative acumen. Essentially, Henn sees the poet in British universities as ground down by administration and marking. His point is a good one. He notes, though, that in America things might appear better, if poets have restricted teaching or greater access to assistants. Henn sees little or no possibility of an academically nurtured poetry:

All that emerges is that the university don, at Oxbridge or Redbrick, is committed to a life that, if he is conscientious in his job, absorbs energy and meditative power on a scale that is not favourable to creative work ... Observation and experience suggest that the artist-don, who is reasonably certain that the springs of creation are clear and unlikely to dry up in the droughts of comparative poverty and domesticity, would be well advised to break away, into whatever wilderness looks inviting.[90]

Henn veers here, in a now familiar way, between classroom and wilderness. From one point of view, as part of an argument about the relationship between poetry and academia which continues today, his

---

[89] Donald Davie, *These the Companions* (Cambridge: Cambridge University Press, 1982), 104.

[90] T. R. Henn, 'University Commentary: The Creative Artist at the University', *Universities Quarterly* 13 (1959), 333–7.

words are shrewdly common-sensical. From another they seem obtuse, patriarchal, and dulled. Henn assumes that the poet in academia is first of all a marker 'conscientious in his job', with 'creative work' a secondary matter. Yet the writers whose work follows in the 'Poets as Dons' anthology clearly think of themselves first and foremost as poets. With what appears in the context of the 1950s as a whiff of misogyny, Henn (who taught at an all-male college) assumes that matters like 'domesticity' mean 'drought'. Works such as *Life Studies*, however, suggested that the familial might be the stuff of contemporary poetry. Lastly, Henn seems to have no sense of the way that the discovery of knowledge in academia might fuel poetry as it had done for Eliot and Pound. Nor can he imagine how teaching might dovetail with this, leading to a nurturing of a writer's own imaginative concerns. The poets whose work follows appear to be aware of such possibilities. Whether or not one rates their work highly, their comments enunciate the opportunities for poets working in universities. Donald Davie attempts to map modern possibilities offered by academia on to older notions of poetry:

It is normal in any age for the poet to be a learned man, and if in our society the universities are increasingly the only places where a life of learning can be carried on, it's proper and natural that more and more of our poets should be connected with our universities, in the only capacity that by and large in Britain (as distinct from America) is feasible: that is to say, as teachers.

Davie insists that the poet teach 'as poet', bringing to the material 'the urgency of intimate concern' rather than giving any impression that the poetry is 'a spare-time occupation or hobby'.[91] John Holloway argues similarly, contending that since to 'teach English' involves a 'life-long call to study' a variety of literatures and writers, this and allied matters are 'essential to most poets'.[92] Laurence Lerner, soon to teach Seamus Heaney at Queen's University, Belfast, emphasizes the need to earn cash. He also stresses the link between creative and critical skills in a way that recalls Eliot.[93] The most interesting response is by Edwin Morgan, whose own work continues the development of a poetry of knowledge into our information age. Morgan hopes it may be possible for poets in academia to 'be left sufficiently at liberty to forget the learning from time to time, or to combine the learning and the poetry in their own peculiar

[91] Donald Davie, untitled statement, *Universities Quarterly*, 13 (1959), 341–2.
[92] John Holloway, untitled statement, ibid. 346.
[93] Lawrence Lerner, untitled statement, ibid. 352.

way'. He sees the potential for a poetry which fuses learning and imagination. Nevertheless, he is very wary:

The university writer discovers that he must guard a certain modicum of unassimilability; even if he is a good teacher, he must not allow himself merely to 'become' a university teacher—he has to keep, and fiercely keep, the kind of independence that every writer has by nature. In so far as a university is an absorbing and protecting world of its own, he must gently fight it...

I am opposed to the American experiment of complete rationalization of the creative writer's position and function within the universities, because it has produced (at least in the United States) a generation of technically advanced and professionally cultivated poets (and their professionalism we might envy) whose response to life itself has atrophied and whose poetry is impotent to move and inspire the human heart. The much-execrated HOWL which arose a few years ago in California was the inevitable counter-attack, and when I read about Ginsberg's angelheaded hipsters who 'passed through universities with radiant cool eyes' and who were 'expelled from the academies for crazy', I felt that perhaps it was high time they did and were.[94]

Encountering these words more than forty years later confirms for me that Morgan occupies the cultural space of the modern poet. Author alike of 'Pleasures of a Technological University' and 'Hyena', he is clearly conditioned and formed by academic knowledge, yet also demonstrates a sympathy with wildness and the primitive.[95] By the time I came to hear Allen Ginsberg read in the mid-1980s, he was wearing a collar, sports jacket, and tie; the venue was St John's College, Oxford. The American Beat poet was introduced as (among other things) a teacher at the Naropa Institute in Boulder, Colorado, where Buddhist studies and poetry were part of the institutional curriculum. Not only was Ginsberg content to be institutionalized as part of a world where poetry and academic systems of one kind or another were increasingly fused. More than that, as the words Morgan quotes from *Howl* indicate, Ginsberg was well aware of the pressure of the universities from the start of his poetic career. Indeed he was part of and moulded by their presence.

Ginsberg would later describe his Columbia University Professor Lionel Trilling as 'Mahogany Matthew Arnold'. Trilling, though, was the most persistent early encourager of Ginsberg's verse. The period around 1945 when he took Trilling's English Romantics class was the

[94] Edwin Morgan, untitled statement, ibid. 359.
[95] Edwin Morgan, *Collected Poems* (Manchester: Carcanet, 1990), 275 and 246.

time when the young poet, through Blake, discovered his own poet-prophet's voice. For Trilling, Blake was a great revelatory initiator, just what Ginsberg sought to become. The location of Ginsberg's 'Blake vision' was Columbia University bookstore. Exclaiming 'I just saw the light!' Ginsberg may well have been entering a heightened state; he was also at the time running into the office of Columbia's English Department.[96] Ginsberg needed an audience. Throughout his career as wild-man he maintained a symbiotic relationship with academia. Like the Pound of the Ezuversity, whose approval he sought, he was attracted to anti-universities. He gravitated towards the wilder side of the system—whether Alexander Trocchi's 'Methedrine University', Timothy Leary's psilocybin Harvard, or Ginsberg's own 'Jack Kerouac School of Disembodied Poetics' at the Naropa Institute. At the same time, the Ginsberg who compared Shelley and Rimbaud for a Columbia essay also constantly touched base with mainstream academic institutions, particularly Columbia.[97] Questioned for the *Paris Review* in 1966, he refers to his *alma mater* repeatedly. The interview just happens to be recorded in Cambridge, England, where Ginsberg has been studying Blake manuscripts in the University's Fitzwilliam Museum.[98] Yes, the American poet gleefully shocked the world's Trillings with his jacking off, his delight in anal fucking, and his relishing of taboo-breaking, but in the heyday of student revolt he was as much a part of campus life as Lionel Trilling, and arguably more so. Many poets now deposit their papers in academic archives, but few so obsessively as the hugely egotistical Ginsberg. By 1980, as his biographer Barry Miles points out, 'twice a year' the papers and books Ginsberg was not using were 'shipped to join Allen's archives on deposit at Columbia University'.[99] Exploiting his own massive experience of public relations, Ginsberg was a media-poet who longed for and courted stardom. Yet he was also formed by academia, against which he revolted and to which he was self-interestedly in thrall. No poet can have been more obsessed with the creation of a university archive-mausoleum than the writer of whom Miles recorded in 1989,

Not only has Ginsberg kept all the sixty thousand-plus letters he has received throughout his life, but he has saved his manuscripts, journals, notebooks, and

[96] Barry Miles, *Ginsberg* (London: Viking, 1990), 37, 58, 79, 98–103.
[97] Ibid. 263, 276, 455, 58.
[98] Ginsberg in Plimpton (ed.), *Poets at Work*, 187–228.
[99] Miles, *Ginsberg*, 487.

doodles. For the last two decades, he has frequently taped his lectures, his conversations with relatives and friends, and, on occasion, his telephone conversations.[100]

Magnificently energetic and supercharged with Blake and Whitman, Ginsberg's 'Howl', as a hymn to those

> who passed through universities with radiant cool eyes hallucinating
>   Arkansas and Blake-light tragedy among the scholars of war,
> who were expelled from the academies for crazy & publishing obscene
>   odes on the windows of the skull[101]

serves as a paean to himself. Unlike Whitman's, this 'Song of Myself' is all the more academically accented for coming with a 'Footnote to Howl' whose 'Holy! Holy! Holy! Holy! Holy! Holy! Holy! Holy! Holy! Holy! Holy! Holy! Holy! Holy! Holy!' is taken from Trilling's Blake, and whose concluding '*Berkeley, 1955*' announces Ginsberg's presence on another campus where at the time he was trying to get an MA.[102]

When Edwin Morgan was attracted to Ginsberg and *Howl*, it was to a poet and a poem seemingly in complete revolt against academia. Yet in retrospect Ginsberg as much as Lowell is a mid-twentieth-century development of the modern poet whose work is formed out of an encounter with campus culture. If Ginsberg was in danger of turning into what T. S. Eliot worried Blake might become—'a wild pet for the supercultivated'—then Professor Robert Lowell remained well aware of a need to cultivate a barbaric aspect alongside his academic one.[103] As a student at Kenyon he shocked some of the College Trustees with an oration in which he rejoiced at a vision of the 'Goths and Philistines' coming to turn out 'the drones' from 'all the golden palaces of learning'. Young Lowell, keen to discover 'knowledge', was also eager to be primitive, or, as he put it, 'sensuous, passionate, brutal...I put in the last adjective because I am modern'.[104] His modernity as a poet was a hyped-up combination of the academic and the wild. Ditto Ginsberg's. Lowell the Harvard Professor, like Eliot the admirer of Mr Apollinax, knew 'Harvard professors' were 'All very pleasant, but...' Recognizing the value of the raw 'poetry of scandal', he was both Professor Lowell

---

[100] Ibid. 536.
[101] Allen Ginsberg, *Collected Poems 1947–1980* (Harmondsworth: Viking, 1984), 126 ('Howl').
[102] Ibid. 134 ('Footnote to Howl'); Miles, *Ginsberg*, 199.
[103] T. S. Eliot, *The Sacred Wood* (1920; repr. London: Methuen, 1960), 151 ('Blake').
[104] Lowell quoted in Hamilton, *Robert Lowell*, 68–9, 279, and 277.

and 'Cal' (short for Caligula), the uncontrollable wildman. Where Ginsberg mixed Columbia with drugs, Lowell veered from Harvard to manic episodes. Each man represents the modern poet in chemical extremity. When in the 1959 *New York Times Book Review* Richard Eberhart wrote that in *Life Studies* 'Savagery and sophistication meet in a style that is original, the Lowell idiom', he was demonstrating how much Lowell's new departure confirmed him as the latest incarnation of the modern poet.[105]

No poets indicate more clearly than Lowell and Ginsberg how strongly gendered is this concept. Bound up in the eighteenth and nineteenth centuries with the evolution of those all-male governing institutions of knowledge, the universities, the conception of the modern poet which this book outlines may have involved from its inception Ossianic elements of feminization, yet it remains predominantly masculine and male. Both Lowell and Ginsberg could be charming with women, but the 1949 photograph of Lowell and his male pals reclining on a bed with their laughing girls draped across them is as revealing as the formal pictures of the all-male Kenyon School of Letters.[106] 'I only fuck girls and learn from men,' said Jack Kerouac to Ginsberg in 1950; Ginsberg was annoyed, and reproached his friend, but the milieu which formed much of Ginsberg's intellect and imagination was generally homosocially male.[107] At issue here are not the differing sexualities of Lowell and Ginsberg, but their shared cultural space as modern poets formed by an interaction with a male-dominated academia. Is the figure of the modern poet now obsolete because confined to an older gender-world? Is the whole notion of a 'poetry of knowledge' so gendered as to be only of historical import? Neither of these questions is answered simply. In modern American poetry, however, there is a tradition of writing by women which has sought to regender the poetry of knowledge. The rest of the present chapter will examine some of its finest poets, and argue that this tradition has been nurtured not least by the opening of college life to female students.

Admission of women to the universities began in the later nineteenth century. It remained the case, though, whether at St Andrews or Oxford, in Cambridge or Columbia that the prevailing ethos was both masculine and male. In Britain, for instance, some of the major institutions carried this ethos until very recently. I can remember the odd sensation of

---

[105] Eberhart quoted ibid. 270.　　[106] Reproduced ibid. opposite pp. 147 and 242.
[107] Miles, *Ginsberg*, 131.

moving in 1981 from the female-dominated English classes at my undergraduate university (Glasgow) to Oxford where in some subjects my college was then celebrating the graduation of its first female students. In various areas of Oxford University a distinctly male, public-school atmosphere still prevailed in the 1980s. This was a world of 'chaps'. I found myself dining one evening in a crowded Senior Common Room where, as snuff was passed round and cigars smoked, there was only one woman in the room. Things may have changed, but if the interaction between the universities and poetry has shaped the development of the modern poet over the last few centuries, then, from the perspective of our gender-conscious present, the milieu in which this has taken place was often strikingly homosocial.

There has been a substantial amount of academic work on what a 1990 critical anthology calls *The Gender of Modernism.*[108] K. K. Ruthven and others have demonstrated ways in which male modernist writers made use of women and female-controlled channels of dissemination to further distinctly masculinist projects.[109] Ronald Bush is only one of the commentators who have drawn attention to Pound's conviction 'that "the female is a chaos," the male a principle of form and order'.[110] The association of modern taxonomies of knowledge with the masculine university structure is one important factor which has led some female poets to reject rational knowledge in favour of an interest in such states as the hysterical, the prelinguistic, the surreal. In different ways Anne Sexton, Penelope Shuttle, and Selima Hill have produced poetries which seek to inhabit spaces not dominated by the male 'logos'. Attempting to articulate a counter-rational feminist poetics within the university system has often been a perilous project. The Parisian example of Hélène Cixous and her efforts to evolve a creative writing alongside the theorizing and study of an 'écriture féminine' may be the most powerful and intriguing contemporary instance of this. Her project operates in an uneasy relationship with the work of Foucault, Lacan, and Derrida. It involves a fundamental questioning of and opposition to an epistemology viewed as not only logocentric but also phallocentric.[111] Where the Ginsberg of the 'Footnote to Howl' exclaimed, 'Holy my mother in the

---

[108] Bonnie Kime Scott (ed.), *The Gender of Modernism* (Bloomington: Indiana University Press, 1990).

[109] K. K. Ruthven, *Feminist Literary Studies* (Cambridge: Cambridge University Press, 1984) and 'Ezra's Appropriations', *Times Literary Supplement*, 20–6 Nov. 1987, 1278 and 1300–1.

[110] Ronald Bush, 'Ezra Pound', in Scott (ed.), *The Gender of Modernism*, 353.

[111] See *The Hélène Cixous Reader*, ed. Susan Sellers (London: Routledge, 1994).

insane asylum! Holy the cocks of the grandfathers of Kansas!' Cixous presents not least a vaginal celebration and an exploration of that femininity so often placed beyond the bounds of male rationality.[112] Her project might call into question my concept of the modern poet. However, the fact that Cixous herself is so thoroughly if uneasily implicated in the struggles and structures of contemporary academia leads me to suggest that work such as hers might lead to a radical alteration of the cultural space represented by the modern poet, instead of to the total obsolescence of the notion. Cixous's interest in combining the discourse of the 'Seminar' with primitive prelinguistic babbling can be seen as a cunning transformation of the modern poet's enabling combination of primitive and sophisticated. But Cixous writes mainly in prose, emerging from a French rather than an anglophone milieu. Her impact on the English-speaking world is increasing. Still, I would contend that there is an older anglophone tradition of a female and regendered poetry of knowledge. That tradition is important in modern American poetry. It represents in contemporary verse perhaps the most significant shift in the concept of the modern poet. Among the writers who are part of this transformation I would point to Marianne Moore, Amy Clampitt, and Jorie Graham.

Reviewing Moore's early poetry in the *Dial* in 1923, T. S. Eliot detected in it a new rhythm, a language born from 'the curious jargon produced in America by universal university education', and 'an almost primitive simplicity of phrase'.[113] Eliot's response may reveal as much about himself as his subject matter. His hearing in Moore's work both the accents of the 'university' and of the 'almost primitive' shows that he found there a poetry that can be related to his own aspirations as a modern poet. At first glance there might seem close connections between the Eliot for whom the poet's 'auditory imagination' fuses 'the most ancient and the most civilised mentality' and the Moore who so admired the 'Archaically New'.[114] Yet the differences between Moore's modern poetry and Eliot's are at least as important as the similarities. When Moore thanked a friend for a gift of 'primitive art', the artwork concerned was not the kind of sculpture Pound so admired—like Gaudier-Brzeska's hard and masculinist, pile-driving *Rock*

---

[112] Ginsberg, *Collected Poems*, 134 ('Footnote to Howl').

[113] T. S. Eliot, 'Marianne Moore', *Dial*, 75 (Dec. 1923), 595.

[114] Eliot, *The Use of Poetry*, 118–19; Marianne Moore, 'Archaically New', in Scott (ed.), *The Gender of Modernism*, 349.

Drill; it was a paper shell.[115] Out of such differences emerged the possibilities of a regendered poetry of knowledge.

The first poem in Moore's *Complete Poems* is 'The Steeple-Jack', which opens with a voice engagingly educated and odd:

> Dürer would have seen a reason for living
>   in a town like this, with eight stranded whales
> to look at; with the sweet sea air coming into your house
> on a fine day, from water etched
>   with scales as formal as the scales
> on a fish.[116]

The oddity is bound up with a precision (those 'eight stranded whales'), but is as easily carried as the education ('Dürer'). Just as there is a pull between whimsy and correctness, so there is one between pointed, factual accuracy and lyrical liquidity (etching, requiring sharpness and incisions on a hard surface, is arrestingly combined with 'water'). Such tensions develop in the poem. It is not entirely surprising to find that along with the figure of the work's title, its townscape also contains a representative from the world of learning:

>   The college student
>   named Ambrose sits on the hillside
>   with his not-native books and hat
>   and sees boats
>
>   at sea progress white and rigid as if in
>   a groove.

The relationships noted above continue here with the slightly pedantic locution 'not-native'. The liquid 'sea' is made 'rigid', yet played against a bobbing rhythm that with wonderful disjunctions sets off line-breaks and stanza-break against the natural speech-rhythm of the sentence. This reinforces a sense of hesitant, off-academic fussiness in the acoustic angularity. Later the poem tells us that 'The hero, the student, | the steeple-jack, each in his way, | is at home.'[117] Bookishness is presented as both foreign and native in the poem's environment. Reading other Moore poems is a way of tuning into a simultaneous attraction to and distrust of the academic. 'Pedantic Literalist' begins

---

[115] Marianne Moore, letter to Louise Crane, 21 Feb. 1937, quoted in Scott (ed.), *The Gender of Modernism*, 338.

[116] Marianne Moore, *Complete Poems*, rev. edn. (London: Faber & Faber, 1984), 5.

[117] Ibid. 6–7.

> Prince Rupert's drop, paper muslin ghost,
>   white torch—'with power to say unkind
> things with kindness, and the most
>   irritating things in the midst of love and
>   tears,' you invite destruction.

As the poem develops, its poet both criticizes and is fascinated by the tones of pedantic literalism; the lines present a conflicting relationship between the mobile and organic on the one hand and the mechanical and rigid on the other . A criticism is being levelled in this poem about an 'immutable production', yet these words may also carry an element of admiration.[118] Moore's quotation marks carry an academic tinge as they alert us to a source recorded by the poet carefully, if with less than total bibliographical detail, in the notes at the back of her volume. This is clearly a voice that emanates from the land of 'The Student', where we hear the voice of a 'lecturer' who tells us how in America 'everyone must have a degree'. Here again a mocking tone accompanies developing admiration for the scholarly world of the student. That environment may involve 'mildews', yet ultimately functions in the poem as an ideal, since 'the student is patience personified', and, if he 'is too reclusive for some things to seem to touch him', then this is 'not because he has no feeling but because he has so much'.[119] Again, spontaneity is played off against rigidity. The voice of Moore's poems delights both in the material and colorations of academia, yet cheeks and interrogates these. The notes to the poem show that it brings together words from a lecture on 'Les Idéals de l'éducation française' by Auguste Desclos, Director-adjoint of the Office National des Universités et Écoles Françaises de Paris, remarks by Einstein made to an American student, allusion to Emerson's essay 'The American Scholar', and other passages from sources as various as the *New York Sun* and a speech by Edmund Burke.[120] Moore's poem is bookishly clued up, yet also aloofly sceptical about the scholarly project in which its author delights. It is not quite allusive in the sense of being connected directly to the literary canon. Rather, it assembles its fragments from high and low culture, print and casual conversation. Though one recent study of her work is entitled *The Savage's Romance*, Moore's poetry exudes less savagery than an alert sophisticated naivety which is the product of her regendering of

---

[118] Ibid. 37 ('Pedantic Literalist').
[120] Ibid. 178.

[119] Ibid. 101–2 ('The Student').

the masculine cultural space of the modern poet of knowledge.[121] It would be quite wrong to suggest that all her poems involve academic figures or an academic environment, but surely correct to discern a tone throughout her work which both invokes and spoofs the culture of the campus.

A student at Bryn Mawr when American college education was allowing increasing numbers of women to acquire a higher education, Moore majored in history and politics, though she also studied English and biology.[122] Once, when asked to name the ten books most influential on her work, she included among them Raymond L. Ditmars's *Confessions of a Scientist* alongside *The English Novel* by the Edinburgh Professor George Saintsbury and the Harvard English Professor Bliss Perry's autobiography *And Gladly Teach*.[123] A later poem makes it clear Moore was quite aware that as a woman she could not have gone to Harvard. Still, she was as intrigued by professorial tones and tomes as she was by the intricate observation present in the work of Ditmars, Curator of Mammals and Reptiles at the Bronx Zoo. If there is something amusing about the juxtaposition of literature professors and a zookeeper, then that is very much in the spirit of Moore's verse, better known to many readers for poems about birds and animals than for lines about academics.

At Bryn Mawr, the young poet was taken aback to hear one of her own poems read aloud. Her words were professorially respoken when the College President intoned them to the assembled students in chapel.[124] Though the poem in question is prentice work, one of the things Moore's mature verse would do is capture something of a professorial voice at the very same instant as ironically criticizing it. Her biographer, Charles Molesworth, locates in a poem by Moore written in honour of a later President of Bryn Mawr a covert criticism of the head of the College when Moore was herself one of the 'Students—foster-plants of scholarship'.[125] Whether or not this is so, a great deal of Moore's later poetry is both nourished by and implicitly admonishing of academic accents. Scholarly tones are juxtaposed with mundane materials, tested against the creatures and experiences of the world. Moore may have

---

[121] John M. Slatin, *The Savage's Romance* (University Park: Pennsylvania State University Press, 1986).
[122] Charles Molesworth, *Marianne Moore* (Boston: Northeastern University Press, 1991), 40–1.
[123] Ibid. p. xi.
[124] Ibid. 44–5.
[125] Ibid. 32.

Men, Women, and American Classrooms

been a 'foster-plant of scholarship', but she maintains a sense of her parentage and home as being elsewhere, at the same time as she is conditioned by the pedagogic. A glance at her poems and their notes confirms how much her work was informed by scientific knowledge. Biological and botanical learning predominate, but her sources are not the grand masterworks of any great tradition. They are often texts either canonically marginal or altogether out of the curricular frame. So the *Illustrated London News* or C. H. Prodgers's *Adventures in Bolivia* mixes with *The Tempest* and Ruskin, destabilizing the male modernists' and New Critics' hierarchies of knowledge and canonical value.[126] Though there is an element of similar mixtures in the work of Eliot and Pound, Moore takes it further. She gives it a new and carrying, informational accent.

Cristanne Miller's *Marianne Moore: Questions of Authority* is most alert to these aspects of Moore's work. Miller argues that this poet, emerging from a family in which women called each other by masculine nicknames, and educated at a college where females at the time were encouraged to develop attributes then gendered as masculine, evolved a non-gendered poetry in which gender politics was nonetheless significant.[127] I would contend that Moore regenders the poetry of knowledge to make possible a new ideal of the female modern poet, as ambitious in the use of learning as her male counterparts. Yet Moore is also very important for the way in which she explicitly mixes 'major' and 'minor' sources. In so doing, she marks the transition from a poetry of knowledge to a poetry of information.

'Where is the knowledge we have lost in information?' worried T. S. Eliot in *The Rock*.[128] As the twentieth century evolved, a movement occurred from knowledge, whose certainties were increasingly undermined and whose 'luminous details' proliferated out of control, to information which was constantly in a process of flux, update, and exchange, ever fluid. In the arena of gender this shift (which in Foucauldian terms we might argue is of epistemic importance) took place alongside a questioning of those hierarchies of value which elevated, for instance, painting on canvas above embroidery, or public statement over private diary. Knowledge was regendered by a line of American women poets at the same time as it was passing into information.

---

[126] Moore, *Complete Poems*, 263–98.
[127] Cristanne Miller, *Marianne Moore* (Cambridge, Mass.: Harvard University Press, 1995), 93–127.
[128] T. S. Eliot, *The Complete Poems and Plays* (London: Faber & Faber, 1969), 147 (*The Rock*, I).

Though the bulk of her work does not seem to me quite to belong to the evolving poetry of learning developed by Moore, Clampitt, and Graham, Elizabeth Bishop, teacher at Harvard and poet of 'The Gentleman of Shalott', was clearly aware of issues of gender and ways of knowing.

Bishop's poem 'At the Fishhouses' brilliantly presents an otherworld of knowing that is fluid, relativistic, and lyrically protean. Hers opposes the Poundian epic knowledge-world with its emphasis on strength, manly control, and hardness. For Bishop the sea is an image of death, distance, and otherness, as well as of the knowledge towards which we reach. That knowledge may be 'drawn' from hardness and solidity. Yet, in an age so aware of relativism and in the work of a poet so alert to gender, it is presented as oceanically vast. Knowledge here is potentially deathly and submerging in the way that information in an information-obsessed society can be. Yet it is also (like the submerging and emerging seal to whom the speaker sings earlier in the poem) full of a protean persistence which evades rigid classification. This fluid rather than taxonomically gridded knowledge has come to characterize a regendered poetry attuned to our information age where it is not simply the luminous details, but even more the bodiless yet also perceivable texture of knowledge itself which fascinates the modern poet.

> If you tasted it, it would first taste bitter,
> then briny, then surely burn your tongue.
> It is like what we imagine knowledge to be:
> dark, salt, clear, moving, utterly free,
> drawn from the cold hard mouth
> of the world, derived from the rocky breasts
> forever, flowing and drawn, and since
> our knowledge is historical, flowing, and flown.[129]

In one sense, this perception of knowledge as near-bodiless flow is something which Bishop shares with some of the poetry of Stevens, and much of that of John Ashbery. It has informed the writing of younger poets, but I would contend that in terms of the regendering of a poetry of knowledge, it has merged particularly with the legacy of Marianne Moore in the poetry of Amy Clampitt. Moore was a hugely important precursor for younger female American poets, not least because she was one of the few women to have a high public and poetic profile in the

[129] Elizabeth Bishop, *Complete Poems* (London: Chatto & Windus, 1983), 66 ('At the Fishhouses').

earlier twentieth century. Beyond that, though, her tone of sceptical, book-freighted enquiry made available an intellectually ambitious voice to subsequent writers who wanted to write a modern poetry that might compete with or even supersede that of Eliot and Pound, yet which would not be taken over by a masculinist voice. Clampitt is one of these later poets who have synthesized something of the conclusion of Bishop's 'At the Fishhouses' with the aspects of Moore's technique.

Though Moore's ocean in 'A Grave' 'is a collector', and so, implicitly, a manufacturer of archive, it is additionally, as that poem's title reminds us, a place of death which 'has nothing to give'.[130] Still aware of the sea as linked to mortality, Bishop modifies this view, connecting its waves also to the fluidity of knowledge. Clampitt's poem 'Beach Glass' develops such a vision as it moves from an observed speaker who is walking 'the water's edge, | turning over concepts | I can't envision' to the ocean whose 'business' runs counter to the economic logic of a modern information society since it keeps open 'old accounts | that never balanced'. This initiates a transition towards a view of ocean as transformer of the products of capitalist modernity—tins, product bottles—into beautiful gems as it reshapes their glass. Bound up with eternal 'process', the aquatic world may appear to be figuring the imagination of those Romantic poets Clampitt so much admired. Yet, without renouncing the attractiveness of oceanic fluidity and the vivifying randomness of the sea as it remakes solid, apparently fixed structures, Clampitt also bonds these facets of marine allure with a view of the ocean as linked to modern channels of intellectual knowledge:

> The process
> goes on forever: they come from sand,
> they go back to gravel,
> along with the treasuries
> of Murano, the buttressed
> astonishments of Chartres.

Later lines in the same verse paragraph make it clear that this unending process is imaged as cognate with the evolution of knowledge, since it progresses

> gradually as an intellect
> engaged in the hazardous

---

[130] Moore, *Complete Poems*, 49 ('A Grave').

redefinition of structures
no one has yet looked at.[131]

Moulded glass, transparent as liquid, yet also solid, combines the aspects of knowledge which Clampitt's poem admires. Here is one of many of her works that can be related to her interest in scientific research. She desires a poetry which will be in touch with modern learning, yet not in thrall to its masculinist institutionalization. An English graduate, Clampitt is conscious of the way poetry was presented as part of a male-dominated classroom system which may have moulded her own writing. She speaks in interview of 'the advice I've more or less absorbed from the whole Brooks and Warren approach to writing poetry'.[132] Yet she has also reacted against such advice and has used her verse to interrogate and regender systems of knowledge. This is one of the things that happens subtly in 'Beach Glass', though it may occur more overtly elsewhere, as in her poem for the tercentenary of the College of William and Mary, 'Mataoka', where, of the title character, she asks

Who was she?
Ask Paul De Man,

for instance. Ask Nietzsche, Freud,
or Lévi-Strauss. Ask Parson
Weems, while you're about it.
Ask any woman…[133]

Here great male names of doctors and professors are presented as on a par with 'any woman'. In a poem directed first of all to a university audience, Clampitt shows an interest in the gendering of knowledge itself. When Marianne Moore addressed Harvard, an institution which gave her an honorary degree in 1969, she did so in a poem entitled 'In Lieu of the Lyre', which opened by pointing out that because of her sex she had been 'One debarred from enrollment at Harvard'. Mentioning the names of various of her male academic hosts, she speculates that they might have liked instead of a lyre various scientific axioms, or reminders of the name of some male inventor.[134] Moore here seems to be mounting a critique of gendered knowledge, yet by identifying in the

---

[131] Amy Clampitt, *Collected Poems* (London: Faber & Faber, 1998), 13 ('Beach Glass').
[132] Amy Clampitt, interviewed by Emily B. Todd, in Robert Crawford et al. (eds.), *Talking Verse* (St Andrews: Verse, 1995), 51.
[133] Clampitt, *Collected Poems*, 422 ('Mataoka').
[134] Moore, *Complete Poems*, 206–7 ('In Lieu of the Lyre').

poem with the figure of Thomas Bewick as a 'verbal pilgrim', she also masculinizes herself. The effect is that, while remaining an outsider (a pilgrim rather than a professor) and making clear the consequences of her sex as far as the Harvard of her youth was concerned, Moore engages with the academics on their own ground. She is both feminized and masculinized in the poem. This makes possible an inclusive regendering of knowledge and an engagement with the world of academic learning by a poet who wishes to be able to use that scholarship, yet to do so from a sceptical standpoint. Moore's opening reminder of her own sex acts as an earlier male poet's 'primitivism' might have functioned, by stating a marginality simultaneously with an engagement with the core of academic scholarship. Similarly at William and Mary, stressing her attraction to the marginal and 'primitive' female figure of the native American Mataoka, someone of whom 'we know so little', Clampitt chastens, even as she celebrates, the overwhelmingly male founders and benefactors of the College, making them share with Mataoka 'the mystery of what we are'.[135] Yet her poem is far from a clear-cut celebration of the mysteriously instinctual. Rather, as its content and its notes make clear, it is a work made out of processes of academic research. Clampitt served as writer-in-residence at many academic institutions, including the University of Wisconsin, Milwaukee, Amherst College, William and Mary, and Smith College. She thought of herself as 'like most bookish people', yet she also liked to be called a 'nomad'.[136] In this again she functions as a modern poet, deeply imbricated in institutions of knowledge, yet still wanting to assert the freedom of the unclassroomed outsider.

It may be that the notion of 'marginality' most accurately represents what the 'primitive' side of the modern poet has become for the writer at the start of the twenty-first century. Certainly, for women poets, asserting their femininity in the face of a knowledge industry developed so largely by men, protestation of 'marginality' has been as strong a gesture as Wordsworth's flaunting of the 'ordinary' in the face of the Cambridge sophistication which shaped him. As a freelance researcher, working for many years as librarian for the National Audubon Society in New York City, Clampitt is again trained in scientific habits which lead her, Moore-like, to provide 'back-of-the-book annotations' of the

[135] Clampitt, *Collected Poems*, 429 ('Mataoka').
[136] Clampitt, interviewed by Todd, in Crawford et al. (eds.), *Talking Verse*, 52–3.

sort which have helped her in researching as well as in imagining her poems.[137] Yet while she speaks out of and through a scholarly culture (as so obviously in the William and Mary poem and more subtly in many others), she remains critical of it. She wishes to enunciate a sense of 'mystery' which involves a use of both the primitive and the female, to assert a marginality even as she speaks from the academic lectern. In doing so she functions as a female modern poet, and encourages a more general regendering of the poetry of knowledge which will involve men poets (both living and dead) just as much as women.

Clampitt's poem 'Imago' bonds the creative imagination of the feminine discoverer of 'tomahawks' (which belong to that native world once classed as 'primitive') and remnants of white Mormon settlers (who would have been seen once as 'advanced') to a mysterious, genderless imago. Here is a poem which, among other things, celebrates the power of the creative sensibility and of ruin, whether the destruction of a civilization or the individual damage of eating disorders:

> 'But it has no form!' they'd say to
> the scribbler whose floundering fragments
> kept getting out of hand—and who, either
> fed up or starved out of
> her native sloughs, would, stowed aboard
> the usual nomadic moving van, trundle her
> dismantled sensibility elsewhere.[138]

The 'fragments' here are not quite those of Macpherson, nor are they those of *The Waste Land*, but Clampitt too is writing out of a sense of having to claw one's way back from near-obliterating defeat. Her vanquishing involves not only a profound sense of shattered civilizations, whether European or native American, but also an awareness of the struggle needed to regender knowledge and art on the part of the female poet, whose sensibility can be bashed by predictably gendered criticism—' "But it has no form!" ' Interrogating gendered forms, particularly those of learning, Clampitt seeks to make something positive out of a 'dismantled sensibility'. Hers is a grand poetry of knowledge, rich in the fragments and textures of scholarship (she loves listings, catalogues, notes, and learned terms), which is also concerned to rewrite male narratives of knowing.

---

[137] Ibid. 53.   [138] Clampitt, *Collected Poems*, 70 ('Imago').

So, for instance, poems like 'Imago' and 'A Procession at Candlemas' can be read as feminine-accented examinations of the relationship between tradition and the individual talent. If Eliot, suspicious of a poet such as Keats whose work has been gendered as feminine, insisted on the damage done by a 'dissociation of sensibility' and preached the virtues of an aggressively male poet like Donne, then Clampitt, author of a play about Dorothy Wordsworth as well as a poem about Mataoka, seeks the suppressed or scorned feminine elements which may help regender a poetry of knowledge. Her quest is far-reaching and funda-mental. Where Marianne Moore admired in the epistemologically ima-ginative Elizabeth Bishop something 'Archaically New', Clampitt seeks an 'Archaic Figure' which may carry a subtly feminine and feminist charge.[139] This is the Clampitt who is unable to return to Oxford without a persistent memory of herself as a young woman, so conscious not only of its library allure, and its masculine attractiveness, but also of its 'centuries of enclosure' somehow opposed to her own imagina-tion.[140] A feminine poet of knowledge, she structures her collection *Westward* so that she moves from Oxford to the Highlands, 'the raw edge | of Europe' where, on Iona, she finds 'the mind's counterpart'.[141] Clampitt is aware of Keats as a predecessor here, yet her journey also follows that of Clough, and of the Macpherson who moved between Hugh Blair's academic Edinburgh and the Highlands. Strikingly, as so often elsewhere, Clampitt, in her regendering of modernist cybernetics, makes use of those key elements—the university and the 'primitive' or marginal—which had established, over two centuries before, the figure of the modern poet.

The examination, or, better, the turning to and fro of knowledge that takes place in Clampitt's work occurs also in the poetry of Jorie Graham. Hers is a very different verse, her recent collections influenced by French poets, by John Ashbery and that heritage of Wallace Stevens which mixes with humour and Paterian sadness in Ashbery's writing. Stylistically, then, and not least because she belongs to a younger generation, Graham, born in 1950, writes a poetry considerably re-moved from the work of Moore, Bishop, and Clampitt. Yet she has in

---

[139] Moore, 'Archaically New', in Scott (ed.), *The Gender of Modernism*, 349–50; Amy Clampitt, *Archaic Figure* (London: Faber & Faber, 1987).

[140] Amy Clampitt, *Westward* (London: Faber & Faber, 1991), 23 ('Having Lunch at Brase-nose').

[141] Ibid. 28, 29 ('Westward').

common with Clampitt a fascination with a Romantic (not least a Keatsian) inheritance, while she shares with Clampitt and Moore a preoccupation with the detailing of organic forms. More than that, Graham, educated at the Sorbonne, Columbia, and the University of Iowa (at whose Writers' Workshop she long taught), scripts a verse highly informed by the topics of contemporary academia. Her work is also much concerned with countering the purely intellectual through an often sensuous poetry obsessed with ways of knowing. Graham's verse importantly continues the regendering of learning to the point where knowledge emerges sometimes as feminized, but often as a degendered amalgam of the intellectual and the sexual. Her language strives to bring together both the textures and precision of a scientific, materialist era with a powerful apprehension of spirituality.

In 'Iowa City, 1976', a short prose memoir of the time in her mid-twenties when, four years before the publication of her first collection *Hybrids of Plants and of Ghosts* (1980), she was a graduate student being taught the writing of poetry by Donald Justice, Jorie Graham remembers Justice looking as if he had 'seaweed over his brow'.[142] Her phrasing recalls the head of Mr Apollinax, 'With seaweed in its hair', disturbing and stimulating the graduate student T. S. Eliot.[143] Graham records 'how frightened' she was of Justice, who '*knew* everything'. She presents her own fear of her teacher as shared with other students, faculty members, and secretaries at Iowa, yet also as special to her. The short piece is a homage to Justice, yet it is also uneasy, a critique of his frightening knowledge and his strictures about poetry. He tells the student Graham to 'give in to the destructiveness of the subject'. Yet as Graham's poetry matures it delights in dissolving and floating out from its explicit subject rather than giving in to it. She seems to learn more from intuitively clarifying her own position against that of Justice, than from following his advice directly. As the student Graham leaves her professor's office, she looks back at Justice silhouetted against a window, 'blacked out' by its brightness behind him.[144] She focuses on the odd whiteness of the framed window, and mumbles something which she only imagines that Justice hears. Graham seems in a different world, able to see not simply the blocking figure of her teacher but, beyond him, a blank space from which her own writing may emerge.

---

[142] Jorie Graham, 'Iowa City, 1976', *Verse*, Double Issue 8.3/9.1 (1992), 20.

[143] Eliot, *The Complete Poems and Plays*, 31 ('Mr Apollinax').

[144] Graham, 'Iowa City, 1976', 20–1.

This short memoir of the experience of a creative writing class may represent many students' experiences: it is often by reacting against a mentor who is scary because so freighted with tradition and knowledge, rather than by following that teacher, that a modern poet's voice emerges. Yet there is also a special sense in which the memoir (written in 1991) contains elements especially pertinent to Graham's developed work. For few things are more important to that poetry than the opening of new spaces and the sensuously sceptical consideration of traditional knowledge. Though Graham's memoir does not point it out, it is hard to ignore that the all-knowing teacher-poet here is male and the student seeking her own poetic knowledge in reaction to that of the teacher is female. As a late twentieth-century author, Graham views knowledge not least as scientific theory and learning. Titles such as *The Dream of the Unified Field* proclaim that she is an ambitious poet keen to take on subject matter conventionally gendered as male in both the converging spheres of modern poetry and of academia, making it and remaking it as her own.

Helen Vendler has written with alert critical imagination about the change in style (particularly from the use of short to long lines) that occurs with the publication of Graham's third collection, *The End of Beauty*, in 1987.[145] However, the fascination with knowledge in Graham's work is present both before and after that shift. It is there in such scientifically tinged phrases as 'kinetic flow' and the statement of belief in 'cylinder lock, pully' in 'The Way Things Work', while the poem 'I Was Taught Three' deals in part with the naming of things and with education. In that poem a tree is 'elastic | with squirrels, memory banks, homes'.[146] Like many of the poems in the book, this one hybridizes the tangible and intangible; yet the phrase just quoted is alert also to the convergence of technologies of knowledge, of the electronic with the natural; this is a world in which squirrels and memory banks come together. A strain between cerebral and intuitive ways of knowing and a rich blurring of these characterizes Graham's poetry. She is preoccupied, as the poem 'Mind' from the same collection puts it, with 'the mind entering the ground' of the material world.[147] Often

[145] Helen Vendler, *The Breaking of Style* (Cambridge, Mass.: Harvard University Press, 1995), 71–95.

[146] Jorie Graham, *The Dream of the Unified Field: Selected Poems 1974–1994* (Manchester: Carcanet, 1996), 3 and 6.

[147] Ibid. 14–15.

Graham's poems carry what seem academic titles—'Reading Plato' (the omission of an opening 'on' makes this sound more like a study-guide than a poem such as Keats's 'On First Looking into Chapman's Homer'), 'On Difficulty' (a title shared with a book by George Steiner), 'The Age of Reason' (the title of several history books as well as of a philosophical text by Sartre), 'What is Called Thinking', 'Relativity: A Quartet' (whose title suggests Einstein teaming up with Eliot), 'The Dream of the Unified Field'.[148] The very titles signal her ambition to write a poetry of knowledge which draws freely on academic research and lab learning, while adopting the now familiar postmodern 'intertextual' device of having poems call themselves by the name of other works. Graham is very much a university insider. Yet she is also anxious to deconstruct and intuitively unpick classroom ways of knowing.

Brought up and working in an academic environment, she produces a poetry informed by modern literary and cultural theory, attuned (as Helen Vendler points out) to such ideas as Julia Kristeva's *chora*.[149] Though not mentioned in Marjorie Perloff's acute study *Radical Artifice: Writing Poetry in the Age of Media*, Graham's is an *œuvre* which signals in such apparently minor quirks as its fondness for algebraic symbols or for the 'click' of cameras and electronic keyboards that it is at one with an informational era.[150] Yet, writing a poetry of knowledge, Graham wishes to present her 'field' not as desiccated but as both enriched and enriching. Her 'Self-Portrait as the Gesture between Them [Adam and Eve]' is only one of many of her poems which focus on knowledge.[151] As it was for Clough in his *Bothie*, so knowledge here for Graham is intellectual, sexual, and ethical. To put it more accurately, Graham is writing a poetry that attempts to present an evolution of knowledge which precedes such categories and observes their emergence. Knowledge is not cerebral here, but fleetingly corporeal; it is 'gesture', which in the poem's first section is 'like a fruit', physicalized

---

[148] Ibid. 23, 56, 30, 140, 164, 176; George Steiner, *On Difficulty* (Oxford: Oxford University Press, 1978); Frank Edward Manuel, *The Age of Reason* (Ithaca, NY: Cornell University Press, 1951); Harold Nicolson, *The Age of Reason* (London: Constable, 1960); Jean Paul Sartre, *L'Âge de raison* (Paris: Gallimard, 1945).

[149] Vendler, *The Breaking of Style*, 78.

[150] Marjorie Perloff, *Radical Artifice* (Chicago: University of Chicago Press, 1991); for algebraic symbols, see *The Dream*, 62, 71, 87, 91, 108; for clicks, see *The Dream*, 113, 135, 139, 140, 147, 151.

[151] Graham, *The Dream*, 51–5.

and made incarnate at the same time as being given enthusiastic excitement in a 'springing back' motion. The poem enacts and describes 'the opening' of a space which has sexual connotations, and traces the dawning of a self-consciousness (which in Graham's later poetry is more and more bound up with screens, technology, and a near-preternatural awareness of the act of looking). Graham uses Eve's action in Eden as a way of locating the origins of knowledge in the female, and of seeing her 'error' as both liberating and empowering. Graham is hardly the first writer to make of the Fall a *felix culpa*, but she does so with a lyrical beauty whose language, peripherally at least, takes into account the nature of modern scientific learning. She engages with the field of the 'complex mechanism', as well as notions of paradigm-breaking lateral thought. However, Graham also links these to a traditionally informed lyricism to produce a poetry of scientific investigation in tandem with lyrical discovery. Her rhetoric amalgamates the organic ('the limb') with the abstract or mechanical ('a piece from another set'). Eve remains as mother, but she is also creative thinker. In the movement of the precisely numbered, freeze-framed lines or stanzas a progression and development takes place which is tentative and exploratory on the one hand, arithmetically fixed on the other. The poetry of knowledge has been strikingly regendered:

24
the balance like an apple held up into the sunlight

25
then taken down, the air changed by its passage, the feeling of being capable

26
of being not quite right for the place, not quite the thing that's needed,

27
the feeling of being a digression not the link in an argument,
a new direction, an offshoot, the limb going on elsewhere,

28
and liking that error, a feeling of being capable *because* an error,

29
of being wrong perhaps altogether wrong a piece from another set

30
stripped of position stripped of true function

31

and loving that error, loving that filial form, that break from perfection

32

where the complex mechanism fails, where the stranger appears in the clearing

33

out of nowhere and uncalled for, out of nowhere to share the day.[152]

The ungendered stranger who arrives here might be a child being born, might be the dawning of knowledge, might be a new genetic variant or a new idea or image. His, her, or its identity in this poem of both mathematical precision and lyrical fluidity is not fixed, though partaking of all and more of these possibilities. What is clear, however, is that Graham has effected a powerful regendering of the poetry of know-ledge. She has done so in verse that engages in its own way as much with history, philosophy, and academic learning as does the work of her predecessors. Other poets such as Adrienne Rich have attempted a sometimes angry regendering of knowledge in their work. Graham's poetry may depend too on that of earlier male writers (particularly John Ashbery), as well as on the achievements of feminist critics, activists, and poets. If her prose memoir of Donald Justice is two-edged, that could be because it recalls a time in her career when she was still negotiating with the all-knowing male who blocked the light. Her recent poetry, though, attending increasingly to the space or screen of the light itself, carries a confidently regendered inflection which seems more relaxed than that of Rich, and certainly more attuned to information technologies. Now the technological and the human converge, the body of tradition becoming both lyrically material, but also dematerializing into the electronic.

> The museum hums round me.
> Something else,
>   something niggardly letting the walls stay up for now, hums,
> something speechless and dense and stationary letting
>
>   matter coalesce
> in obstinate illustration—hums.[153]

Graham's work, strikingly representing a regendered poetry of know-ledge, is also one of the poetries most likely to be crucial in the development of a new century's verse when, in an ever-developing information era, human knowledge and machine knowledge coalesce.

---

[152] Ibid. 54–5.   [153] Ibid. 185 ('Manifest Destiny').

It is essential to the modern poet's work to be part of that world at the same time as articulating the kind of short-circuiting poetic perceptions which allow her to express what might distinguish the human from the purely mechanical.

CODA

The Poet's Work

Whether, like Jorie Graham, employed to teach creative writing in a university, or, like Wallace Stevens, to run a commercial company, all authors of verse know that, ultimately, the poet's work is the poem. Yet generally in Britain, unless they have private means or live off uncertain sources like Arts Council grants, poets need to do more than write poetry. This is not a new situation. Though there have always been exceptions, poets in earlier centuries had patrons or private wealth, or else (like Robert Burns or T. S. Eliot) they worked. Poetry alone is rarely sufficient to constitute a living. At the same time, poets may often feel that they would rather be making a poem than doing what others see as their work. In this, they are not alone. Many people have activities that they prefer to their jobs, so they may at least sympathize with the poet's position. In twentieth-century England by far the most celebrated poem on this topic was Philip Larkin's 'Toads'.

Larkin made his living in academia, working as a librarian (latterly at the University of Hull), rather than a lecturer. His poetry suggests a certain attraction to the idea of the man who *'chucked up everything | And just cleared off'*, yet also a wariness about such gestures as too deliberately calculated. In 'Poetry of Departures', he detects a poetry in departure itself, and communicates a hatred of home which strikes me as peculiar, though he claims it is universal. Yet the very dream of departure, in this psychologically acute poem, is what keeps the speaker 'Sober and industrious'.[1] Larkin among his books, running his university library, worked hard. There is a note of pride when, interviewed as a poet in the *Paris Review*, he makes the point that 'My job as University Librarian is a full-time one, five days a week, forty-five weeks a year...But you wouldn't be interested in all that.'[2] If in poems like 'Poetry of

---

[1] Philip Larkin, *Collected Poems*, ed. Anthony Thwaite (London: The Marvell Press and Faber & Faber, 1988), 85 ('Poetry of Departures).
[2] Philip Larkin, *Required Writing* (London: Faber & Faber, 1983), 57.

Departures' or 'Breadfruit' he dreamed of a Gauguinesque clearing off, then this seems to have been a kind of balancing mechanism, a dream of wildness that kept him at his desk.

In 'Toads', imaging work as a venomous toad which squats on his life, and is needed only to pay the bills, Larkin imagines alternative existences, since 'Lots of folk live on their wits.' In the lines that follow, he gives several examples. Tellingly, the first item on his list is 'Lecturers', who are linked alliteratively with 'lispers | Losels, loblolly-men, louts'. Larkin mixes recondite and colloquial vocabularies; only lexicographers are likely to know what 'loblolly-men' are. Specifically, the term means 'surgeon's mates', but Larkin seems to be using it to mean something closer to loblollies, who are boors or louts. He shows himself as learned enough here, but also as someone scornful of those learned persons, lecturers, who are linked to affected talkers ('lispers'), and people who seem able to live on air; later on the poet makes it clear that he could never 'blarney'.[3] The scholars Larkin likes are those 'scholars *manqués*' of the jazz scene in 'For Sidney Bechet'.[4] Elsewhere, academics are dismissed as 'a weed from Plant Psychology', or, with a touch of that casual misogyny that can be Larkin's hallmark, 'a Ph.D. with a beard | And nympho wife'.[5] This manifest hostility may be most evident perhaps in 'Posterity' where the speaker's biographer, the academic Jake Balokowsky (Jake as in 'jakes' or chamber-pot, 'Balok-' as in bollocks), works in an 'air-conditioned cell'. Balokowsky denounces his subject as an 'old fart', with whom, nonetheless, the 'research line' insists he must persist in order to get academic 'tenure'. Though there may be self-loathing in 'Posterity', more apparent is the poet's detestation of a particularly American-accented academic mill, against which, in one sense, his poetry is aimed; yet in another way, Larkin knows his work is also aligned with the system in which pages are microfilmed and students learn 'crummy textbook stuff from Freshman Psych'.[6]

Such an awareness is part of Larkin's career over several decades. He knew that his work, in the different senses of that word, was bound up with academia. He studied English at Oxford, yet detested much of the course. Ill at ease with public schoolboys, he recalled tutorials as a 'farrago', denounced Old English literature as 'ape's bum fodder', and

[3] Larkin, *Collected Poems*, 89–90 ('Toads').   [4] Ibid. 83.
[5] Ibid. 156 ('The Dance') and 160 ('Ape Experiment Room').
[6] Ibid. 170 ('Posterity').

avoided most lectures.[7] Yet Larkin did make use of aspects of the academic system, most notably the Bodleian Library, to further his own interests in Auden and Baudelaire, for instance.[8] If his enthusiasm for D. H. Lawrence seemed not to come from his tutors, then it would be wrong to think it was unconnected with contemporary developments in academic criticism. Larkin was delighted and shocked to get a first-class Honours degree in English (engagingly, he confessed in 1943 that he did not have a genuine love of literature and did not know a shop where they sold them).[9] Yet his examiners recognized him as someone who could work within an academic system as well as chafe against it. This would be the pattern of his working life.

Larkin liked simultaneously to inhabit an academic milieu and to mock it. So, for instance, in 1954, he published in the Oxford academic journal *Essays in Criticism* a poem which takes its title from Cambridge academic Q. D. Leavis's 1932 study *Fiction and the Reading Public*. Larkin's 'Fiction and the Reading Public' has a cynically demotic tone. Presented as written by readers, rather than an academic who studies them, it ridicules notions of the 'truly great' (F. R. Leavis's *The Great Tradition* had appeared in 1948).[10] Like his poem 'The Literary World', written in the same year, this piece has a tone of being browned off with the paraphernalia of writing. In 'The Literary World' poetic business is imaged as shit.[11] Larkin shuffles uncomfortably. In 'At thirty-one, when some are rich', he complains that he 'has a job instead'.[12] His 'job' is not so much 'poetic business' as earning a living. 'The Literary World' remains an unfinished poem. In a sense it will be completed by 'Toads', except that 'Toads' itself will demand a sequel, 'Toads Revisited', which again contemplates those who are 'dodging the toad work'. That verb signals disapproval, and the poet returns to his 'loaf-haired secretary' (a brilliant, slighting adjective), and famously exits, arm in arm with his toad, 'down Cemetery Road'.[13]

Larkin's, for all its flashes of humour, lyric brilliance, and verbal unexpectedness, is a dour sensibility. Though they fight one another, his poetic work and his salaried employment are bonded. He may scorn the jet-setter whose 'pal' is a 'Professor' in 'Naturally the Foundation will Bear your Expenses', just as, in a related poem, he ridicules 'The

---

[7]   Andrew Motion, *Philip Larkin* (London: Faber & Faber, 1993), 41–2.   [8]   Ibid. 43.
[9]   Philip Larkin, *Selected Letters*, ed. Anthony Thwaite (London: Faber & Faber, 1992), 57 (to Norman Iles, 7 Apr. 1943).   [10]   Larkin, *Collected Poems*, 34.
[11]   Ibid. 38.   [12]   Ibid. 69.   [13]   Ibid. 147.

Light Horse of L. S. E.' (the London School of Economics).[14] However, Larkin's ridicule first appeared in an educational manifesto. He once wrote that he had spent his 'second quarter-century | Losing what I learnt at university', and denounced anyone who had stayed on in Oxford as an 'arselicker'.[15] Yet the same poet hymned in Hull 'Knowledge; a University; a name'.[16] In 1940 Larkin had written a poem, 'Schoolmaster', which set 'the job' against 'living'.[17] He went on to do so throughout his life. He recalled being narked in 1943 when, trying to write a novel, he was interrupted by an official letter from the Ministry of Labour, asking what he was doing; he went straightaway to find work in a library.[18] 'I work all day' grumble the opening words of 'Aubade', several decades later, and Larkin does not mean he spends all day writing poetry.[19] He may have fantasized in 'The Life with a Hole in it' about 'the shit in the shuttered chateau' who is able to produce 500 words, then spend the rest of the day 'Between bathing and booze and birds', but Larkin knew he would never enjoy such an existence, and that for him there was instead 'The unbeatable slow machine'.[20] Larkin ran his library, and rebelled against the academia in which he slogged. In its title, no poem sounds more like a work from Eng. Lit. academia than 'A Study of Reading Habits'; its last line, as pointed out in my previous chapter, is 'Books are a load of crap.'

While an undergraduate in wartime Oxford, Larkin had met the poet Vernon Watkins. The student was impressed alike by Watkins's 'devotion to poetry' and by his not having 'the slightest intention of "living by writing"' (Watkins worked as a bank clerk); for Larkin, perilously perched 'on the edge of the world of employment', Watkins's example was 'almost encouraging'.[21] As early as 1945, Larkin was complaining in a letter to Kingsley Amis that no one would give him money if he did anything for them that made him happy while he did it.[22] Characteristically, he warned his correspondent not to interpret that as a *double entendre*, but a division persisted throughout Larkin's life between his work in academia and his work as a poet. He liked the idea that there

---

[14] Ibid. 134 ('Naturally the Foundation will Bear your Expenses') and 172 ('When the Russian tanks roll westward'); the latter first appeared in *Black Paper Two: The Crisis in Education* (1969).

[15] Larkin, *Collected Poems*, 211 ('The Winter Palace') and 179 ('Poem about Oxford').

[16] Ibid. 220 ('By day, a lifted study-storehouse').   [17] Ibid. 248.

[18] Larkin, *Required Writing*, 31.   [19] Larkin, *Collected Poems*, 208.

[20] Ibid. 202.   [21] Larkin, *Required Writing*, 42.

[22] Larkin, *Selected Letters*, 108 (to Kingsley Amis, 22 Aug. 1945).

were subjects for poetry that lay beyond the Honours School of English, and he had little time for a poet like Charles Tomlinson, who admired 'bookish young Yanks' and denounced that 'Middlebrow Muse' to which part of Larkin was attracted.[23] It is ironic that the librarian Larkin should scorn someone else as 'bookish', but it is also characteristic. Larkin was annoyed by Tomlinson's suggestion that he had not read Eliot's 'Tradition and the Individual Talent'. Larkin, with his First in English, girned that he had read it, and considered it 'piss'.[24] The demotic here is a form of primitive anti-highbrow attack. It is uttered by someone all the more desperate to pose as anti-intellectual because he has to work every day in a university library.

Larkin's work as academic librarian and as poet makes him resentful towards lecturers. So Frank Kermode is a 'book drunk ponce', damned as one of the 'salaried explainers of poetry' who have a professional interest in making sure that verse stays difficult, allusive, and in need of academic explication.[25] Larkin's flyting with campus culture is bound up with his quarrel with modernism. However, just as I have argued elsewhere that his own verse owes a debt to modernism, so I would contend here that his poetic *œuvre* is inextricably bound up with his work in academia.[26] Larkin disliked taking part in seminars about poetry. He once said that 'The academic world has worked all right for me, but then, I'm not a teacher'; to teach in a university, he maintained, would put him off literature.[27] When his *Paris Review* interviewer asks him about his study of poets, the author of 'A Study of Reading Habits' replies, 'Oh, for Christ's sake, one doesn't *study* poets! You read them.'[28] In 1972, when he took up a short-term post as a university Writing Fellow, Anthony Thwaite was cautioned by his friend Larkin about problems of contact between students and poets; yet the warning Larkin delivered is in a letter dictated to his secretary in the librarian's office, University of Hull.[29] Larkin perceived with scepticism 'a cunning merger between poet, literary critic and academic critic (three classes now notoriously indistinguishable)', resulting in a situation where poets could explain their own poetry in the classroom.[30] Working as a university librarian kept Larkin out of seminars; yet it situated him unignorably in academe. In

---

[23] Ibid. 242 (to Robert Conquest, 28 May 1955) and 274 (to Robert Conquest, 7 May 1957).
[24] Ibid. 274.   [25] Ibid. 307 (to Robert Conquest, 15 Sept. 1959).
[26] See Robert Crawford, *Devolving English Literature*, 2nd edn. (Edinburgh: Edinburgh University Press, 2000), 271–7.   [27] Larkin, *Required Writing*, 60.
[28] Ibid. 67.   [29] Larkin, *Selected Letters*, 456 (to Anthony Thwaite, 25 Apr. 1972).
[30] Larkin, *Required Writing*, 81.

1974 he sounds pleased but bemused by his treatment at St Andrews, where he had been given an honorary degree, and fed up with the prospect of having to go and speak at the University of Sussex.[31] In the same letter what he invokes with longing are the modernist James Joyce's watchwords: 'silence exile and cunning.' Larkin's silence takes the form of academic correspondence; his exile is an office in a university building; his cunning is to capture a creative spark generated out of a clash between his different kinds of work. He knew that he 'belonged to an academic community', and part of him forever hungered not to.[32]

Larkin paid considerable imaginative and analytical attention to the problem of the poet's work. 'Aren't you, really, asking about *work*?' he questions an interviewer, making clear his own reluctance to 'join the cultural entertainment industry' or 'take hand-outs' from Arts Councils. All Larkin's poetry is written, he makes clear, 'after a day's work'. There is an element of pride in that statement, and a note of acceptance; but there is also annoyance in his realization that despite the honour his poetry has attracted, all that society is willing to pay him for is being 'an undistinguished university administrator'.[33] His lecture on 'Subsidizing Poetry' indicates concern with a poet's work, and wariness of how in 1970s England poetry was moving into 'the education world', so that poets were being welcomed onto many a university campus, even to engage in the teaching of creative writing. Larkin sees some economic advantages here, but warns against the poet becoming a 'university teacher' to the extent that 'by acting like a critic he may come to think like a critic', and so produce the sort of poems that are dutifully in line with the professional conduct of seminar-room exegesis.[34] Larkin did succeed in engineering short-term fellowships for several poets at Hull University in the late 1960s and early 1970s. For him this was not only a channel for getting money to writers; it was also a way of keeping the university in touch with poets from the outside world, even if 'poetry has been increasingly the preserve of academic English teaching'.[35] The last holder of this fellowship, Douglas Dunn, would receive Larkin's special encouragement, and win substantial admiration; he would also accept a Chair of English, which may not have been what Larkin had in mind. Larkin's own biographer, Andrew Motion, became the first university professor to be appointed Poet Laureate.

---

[31] Larkin, *Selected Letters*, 511 (to Anthony Thwaite, 11 July 1974).
[32] Larkin, *Required Writing*, 39.   [33] Ibid. 61–2.   [34] Ibid. 88–9.
[35] Larkin, quoted in Motion, *Philip Larkin*, 381.

Larkin's admiration for John Betjeman is bound up with his attraction to a poet for whom there seems to have been no Pound nor Eliot, 'no *Seven Types* or *Some Versions*, no works of criticism with titles such as *Communication as Discipline* or *Implicit and Explicit Image-Obliquity in Sir Lewis Morris*'.[36] The Larkin who, as a child, 'wanted to be a drummer' hungers after the 'primitive vivacity' which he hears in Betjeman's work.[37] For Larkin, as for Eliot, Pound, and other modernist poets, the concept of poetry was at root what he called 'primitive'.[38] However, his very invocation of Empson's academic studies, *Seven Types of Ambiguity* and *Some Versions of Pastoral*, makes manifest Larkin's academic filiations. His solution is to spoof, to insult, to swear, and to attempt (albeit limited) escape. Sitting at a Board of the Faculty of Arts meeting at Hull University in 1981, he doodled a series of cubes on the back of the agenda paper. These include a bird cage, a 'Condemned Cell', and a 'Librarian's Office'. There is also a smaller box marked 'The secret stairs'.[39] Metaphorically speaking, these are the stairs that connect the two senses of Larkin's 'work'. His poetry and his academic employment always existed in an uneasy state of mutual implication and stand-off. He knew that the poet who works in academia must preserve just such a secret staircase if his or her poetic work is to flourish. Larkin might be caricatured as an anti-academic poet; such a view would be at best a partial truth. More accurately, he represents the poet who labours hard within academia and who therefore becomes aware of the need to inhabit the machine with skill and to evolve escape-mechanisms from his job, protecting areas of his or her imagination from numbing bureaucratic routines. The very origins of Larkin's poetry are bound up with the education system. He recalled that the first poem he ever wrote 'was set for homework' by his schoolteacher, and that, after that, he went on writing both prose and verse each night 'after homework'.[40] This writing additional to his 'required writing' (to invoke the title of one of Larkin's books which parodies academia's 'required reading'), this work after work, set the pattern for Larkin's mature poetry. However dutiful, he knew, like his very different Scottish contemporary Edwin

[36] Larkin, *Required Writing*, 209.
[37] Ibid. 286 and 209.
[38] Larkin, quoted in Motion, *Philip Larkin*, 380.
[39] Philip Larkin, 'Some Doodles', in Harry Chambers (ed.), *An Enormous Yes* (Calstock: Peterloo Poets, 1986), 45.
[40] Larkin, *Required Writing*, 48; Larkin, quoted in Roger Day, *Larkin* (Milton Keynes: Open University Press, 1987), 1.

Morgan, that a part of the poet who works in academia must always retain a 'modicum of unassimilability'.[41]

This awareness makes Larkin, rather than, say, Donald Davie, exemplify the necessary strategy of the modern poet for whom some relationship with academia is well-nigh inevitable. Though Davie might write in his autobiography of 'we poets' and of 'my friend Philip Larkin', he sounds throughout far more of a critic than a poet. Yet there are occasional flashes of something else. He rejoices in a lifelong sense of 'living dangerously, outwitting the examiner/reader', proclaiming himself 'a poet who has spent his life in universities'. As such, he contends, he 'always shall attack those who would set the life of poetry against the life of intellect and the life of learning'. Yet even Davie is concerned to protest that he is alert to 'the blight of academicism' which can refuse to treat poetry as anything more than 'a wayward variant on discursive prose'.[42] There may be something sadly revealing in the academic Davie who has to protest in prose, 'I want to be a poet of *feeling*,' a quality that can seem lacking in his verse. Nonetheless, this committedly academic poet defends poetry against a 'literary criticism' that has 'got too big for its boots', and is aware of the voices of poet friends questioning his own fascination with academic criticism.[43] Elsewhere, Davie evinces a continuing anxiety that 'That awkward amphibian the poet-critic runs the danger . . . of having the poet in him immolated for the sake of the critic'; a vital question to ask of poet-critics is 'what is the poet inside the poet-critic doing, if not out-witting the critic in him?'[44] Though one might retort that the poet not so much out-wits the critic as out-dreams him, it is reassuring to find, even in so professorial a poet as Davie, this awareness of poetry's need to strive to elude the institutional intelligence.

In retrospect, Davie presented such 1950s critical works as *Purity of Diction in English Poetry* as 'a sort of concealed manifesto', claiming he wrote his earlier prose 'in order to explain to myself what I had been doing in the poems'.[45] This statement indicates just how academically formed was Davie's mind. Few poets feel a strong desire to explain to

[41] Edwin Morgan, *Nothing Not Giving Messages*, ed. Hamish Whyte (Edinburgh: Polygon, 1990), 194.
[42] Donald Davie, *These the Companions* (Cambridge: Cambridge University Press, 1982), 22, 106, 123, and 129.
[43] Ibid. 129 and 168.
[44] Donald Davie, introduction to *The Collected Poems of Yvor Winters* (Manchester: Carcanet, 1978), 3.
[45] Donald Davie, *Trying to Explain* (Manchester: Carcanet, 1980), 208–9.

themselves what they have done in their poems. The latter must stand independently. They might attract from the older poet commentary or contextualization, but surely not academic exposition. Davie may seem an instance of the sort of poet Larkin warned against—the one who explains his own poems in the classroom. Where Larkin avoided 'creative writing', Davie taught it. He readily embraced academia. Yet he did not claim that the teaching of writing could achieve more than 'rules of thumb'. The 'artificial' conditions of his workshop allowed fledgling poets simply to engage with an audience.[46] Davie's finest work, his adaptation of Mickiewicz, 'The Forests of Lithuania', owes as much to his experience outside college as to his time in lecture halls.[47] Few English poets have been more academicized, but Davie preserved a certain scepticism about poetry and the seminar. He sought to negotiate between an American 'vice' of 'excessive professionalism' in poetry's relationship with academia, and an English view that poetry should remain 'wholly amateur'.[48] Even Davie made it clear that the poet must be prepared to be numbered among 'the barbarians' as well as among the 'administrators'.[49] He and Larkin in their different ways indicate how poetry in the later twentieth century increasingly had to come to terms with the campus climate which enveloped it. Larkin, working in a university, posed as anti-academic; Davie presented himself as transatlantic scholarly professional, yet sought to allow that the overlap between poet and academic critic was less than total. Among more recent poets, similar strategies have been deployed. All, however, have had to come to terms sooner or later with academia as a presence.

For Ted Hughes, this meant as a student of English a dramatic confrontation with his subject matter. A few years before he died, that poet wrote how, as an undergraduate at Cambridge, he came to change from English to Archaeology and Anthropology. He sensed a resistance building up in him towards the writing of analytical essays on literary texts. Just before his Part I examinations, he dreamed that a creature with a man's body but a fox's head came to him, apparently on fire. It placed its pained, bloody hand on the blank page of his essay, and pleaded, 'Stop this—you are destroying us.'[50] After this, Hughes gave

---

[46] Ibid. 211–12.
[47] Donald Davie, *Slavic Excursions* (Manchester: Carcanet, 1990), 54–94.
[48] Davie, *Trying to Explain*, 213.   [49] Davie, *These the Companions*, 80.
[50] Ted Hughes, *Winter Pollen*, ed. William Scammell (London: Faber & Faber, 1994), 9.

up the academic study of English. Reading his poem 'The Thought-Fox' (born from that dream), one assumes the poet's 'blank page' in the first stanza is the result of trying to write verse, rather than an abortive student paper. According to Hughes's recollection, though, 'The Thought-Fox' marks the conversion of his university essay into poetry that celebrates wildness. Perhaps the only academic element that remains is the word 'Thought'. With its 'sharp hot stink', his fox seems far more feral than cerebral, yet his poem's title maintains there is an intellectual as well as a purely dream-element to the experience. At one level the poem is about abandoning the Eng. Lit. study of poetry for the shamanistic identification with the wild; at another level, though, it is about the poet's desire to fuse what is 'Thought' with what is 'Fox'. The success which is celebrated is signalled by the hyphen in the poem's title. The modern poet can be neither 'Thought' nor 'Fox', but must be 'Thought-Fox'.[51] Though Hughes, nicknamed by Larkin 'the Incredible Hulk', is famous for his poems of animality, there are moments when we might recall that behind them lies an Anthropology graduate.[52] It is surely this poet's particular academic training that leads him, for instance, to describe a jaguar as 'Like a thick Aztec disemboweller'; the construction of the *Crow* sequence shows Hughes the poet putting into practice lessons about totemism and shamanism which he had learned at Cambridge.[53] Hughes liked to write as a poetic shaman; yet other works, most notably the Gravesian *Shakespeare and the Goddess of Complete Being*, postulating 'a basic structural pattern' in many of Shakespeare's plays, appear very much like the quasi-professorial productions of a former student who had studied English as well as anthropology.[54]

For poet after poet over the last few decades there has been an often effortful search for how to combine elements of the sophisticated knowledge-world of the universities with the 'primitive' or 'marginal' zone which seems vital to poetic work. Seamus Heaney's 'Hercules and Antaeus' is usually read as a poem about the overcoming of the marginal by colonizing powers, but also involves a struggle between 'intelligence' and a darker, more primitive world of 'origins'.[55] Written around the time Heaney gave up his job as a Lecturer in English at Queen's

[51] Ted Hughes, *New Selected Poems* (London: Faber & Faber, 1995), 3.
[52] Larkin, *Selected Letters*, 636 (to Kingsley Amis, 11 Jan. 1981).
[53] Ibid. 60 ('Second Glance at a Jaguar').
[54] Ted Hughes, *Shakespeare and the Goddess of Complete Being* (London: Faber & Faber, 1992), 1.
[55] Seamus Heaney, *Opened Ground* (London: Faber & Faber, 1998), 129 ('Hercules and Antaeus').

University, Belfast, and moved south to the Irish Republic to live as a freelance writer, it can be read as a struggle between his two selves. The poet's sympathies tend towards Antaeus, yet it is the figure of 'intelligence' who is victorious. The best known of Heaney's early poems, 'Digging', tries to reconcile the paternal mud-world of the farm with the milieu of the pen in which the writer, by definition, finds himself. However, Heaney was not only using his pen to make poetry; he was also writing lectures and marking essays. He is a poet celebrated alike for his evocations of bog, soil, and farmscape, and for holding some of academia's most distinguished literary appointments at Harvard and Oxford. These two aspects are mutually reinforcing. So, for instance, the emphasis in the work of his Scottish Professor John Braidwood on dialect as 'the mark of our history upon our tongues' has been important to Heaney's overarching sense of word-music, while precise details from Braidwood's inaugural lecture have found their way into Heaney's poem 'The Backward Look', with its loving attention to 'dialect' and 'variants' in 'a fieldworker's archive'.[56] 'Field Work', title of Heaney's 1979 collection, is a term which allows him to bring together his rural background and his academic training, to be at once marginal and sophisticated, as if, like his friend Hughes, he were both wild earth-creature and trained anthropologist. That dynamic continues in different guises throughout much of Heaney's *œuvre*, most recently in his celebrated translation of *Beowulf*. Dedicated to Hughes, this volume allows Heaney to tap into the 'primal' at the same time as making use of material that came to him first as one among 'generations of undergraduates'; it is a production both professorial and primitive. Heaney pays tribute in his introduction to his own training at Queen's and to 'Professor John Braidwood', yet he also imagines himself in a more intemperate, Hughes-like world of 'dog-breath in the dark'.[57] His stance here, one foot in the cavern and one in the classroom, confirms at the heart of modern poetry the enduring figure of the modern poet as presented in this book.

Nor is such a phenomenon confined to the generation of Heaney and Hughes. If Heaney is the most influential Irish poet of his era, then the

[56] John Braidwood, 'The Ulster Dialect Lexicon' (Belfast: Queen's University, 1975), 4; Heaney, *Opened Ground*, 56–7 ('The Backward Look'); see Nils Eskestad, 'Negotiating the Canon: Regionality and the Impact of Education in Seamus Heaney's Poetry', *Ariel*, 29/4 (1998), 7–20.

[57] Seamus Heaney, *Beowulf* (London: Faber & Faber, 1999), pp. xvii, x, xxiv, and xviii.

leading Irish poet of the generation that follows, Paul Muldoon, has developed a whole career in which he balances between the shamanic and the anthropological. Awarded a third-class degree in English by Queen's, Belfast, Muldoon may, like Auden, have taken his revenge on the academic mindset in *Madoc: A Mystery* (1990), with its recondite, square-bracketed subheadings referring readers to '[Burnet]', '[Aenesidemus]' or '[Feuerbach]'.[58] Though this collection begins teasingly with 'The Key', the 'mystery' that is 'Madoc' seems designed to lure academics to their doom. Named after a work by Robert Southey which deals with an encounter between a white Welshman and the 'primitive' world of the native Americans, the book inhabits simultaneously the territory of the barbarous and the academically gowned. In its stance towards institutional knowledge, it seems like a late twentieth-century sequel to Auden's *The Orators*, and, though it lacks the passion of Muldoon's 'Incantata', its blending of the primitive and the sophisticated is typical of his often coolly postmodern verse. Elsewhere, in 'Trance', he splices the culture of his childhood in Northern Ireland with the world of Siberian shamans. At one point in this druggy poem Muldoon seems to inhabit with relish a language of rich shamanistic practice—'Someone mutters a flame from lichen'—while at another his language sounds more like that of the anthropologist taking notes—'to drink his mind-expanding urine'.[59] Here, linguistically, Muldoon is insider and outsider at once, both tribal initiate and academic observer. Continually he blends cultures in unexpected ways. He juxtaposes languages, not least Gaelic and English. To move fluidly between the stances of shaman and anthropologist may be but another of Muldoon's insider-outsider manœuvres, but it is a significant one. Holder of a chair at Princeton University, and currently Professor of Poetry at Oxford, he inhabits the academic machine, yet delights in spoofing its procedures. His recent Clarendon Lectures carry into print a mock-professorial tone and mannerisms: 'I digress . . . But I digress again . . . I remind myself.' There is a delight in proposing to an academic audience suggestions which emanate from a poet's punning sense of the subterranean currents of language, even as they pose as New Critical close-readings. So in Joyce's story 'The Dead', Muldoon finds the 'ghostly presence' of the Arthurian folklorist Alfred Nutt in the word '*nut*meg', while proceeding to say, 'I'm not going to try here to crack Nutt, or Arthurian motifs in "The Dead"',

[58] Paul Muldoon, *Madoc: A Mystery* (London: Faber & Faber, 1990), 101, 42, and 159.
[59] Paul Muldoon, *Quoof* (London: Faber & Faber, 1983), 10 ('Trance').

except perhaps to mention the standing army of Fenian bottles, "black, with brown and red labels", dedicated to Arthur Guinness, because I know you already think I'm totally nuts.'[60] Balancing precariously between parodic 'mad professor' and subversive bard operating in his linguistic trance, Muldoon before his Oxford audience presents a further variation on the figure of the modern poet who attempts to stay true to the sources of his own magic at the same time as relating to the labyrinthine knowledge-world of academia. His position is, to a greater or lesser degree, that of an array of contemporary poets, not only in Britain and Ireland, but throughout the English-speaking world from American 'Language' poets to 'Scottish Informationists'.[61]

Several male Scottish and Irish poets, including Seamus Heaney, Tom Paulin, and Douglas Dunn, have sought to fuse a 'barbarian' stance with academic authority. For many women writers, the tactics have been different, and have often involved a striking use of anti-rational elements (building on such commonplace male put-downs as 'the hysterical woman') alongside a sophisticated and informed sense of literary decorum. This is evident in Sylvia Plath's work as well as in the later poetries of Medbh McGuckian and Selima Hill. These are modern poets whose primitivism comes not so much from a calculated assertion of local, national, or regional resources as from a deployment of their perceived marginality as women contesting the structures of male rationality. One fine example of this is Hill's poem 'The Significance of Significance' which draws on the poet's family connection with Dorothea and I. A. Richards (co-author of the impressively titled *The Meaning of Meaning*) in order to make a poem which presents a woman who 'couldn't spell' and a ' "Great Man" ' who is obsessed with 'Plans, and plans about plans'. As the poem unfolds, its female character appears to fall ill and be consigned to the care of nurses, while the male's rather aridly intellectual pursuits develop,

> Their children were his books.
> She understood that.
> O *Significado De Significado*,
> lecture notes.[62]

[60] Paul Muldoon, *To Ireland, I* (Oxford: Oxford University Press, 2000), 17–18 and 63.

[61] See Robert Crawford, 'Contemporary Poetry and Academia: The Instance of Informationism', in Andrew Roberts and Jonathan Allison (eds.), *Poetry, Value and Contemporary Culture* (Edinburgh: Edinburgh University Press, 2001).

[62] Selima Hill, *My Darling Camel* (London: Chatto & Windus, 1988), 13 ('The Significance of Significance').

What emerges is a critique of a relationship which may be not only the connection between two individuals, but also the once conventional stand-off between women and gendered institutional knowledge. Hill's is an often arresting poetry with a surrealist tincture. It is interested not least in the balance between organic and mechanical form, as well as that between female and male. As in the work of Medbh McGuckian, there is a tendency to take over older cultural assumptions about the status of the female (women as 'delicate flowers', or 'shrinking violets', for example) and replay them so as to disturb the reader. In 'Orchids', for instance, a male orchid hunter lies injured after his plane has crashed. He listens to gunfire, while nearby his daughter lies 'guarded by sweet machines like a rare flower'.[63] It would be easy in this poem to equate the mechanical with the male, the floral with the female; yet the unusual use of the adjective 'sweet' with the noun 'machines' complicates this, while the 'limp white penis' of the man clothed in white makes him a little like an orchid himself. Hill's poetry seems much concerned with destabilizing notions of gender, as is the verse of McGuckian who moves from such early books as *The Flower Master* (where again the flower is linked to male, not simply female) to *Marconi's Cottage* in which the relationship between the organic and the technological is hinted at, though hardly explored.[64] Only recently has criticism begun to come to terms with the way in which for the female modern poet gender may interact with national or regional voice, as it does in the poetries of McGuckian, Liz Lochhead, and Kathleen Jamie.[65] All these poets make use not simply of the primitive (manifest in their interest in kinds of magical knowledge), but also of forms of what the jargon of academia has designated 'marginality' (in terms of gender, nation, and region), as well as drawing on that sophistication offered by the universities which can give to their initiates a liberating, though also potentially estranging 'sail' or 'visa'.[66]

[63] Selima Hill, *Trembling Hearts in the Bodies of Dogs* (Newcastle upon Tyne: Bloodaxe, 1994), 143 ('Orchids').

[64] Medbh McGuckian, *The Flower Master* (Oxford: Oxford University Press, 1982); Medbh McGuckian, *Marconi's Cottage* (Newcastle upon Tyne: Bloodaxe, 1992).

[65] Clair Wills, *Improprieties* (Oxford: Clarendon Press, 1993), 158–93; Robert Crawford and Anne Varty (eds.), *Liz Lochhead's Voices* (Edinburgh: Edinburgh University Press, 1993); Dorothy Macmillan, 'Twentieth-Century Poetry II: The Last Twenty-Five Years', in Douglas Gifford and Dorothy Macmillan (eds.), *A History of Scottish Women's Writing* (Edinburgh: Edinburgh University Press, 1997), 549–78; Aileen Christianson and Alison Lumsden (eds.), *Contemporary Scottish Women's Writing* (Edinburgh: Edinburgh University Press, 2000).

[66] Kathleen Jamie, *Jizzen* (London: Picador, 1999), 4 ('The Graduates').

Male or female, the poets of the generation of Heaney, Hill, Dunn, Harrison, and McGuckian seem less profoundly affected by the culture of information than are Muldoon, the younger Scottish 'Informationist' poets, or their American predecessors and counterparts. Several of the last group are presented by Marjorie Perloff in her study of poetry in the age of media.[67] Here, considering the older American avant-garde of Louis Zukofsky, John Cage and George Oppen, Perloff connects mid-twentieth-century experimental work with that of a newer avant-garde which includes Charles Bernstein and the Language poets. She is acute in discerning that in much of this writing 'The poets' repeated denial of "normal" word order or syntactic integrity, their introduction of arcane vocabulary and difficult, indeed confusing reference, functions, I think, to mime the coming to awareness of the mind in the face of the endless information glut that surrounds us.'[68] She detects this particularly in the output of John Cage. Yet Perloff masks or ignores the extent to which such poetries evolved as part of a debate with academia. Pieces like Cage's 'Lecture on Nothing' (1959) or his 'Lecture on the Weather' (1976) are, at least in part, parodies of academic form. Cage's *I–VI*, a key text for Perloff, was delivered as the Charles Eliot Norton Lectures at Harvard in 1988–9, and its full title reads like a spoof of a lecturer's 'keywords':

**MethodStructureIntentionDisciplineNotationIndeterminacyInterpene-
trationImitationDevotionCircumstancesVariableStructureNonunder-
standingContingencyInconsistencyPerformance**[69]

Made out of quotations rearranged from files and computer random-ized, Cage's 'lectures' function as a parodic interference with and send-up of the academic milieu in which they are delivered and on which their form partly depends, as he tells his Harvard audience in gowned-up, mock-professorial style (which Auden or Muldoon might have rel-ished), *'you have the opportunity with these lectures to discover how to pay attention to something that isn't interesting'.*[70] There seems a mind-expanding purpose to Cage's work, extending the horizons of music into sound, literature and its commentary into the condition of a redefined music. Yet there is also a virtuoso cheekiness which builds the work out of a tweaking of

---

[67] Marjorie Perloff, *Radical Artifice* (Chicago: Chicago University Press, 1991).
[68] Ibid. 205.
[69] John Cage, *I–VI* (Cambridge, Mass.: Harvard University Press, 1990), title page.
[70] Ibid. 316.

academic conventions. Whether Cage's productions are seen as anti-academic or as in tune with pedagogical discourses, their destructuralism is part of American poetry's symbiotic relationship with college culture, a bond made all the closer by an awareness of living in an information-saturated era.

Though it is often seen as a mode of writing developed outside universities, something similar can be said of Language poetry, which so frequently appears written both to demand explication (to fuel academic critics) and to defeat explanation (poet beats critic). This is a technique inherited from modernist works such as *The Orators* and *The Cantos*, and one linked to an entanglement with professional academia. In this engagement, as they have done since the eighteenth century, anthologies play their part. Visiting California in the mid-1990s I bought a huge collection of experimental American poetry whose back-cover blurb pronounced it to be based on Donald Allen's 1960 gathering *The New American Poetry*, which ran counter to 'the American Academy in general'. Yet as I examined Douglas Messerli's *From the Other Side of the Century: A New American Poetry 1960–1990* I was struck by the way the editor made clear how his book had evolved through extensive consultations with Marjorie Perloff (a professor at Stanford) and Charles Bernstein (a poet and professor at the State University of New York, Buffalo).[71] Even the poetry that might be considered counter-cultural in contemporary America is permeated by a profound consciousness of academic readers. This fact can be as evident in the case of Language poetry as it is in the situation of more conventional verse. So, for instance, not only has Douglas Messerli edited a large Language anthology for New Directions (a house well regarded by the American academy), but there is already a *Norton Anthology* (the poetry imprint most closely keyed to US universities) given over largely to Language poetry.[72]

This comes as no surprise to the observer of the dialogues between poetry and academia. For Language poetry draws on aspects of the French Oulipo school with its structural games, and preoccupation with the making and breaking of new kinds of formal rule; as Oulipo evolved in conjunction with Tel Quel in France, so Language poetry (though

[71] Douglas Messerli (ed.), *From the Other Side of the Century* (Los Angeles: Sun & Moon Press, 1994), 34.

[72] Douglas Messerli (ed.), *'Language' Poetries* (New York: New Directions, 1986); Paul Hoover (ed.), *Postmodern American Poetry* (New York: Norton, 1994).

many of the poets might deny this) has developed not just out of the French-influenced work of the early Ashbery but also alongside the growth of poststructuralism in US academia, Language writing being closely linked to the exfoliation of interest in modern literary theory.[73] While Linda Reinfeld, author of a helpful introduction to Language poetry, sets apart the Language poets from 'their academic counterparts', that very phrase hints at a relationship, and Reinfeld clearly connects Language poets' work to kinds of literary theory fashionable in American universities.[74] Bernstein's editing of a 1987 issue of the poststructuralist State University of New York journal *boundary 2* is of a piece with the cut-and-paste, self-interfering texts of his own poetry. If the earlier work of Ashbery is attuned to the technologies of the cinema and television, the later Language and related poetries are more keyed to the computer screen, which provides formal encouragement to the generation of randomized works, electronic cutting and pasting, and poetry as amalgams of 'text'. That very word 'text', so redolent of the classroom, has become a key one in the computer age, and has furthered a convergence of poetic and critical productions in such different works as Harold Bloom's *The Anxiety of Influence*, Cage's 'lectures', and innumerable Language computer cut-ups. Prefacing the 'Postmodern Poetries' issue of *Verse* in 1990, Jerome McGann (himself a critic, hypertext maker and experimental poet) draws attention to postmodern poetries' 'commitment to ideas and critical thinking'. His own introduction subtly links the different facets of his work, and suggests just how strongly implicated in academia these experimental poetries have become.[75] The wild sophistication of the Language poets propels them towards, not away from, universities.

This may be why some readers often find Language poetry more compelling in theory than in extended practice. The Language poets are of interest not because they instigate a break away from academia in American poetry (such a thing may be no longer possible in the American tradition), but because they mark a different engagement with it. Furthermore, both in technique and in content, they show such a strong awareness of the computer and of the informational. So we have the

---

[73] Mary Ann Caws (ed.), *About French Poetry from Dada to Tel Quel* (Detroit: Wayne State University Press, 1974); Linda Reinfeld, *Language Poetry* (Baton Rouge: Louisiana State University Press, 1992), 3, 25, 33.
[74] Reinfeld, *Language Poetry*, 3.
[75] Jerome McGann, 'Postmodern Poetries', *Verse*, 7/1 (1990), 7.

exciting, funny, yet also at times arid world of Bob Perelman's 'Neonew' with its

> the only stimulus   delete
> the proper body   delete
> the canon of inspiration delete[76]

In the world of Language poetry, informationism, and a myriad of competing poetic voices, one thing becomes increasingly clear. Poetry has come to exist in an ongoing relationship with academia, which may take the form of a dialogue or a flyting or both. Poets and academics will woo and, at times, execrate one another. Poets working within universities will use the voice of the lecturer and of the poet; sometimes, indeed, they may employ the voice of the academic in order to defend the voice of the poet. If academia can offer financial security, it can also threaten the deletion of inspiration. Hence, the strategy of the modern poet, the writer who seeks to engage with college life and make use of its resources, yet also evolves ways of preserving in the face of the reductively analytical some access to the 'primitive', the world of dream, magic, wildness, and 'marginality' which poetry both guards and offers. This too must be part of the poet's work in the university. There he or she acts not just as a custodian of inherited knowledge but also as a witness to the technical and spiritual force which helps preserve poetry as a distinct medium. Himself or herself a medium through which the medium of poetry can pass, the modern poet seeks to juggle the roles of shaman and professor, bard, administrator, and barbarian. To do so is not easy. Simply, in our civilization, it is necessary. Those who find themselves in such a position may not find that it is always smoothly negotiated. The work of the poet on campus can chafe against the work of the poem. However, there may be some comfort in realizing that this predicament is scarcely of recent making. On the contrary, it is centuries old, and the figure of the modern poet, involved at once with poetry, academia, and knowledge, has become not only our contemporary, but also our tradition, our inheritance. To move on, it helps to know where we stand.

---

[76] Bob Perelman, 'Neonew', *Verse*, 7/1 (1990), 42.

Index